APART

JUSTIN GEST

APART

*Alienated and Engaged Muslims
in the West*

Columbia University Press
New York

Columbia University Press
Publishers Since 1893
New York   Chichester, West Sussex
Copyright © Justin Gest, 2010
All rights reserved

Library of Congress Cataloging-in-Publication Data

Gest, Justin.
  Apart : alienated and engaged Muslims in the West / Justin Gest.
      p. cm.
  Includes bibliographical references and index.
  ISBN 978-0-231-70188-4 (alk. paper)
  1. Muslims—Non-Muslim countries. 2. Muslims—Non-Muslim
  countries—Interviews. I. Title.

  BP52.5.G47 2010
  305.242088'297091821—dc22

                          2010018299

∞

Columbia University Press books are printed on permanent and durable acid-free paper.
This book is printed on paper with recycled content.
Printed in India

c 10 9 8 7 6 5 4 3 2 1

References to Internet Web sites (URLs) were accurate at the time of writing.
Neither the author nor Columbia University Press is responsible for URLs
that may have expired or changed since the manuscript was prepared.

CONTENTS

CONTENTS

LIST OF FIGURES

ACKNOWLEDGEMENTS

The greatest understatement in Apart resides in its by-line. This book was only possible thanks to the sustained belief and generosity of various dear friends, colleagues, advisors, family members and small acts of kind assistance from scores of others. Like the political communities I examine, this book is the product of innumerable favors, countless questions answered, and general goodwill—all exercised in the context of everyday life. On its own, each contribution seemed trivial at the time. However, as democratic politics can demonstrate, the grandest achievements are the sum of many pedestrian feats.

My great grandfather Philip Halperin always said, 'Surround yourself with people who are smarter than you, and keep the company of those you admire.' Considering my attempts to heed his guidance, the following list is indeed humbling.

First and foremost, this work was guided by the experienced and delicate hands of my mentors David Held and Henrietta Moore. From the moment we met, David embraced me and my ambitions. He gave me new opportunities to succeed and rewarded me with his concern for my welfare and faith in my ability. Henrietta always harnessed my energy and ideas, and helped me pursue a thoughtful, creative, rigorous investigation. Erudite and extraordinarily dynamic, she always managed to strike a balance between thorough criticism and benevolent warmth. The two of them rendered me full independence and full support, conditioned only on my persistent effort and dedication. I could not ask for better guidance.

If David and Henrietta occupied the boardroom, I was privileged to receive a significant amount of unofficial advice in the workshop. Meera Sabaratnam is a dear friend who regularly shared her profound wisdom and tolerated my sense of humor in exchange for the opportunity to brutally roast my preconceptions and ideas. Her input was invaluable at every stage of writing. Michael McMahon made time to placate my insecurities. I am very grateful for his pragmatic guidance and calming optimism. Anna Boucher is one of the most driven, talented intellectuals I know, and yet she never hesitated to make generous space to assist my efforts. She clearly has enough energy for the two of us. Mike Seiferling kindly shared his wisdom and expertise at various stages. And John Gledhill always made time to understand my work and make it better, to understand my pursuits and help me achieve.

In the course of thinking about the issues addressed in the book, I was further aided by the generous support and friendship of Nick Broadway, Chris Kyriacou, Arthur Schilling, Gideon Bresler, Markus Wagner, Simon Hix, Ignazio De Ferrari, Ravi Agrawal, Federico Baradello, Azim Hussain, Mick Cox, Gita Subramanyam, George Lawson, Mary Kaldor, Meg Bailey, Judy Kisor, Stephen Noble Smith, Fredrik Sjoberg, Fred Halliday, Matt Bai, Eiko Thielemann, Pat McGovern, Michael Lister, Stuart Croft, Kate Daubney, Debra Hauer and Michael Dwyer.

My research and professional endeavours were financially supported by the generosity of the Abbey Santander Group, the Newby Trust, the Ralph Miliband Programme, the Bernard Levin Trust, the William Robson Prize Fund, the Baroness Birk Scholarship and the Department of Government at the London School of Economics and Political Science. At the LSE, I was further reinforced by the efforts of Joanna Stone, Madeleine Bothe, Nicole Boyce, Martina Langer, Harriet Carter and Dominika Spyratou.

My fieldwork in London's East End was facilitated and aided immensely by the kind support of Sayed Khan, Badrul Hussain, Khalid Ali, Kevin Munday, Usama Hasan, Antonia Dixey, Mostak Ahmed, and Blossom Young. In Spain, I am deeply grateful for the help of Ana Planet, Berta Álvarez-Miranda, Héctor Cebolla Boado, Polo Camacho, Francisco 'Pancho' Alonso, Paz Fernandez, José Javier Olivas Osuna, Juan Antonio García, Javier Gomez, Jordi Moreras, Renzo Llorente, and Joan Monras Oliu.

London is a long way from Los Angeles. But I felt at home from the moment I began this journey. I was immediately embraced by Susan Wilen and Jeffrey Weingarten, who adopted me as a surrogate son and integrated me as a part of their family. Amanda Weingarten is a sister, Justin Fraterman is a brother, and I have always known that they will be at my side through more daunting challenges than the completion of this book.

Finally, this book would not have been possible without the unconditional support of my most precious partner Monika; my brother and best friend Darren; my wonderful grandparents Jeannette and Alvin Litt, Ann and Matt Vande Wydeven, and Tema and Sigmund Gest; and my inspiring parents, whose limitless love makes me truly believe that I can achieve anything.

From the bottom of my heart, thank you.

London   Justin Gest
April 2010

PREFACE

For social scientists, it remains unclear why similar people, in similar circumstances, behave as political actors in such divergent ways.

Zak is the poster image for diversity and difference in the West today.

Indeed, he is the young man portrayed on the cover of this book.

He perches on three cinder blocks—the foundation of an unfinished public housing project in Mile End, East London. His face in the shadows of a neighboring project, he extends his legs to absorb the mild April sunlight through his Nike sweatpants. He wears a pair of loosely strapped, white Velcro sneakers and a charcoal grey Puma hoody. Even in the shade, he covers his head as he peers out toward the sun-drenched empty lot where he played football after school as a child, emulating Manchester United's Roy Keane.

The older boys would lean along the metal poles that line the weeded front yards of the estates, just like boys of the same age do today. They would sit back and chat, commenting on funny stories, passers-by, and grand plans for the weekend that would probably not come to fruition. The kids would disperse when police officers neared. For a thrill, they often ventured into nearby Bow Cemetery, where there are hundreds of 170–year-old graves to inspire eerie tales, rumors of possession, and adolescent dares.

His reverie is interrupted by the piercing treble of his mobile phone ringtone, a hip hop song by Tupac entitled 'Bury Me a G.'

'You get my text?' he asks, pulling the phone away to check the time on the screen.

'Well we was at the chicken and chips shop, in'it.'

'I can't. My mum needs me to stay with my little brother.'

'A'ight, safe,' he says, pocketing the phone.

Fried chicken and French fries to snack. Soccer after school. Hip hop music. Nike threads. Family obligations.

Difference has rarely been so strikingly familiar.

And yet Zak is treated differently. He hears and reads that he actually is quite different. And Zak says, indeed, he feels different.

'No I don't feel British,' he asserts forcefully, almost to himself as much as to anyone else. 'Their values have nothing to do with mine.'

'The way we've grown up here in the big country of the UK,' he says, as he gestures back toward the empty lot, 'we've only ever really seen Mile End.'

He goes quiet, and nods in the direction of a neighbor in a flowing white prayer gown, passing by on the uneven pavement.

Lowering his voice, he says, 'You know, yeah, I would love to change the world, but when you think about it, it's not going to happen. I can't worry about them, because I got other things. I gotta feed my family...'

He pauses pensively.

'Besides, you're just a pawn in their game. They just want your vote. They don't give a [damn] about you.'

And so Zak is apart—alienated from the democratic government and society of the only country he has ever known. This book seeks to find out why.

Since the rapid growth and expanding influence of European Muslim minority groups in the late 1980s, a vast variety of studies have examined different communities' political and social relations. These studies were significantly concerned with Muslim individuals' integration and participation in local democratic institutions. They observed individual struggles to belong, to make claims, to occupy public space, and develop identity forms. But since the terrorist attacks of 11 September 2001, 11 March 2004, and 7 July 2005, a large amount of research has focused on destructive political behavior—the causes of the extremism or 'radicalization' that is currently said to threaten Western democracies. Discursively, much of the language about Islamic extremism has objectified the individual as a subject of indoctrination or circumstances beyond his or her control. The individual is cast as an empty vessel, 'vulnerable' to others' persuasion and the effects of socio-economic, discursive, or religious forces.

This study represents a departure in two key ways. First, it is based on the premise that Muslim individuals—like all others—approach the political sphere with disparate perceptions and interpretations of an otherwise shared reality. It is based on the understanding that individuals are never empty vessels, and that each of us makes political choices according to instilled paradigms of morality, felt sentiment, and principal understandings about the structure of our society. In other words, the way agents reflectively monitor and constitute their personal realities is to some extent *sui generis*. In the light of this argument, there is no such thing as abstract vulnerability, only conditioning. Human agency is pivotal. Second, this study contends that the greatest threat within Western democracies is not terrorism, but the sustained marginalization of citizens from their political system. In this way, violent extremism is understood as a manifestation of the same outlook that informs individuals who choose to withdraw from the public sphere, rather than attack it. Both the withdrawn and the destructive defect from the political system and its capacity to facilitate change. Like Zak—or Zakaria—the former reacts by living outside of it; the latter chooses to disrupt it. Neither reproduces the democratic political system or contributes to the process of responsive claims making.

We will journey into neighborhoods like Zakaria's and attempt to understand better the spectrum of political engagement and disengagement among other young Muslim men. Because political behavior, like all behavior, is connected and contextualized by the surrounding factors and environments, this study focuses closely on the nature of daily life for modern Western Muslims. We shall examine constructions and projections of individual identity and its conflicts. And we shall use these observations to construct a new way of explaining the withdrawn and destructive anti–system behavior addressed above—apartism.

1

INTRODUCTION

DEMOCRACY'S CHALLENGE

This is a study of democracies that asks what distinguishes individuals who engage with the political system and act within its institutional channels from those who reject the political system and withdraw from it or act to undermine its functioning. In proposing new theoretical approaches that address this question, I test hypotheses in the field and provide initial empirical evidence from communities of British Bangladeshi men in London's East End, Spanish Moroccan men in Southern Madrid, and the nature of their involvement in political life. Since the destabilizing terrorist attacks that took place footsteps from these two communities, Western polities have been faced with the reality that a small proportion of citizens are marginalized to the extent that they would circumvent democratic processes and violently attack members of their own society to advance a political objective.

While the isolated terrorist has been and certainly remains the main security concern within Western democracies, the following book is premised on the belief that the main concern to the proper functioning of such liberal democracies is the growing community of Muslims withdrawn from civil society and the structures of democratic activism. In Europe, although many second generation Muslims have continued to invest in local political systems despite such policies, others have become disaffected from the only society in which they have lived and the only government positioned to help them. This study asks why this has occurred, and why public policy has been unable to address this problem effectively.

These are perplexing questions. We must address the distinct circumstances and background of these particular communities—not just their ethno-cultural and religious heritage, but also the inherent differences between two democracies. And until now, no study has attempted conceptually to address Muslims' alienation from their local political system and concern itself with the everyday political engagement of ordinary individuals in these two communities.

In doing so, this book endeavors to build a typology for understanding political behavior. We shall interrogate two of social theory's most referenced and misunderstood ideas—alienation, and its antithesis, engagement—and we shall utilize a unique comparison to test new ideas. In the process, we shall acquaint ourselves with the culture, lifestyle, history and politics of two neighborhoods and two communities of European Muslims at the center of public debate—all to help us address imperative questions about the future of civic relations in Western democracies. Are Muslims intrinsically different from other minority groups in the West? What is the role of Islam in shaping European Muslims' reconstructed identities? What is the impact of different regimes on Muslims' choice to engage with the political system? More broadly, why, among people under similar circumstances, do some act within the political system and others divest themselves of it? Why, among those who divest, do some actively disrupt the political system while others withdraw?

The objectives of this study are largely conceptual. However, its means are empirical, as we shall rely heavily on illustrative evidence from interviews and observation deep in the alleyways, street corners, living rooms, and prayer rooms of London and Madrid. And while the results cannot claim to be representative of all Western Muslims, it is hoped that the arguments and evidence from participants' daily realities advance our understanding of a misunderstood population. First, our exploration begins by introducing Western Muslim communities and the complexities that they elicit in contemporary democracies.

On the Muslim Question

Approaching the question of European Muslims' alienation objectively, we cannot be certain about who exactly is alienated from whom. From our proliferating sources of news and commentary, it is clear that the Islamic faith and some Muslims' lifestyles are commonly thought to be incompatible with daily existence in the West. However, is it that many Muslim individuals and communities are having difficulty reconciling their customs, moral frameworks, tastes and culture with those of their surrounding state? Or is it that many non-Muslim members of the state are having difficulty reconciling the presence and practice of Muslim customs, moral frameworks, tastes and culture in what may retrospectively appear to have been a relatively more cohesive—perhaps even homogeneous—environment?

Immigrants entering new countries and cultures have no choice but to transform their lives in a variety of ways—for practical reasons, if not legal reasons. Cooking, fashion and architecture are convenient examples. British oral histories about South Asian cuisine describe how earlier generations of migrants had to mix ketchup and mayonnaise with herbs and curry powder obtained from pharmacists to recreate familiar dishes. In terms of fashion, even if an Indian migrant wished to wear a silken sari in Scotland, she would ultimately opt to cover it up with a locally produced wool coat come December—or September for that matter. Architecturally, there were few purpose-built mosques when the first Maghrebis ventured to France and Spain. So an abandoned commercial space with a southeastern-facing wall sufficed, once a group of friends bought a few square meters of carpeting. Adaptation, if not assimilation, is to a certain extent a natural, unlegislated part of migration.

Adaptation, however, is not conventionally perceived to be a necessary reality for indigenous individuals and the state society that initially recruited migrants in the interest of national economic growth. Though many new migrants have struggled to learn local languages, some governments have resisted making official documents bilingual. In England, though Pakistanis have few cultural spaces, Newham residents have successfully blocked the rendering of building permits for a new 'mega' mosque. And although non-naturalized Moroccan migrants in Spain are subject to municipal rules, city councils have avoided extending municipal voting rights to them. By opening borders to labor migrants and asylum seekers, destination democracies made the conscious choice to diversify the composition of their societies in the interest of prosperity and humanitarianism. However, in various ways, states are proving to be reluctant to facilitate corresponding changes to their electoral and cultural composition as well.

As the years have passed, migrants' children and grandchildren have grown up in these states. Members of the so-called 'second' and 'third generation' are accustomed to local trends and routines in households attempting to maintain homeland norms and habits, and they have reason to feel entitled to full liberties and rights in societies still hesitant to extend recognition. In this way, the emerging generation of migrants' children are maturing in families and societies which are simply not prepared for their modernity. Their capacity to reinterpret and then reclaim their roots and surroundings in ever-powerful ways perplexes their parents—but it also confounds the governments which oversee the modern societies that facilitate these defiant assertions. Parents' reactions range from capitulation to control, and governments are hardly different.

In the past 20 years, national political discourses have been characterized by passionate debates about the diversity and integration of migrant peoples. Many governments have been castigated for being too acquiescent. Simultaneously—and perhaps in response—there has been significant growth in public policy mandating specific adaptations by minority groups. While some laws require migrants to change in ways that facilitate their transition and contribution to the new society—like a grasp of the national language, an employment contract, a satisfactory criminal record, and an understanding of civic institutions and participation—others require migrants to adapt in ways that make their difference more palatable to their new society—like prohibitions of particular dress, tests that ensure knowledge of local holidays and other national trivia, and bans on certain forms of religious architecture. Although a variety of anti–discrimination and equal rights corollaries have also been sanctioned, other laws mandating the tolerance and incorporation of new citizens have proven more difficult to pass and enforce. This has been excused largely because—as in the past—contemporary ethnic and religious difference has been successfully equated to existential danger.

The difference that characterized the attackers of the 11 September 2001 bombings (and subsequent political violence) has been broadly attributed to other Muslim individuals and communities living in the West. Murder was performed in the name of Islam and in the interest of its religious conquest, and as a result other followers have been suspected of complicity—on the basis that their continued faith suggests their adherence to the same values that rhetorically justified the horrific attacks. This has polemicized Muslims' residence in the West in ways that poignantly question the efficacy of inclusive democracies and complicate the individual's relationship with the state.

Muslims in Europe

Muslim communities represent the fastest growing segment of the European population today. Recent studies estimate there to be twenty million Muslim individuals currently living in the European Union.[1] Though they do not currently comprise more than 10 per cent of any one country, demographers expect their total population to double by 2015[2] or 2020,[3] and expect Muslims to make up 20 per cent of the EU's total population by 2050.[4] Though often classified by their shared religion, European Muslims are remarkably heterogeneous. Many Muslim minorities' countries of origin correspond to direct colonial ties, such as South Asians in the United Kingdom, Moroccans in Spain, Indonesians in the Netherlands, and Algerians and Moroccans in France. Other countries have established non-colonial relationships with early migrants who settled in their cities and later attracted future migrants from the same country of origin, such as Iraqis in Sweden, Moroccans in Holland, Tunisians in Italy, and Turks in Germany, Sweden and the Netherlands. Amidst such different nationalities, there are even further divisions with regard to religious sect, with Barelwis, Deobandis, Wahhabis, Tablighis, Ismailis, Shi'is, Sufis and many others represented.

Each national and sectarian group in each destination country has a distinct history of settlement, though most originally arrived in the three decades after the conclusion of World War II—some to supplant depleted labor forces, others to provide cheap labor to growing economies, and still others escaping oppression and poverty. To a large extent, migrants were encouraged by lenient Northern European border policies that occasionally rendered citizenship rights to colonial subjects, but typically viewed them as a temporary stopgap for labor needs. Such groups were met in their destination countries by a substantial flow of Southern Europeans also moving to the more prosperous North. Of course, the vast majority of migrants settled and stayed in their new European societies. And by the time of the 1970s oil price shocks and economic downturn, many states restricted migration to adjust to the slowing demand for labor and focus on the integration of those who had arrived over the past few decades.

Since the beginning of the 1980s, however, the globalization of capital and labor facilitated the greater integration of the world economy and galvanized new, irregular migrant flows to Northern Europe and the fledgling economies of Southern Europe. Migrants came from more distant regions, to multiple destinations before settling, and often entered without proper documentation. This is the time when Southern Europe received their first significant influx of Muslim immigrants from North Africa and the Middle East. With the simultaneous liberalization of trade and domestic markets, national governments saw their control over capital and labor flows attenuate, as investments and the need for skilled and unskilled migrants rushed money and people across borders with high frequency. This interchange would only accelerate when the communist systems of Eastern Europe caved in by 1989, and population move-ment crisscrossed the continent—via proper channels, smuggling routes, or simply by overstaying student and tourist visas.

Across nearly all cases, Muslim individuals have faced a significant amount of discrimination and social exclusion since their arrival, and, like other migrant communities, many have sought protection through local interdepen-dence and geographic concentration. Economic downturns and unemploy-ment rates have inspired resentment from native populations, while cultural and ideological differences have tested the tolerance and flexibility of European societies.

It was only by the late 1980s and early 1990s that communities of migrant origin Muslim individuals began to embrace their 'Muslimness' as a political identity at the national level. In Britain, the first steps away from the Asian identity and political 'blackness' were a consequence of the uproar following the 1989 publication of Salman Rushdie's novel, *The Satanic Verses*. The reper-cussions, of course, became international with the subsequent intervention and *fatwa* by Iran's Ayatollah Khomeini. Describing the circumstances in the United Kingdom, Tariq Modood wrote, 'It generated an impassioned Muslim activism and mobilization that no previous campaign against racism had been remotely able to stir. Many "lapsed" or "passive" Muslims (especially non-reli-gious Muslims, for whom hitherto their Muslim background was not particu-larly important) (re)discovered a new sense of community solidarity.'[5] From this point forward, future demonstrations with regard to the Gulf War, Bosnia, Chechnya and Kosovo were understood as issues of Muslim, as much as humanitarian, concern.

Subsequently, rifts began to develop with the emergence of protective asso-ciations and collective movements defined by particularistic Muslim and South Asian identities. These were often connected to people's countries of origin or the global Islamic brotherhood (the *ummah*), and unrestrained by the borders of national citizenship. By the millennium, Muslims were a generation deep in nearly all countries west of Berlin—legally recognized citizens of their poli-ties or at least eligible for citizenship. But despite their deepening roots in the West, Muslim individuals continued to be regarded with a strong degree of suspicion and ignorance. During these years of adjustment, highly visible rac-ism, xenophobia and outright discrimination occasionally entered the public realm, and societies were confronted with controversies about minority rights and hate speech. The tension was occasionally manifested publicly, as with the string of riots that erupted across the United Kingdom in the summer of 2001, pitting South Asian communities against white neighbors. Each incident held some degree of social relevance as Europeans were asked to define equal treatment in their diversifying democracies.

But this tension did not create the polarity between the Western and Muslim worlds that was kindled by the 2001 terrorist attacks and reproduced by discursive interpretations of subsequent non-violent, European Muslim activism (even when, as with Iraq War protests, Muslims were joined by large assemblages of non-Muslims). As a result, anti–racist movements and demonstrations undertaken by Muslim groups were often less associated with a democratic struggle for civil rights, and more commonly forced into the rigid bipolarity of Islam–West relations. This bipolarity has only been reinforced by the post-9/11 political climate, which has obligated ordinary Muslims and their community leaders to monotonously condemn terrorism and disclaim extremism at every opportunity, and carefully consider the symbolism of every public choice—from mosque decisions on whom their congregation admits to what paperbacks their bookshop sells.

To define an alternative, governments have constructed competing fundamentalisms of freshly re-imagined European national identities—pristine cultural paragons like 'Britishness', *fraternité* and *hispanidad*—around which new policies of integration have been cobbled. Much of these new citizenship ideals have been styled with values that directly counter those set by Islamic identities. Muslims have thus, in many ways, become a litmus test for patriotism, as the character of true democratic equality and fellowship is questioned.

The estranged status of such individuals may be the real legacy of this era in social policy: a generational subsection of Muslims living outside the realm of the state and society, a gaping void in the democratic representation of Europe's fastest growing constituency. Indeed, despite their deepening roots, better orientation and growing numbers, Muslims in Europe have been increasingly reporting heightened levels of social isolation and political alienation. In a 2009 survey of Muslims in fourteen European Union member states, the Agency for Fundamental Rights reported that one in three Muslims had faced discrimination, and 11 per cent of those questioned said they had experienced a racially motivated crime.[6] In Germany, a 2009 study by the Berlin Institute for Population and Development found that Muslims tend to 'remain strangers, even after fifty years and three generations in some cases'.[7] In the United Kingdom, a 2006 survey reported that one-third of 18– to 24–year-old Muslims would rather live under the provisions of shari'a law than under British law.[8] Another 2006 survey, which questioned Muslims the world over, found that 81 per cent of Muslims living in Great Britain identify themselves as Muslims before identifying themselves as citizens of their country.[9] In 2008, a British government minister said that many British Muslims now felt like 'aliens in their own country'.[10]

This study is interested in addressing this democratic failure—one that is currently veiled by overwhelming concern at the spectacle of terrorism. It seeks to distinguish those second generation European Muslims who continue to engage with the democratic political system, and those who reject it. In addressing this challenge, this study will contribute arguments to the overarching debates defining European discourse and policy today.

Principal Debates

(How) Are Muslims intrinsically different from other minority groups in Europe?

After decades of migration to the European continent by millions of other individuals, Muslim communities have elicited reactionary government policy, inflammatory discourse, and an extraordinary amount of attention. Laymen and scholars alike have subsequently sought to understand what makes this particular minority purportedly different, why this group's integration might be unlike the process experienced by previous generations. Much scholarship and popular press on the matter has identified the most apparent answer: Islam. If we return to London—a European capital with one of the longest histories of immigration—we see a lineage of 'different' communities: French, Catholic, Jewish, Black, all of whom have 'integrated' sufficiently into British society. However, Britons fretted with each new arrival over the centuries, as the 'foreignness' of the migrant population became increasingly exotic. First, it was a different ethnicity and nationality within Europe; then a competing religious sect of Christianity; next a separate religious tradition along with cabals of communist radicals; later, it was a different 'race'. Finally, with today's Muslims, difference has reached the level of 'civilizational' proportions.[11]

Questions about Muslim exceptionalism abound. And while many emerge in line with the scare tactics of nationalist groups, others merit legitimate social inquiry and require a close examination of this group of people. The core question that underlies the exceptional treatment and consideration of European Muslim minorities in policy, discourse and interpersonal interaction is: are Muslims intrinsically different from other minority groups in Europe today, or in the history of migration to Europe? And if so, how? Does the character and nature of Islam change Muslim migrants' capacity to assimilate or integrate or take part equally in diverse political fellowships? Many concerned about the state of national traditions and identities ask whether the precious histories and images can endure in an environment where they are competing with divergent, heterogeneous cultural images on an equal footing.

What is the role of Islam in shaping European Muslims' reconstructed identities?

For many prominent observers, Europe is the center of a revivalist Islamic movement. Gilles Kepel argues that the associationalism and civic organization of European Muslims who hail from a diverse range of countries around their shared religious beliefs represents a revolutionary medium for the proliferation of Islamic influence and faith worldwide.[12] Tariq Ramadan contends that Europe can serve as such a base because Muslims there are able to develop a 'pure faith' that is liberated from the ethnic rituals and cultural accoutrements that have been the source of petty regional subdivisions from Morocco to Indonesia.[13] Is the European Muslims' embrace and employment of their revitalized Islamic identity characterized by the coordination suggested by these authors?

Tariq Ramadan, in particular, perceives an opportunity in Europe for Muslims to bypass their anachronistic national and ethnic cleavages and progress closer to the Prophet Mohammed's conception of the *ummah*. Are we witnessing a greater pan-Islamism across Europe that connects Muslims more transnationally than they are connected to their local societies and states? How sterilized is European Islam from the local societies where migrant-origin Muslims now reside and live every day? The answers to such questions will help define whether the evolution of an individual-state relationship is more about Islam than the transformational factors referenced earlier.

What is the impact of different regimes on Muslims' choice to engage with the political system?

Until now, much of the political science and sociological work examining Muslims' integration has worked within an institutionalist framework that conceptualizes the variable governmental regimes designed to integrate diverse citizenries. The key models are the 'multicultural' approach exercised in the Netherlands, Sweden and to some degree in the United Kingdom; the 'assimilationist' or 'republican' approach utilized by France; and the 'exclusivist' ethnic approach influencing Germany, Switzerland and Spain. These different institutional strategies have framed many earlier (primarily normative) citizenship studies, which seek to identify what policies better facilitate political mobilization.[14] An intriguing stream of research by Ruud Koopmans and Paul Statham has investigated the role of 'political opportunity structures'. Tarrow defines these as 'consistent—but not necessarily formal or permanent—dimensions of the political environment that provide incentives for people to undertake collective action by affecting their expectations of success or failure'.[15] This builds on the contentions of Patrick Ireland's 'institutional channeling theory' and others, who cite legal and political institutions as a key variable that determines migrants' political engagement.[16] However, it is readily observable that—despite their differences—none of these different policy models seems to be working well with the heterogeneous communities of European Muslim migrants—particularly among their second generation. After two or three generations of settlement, significant portions of Muslim communities across European countries reportedly remain disaffected or excluded from their local democratic societies—regardless of what integration philosophy the national government implements.

Other institutionalist studies address European Muslims' marginalization within a secularist framework that scrutinizes their religiosity and its relationship with the democratic political sphere. Rather than focus exclusively on the overarching structure of state policy, this way of conceptualizing the field of ethnic relations balances an institutional interest with individual behavior. However, it also reduces social and cultural difference in Europe to a matter of religion and its role in government and civil society. Young European Muslims' identity and their struggle in the political sphere are much more about self-definition than about religious practice. Indeed, as we continue to witness, religious leaders are not the only representatives of young Muslims, and religious affiliation is only one aspect of their identity. In fact, as this study confirms, young Muslims often ignore their local imams' tuition about Islam and its application to daily life. If anything, hanging the debate on secularism reinforces the civilizational barriers that radical Islamists and right-wing xenophobes are attempting to make relevant. The ideological divide about secularism does not only concern the presence of Islam, but Christianity too.

While the institutionalist literature has proven to be very useful and convincing in other areas of policy studies, it has not been used systematically to look at more extreme forms of political behavior.[17] Indeed, in the examination of actors who are significantly divorced from the political system, it is questionable how much institutions and structures affect their behavior anyway. For this reason, this study does not evaluate the merit of the various institutionalist philosophies and approaches. It acknowledges the general, cross-national, cross-policy inefficacy of 'secular' European democracies to integrate fully and incorporate politically their growing Muslim minorities, particularly since the 11 September 2001 terrorist attacks—even if it does not reveal precisely how alienation develops separately under each regime. It suggests that certain characteristics of modern political estrangement may be common across the spectrum of institutional strategies. Consequently, this examination shifts the focus away from the institutional, and instead analyses the phenomenon of European Muslims' alienation from below—at the level of the individual, whose relationship with the state is being transformed. This is not to argue that secular governance and competing integration philosophies are unimportant to the daily existences and political life of most European Muslims. They *are* important and earlier studies have demonstrated their variable impact. But alienation within migrant-origin Muslim communities is taking place either way and transcending the different integration policies.

In this light, my research investigates the other side of the 'political opportunity structures' approach underscored earlier. In examining institutions' capacity to promote people's expectations of successful civic activism, the approach inherently assumes that government policies determine the expectations of citizens. Instead, my research is predicated on the idea that individuals' expectations represent an independent factor that distorts and interprets the effects of policy, just as much as policy approaches affect individual expectations. Indeed, it is reasonable to construe the opportunity structure approach as one which already recognizes that the efficacy of political and legal institutions is contingent upon the subjective expectations of their citizens. It is the objective of this study to understand better the nature of these expectations, their formation, their influences and related outcomes. In turn, such conclusions will also enable us to judge the efficacy of policies, empirically and from the perspective of implicated individuals. To do so, this study reconceptualizes individuals' engagement in—and alienation from—modern democracies, given the transformational effect of global communication and transportation technologies. Rather than interrogate how states promote participatory civic behavior and mitigate socio-political marginalization, it investigates what underpins individuals' daily decisions about their relationship with their political system—the decision to join or withdraw, to believe or divest. By comparing two groups of young European Muslim males living under different policy regimes, I hope to identify cross-cutting trends that connect the European phenomenon of Muslims' marginalization and answer my primary research question: What are the characteristics and causes of political alienation among young Muslim men in European democracies?

Outline of the Book

Addressing this question first requires the establishment of a conceptual framework that can be utilized in subsequent empirical studies. For this reason, the next chapter seeks what we can learn from theories of alienation and engagement that would bear on the problem of Muslims' disaffection from the political systems of modern democratic states. In taking this first step, I critically review the classic conceptions of 'alienation' and their counterfactual ideals of 'engagement', and appraise their relevance to the modern democratic political sphere and the challenge posed by diverse new citizens. In the end, I find that disaffected European Muslims fit neither the classical conception of 'alienation' nor 'engagement'. In response, I introduce a typology of political behavior, derived from the empirical reality, which fills this theoretical void—anti–system behavior.

In Chapter Three, I critically review the empirical sociology that seeks to explain anti–system behavior. The four primary streams of argumentation point to a series of causal factors citing certain structural circumstances, each of which I find to be insufficient in determining why, among young Muslims facing largely the same circumstances, some engage or accept the political system and others reject it. In response, I hypothesize that different behavioral reactions to the same set of sociopolitical conditions are dependent on individual perceptions, which tint interpretations and expectations about shared disadvantages. I hypothesize that while one set promotes the reproduction of democratic institutions, another set of perceptions leads individuals to disrupt or withdraw from the democracy—I call these perceptions *apartist*. My empirical research thus embarks on qualitatively developing these hypotheses and their corresponding observable implications, by relating different perceptions to anti–system behavior and democratic engagement.

Chapters Four and Five present content from separate case studies of young British-Bangladeshi men from London's East End, and young Spanish-Moroccan men from the southern barrios of Madrid—key Muslim communities in liberal European democracies in their second generation of residence. Interviews exhibit two remarkably different political communities, both irreversibly transformed by horrific terrorist attacks. In London, we encounter an extraordinarily civically active and cohesive 'village'. There is high public awareness and a keen sensitivity to societal discourse and democratic politics, which produces a sense of political entitlement. This takes place amid a cacophony of competing identity structures, moral paradigms and means of civic organization—including a high incidence of apartist activism. In Madrid, we document significant atomization and low levels of social trust—for Spaniards and other Moroccans. Participants demonstrated utter divestment from and disorientation in the Spanish political sphere, along with extremely low levels of civic participation. The myth of return to Morocco endures strongly, even among those with no or little experience in their country of origin. And contrary to London, there is a high incidence of apartist withdrawal.

Chapter Six compares the cases, as they relate to the empirical sociological arguments noted in Chapter Three, and evaluates my hypotheses in a reassessment of the original question. Information collected suggests that previous answers which point to structural differences between Muslims and indigenous majorities—like political disorientation, income, discrimination, and identity constructions—are flawed. Instead, this chapter proposes an association between political behavior and the discrepancy between individuals' subjective expectations of their political system and their perceived fulfillment. It contends that personal attitudes thus serve as an important causal mechanism, altering how subjects perceive the state and greater society. Those who can reconcile their disadvantages and acknowledge the system's capacity to reform were more likely to display engaged behaviors. Those who generalize democratic losses and perceive stagnancy are more likely to be either actively or passively apartist. This chapter also finds that integration is actually characteristic of individuals who spurn the political system of their democracies, as much as it may otherwise characterize those who participate in the system. Indeed those most aware of the rights, liberties and cultural mores of their democratic system were those most likely to have the deepest sense of disappointment about their un-fulfillment. Both cases exhibit young Muslims' need for norm-based stability in an era characterized by contested beliefs about nation, state and faith.

Chapter Seven closes this study by reviewing the primary findings and identifying a variety of significant implications on state policy and social thought. Drawing from these conclusions, we will examine the common argument that the challenge of Muslims' alienation and 'home-grown terrorism' is an exclusively European problem—that a country like the United States is immune by virtue of its immigrant history and inclusive identity. Current, irrational fears about the allegiances of Muslim citizens provide America with a real test of the diversity and inclusion on which it hangs its exceptionalism. We shall consider America's struggle in the light of our observations from Europe, and weigh corresponding policy recommendations. These ideas will then inform a reconsideration of the polemical questions that underlie the transcendent debates underscored in this first chapter.

2

ALIENATION, ENGAGEMENT AND ANTI-SYSTEM BEHAVIOR

In the light of this study's concern with that which promotes and prevents political engagement by Muslim individuals in Western democracies, this chapter seeks to clarify the terms we shall need. It asks what we can learn from archetypes of alienation and models of engagement that would bear on the problem in front of us. The idea of alienation has a reinvigorated significance amidst the disorienting technologies and fast-moving social trends of modernity, yet it is a term rooted in antiquity. The ancient Greek concept of *ekstasis* (*superstitio* in Latin), the leaving of one's body in the mystery rites, or ecstasy, was considered by Roman contemporaries as a socially reprehensible form of 'mental alienation' (*abalienatio mentis*).[1] To early Christians, alienation signified the estrangement of man from God.[2] Further precursors in Greek literature and the Old Testament are as old as literary history.[3] Indeed throughout human history, individuals and groups of people have been separated from their sense of self, their sense of community, and their sense of control.

Today, alienation appears to possess a particularly modern relevance to an increasingly competitive, interconnected, and faster-paced world. Earlier scholars recorded expressions of anxiety and disorientation in the competition of classes and generations. Contemporary alienation also relates to a competition of cultures, as diverse transportation and communication media proliferate images of the previously foreign Other and its alternative existences with extraordinary vividness and alacrity. Beyond such iconography, human migration has blended previously contrasting societies by bringing them face to face with the Other in an interdependent economic and democratic relationship—creating whole new sets of communities, identity constructions and alienation.

Through its history, alienation has always spoken to an implicit counterfactual. As Joachim Israel observed in his 1971 analysis, 'If one declares that an individual is alienated, it is implied that he must be alienated from something. Even if not made explicit in theories of alienation, the very term refers to a state or a process that deviates from a state considered to be normal.'[4] And indeed, no matter how rational, all theories' identification of that which is 'normal' illuminates the subjectivity of determining whether an individual, group or society is experiencing alienation. The requisite question therefore becomes not simply 'Alienated from what?' but 'What is normal?' In this study of sociopolitical alienation, the 'normal' counterfactual is sociopolitical engagement.

Over the course of its employment as a term of political behavior, alienation has been regarded as synonymous with political violence, poverty, social positioning, atomization, apathy and also the sentimental or metaphysical estrangement that leads to such manifestations. In this way, it has both described the outcome and explained the outcome, demonstrating the lack of a concrete understanding. The dilemma is that alienation has been under-theorized and over-utilized. This chapter will demonstrate the contested natures of alienation and engagement, before incorporating them to explain the nature of anti–system behavior and its use as a specific term of alienation to be employed generally, and also specifically among Muslim individuals in Western democracies.

It will begin with an analysis of alienation as an empirical phenomenon and an instrument of sociological explication. It will then critically review the principal political understandings of individual and social disaffection with an eye to their contemporary relevance, and find that none of them directly applies to the problem before us. We shall consider alienation in Marxism, anomie in Durkheimian thought, non-participation in liberal frameworks, and disengagement in social capital theory. And through each discussion, I will build my core argument—that structuralist accounts of alienation are outdated because sociological conditions and possibilities for connectedness have increased and deterritorialized. In the light of this contention, the chapter then explores the equally contested nature of the counterfactual, 'engagement', before explaining the criteria of 'normality' employed here. In the end, I shall conclude by re-introducing the term 'anti–system behavior' as a useful typology to understand the dependent variable of this study and related contemporary phenomena.

The Individual and State in Modernity

Alienation has been conventionally framed according to an established relationship between the individual and the state. However, in the past 20 years, the conceptual foundations of this relationship have been complicated by the expansion of new technologies of communication and global immigration in modern democracies. It is worth considering what these changes have entailed, before we review the archetypes of alienation and normality that still purportedly apply to this transforming sociopolitical sphere the way they did when they were first conceived.

According to John Locke's original conception, the state is a civic creation that requires no common heritage amongst its citizens, but a common commitment to one's countrymen and a common understanding about how to govern a given territory. If anything, the construction of a self-determined nation of citizens is dependent on the integration of what is initially a hodgepodge of people into a collective identity that reaches beyond inherited loyalties to village, family or clan.[5] As states purportedly formed on a foundation of political fellowship, democracies are therefore supposed to be societies qualified by the integrated consent of their constitutive members—and not their shared ethnic or cultural heritage.

However, over the centuries, the requirements of political leadership and action have led to attempts to deploy national identity as a means of ensuring the coordination of policy, mobilization and legitimacy.[6] In practice, the consensual agreement has often been a product of shared norms, sacrifices and past experiences in bloody struggles that are only possible with a common genealogical lineage.[7]

Immigrants challenge such rooted societies to render them equally their rights, liberties and benefits—just as societies would to any other citizen whose ancestors gave their lives on battlefields, contributed hard-earned wealth to the welfare state, and shared certain social customs and lifestyles typically grounded in a common ethnic, religious and cultural tradition. Indeed if national bonds were purely a product of shared ideals, then qualification for nationality would never be based on lineage at all, but on political outlook. But in today's world, not a single state can claim that as true.[8] The general consent to a shared legal structure, which was originally necessary for the inauguration of fellowship, is apparently insufficient. Nevertheless, in the interest of gaining the benefits of immigrant labor, many states have since reconciled migrants' cultural differences by establishing rigid naturalization and assimilation policies that attempt to sustain the normative and cultural lineage of the country. This has entailed inventions like citizenship tests.

However, today's minority groups have developed better means to assert their right to individual choice and resist such assimilation policies, thanks to processes of globalization that undermine both the nation-state's institutional monopoly on civic activism and its capacity to define a national identity discourse.[9] As Arjun Appadurai argues, the problem is the tension between diasporic pluralism and territorial stability in the project of the modern nation-state.[10] 'What diasporic pluralisms particularly expose and intensify,' he writes, 'is the gap between the powers of the state to regulate borders, monitor dissent, distribute entitlements within a finite territory and the fiction of ethnic singularity on which most nations ultimately rely.'[11] Diasporic pluralism tends to undermine the narratives of ethnic singularity that try to naturalize these histories. And this undermining is only reinforced by the plethora of non-state actors, non-governmental organizations and various forms of allegiances. Appadurai observes that where states used to be the legitimate guarantors of the territorial organization of markets, identities and histories, they are now to a large extent only one of many arbiters of various forms of global flow.[12] Therefore, territorial integrity becomes crucial to state-sponsored ideas of sovereignty, which may be in the interest of no other organization than the state apparatus itself.[13] This augmented ability to resist is as true for migrant groups as it is for indigenous minorities of ethnic, religious, political and ideological difference. The various transportation, commerce and communication enhancements of globalization have undermined the state's ability to control the domestic public sphere in a most general way. Under such circumstances, the relationship between the individual and the state is undergoing a significant transformation—one which challenges democracies to fulfill the blind fellowship dictated by their original conception.

Of course, certain things like welfare policy and street maintenance remain very much subject to state control. And despite tugs from external affiliations and loyalties, minority citizens remain engaged in a variety of ways with their destination community and its institutions one way or another. Even if they are not voting, serving on local governmental organizations or joining social clubs, the vast majority of people must still interact with host education bodies, housing estates, public transportation, tax collection, police organizations, and are subject to the effects of host foreign and trade policy—all whether they identify with the ruling state or not. Taken in scope, the practical need for such state-based functions has not deteriorated nearly as rapidly as the rhetorical strength of state-constructed identity and its imagery. And while the individual has been enchanted by his and her new freedom to connect, associate and belong across national borders, the state remains emboldened by the multitude of policy powers it still maintains and the proverbial social contract to which it enforces citizens' adherence. The result is a tug-of-war for political control.

There is thus a widening disconnection between the state's position as mediator of the normative community and the individual's enhanced capacity to defy the state in his activism or disengagement. This disconnection becomes clearer when we contrast observable trends in empirical studies with certain political conventions that informed the historical reality of how democratic political systems portray themselves. Three conventions germane to this discussion are:

1) the nationalist aspiration of congruence between a stable nation of people and the outline of the state;
2) the Lockean expectation that new consenters will be welcome in new societies by fellow consenters; and
3) the equally Lockean calculation that majoritarianism validates the disadvantage of the minority.

Such nationalist and liberal images of nation-states inspired a number of reforms during the past 150 years that have endured in modern democratic states, such as the expansion of suffrage, constitutionalism and national self-determination.[14] However, the concept of the state is changing. So is the idea of statecraft. As citizens acquire greater independence from such frameworks, their structural undergirding stretches to the point that empirical realities appear manifestly different.

The Changing Composition of Nation-States

Conflicts over identity can galvanize such passion because there is a distinct need for identity,[15] and because there is a perception that it is inherited and therefore enduring. Stuart Hall writes that the logic of the discourse of ethno-cultural identity assumes a stable subject—something which, in a rapidly changing world, has the great advantage of staying still.[16] This fixity renders identity a sort of positionality, from which a subject can express him or herself. Hall writes that there is no way people can act, speak, create, come in from the margins and talk, or begin to reflect on their own experience, unless they come from some place, some history, or inherit some cultural traditions.[17] In this sense, positionality is a prerequisite for expression. The problem is that this understanding of ethno-cultural identity has been historically extended by nation-states to define civic (or political) identity—the basis of citizenship. This violates the aforementioned Lockean ideal that the foundation of territorial fellowship is mutual consent to shared principles and laws—not common heritage.

Instead, over the past two centuries, states have increasingly been organized according to nationalist principles to create a 'neat fit' between international boundaries and the politically significant identities therein. This concept of a nation-state was justified by the Wilsonian doctrine of national self-determination, which asserted that every nation has a right to independent political control over a given territory and its people. States' recognition of the fact that there would inevitably be some degree of dissatisfaction, however much borders are redrawn, produced 'the pragmatic reconciliation between the prescriptive principle of state sovereignty and the popular principle of national self-determination.'[18] This accommodation created over 100 new states, but did not end nationalist disputes.[19]

Many minority nations remain in territories ruled by separate, larger groups, and this has been further complicated by extensive global migration that has further diversified the composition of national citizenries—demonstrating that identities are neither stable nor pure. With growing immigration and higher immigrant-origin birth rates, states are now subject to the changing make-up of an increasingly patchwork citizenry, which is consistently altered thanks to the ceaseless movement of people. So while both the ethno-cultural and civic notions of identity retain their false association with stability, today's globalizing forces have rendered them a new paradoxical variability, thus begging the question: 'Who *are* the people?'[20]

Classic liberal theorists not only accounted for, but sanctioned political exclusion, both to ensure sound decision-making by including only 'rational' subjects, and to ensure the cohesive homogeneity of the society. Within a similar frame of thought, the ruling elite could historically consider itself the only authentic source of input into the process of determining the direction of the state.[21] However, particularly since the conclusion of World War II (and due to a desire for self-determination at the individual level), access to the political system has been steadily expanded to 'Other' groups that were previously disqualified, disadvantaged, or otherwise excluded from political influence. And while these 'Others' previously suggested members of the non-bourgeois masses, it has recently been further expanded to finger ethnic and religious minorities that have immigrated into relatively homogeneous societies. Such multicultural and increasingly individualized societies demand the end of the symbiosis between the constitutional state and 'the nation' as a community of shared descent, and the abstraction of civil solidarity to include those perceived as intrinsically different.[22] In this light, globalization has whittled the criteria of fellowship so far down that, common ancestry is now inadequate as a criterion for identification.

This places the contemporary national government in an awkward position, because the majority national identity it embodies is decreasingly reflective of the constituency it oversees. As David Jacobson writes, the state is not only the government: 'It embodies the national myth, a sense of the national self, even a soteriological promise. If the state is unable to represent or symbolize "the people", then its authority, and its sovereignty, is in question.'[23] But while there remains a clear-cut ethno-religious majority in most democratic countries, globalization and the migrants it empowers have gained the numbers and capacity to demand more representation and adaptability from the seemingly monolithic state identity. Migration has thus revealed a fundamental contradiction in the conventional practice of citizenship. On the one hand, the principle of 'citizenship for all members of society' demands the inclusion of new ethnic minorities into the political community. On the other hand, the principle of national belonging demands the exclusion of those who are 'different'.[24] As citizenship in states pertains less to common ancestry or culture, states cannot be oriented around the development and progress of a singular nation of people.

Third-Party Rejection of New Consenters

In his *Second Treatise of Government*, Locke describes the individual's entering into a new or established political fellowship as a voluntary endeavor.[25] It is the individual's choice either to relinquish certain freedoms he would enjoy in the state of nature or to obtain the security offered by the organized society. The individual's entrance into a social contract is conditional upon his consent to the rules that have been agreed upon by those who are already members of the society. For this reason, acknowledgement of a new consenter as a member of the polity is not required from a third party, precisely because the state represents the 'greater force' of the populace.[26] Once a new consenter is legally accepted into the polity, his or her entry is official and complete. Since states began increasingly to open their borders to new consenters—migrants—the Lockean principles of conditional entrance have grown increasingly relevant.

Migrants' membership has been based on their consent to a national constitution or set of laws. However, their legal acceptance has not fostered the social acceptance that Locke took for granted. Indeed, just because a new consenter is accepted into the fellowship of citizens by the government, that does not mean he or she is accepted by the citizenry at large. And while legal acceptance is official, social rejection is often equally powerful.

Rejection and qualification have often been rendered according to ethnocultural difference and similarity. This reflects identities' tendency to be defined by juxtaposition with an Other, but also a powerful nativism that responds to fears that the dominant national identity will be diluted with the change of political composition. For as national identity is extended to new immigrants and their children, the nature of that identity becomes more voluntarist (civic) than ethno-traditional (organic). The frequency and facilitation of immigration from place to place contributes to a lost sense of origin, and exhibits the subjectivity of identity in that it can be switched with such ease.[27] While that undermines the power of the 'citizenship' label rendered to worthy immigrants, it also undermines the worth of the host identity because it is being manufactured or acquired so simply.

In a struggle to maintain their dwindling national constituency and their increasingly diluted sense of identity, some states are seeking to monopolize normative power over the community. While some flatly claim perfect concert between the state and the populace therein, others systematically museumize internal subdivisions in a variety of heritage politics.[28] Like the fundamentalist groups they combat, some nationalists perceive identity to be zero-sum, whereby one ethnic group's expanded cultural representation saps the strength of the other. But unlike fundamentalist groups, democratic states have a harder time repressing the ideas of new identities that are threatening to dilute their ideas. The reason is that democratic states find themselves pressed to stay open to such identities by the forces of media, technology and travel, which have fueled consumerism worldwide and increased the craving for new commodities, ideas and spectacles.[29] Like fundamentalist groups, certain members of nation-state majorities are reluctant to embrace the evolving character of their diversifying society and have responded with a return to the local. This return represents a reaction against modernity that appeals to those members of the majority ethnicity seeking to maintain their roots, even as many of them embrace and dabble in global mass culture—a sphere that they may enjoy, but perhaps subconsciously fear.

The rejection of the new consenter (immigrant) is a part of nationalists' reactionary revitalization of the nationally familiar. It is usually manifest as an anachronistic (if jingoistic) nostalgia for seemingly simpler times, which produces a nativist backlash against the attenuating forces of globalization and the accompanying exposure to diversity. The backlash is commonly expressed through paranoia about the infiltration of alternative sources of identity—a sort of identity protectionism that is often manifest in attempts to define more narrowly the national identity against an established Other. As each generation of migrants integrates and alters states' demographic composition, one would imagine that rejection and the strength of identity protectionism will wane.

Majority Rule and Minority Rights

In discussing the empowerment of a community, Locke writes that the act of the majority passes for the act of the whole and determines the power of the whole. Thus every man, he writes, by consenting to make one body politic under one government, puts himself under an obligation to submit to the determination of the majority.[30] But ultimately, majoritarianism—democracy's mechanism of popular control—is also its most significant impediment to inclusion. Of course, this is hardly a new issue. Famously, John Stuart Mill guarded against the tyranny of the majority in arguing that the individual should have the right to put his or her choice into practice so long as no one else is subsequently harmed.[31] Mill disliked the idea that the will of a majority of people, which could just as effectively govern themselves, can govern the actions of a sizeable minority that wishes, and ought to have the right, to do as they desire. Put simply, Mill states, 'In things which do not primarily concern others, individuality should assert itself.'[32] Such an argument gains new salience among populations of newly empowered migrants, who are sensitive to their disadvantages and feel entitled by global human rights discourse.

If the manifold processes of globalization empower minority groups with the capacity to express and follow their individual preferences in the face of dissenting majorities, the global human rights regime has given them the *license*.[33] Yasemin Soysal writes that, for years, national belonging constituted the source of rights and duties of individuals, while the nationally circumscribed public sphere constituted the locus of people's claims and contentions.[34] However, she continues, as national citizens' rights are increasingly recast as human rights, those rights previously associated with national belonging become more abstract, and defined at the transnational level. This has undermined the state's legitimacy in citing a majoritarian mechanism to control the activities and attention of its citizenry, and has inspired diverging perceptions about what the proper role of the state should be. As individuals recognize their own capacity both to express their views and to act on them, minority viewpoints gain strength.

From this brief analysis, we see that state political systems have 'ethnicized' membership and been qualified by third-party coercion. And we see that new consenters have increasingly hybridized the state's civic identity and championed its minority rights to resist state control. As a result, three primary means of promoting individuals' 'belonging' to a given democratic society (from which flows their position in that society's political sphere) are increasingly resistible:

1) The full assimilation of new citizens to a state's identity and normative system seems like an impossible demand to make of newcomers who may more easily maintain old connections and create new connections with alternative ways of life.

2) Third-party recognition of fellow citizens is optional, as global technologies enable new citizens and native-born citizens alike to construct their own identity independent of local expectations.

3) Civic community is no longer exclusively held within states, as citizens who may be in the minority within one state can construct their own localized or deterritorialized communities of consent *across* states.

The next task of this chapter is to evaluate the capacity of social theory's archetypes of human relations to adjust to these contemporary transformations. Much of social theory offers us ideals about the good life and understandings of the marketplace. But the question of some Muslims' alienation demands an examination of theories of deviance and societal fracture. What does such theory have to say about social failure?

Marx and Alienation

Much of what is meant and connoted by the modern social scientific use of the term 'alienation' derives from the work of Karl Marx. In his critiques of capitalism, Marx portrays alienation as a product of the capitalist division of labor. He contends that all economic processes are actually social processes, predicated on a class division separating the proletariat from the bourgeoisie. This, Marx writes, creates an exploitative relationship between superior and subordinate—a 'bitter struggle between capitalist and worker'.[35] According to Marx's theory, as capitalism expands, the worker loses control over the means of production and the products he produces. Whereas before, the fruit of man's labor represented man's power over natural objects, capitalism reverses this relationship as the product of man's labor becomes external to his capacities and the worker himself is objectified by the process of labor. Though Marx notes that this set of circumstances is experienced by all workers, it is felt more strongly by the proletariat than the capitalist bourgeoisie, the members of which own capital and are rewarded with greater material benefits for their objectification. This fosters an antagonistic rift in the economy and society, which for Marx suggests that the true objects of analysis ought to be men themselves rather than the greater economic system. Alienation is thus an intellectual construct through which Marx displays the devastating effect of capitalist production on human beings.[36] There are five principal entities from which Marx argues man is alienated: 1) from the species-being; 2) from the product; 3) from the means of production; 4) from his fellow man; and 5) from the state and political community.

As emphasized earlier, each concept of alienation points to a counterfactual of subjective normality that illuminates the assumptions and ideals of the author. Marx's judgment that capitalism alienates man from his *species-being* reveals his vision of man's natural 'normal' condition, before it is corrupted by the market economy and its oppressive division of labor. Anthony Giddens writes that, for Marx, 'History is a process of the continuous creation, satisfaction and re-creation of human needs. This is what distinguishes man from the animals, whose needs are fixed and unchanging. This is why labor, the creative interchange between men and their natural environment, is the foundation of human society.'[37] In this idealized state, man lives a communal existence. Individualization, for Marx, is a result of a specific history of capitalist processes that institute a specialized division of labor and create a production surplus that places material wealth and power in the hands of the few. By losing touch with human specificity, the alienated man's actions are dictated by his concern for money and the 'alienated life elements' he produces—property, industry and religion[38]—each of which simply reinforces the capitalist system that initiated this transformation to alienated life. In tearing man away from the object of his production, Marx writes that 'estranged labour tears him from his species-objectivity, his real species-objectivity, and transforms his advantage over animals into the disadvantage that his organic body, nature, is taken from him. Similarly, in degrading spontaneous activity, free activity, to a means, estranged labour makes man's species-life a means to his physical existence.'[39] In this manner, man loses the characteristics that earlier distinguished him from other living creatures and depicted his species-being.

Not belonging to his essential being, man becomes alienated from the *means of production*, the *product* itself, and his *fellow man*. The division of labor specializes man within a constricted expression of his full ability. It exercises man's relative strengths, and retards his other capacities that lose their worth. Subsequently, man loses his sense of self-worth. Man simply engages in monotonous, arduous, sometimes backbreaking tasks, while his other potential contributions go unfulfilled. Marx contends that capitalism consumes man's natural powers without sustaining them, before discarding man as a depleted, exhausted instrument—objectified by his labor, without control over that which he produces. 'The alienation of the worker from his product means not only that his labor becomes an object, an external existence,' he writes, 'but that it exists outside him, independently, as something alien to him, and that it becomes a power on its own confronting him.'[40] Marx points to man's dependence upon nature for the manufacturing of his products, but laments the transformation of this relationship under capitalism: 'Thus the more the worker by his labour appropriates the external world, sensuous nature, the more he deprives himself of the means of life in the double respect: first, that the sensuous external world more and more ceases to be an object belonging to his labour—to be his labour's means of life; and secondly, that it more and more ceases to be means of life in the immediate sense, means for the physical subsistence of the worker.'[41]

If the product of labor does not belong to the worker and confronts him as an external force, Marx argues, then this can only be because that product belongs to some other man: 'Man's relation to himself only becomes objective and real for him through his relation to other men. Thus, if the product of his labour, his labour objectified, is for him an alien, hostile, powerful object independent of him, then his position towards it is such that someone else is master of this object, someone who is alien, hostile, powerful, and independent of him.'[42] This antagonistic relationship is the result of the division of labor, which creates a surplus in the hands of the class of capitalist elite, who own both man's means of labor but also his means of subsistence and his dwelling. The worker's product and even the reward of his labor are therefore very much subject to his relations with an external ownership. In this way, all men view one another only from the position they occupy in the class division.

Given Marx's understanding of the social and economic system, there exists what Giddens calls an 'equilibrium' between the superstructure of class domination, social relations and the modes of production.[43] And at the top of this superstructure, the state presides as perhaps the most estranged entity dictating the nature of man's alienated life under capitalism. Despite its portrayal as the source of man's collective power, Marx describes the state as an instrument of the bourgeoisie, through which they may further exercise their domination over the subordinate working class. Picking apart the facade of the state, Marx argues that the legal freedoms that exist in bourgeois society actually serve to legitimize the reality of contractual obligations in which propertyless wage-labor is heavily disadvantaged relative to the owners of capital.[44] In this position of disadvantage, man must censor any views that may challenge the prevailing opinions of the dominant class. The state relies on man's rationality passively to yield to the state's order and restrain their participation. Regard for the state thus becomes prior to regard for the individual, who is reduced to deciding petty personal matters that remain beyond the government's purview. More pertinent issues are addressed by others, and man becomes 'publicly administered' just like government services. Rather than empowering man to rule himself, Marx argues that the state actually impedes the expression of man's public capacities, limiting them to the private sphere, and severing them from public life. And in this manner, man is alienated from his own personal administration as much as he is alienated from the structure of governance.

However, man also becomes equally alienated from the political community that purportedly constitutes the power and legitimacy of the state. For Marx, the realization of 'true democracy' entails resolving the dichotomy between the 'egoistic' interests of individuals in civil society and the 'social' character of political life.[45] Without universal suffrage and equality, Marx argues, communal interest can only be produced by the interdependence inherent in the division of labor, which is merely a set of competing interests, one of which always wins.[46] Under such circumstances, society would be a battleground of disconnected interests, and the framework of state power would become a manifestation of class domination. For Marx, capitalism's communal interest in the general welfare is simply the interests of the bourgeoisie in disguise.

While there is strong evidence to suggest that Marx's criticism of the state's susceptibility to the power of the bourgeoisie endures today, the alienation that underpins the proletariat's estrangement from the state appears less germane. Marx's concept of alienation derives from a worker who has lost interest and control over his work, and has therefore lost control over his nature, his relationship with other men and his relationship to the state. However, the Muslim populations analyzed in this study are disproportionately unemployed. Many are eager to find work and enter the market economy. In the most recent census, British Bangladeshis have the highest levels of unemployment in the

United Kingdom (20–24 per cent). Among Bangladeshis between 18 and 25 years old, 40 per cent are out of a job.[47] In Spain, Moroccan unemployment has been calculated to be anywhere between 20 and 30 per cent, and in 2009 the Spanish government offered unemployed Moroccans money to return 'to their country of origin'.[48] In the light of such circumstances, many of the European Muslims examined here are actually living outside the capitalist system and/or benefiting from the social welfare state. Indeed, very few Moroccans have since accepted the offer of return, because rather than being the victims of capitalist class division, it is the upward mobility of capitalism that renders them hope. A proletariat job in Spain can support an extended family across the Strait of Gibraltar. For many immigrant citizens, the division of labor represents a ladder to opportunity.

Of course, the majority of European Muslim men are employed within the capitalist system that Marx castigates. And predominantly occupying proletariat positions, they may well be alienated from their labor, their product, their species-being and their fellow man. Marx's theories would subsequently expect such workers to be disengaged from the local political system that allegedly institutionalizes their disadvantage and objectification. However, later in this book, I will show that many members of the European Muslim workers examined not only participate actively, but that it is often the educated bourgeoisie who seek to disrupt the system. (See 4.2.5 and 6.2.)

Durkheim and Anomie

Émile Durkheim contends that economic phenomena cannot be considered separately from the regulatory norms and beliefs of individuals. For this reason, while Marx is preoccupied by the alienation produced by the division of labor, Durkheim is more concerned that the division of labor hinders societies' ability to integrate cohesively. This, Durkheim suggests, is a product of increased 'anomie', a term he employs in a manner similar to Marx on 'alienation'. Durkheim consequently treats class conflict not as providing a basis for the revolutionary restructuring of society, but as symptomatic of deficiencies in the moral coordination of different occupational groups within the division of labor.[49] By emphasizing the relative advantages among different individuals, the division of labor undermines the morality of all individuals following the same social ideals, and instead pressures them toward individual self-fulfillment. 'In a general way,' Durkheim writes, 'the precept which commands us to specialize appears everywhere to be contradicted by the precept which commands us all to follow the same ideal.'[50] There is therefore a trade-off between individualism and the sharing of common beliefs, between the atomizing effects of the division of labor and social solidarity.

In the light of this relationship, Durkheim presents two primary forms of social solidarity. Societies with 'mechanical solidarity' are composed of groups of people with familial or clan-like relations, sharing a similar social structure and cultural values. Such polities are depicted as an 'organized totality of beliefs and sentiments common to all members of the group.'[51] With little differentiation, social solidarity is based on a set of shared norms and values that facilitate the collective ownership of public goods and relatively little individualism.[52] A society with 'organic solidarity' is a more modern 'system of differentiated and special functions united in definite relationships.'[53] While such a society is still solidified by shared beliefs and sentiments, these bonds are underpinned by the interdependence of the division of labor.[54] Despite associating the division of labor with greater individualism, Durkheim thus acknowledges the reconcilability between class conflict and social solidarity. The division of labor can therefore be validated by the coexistence it fosters among otherwise competitively positioned men, by placing them in cooperating trades. For Durkheim, cooperation possesses its own intrinsic normative morality—even in a modern world characterized by class conflict—as long as individuals have the equal right and opportunity to fill different market roles.

That which preoccupies Durkheim is the occurrence of human suffering and frequency of social unrest, indicated by the rates of suicide in economically developed countries. He hypothesizes that suicide 'varies in inverse ratio to the degree of integration of the social groups of which the individual forms a part' and in relation to the extent of normlessness or anomie characterizing man's economic and social relationships.[55] In this sense, Durkheim argues that suicide itself represents a sort of freedom from the moral restraint and regulation that stabilizes man in moments of disorientation. In modern societies characterized by the division of labor (and today globalized communication technologies as well), the exclusive influence of certain collectively restraining traditions has all but disappeared. This leaves a cacophony of beliefs and norms that situates the state as a primary spring of normative stability. For Durkheim, a state is only democratic when there is two-way communication between the government and other levels of society—enabling the state not only to summarize and express their views but also to serve as the social ego.[56] For without such regulation, anomie will prevail.

Durkheim's ideas about the cohesive value of the interdependence intrinsic to the division of labor remain useful to understanding the organization of modern societies. Today, communities and states have regularly been brought together by the prospect of mutual gain from economic cooperation. And indeed, as Durkheim predicts, the state's ability to manage and regulate societal norms has modulated. However, as states and their economies have expanded and become increasingly normless, citizens empowered by new means of communication and association have recreated norm-based communities more locally. Historically, migrant communities have always exercised extraordinary solidarity in the interest of reciprocal support and protection. And today (as we shall see in Chapters Four and Five), few communities in Europe are as cohesive as British Bangladeshis, and few normative systems have benefited more from the interconnections of globalization than Islam.[57] Across the two cases, we witness an attachment to a globalized but village-based community, and an atomized group of people who remain connected by a shared diasporic ideal. In some cases, national counter-solidarities like *hispanidad* or Britishness have alienated those who are excluded from such normative communities. This stands Durkheim's argument on its head, as strong normative integration is able to alienate as much as weak normative integration.

Increasingly, re-created communities span beyond the state, across borders and continents, but they do not necessarily lead to domestic strife (see 4.2.3 and 5.4)—as Durkheim's ideas suggest. The sphere of normative connection has simply shifted and diversified. They are neither opposed to the state nor necessarily supportive of it. They simply exist as moral communities competing with the state for adherence. For this reason, the anomic form of alienation that Durkheim depicts is less applicable to a world with new means of normative connection. If anything, individualism and modern technology have produced a distribution of norm-based solidarities competing as (re)constructed 'cultures', 'sects' and 'ideologies'. The purportedly alienated are among them.

Liberal Thought and Non-Participation

For liberals like Max Weber and Josef Schumpeter, man is differentiated from animals by a free will that is influenced by his own rational and strategic needs, rather than his social relations with others.[58] Individualism and self-interest are not only social facts; they embody a state of nature that is only characterized by the dissonance of competing interests once men interact with each other. For this reason, liberals are more concerned to effect the most efficient accommodation of these opposing wills, by facilitating a contractual exchange of man's inherent liberty for certain secured protections. As the division of labor is viewed to be an effective way to manage competing economic interests, the state analogously serves as the instrument that constantly negotiates and renegotiates the social contract managing the competition of political interests. To strike this balance and monitor the changing pulse of opinion, the state requires the active involvement of its constituents. Without a participatory citizenry, the liberal suspects tyranny and social exclusion to prevail over the expression of the common will—a fear somewhat analogous to Marx's alienation and Durkheim's anomie.

In the light of this need to find and accommodate society's common will, liberal thinkers address non-participation in different ways. To a certain extent, non-participation is factored into the liberal idea of the state. Citizens permit the state to make decisions without their direct influence or specific consent, and only with their general acquiescence to legitimate political authority. This is precisely why the founding of a common will is essential. Once general interest convergence is solidified, issue-specific disagreement can be rationalized within the structure of the agreed regulatory framework. Here, such debate may take place, but not with regard to the overarching system of governance instituted with the general welfare in mind.[59] Within the day-to-day issues of public policy, the act of the majority passes for the act of the whole and determines the power of the whole. Alienation is only observable with a citizen's subjection to laws *without* the citizen's membership in the demos.

However, Weber argues that even those who are subjected to civil laws and *are* members of the demos often lose control over the process of governance. Firmly committed to the liberal ideals of individuality and social difference, Weber feared for their endurance in an era of increasingly larger companies, unions, parties and governments.[60] For Weber, the greatest threat to participation and personal choice was the expansion of an immense, impersonal and unaccountable bureaucracy—controlled by those in higher echelons, operated by internal workers blind to the work of other divisions, and cut off from interaction with the very people they are positioned to serve. This, Weber estimates, is simply the price to be paid for living in an economically and technologically developed world with mass citizenship and a modern economic system.[61] Therefore, to maintain societal order and the provision of public goods, non-participation is enforced by bureaucracies as necessary for the proper functioning of modern democracies and their market economies.

Joseph Schumpeter recognized the destructive nature of impersonal industry and growing capitalism like Marx, Durkheim and Weber, and expected the resolution of the ever-expanding citizenry and market to come from socialism. As Held discusses, 'Schumpeter was a reluctant socialist. Socialism had to be understood as the result of a series of social trends; it was essentially a prediction, not an ethical ideal. In addition, socialism did not necessarily mean social or state ownership of property. Rather it connoted above all a solution to the technical problem of maximizing national output in an efficient way in the context of an economy dominated by large companies.'[62] In fact, for Schumpeter, socialism represents a cynical answer to 'classic' democracy that rationalizes non-participation as an inevitable consequence of democratic politics, in a manner that does not necessarily affect the system's ability to govern effectively. 'Democracy,' he writes, 'does not mean and cannot mean that the people actually rule in any obvious sense of the terms "people" and "rule". Democracy means only that the people have the opportunity of accepting or refusing the men who are to rule them.... Democracy is the rule of the politician.'[63]

For Schumpeter, democracy was simply a political method—'an institutional arrangement for arriving at political decisions in which individuals acquire the power to decide by means of a competitive struggle for the people's vote'[64]—to avoid tyranny by entrusting people to participate in the selection of alternative governments. That said, Schumpeter has an unenthusiastic impression of the capacity of individual activism. Citing literature on the psychology of crowds, he notes politics' ability to galvanize the 'sudden disappearance, in a state of excitement, of moral restraints and civilized modes of thinking and feeling, the sudden eruption of primitive impulses, infantilisms and criminal propensities'.[65] He writes that human decision-making is 'indefinite', and that their actions upon their desires are 'nothing like as rational and prompt'.[66] This, he estimates, deals a 'serious blow' to the depiction of man's nature, underlying the classical doctrine of democracy.

Accordingly, Schumpeter places little value in the conception of a 'common will'. He writes that there is no such thing as a uniquely determined common good that all people could agree upon or be made to agree on by the force of rational argument. Different individuals and groups will have diverse interpretations of the common good, because questions of values and principles are beyond the range of commonly shared logic.[67] In the light of the expansion of industry and bureaucracy, Schumpeter contends that the demos is decreasingly connected to the actions of the state, and therefore more easily manipulated by propaganda. So how great is the problem of non-participation and exclusion to the liberal model?

On the one hand, man's exclusion from the demos could mean his exclusion from the sphere of enforcement. For example, Dahl writes that those who do not participate or are prohibited from participating are typically given less consideration by the state. As a result, he suggests rendering civic membership at the moment when civic obligations are assigned.[68] This follows up on the contractual obligations of the state to serve and protect its citizens, as much as citizens are obligated to acquiesce to the restrictions of the state. An unequal bargain will lead to a severe deficiency of communication between the state and certain minorities within it. A lack of public consultancy about policymaking produces discriminatory or inadequate services and action, which will only serve to estrange the excluded further from their structure of governance.

On the other hand, certain forms of non-participation can be necessary to the proper functioning of a democratic government. Schumpeter argues that certain decisions that are made non-democratically may occasionally prove to be more acceptable as compromises that public debate would not have reached.[69] And indeed in many cases non-participation indicates a degree of complacent satisfaction. More logistically, the state must resist all forms of personal interaction beyond a certain point because it cannot face its citizens as real interlocutors.[70] In this way, while democracy may be effective at advancing the interests of activist groups and protecting equal rights, it does not promote forms of political community. Instead, Henrietta Moore writes, democracies require individuals and communities to think of themselves as abstract and notional, as being in some sense equal to all other individuals and communities, as being in the same relation to law, rights, justice, redistribution. This is a challenge and, in the context of a world that is manifestly unequal, one in which resources and opportunities are so unfairly distributed that it requires a serious commitment of faith.[71]

With Weber's concerns about the impersonal and disconnected nature of bureaucracy and Schumpeter's concerns about an increasingly complacent, malleable and impotent citizenry, alienation is here a product of the reduced opportunities and gains of political participation. Such arguments prove very relevant to rising population figures and constituent-representative ratios in modern states. Democracy appears increasingly indirect and the state increasingly distant from the citizen. That said, the modern citizen is equipped with new means of political communication and action. The explosion of weblogs, non-governmental organizations (NGOs) and online social networks facilitates accessible self-expression and public association—and they are of particular use to minority groups. As some of the primary consumers of these new mechanisms, the European Muslims considered in this study are less restricted to the non-participation with which Weber and Schumpeter depict alienated individuals.

Associationalists and Atomization

Associationalism idealizes the communitarian value of fostering small associations of voluntary membership engaged around particular shared interests. With adequate support, it is argued that these small associations can create the basis of a normative consciousness that facilitates greater community cohesion. They can also render individuals a means to express collective opinions and participate in greater civic dialogue. In his 1835 and 1840 studies of American politics, Alexis de Tocqueville championed associationalism as a means of binding citizens to a cause greater than their individual objectives, and yet independent of the state.[72] This ideal was more recently understood as 'social capital'. The term first appeared in L.J. Hanifan's description of local support for rural schools in America.[73] It was recovered from dormancy by Robert Putnam's 1993 study of Italian villagers and 2000 analysis of the United States, in which he reintroduces the concept to describe means of civic engagement like unions, sports teams, bridge clubs, music groups, and other associations that promote greater public activism. 'Networks of civic engagement,' Putnam writes, 'are an essential form of social capital: the denser such networks in a community, the more likely that its citizens will be able to co-operate for mutual benefit.'[74] Throughout his work, Putnam is conscious of the difference between 'bonding' social capital (networks of association *within* established segments of a population) and the more civically beneficial 'bridging' social capital (networks of association *across* segments of a population). Though he emphasizes that building either type of social capital is always useful for the groups involved, Putnam also acknowledges that the strengthening of certain in-group (bonding) relationships is not always in the best interests of wider society. Groups such as gangs, mafias and supremacists represent this 'dark side' of social capital.

Putnam and others since have lamented the decline in these networks of civic engagement. Societies, it is argued, are becoming increasingly atomized as citizens become increasingly self-concerned, distrusting, and discount the impact of individual action on their societies and state. In his 2007 article, 'E Pluribus Unum: Diversity and Community in the Twenty-first Century', Putnam underscored immigration and ethnic diversity as causes for lower social solidarity in the short term.[75] In regions with high levels of immigration or ethnic heterogeneity, Putnam finds lower levels of both kinds of social capital. Putnam finds that in the more heterogeneous regions, people are more likely even to withdraw from their in-group relationships, leaving an atomized society.

While a good amount of debate continues about whether there has been a decline or increase of membership in voluntary associations, social clubs and activity groups, the nature of civic organization is steadily changing. Community is increasingly virtual and deterritorialized, even while it also remains localized and congregational. Groups that once protested in front of a local political office can now increase their numerical strength exponentially with an internet petition. Poker nights have been replaced by online gaming communities. Neighborhood groups can relay information via chat rooms. School alumni no longer depend on reunions to find a lost friend when they can search social networking websites. Young Muslims in the West utilize, indeed they depend on, these new means of associating—thus challenging the argument that they are alienated due to a drop in association. In many ways, the competing transnational identities that many young Muslims are forming in protest against their European societies are housed in the virtual, deterritorialized associations of the web. Undeniably, the 'ummatic' Al-Qaeda has bridged and bonded like few other organizations in the world.

Synthesis

To sum up this review of different forms of alienation in classic social thought, it is clear that the concept has evolved. In its original Marxist construction, alienation is an objective set of circumstances, intrinsic in the social relations of capitalism. However, later thinkers have reinterpreted social and economic relations and concerned themselves with underlying phenomena (anomie) and habits that demonstrate alienation (non-participation or atomization).[76] However, none of these ideas are particularly germane to alienated individuals within the West's growing Muslim population. Pace Marx, this group is politically active despite their purported oppression by the capitalist division of labor. Pace Durkheim, they connect to a range of norm-based solidarities, none of which need be produced by the government. And pace various liberals, Western Muslims are well equipped with the technology both to participate in the public sector without going through state institutions and to construct their own public identities without adhering to the local tradition. These classical ideas about social failure are therefore difficult to operationalize empirically.

Given the changing nature of the state, alienation is now of a different nature. Contemporary alienation is sometimes expressed through association and activism—albeit in exclusivist groups which seek to divide or undermine the democratic political system. Contemporary alienation is often less a matter of 'can't' (capacity), and more a matter of 'don't want to' (choice). Marvin Olsen refers to this distinction as 'attitudes of incapability' and 'attitudes of discontentment.'[77] Finally, contemporary alienation's deprivation is less economic in nature, and more political. This is partially because modern democracies champion equality of opportunity more than equality of resources. More generally, what separates today's alienated individuals from the characteristics envisioned by earlier thinkers is that today's citizens are less subject to and dependent upon the structural constraints of the state. Increasingly, it matters how the individual perceives the state—and how the individual perceives himself.

Globalization has sensitized individuals to personal identity because, in the past 20 to 30 years, we have been increasingly bombarded with vivid, foreign cultural representations through the advent of online profiles, the wider spread of exotic products and commodities, the reach of transnational associationalism and the immediacy of global media. The introduction to other lifestyles, cultures, religions, personas and habits forces the individual to reconsider and ultimately classify his own. Classification usually is a matter of a trait being 'similar' or 'different' according to criteria that are less grounded in the national than in the personal. Globalization has the capacity to introduce and then humanize the Other. And in portraying characteristics like birthplace and ethnicity as arbitrary, and portraying one's persona as self-constructed, we are permitted to build our own identity rather than accept what we are told it is naturally 'meant' to be.

This concept of agency-over-structure undermines the established discursive superiority of colonizing, industrial powers and their civilizations, and emboldens those previously resigned to their submission. Because of this, we have witnessed a significant reinvigoration of international cosmopolitanism, but also incidents of extreme and violent particularist backlash. So whereas previous generations of immigrants could only respond to the domestic hegemony of national identity construction by retreating to suppressed particularist communities in the cracks of the nationalist facade, today's people of immigrant origin have the option of defying the national completely, emerging above the cracks. The evolution of such personal choice has reinvigorated individual agency.

Ironically, individual agency and political engagement seem to be most commonly expressed in collective form. The ability to construct one's identity still leaves the individual subjected to group membership—only now they are groups of his or her choosing. One only needs to view a few personal web profiles to see that it is not enough to identify who one is, but that the next step is to find others who can relate—networks. Just as these communities foster collective pride, they can also lend themselves to collective injury, whereby one person's moral behavior impugns another person's moral standing. This reinvigoration of individual agency, the range of personal choice and the greater scope of individual activism merit an examination of not only how people perceive the state, but first how this individual empowerment transforms the nature of engagement in society.

Ideals of Engagement

Thus far, this chapter has reviewed a variety of the principal understandings of social, economic and political 'alienation'—revealing its contested nature and the myriad manifestations of the phenomenon. This section will explore alienation's counterfactual concept—'engagement'—equally contested and with an array of interpretations. If alienation depicts man's estrangement from his society, work or self, the principal archetypes of engagement speak to a social cohesion grounded in different communions. Unlike alienation, engagement exists mostly as an ideal, rather than what its designers believe to be an empirical reality. Most contemporary references to engagement underscore its deficiency, and the few paragons by which engagement might be measured are anachronistic, imagined or conceptual models:

Marxist Collectivism

Marx's primary ideal of a cohesive society rested with his dream of a communist state, which healed the rifts created by the class conflict inherent in capitalist systems. He argues that the communist state would re-engage man's nature as a collectively conscious being, reunited by a struggle against the objectification of the market economy and its gross inequality. While this dream has not been fulfilled in the markets of liberal democracies, states have hedged capitalism's inequality with socialist programs that redistribute individual wealth and cooperatives that protect the vulnerable from the swings of the market. Through this desire to remedy or balance the inequities of capitalism, the Marxist counterfactual of collectivism endures, but in limited fashion. Contemporary forms of engagement that would satisfy the Marxian criteria for collectivism would be:

– Participation in a commune, union or cooperative
– Volunteer or community service work

Durkheimian Solidarity

Durkheim attributes 'mechanical solidarity' to primitive civilizations of man. Here, the bonds of engagement are forged with familial or clan-like relations threaded with shared beliefs and moral sentiments that are passed from generation to generation, family to family. In this manner, each individual represents a microcosm of the whole society, and can be removed without affecting its normative composition. However, Durkheim dismisses this as an unattainable archetype. The technology and diversity of the modern world have undermined the normative unity of earlier civilizations, and the division of labor has underscored man's relative differences. Amidst this individualization, Durkheim idealizes an 'organic solidarity' stitched together by a cooperative interdependence overlaying a set of common values.[78] In the contemporary era, Durkheim's dismissal of the likelihood of mechanical solidarity has proved prescient. Migration and individualization have expanded dramatically since his writings, and the diversification of society has placed a new premium on the formation of normative communities that promote social cohesion. However, the state is but one entity that provides a moral compass for its citizens— one alternative among many that should conceivably satisfy the Durkheimian criteria for normative solidarities:

– Party membership
– Participation in a commune, union, cooperative or chamber of commerce
– Affiliation with an NGO, a special interest or advocacy group
– Membership of a church or mosque organization, civil society, or other inclusive club/group that builds normative agreement

Liberal Equal Rights and Participation

The counter to collectivist frameworks of engagement, the tenets of traditional liberalism, contend that cohesion flows from equality and protection for individual rights. This facilitates individual participation by way of membership of councils, claims-making, advocacy, protest and expression—each of which contributes to the macro-discourse and negotiation of the public sphere. In this sense, cohesion is a product of aware and active citizens fulfilling their individual responsibilities like jury duty and voting. For Weber and Schumpeter, any act that cuts through the numbing bureaucracy and complacency of the public sphere is a step toward democratic engagement. Individuals' enhanced ability to express themselves does this precisely. Contemporary forms of engagement that would satisfy the Weberian or Schumpeterian criteria for participation would be:

- Voting and jury duty (as a baseline)
- Affiliation with an NGO, a special interest or advocacy group
- Participation in community activity or a peaceful protest, strike, sit-in, etc.
- Writing or corresponding with an elected representative or official
- Attending meetings of community authorities, or other local boards
- Serving in or running for a position as an elected official
- Regularly reading news publications and following political/community news
- Writing letters to the editor, blogging, or engaging in other means of public or political expression

Associationalism and Social Capital

The counterfactual of atomization is association and high levels of social capital. Putnam writes that social connections are important for the rules of conduct they sustain. Networks, he argues, involve mutual obligations and therefore foster norms of reciprocity, which is good for society: 'A society characterized by general reciprocity is more efficient than a distrustful society, for the same reason that money is more effective than barter. If we don't have to balance every exchange instantly, we can get a lot more accomplished. Trustworthiness lubricates social life. Frequent interaction among a diverse set of people tends to produce a norm of generalized reciprocity.' For Putnam, social capital comes in a 'variety of shapes and sizes' but most pertain to associations, organizations, clubs and other congregational forms of interaction for a common interest that render a sense of belonging. Putnam questions the value of 'virtual' communities, because it is uncertain whether or not their anonymity undermines their potential to instill norms of reciprocity. Nevertheless, he has maintained an open mind to internet chat rooms and online 'meet-ups'. Contemporary forms of engagement that would thus satisfy associationalist criteria would be:

- Party membership
- Participation in a commune, union or cooperative

- Affiliation with an NGO, a special interest or advocacy group
- Membership of a sports team or league, church or mosque organization, music band or choral society, or other inclusive club or group that builds social capital
- Writing letters to the editor, blogging, or engaging in other means of public or collective political expression

This review of ideals of engagement is by no means exhaustive. Indeed, for the purposes of this study—one that examines cases of sociopolitical engagement in Western societies—I have consciously limited the concepts considered to Western forms of engagement. Within this cross-section, concepts of engagement are nevertheless disputed and remarkably variegated.

New Meanings of Engagement

In today's liberal democracies, the 'common will' is complicated by the diversity of citizens as areas of commonality are attenuated by the processes of globalization. As described above, communications technologies, quicker means of transport and human migration have flooded the public sphere with alternative norms and lifestyles that dilute solidarities based on homogeneity and shared heritage. In their disorientation, many liberal democratic societies are depending on collectivist structures for social cohesion, while paradoxically promoting policies that emphasize individual responsibility and individual rights according to universalist value sets. This is observable in some governments' construction of communitarian ideals that are specific to the given locality—like Britishness—cloaked in rhetoric of universal values and equal respect for diversity. Such a paradox is intended to absorb difference, but in practice the reassertion of mechanical solidarity often relegates minority groups to the private realm, while also presenting hybridizing societies with a misplaced monolithic identity. Migrants and outsiders are often left alienated from the society's primary channels of engagement, and are often simultaneously perceived to be undermining them. Concurrently, native communities are rendered increasingly normless, as they lack the communion of minority groups and fail to relate to false and often anachronistic meta-narratives like Britishness. In this way, the cacophony of 'shared values' could foster greater alienation *or* engagement.

This study examines communities that straddle this edge of these two phenomena, which is why it is important to establish what we mean by each phrase before embarking on further examinations. The variety of conceptions of engagement exhibited above offers an equally wide spectrum of empirically observable modes of engagement. A cross-referential but not necessarily exhaustive list of the overlapping ideas above includes the following:

a. Voting and jury duty
b. Party membership
c. Participation in a commune, union or cooperative
d. Affiliation with an NGO, a special interest or advocacy group
e. Participation in community activity or a peaceful protest, strike, sit-in, etc.
f. Writing or corresponding with an elected representative or official
g. Attending meetings of community authorities, or other local boards
h. Serving in or running for a position as an elected official
i. Regularly reading news publications and following political/community news
j. Non-compulsory volunteer or community service work
k. Membership of a sports team or league, church or mosque organization, music band or choral society, or other inclusive club or group that builds normative agreement or social capital
l. Writing letters to the editor, blogging, or engaging in other means of public or collective political expression

All such actions represent a commitment to the system and its functioning. It is worth noting that accepting public goods and provisions afforded by the political system (like health services, welfare, education or housing) is not considered an act of engagement. Consumption does not indicate support or participation as much as it suggests instrumentalism. Also, as this book is more concerned with disengagement, the relative quality of the different modes above is less important than their basic employment. Problematically, there is no singular activity above that necessarily triggers the state of ideal engagement. Instead there are various that suggest a certain degree of engagement, and the absence of the political alienation that the next section will address. So for the purposes of this investigation, any combination of activities from the list above will suffice to suggest that a subject is engaged in behavior that reproduces the democratic system and its spheres of discourse and dialogue.

Of course, in practice, engagement does not typify a state of existence in the way that concepts of alienation do. Engagement tends to entail occasional or regular acts that punctuate otherwise non-civic existences. Most individual actors lead lives focused on the obligations of work and family, during which they are indifferent to the activities of the civic sphere or too otherwise occupied to be concerned about them. Political engagement occupies the space between work, family, care and logistics. Therefore, an individual is not alienated in the moments when he or she is not engaged in the activities of the state or society. Alienation can only refer to those who cannot or are disinclined to *ever* engage. For this reason, documenting engagement is a question of whether each individual does (or is willing to) participate in the civic sphere—regardless of frequency, fervency or method.

Conceptualizing Contemporary Alienation and Engagement

We are able to embrace a variety of forms of political engagement because each indicates a general connection to the political system. We do not have the same luxury with the various concepts of alienation described earlier, each of which suggests a different relationship to society and state. Those available mean very different things, flow from different assumptions, and are difficult to operationalize on the ground. There is a distinct need for a conception of alienation that draws upon these classic theories of social failure, but relates to contemporary circumstances in the field.

Deriving Anti–System Behavior

The meaning and impact of alienation has been continuously examined throughout different historical periods. However, the bulk of scholarly attempts to conclusively define its *contemporary* nature and expression were carried out in the 1960s and 1970s.[79] It was in this era that Robert Nisbet mused, 'Synonyms of alienation have a foremost place in studies of human relations. Investigations of the "unattached," the "marginal," the "obsessive," the "normless," and the "isolated" individual all testify to the central place occupied by the hypothesis of alienation in contemporary social science...It has become nearly as prevalent as the doctrine of enlightened self-interest was two generations ago.'[80] Melvin Seeman provided grist for the mill when he published his influential article, 'On the Meaning of Alienation' in the *American Sociological Review* in December 1959. In this piece, Seeman proposes five variants of alienation: powerlessness, meaninglessness, normlessness, isolation, and self-estrangement.[81] In the interest of paving the way for future studies that correlate these alternative meanings with social conditions and behavioral responses, Seeman compared the employment of alienation in previous works.

Since then, the vast majority of literature has sought to refine Seeman's list of understandings or apply them socio-psychologically. Zeller, et al. sought to explore alienation's multidimensionality and demonstrate its quantitative separability into the four Seeman-inspired variables of powerlessness, meaninglessness, normlessness, and social isolation. Their data suggested substantial stability in the dimensions of alienation over an eight-year period.[82] In a significant empirical contribution, Finifter connected four similar dimensions of alienation to existing political attitudes.[83] Later, in arguing that political alienation is actually a significant element of political systems, David Schwartz wrote that 'recent empirical research has found alienation to be significantly associated with a wide range of important political attitudes and behaviors,' including revolutionary activities, low or withdrawn political interest and participation, negative attitudes toward governmental organizations, rioting, support for demagogues, non-voting and protest voting, and participation in radical right-wing activities.[84]

However, in establishing the many variants and expressions of alienation, the term has ceased to serve as a useful reference for social scientific enquiry. The different 'dimensions' described and measured by Seeman, Finifter and Zeller, et al all simply suggest that 'alienation' is ultimately too plastic to facilitate explicit reference or any real examination of its effects. This ambiguity enables a plethora of versatile, if not utterly paradoxical employments of the term. Following a thorough discussion in Johnson, principal points of contestation revolve around questions of (1) whether alienation should be used as an active transitive verb ('one person alienates another') or in passive constructions ('something or someone is alienated,' or 'is being alienated'); (2) whether the individual or group deliberately rebuffs the efforts of its society to include or—and not mutually exclusively—if the society is actually the exclusionary actor; (3) whether the alienated entity is conscious of its occurrence or not; and (4) whether alienation is experienced individually or collectively.[85] In light of this ambiguity, Johnson wrote that the term exists as a 'panchreston'—a word which, in attempting to explain all, essentially explains nothing.[86]

Beyond ambiguity, the previous employment of 'alienation' is problematic for three further, crucial reasons:

1) In separate scholarly works, alienation now fills the role of both dependent variable and causal factor—a simple impossibility. Indeed, if the dependent

variable and causation are one and the same, then the reasoning of causality becomes tautological (e.g. 'Individuals that are alienated are typically alienated'; or 'Alienation is caused by alienation.')

2) Those who qualify as 'alienated'—according to many definitions—often paradoxically invest in and participate in the very political system from which they are purportedly alienated. In one study measuring feelings of powerlessness, three quarters of those deemed to be alienated actually voted in the examined election.[87] In the same study, alienation was tested according to whether subjects trusted public officials and whether subjects believed they influenced public debate. Not surprisingly, about half of the respondents were deemed to be alienated.

3) The dimensions of alienation—powerlessness, normlessness, meaninglessness, social isolation—are conventionally thought to occur co-dependently.[88] But in the contemporary era, this is not necessarily true. Indeed, there are diverse counterexamples demonstrating powerlessness in a strongly integrated normative community (many minority communities or devolved nations), or normlessness among a collective (perhaps yuppies or trade colleagues).

One of the reasons that this has not been a major problem thus far is because alienation has been mostly considered theoretically. Indeed, without a semblance of agreement about the meaning of alienation, Roberts explains that investigations into the subject thus far entail little empirical evidence in support of their contentions.[89] There is therefore a distinct need for a conception of alienation that draws upon classic theories of social failure, relates to contemporary circumstances in the field, and identifies specific empirical expressions to be examined and explained. The following section of this article begins to develop a practical path forward.

Introducing Anti–System Behavior

Given the dissonance about the definition of alienation, social scientists appear obligated to specify the exact manifestation or nature of the alienation about which they are concerned. Émile Durkheim did just that with his famed examination of the high incidence of suicide in developed, industrialized countries. In that same spirit, this study examines a specific expression of alienation in the form of anti–system behavior—citizen's passive withdrawal from political life, and citizen's *active* disruption of political life.

Anti-system behavior has few antecedent definitions in political science and political sociology, particularly in studies of democracies. Perhaps the most significant use was by Edward N. Muller, Thomas O. Jukam, and Mitchell A. Seligson, in their 1982 article, 'Diffuse Political Support and Antisystem Political Behavior.'[90] In this paper, the authors define 'antisystem behavior'—like others—as exclusively active or aggressive. It included: '1) fights with police or other demonstrators, 2) a wildcat or unofficial strike, 3) a group who refused to pay taxes, 4) taking over factories, offices, or other buildings, and 5) a group which wanted to overthrow the government by violent means.' While I would argue that there is nothing anti-democratic about sit-ins, unofficial demonstrations, or civic disobedience in the form of tax evasion—even if they may be illegal—such was their idea. Most other works of scholarship use the term without definition, normally in reference to rioting or protest behavior.

In the model I propose, the passive anti-system individual does not voluntarily participate in democratic political life. He or she is withdrawn. As previously discussed, apathy in the form of non-participation does not necessarily mean a person is alienated. They may be satisfied, complacent, ignorant or lack the resources to participate. So passive anti-system behavior necessarily entails the individual's cognizant withdrawal from and rejection of the political system. Such withdrawal leaves a lack of government accountability, a less representative political system, and a widening social rift between those citizens who make claims of the system and those who do not.

The active anti-system individual is committed to behavior that undermines or attempts to topple the democratic system. He may engage in clubs, organizations, and other political efforts that become substitutes for the democratic political system or are detrimental to it. His form of protest is not intended to reform the system, but to defeat it. An example might be someone espousing or practicing political violence, but also an individual who encourages others to not vote or otherwise participate. This of course removes the active anti-system individual from political claims-making within formal institutions, along with those they are able to persuade. Both active and passive anti-system behavior depict individuals whose actions or inaction do not reproduce the democratic system, or are manifestations of a general rejection of democratic principles.

In this framework, anti-system behavior thus exists in the democratic system authentically (even if illegally), but such activity (or inactivity) is in revolt against it. From a critical perspective, such a course of action is not objectively wrong, but it does threaten the strength or efficacy of the democratic system.

For this reason, anti–system behavior is often illegal, banned, or called a 'menace.' However, it should be acknowledged that anti–system behavior is also threatening to the ability of the anti–system individuals themselves to make claims and thrive in the democratic system. It is not unique to Muslims or Western democracy.[91]

Figure One is a dynamic model of analytical types of engaged and anti–system behavior, given these passive and active distinctions.[92] It is separated into four quadrants delineating activity and passivity, engagement and anti–system behavior. In Quadrant I, those citizens engaging in conventional and unorthodox forms of political and civic engagement are represented. This list is derived from the previous section's outline of different modes of activity associated with engagement. While they may be engaged for normative, instrumentalist or traditionalist reasons, they nevertheless believe their activism is merited, effective, useful or otherwise a good idea.[93]

Quadrant II contains those citizens who are actively attempting to undermine, disrupt or destroy the political system. These individuals are actively anti–system.

Quadrant III is composed of those citizens who are inactive in the democratic political system, but still satisfied with it. Some of these individuals feel no motivation to participate. Others might believe that their participation is costly or not effective enough to merit action on a given issue. Still others might be fully satisfied, or might simply not know the means of participation. As discussed earlier, democratic governance—to some extent—depends on all citizens being complacent and trustful enough not to engage in every political issue, but only those chosen with discretion.

Finally, Quadrant IV encompasses those citizens who have withdrawn from the sphere of democratic activity because they reject the system and are alienated from its institutions. These individuals are passively anti–system.

As I emphasize earlier on pages 40–41, in practice, individual actors lead lives occupied by the immediate requirements of work, family, care and logistics. Activism punctuates these busy existences with the obligations of civic life and a concern for the political direction of one's society. Figure One helps us classify how individuals act or choose not to act. Rather than characterize their entire sociopolitical existence (as earlier conceptualizations of alienation do), this understanding of engagement and anti–system behavior limits its concern to individual's civic sphere, and characterizes their choices therein.

While these categories are constructed to be mutually exclusive, their exercise requires some explanation. It is quite possible that an examined individual

	ENGAGED		ANTI-SYSTEM
I. Active:	Activity within the democratic system:	II. Active:	Activity within the democratic system intended to undermine, disrupt, or overthrow the democratic system:
	a. Voting b. Party membership c. Commune, union, cooperative d. Advocacy group, NGO e. Non-violent protests, strikes f. Correspondence with an elected official g. Civic meeting attendance h. erving in or running for public office i. Follow political news regularly j. Volunteer or community work k. Social capital-building activity l. Political self-expression		a. Violence for political purpose b. Membership of an exclusivist organiza- tion c. Revolutionary action d. Clandestine activity
III. Passive:	Inactivity within the demo- cratic system:	IV. Passive:	Inactivity and disengage- ment within the system:
	a. Satisfied with the system b. Complacent c. Ignorant, uninterested		a. Rejecting the system b. Withdrawal

Figure One: Anti–System Behavior and Engagement The four quadrants model the attitudes and behavior of different individuals who are apartist or engaged, passively or
actively.

partakes in both democratic channels (active engagement) and those which
undermine the democracy (active anti–system behavior). In fact, it is likely
that anyone who seeks to disrupt or undermine the political system at some
point (or perhaps concurrently) tries to pursue their agenda through its institutions. Because this study is concerned with anti–system choices, I deem those

individuals who circumvent the system (even while engaging it) to be defecting from the system. This is because the choice to disrupt or undermine the political system exhibits an individual actor's loss of confidence in the capacity of the democracy to facilitate the change they seek.

A second complexity of this system of classifying political behavior is that the difference between the passivity of individuals engaged within the democracy (Quadrant III) and the passivity of anti–system individuals (Quadrant IV) is not behaviorally observable. Indeed, both are inactive. Instead, the difference is that passive anti–system individuals do not intend to ever become active democrats, while the passively engaged individuals still may, given a change in circumstances or resources. While the former are effectively defecting from participatory opportunities, the latter are effectively abstaining. This distinction suggests the need to solicit individual actors' ideas and impressions.

Further to this point, it is important to note that the model's boundaries are by no means rigid. The primary analytical types are abstractions from reality, capturing important behavioral aspects. There are possibilities for movement between categories. Indeed, it is possible that individuals who normally work within the democratic system may on occasion stray into exclusivist organizations or efforts undermining democratic process. And it is possible that those once committed to the destruction of the democratic system find a way to satisfy their goals by reforming the system, rather than by upending it. It is equally possible that citizens may move from passive withdrawal to inspired anti–system behavior, at different times and with regard to different issues. This model therefore suggests that political behavior—both engagement and anti–system—may have an attitudinal basis. If so, it could be hypothesized that anti–system behavior is to some degree dependent on how the world is interpreted by the agent.

For now, this model illustrates the range of this study's dependent variable: political behavior. In the next chapter, the attitudinal hypothesis pertaining to the causes of democratic and anti–system behavior will be elaborated and juxtaposed to a set of causal arguments prevalent in the field today.

3

APARTISM

EXPLAINING ANTI-SYSTEM BEHAVIOR

In re-introducing the concept of anti–system behavior, the previous chapter characterizes a specific type of political behavior, which complicates earlier ideas about alienation because it is enabled by particularly modern phenomena and social trends. This first attempt to understand such contemporary factors and behavior conceptually opens the door to a reconsideration of the institutionalist-structuralist account of alienation, toward the development of a more reflective and normative depiction that engages the political beliefs of the individual. Accordingly, in this chapter, I argue that the level and fulfillment of individuals' expectations about the political system are the central determinants of anti–system political behavior. I have arrived at this hypothesis after considering a range of existing explanations attributing anti–system behavior to certain structural variables. Indeed, while this is the first known attempt to classify such behavior typologically and contextualize it in the classical thought on alienation, this subject is hardly understudied. Many social scientists have sought to address its underlying causes. Over the past twenty years, these studies have examined the same general dependent variable—alienation and disengagement among European Muslim individuals—using different disciplines and methods, yielding a set of four streams of thought about independent causational factors:

a) Politico-theological factors
b) Socio-economic status

c) Public discourse
d) Identity constructions

This chapter presents a critical review of the burgeoning field of empirical and conceptual work, proposing reasons for why some Muslim people maintain an adversarial relationship with their national society and state within liberal democracies—or to put it more plainly, why some Muslims engage in anti–system behavior. The dilemma is that we are witnessing great structural diversity at the most extreme ends of political behavior. The violent and the withdrawn represent a broad cross-section of social class, ethnicity, religious sect, duration of residence and geographic group. As a result, I argue that anti-system behavior cannot exist without the apartist perceptions I associate with it. And in the end, I contend that anti–system behavior is to some degree dependent on how political systems—and the shared causal factors listed above—are interpreted by individual actors.

Politico-Theological Explanations

Islam's Irreconcilability

The scrutiny and exceptional treatment of European Muslims, especially in the wake of a sequence of 'home-grown' terrorist attacks, has made many Muslims re-focus on a religious identity that has been simultaneously vilified and strengthened by recognition. This trend has been going on for decades, but has recently intensified. Since the mid-1980s, researchers and poll administrators have acknowledged minority communities' assertions of more specific ethnic identities.[1] Some commentators have argued that if this reinvigorated Muslim identity leads to the subordination of civic obligations and disengagement from the democratic polity, then the social cohesion and efficacy of responsive, accountable, democratic governance is placed at severe risk.

Unlike other minority groups of earlier eras, Islam has an institutionalized supranational object of loyalty—the *ummah*—allegiance to which, at least rhetorically, is meant to supersede ties to the local communities of the nation-state. Such an outlook is only further enabled by the revolutionary new forms of communication technology that connect people globally. This relationship and its exceptional manifestation in international Islamist terrorism have created a sense of paranoia in many non-Muslim polities, fearful of an 'enemy within'.[2] And indeed, there have been a number of isolated (but very well-publicized) cases when Muslims have resisted certain obligations of citizenship, citing the violation of personal conviction.[3]

Each example defies the ideal of congruence between man's role as an individual and man's role as a citizen—perhaps because many of the demands of Western citizenship are derived from a Western concept of identity. In any case, for some observers, the superseding of civic roles and national expectations by those based on a theologically established set of values and priorities suggests an utter irreconcilability between the Muslim and Western identities. For these commentators, the question is simple: How can a democracy accommodate certain political or religious movements, the main tenets of which undermine the foundational freedoms of democracy and the individualism it seeks to protect?[4]

The strongest case put forth to challenge claims of irreconcilability has been from Muslim scholars who directly engage the Quran and Islamic tradition, and point to a capacity for Islam and its current minority status in Western democracies to coexist, if not thrive. Tariq Modood writes that most Muslims have no theological or conscientious problems with multi–faith citizenship because, after all, 'the Prophet Mohammad founded such a polity. The first organized, settled Muslim community was the city of Medina which was shared with Jews and others and was based on an inter-communally agreed constitution.'[5] Other scholars have also interpreted Islam to be a religion of tolerance and pluralism that accepts the beliefs of non-Muslims (*kuffar*) and their practice within a shared society.[6]

A complementary strand of argument contends that while Islam has always intermingled the spiritual with the temporal, its political outlook has always been civic in nature. Iftikhar Malik writes that the parameters of a politically organized community were provided early on by the establishment of Muslim polities in city-states with a quintessential emphasis on community-building.[7] Following the same logic, Modood maintains that Muslim notions of citizenship are more communitarian than they are state-centered anyway, much like other non-Western traditions. He writes that 'Islam has a highly developed sense of social or ethical citizenship in which, in line with contemporary Western communitarian thinking, duties as well as rights are emphasized.'[8] Modood here cites the obligation of *zakat*, one of the five pillars of Islam, which requires a portion of one's income to be contributed charitably.

The theological and political argument for Islam's compatibility with liberal democracy is supplemented by some scholars' assertion that Islam is also a malleable religion that adapts to new and modern circumstances. Malik writes that the reconstruction of Muslim communities in the contemporary, non-Muslim world will be successful because Islam's trans-regionalism, in its religious and cultural sense, does not preclude Islamic receptivity to cultural, ethnic and national diversity.[9] This thread of thinking views purportedly invariant *shari'a* not as a body of unchanging law, but as a set of ethical principles with legal conclusions that apply to specific places and times only and are continually reinterpreted—thus placing the ethical over the legal and the political.[10] Proponents of this view argue that Islam makes adequate space for re-interpretation depending on historical and cultural environments via the practice of *ijtahad*—the exercise of independent human reason. Literally meaning 'to exert', *ijtahad* connotes one's maximum effort in ascertaining the intent of Islam applied to any problem or matter in which there is more than one point of view, and then the selection of the preferred view on account of its appropriateness.[11] Bhikhu Parekh argues that because the modern state is too abstract, distant and bureaucratic to hold society together and deal with such problems as the disintegration of the family, a rise in crime, and selfish disregard of others' interests, the state requires moral partners, of which religion and its variable dimensions are one.[12] In this way, Islam and religion in general complement the state by reaching the elements of people's lives that secular government cannot access. From this perspective, Islam is not merely reconcilable, but desirable too.

Political Disorientation

In most Muslim-majority countries, Islam is either the established religion or under the authority of state oversight—continuing a long history of Islam's influence on political and civic affairs. Faith thus transcends the public and private realms in a relationship through which 'the invisible faith sincerely held will lead to correct ethical and ritual behavior and thus public visibility of the underlying faith and, vice versa, adherence to the visible rules of ethnics and ritual will lead to and strengthen faith'.[13] Under such circumstances, Cesari writes that the Muslim state is then almost always the primary agent responsible for the authoritative interpretation of tradition, and Islam thus loses a certain vitality with regard to questions of government, culture and social life. Thus, she explains, 'it's not that "the Muslim mind" is naturally resistant to critical thinking, but rather that analysis and judgment have too often been the exclusive privilege of political authority'.[14]

Some researchers argue that this legacy of intermingling has disoriented Muslims living in the West, leaving them less able to navigate new social and political systems and negotiate a place in civil society. Jorgen Nielsen, for one, contends that it is not therefore the secular context of Western democracies that is the basic challenge to the transmission of faith in the public sphere. He believes that it is more the changes in the social, economic and cultural environment and the effects of these changes which present the challenge.[15] This challenge is total. Nielsen argues that Muslims were a small minority trying to find their way through a foreign set of structures and institutions, in a context developed from a Christian background founded upon the specialization of labor and a rationalism that pervaded the set of sociopolitical norms, ideals and identities.[16] This new system threatened the Muslim hierarchies of authority, introducing the ideal that each individual should seek his or her own authority, effectively making the individual the ultimate authority.[17]

What many in the West might refer to as freedom is thus portrayed as a sort of anarchy—a social and political system turned upside down. In such an environment, one can hardly expect the newcomers to learn how to manipulate the structures of democratic governance in order to make claims and participate effectively. However, with each succeeding generation of Muslims born in the West, this explanation for Muslims' alienation from the state becomes less relevant. The newest generation of Muslims whom this study examines knows no other political system. And while their parents may be less aware and subsequently less shrewd in their civic life, young Muslims are educated in the West and socialized in its civic life. Like many young people in democracies, they are keenly aware of their rights, routinely push the limits of their freedom, and are sensitized to conceptions of justice. So while the politico-theological explanation of Muslims' unfamiliarity with the nature of Western democratic civic life is a useful stream of thought when we consider some Muslims' lack of participation and commitment to the national government and society, it holds less relevance today than it did decades ago. Indeed, if such unfamiliarity was what has held Muslims back from higher levels of democratic engagement, then there would be little in their way today. It is therefore worth considering other explanations.

Socio-economic Explanations

Many social scientists point to the entrenchment of minority Muslim communities in a socio-economic underclass as a main reason for alienation.[18] The idea is that workplace discrimination and the marginalization of European Muslims from the mainstream labor force render them disinterested in the public sphere of a state in which they remain un-invested. And at a more basic level, the argument suggests that the better educated, the wealthier and the more financially stable people are, the more likely they are to engage.[19] Other scholars point to the coincidence between the cutback of social programs and the mass population influx of Muslim immigrants and their children. This has fostered further resentment from poor nationals, and enhanced polarization between ethno-religious groups with a common social cause. Castles adds that as membership of unions and working-class parties has declined, the ideological and organizational basis for an effective response to the attack on living standards has been lost too.[20] Specifically with regard to Muslims, Modood and Berthoud write that British Indians are more likely to identify with the national majority because of their economic success, as compared to their poorer counterparts of Bangladeshi and Pakistani descent.[21]

Despite the wide appeal of socio-economic explanations for political disengagement, there have been strong counterexamples. Several studies have found that poor Turkish migrants in Western Europe have occasionally voted at a higher rate than native nationals.[22] And in his analysis of the 2003 British Home Office Citizenship Survey, Hassan Maxwell found that, contrary to Modood and Berthoud, Bangladeshis and Pakistanis are more likely to feel British than Indians in the United Kingdom. He says that his finding does not necessarily suggest that Indians are especially alienated but rather places them in line with white Britons, for whom higher education is correlated with lower British identification.[23] Maxwell writes, 'The fact that Muslims and South Asians are more likely to identify as British than the more culturally integrated Caribbeans suggests that national identification is a flexible concept not necessarily at odds with non-Christian and non-English cultural practices, and that Muslims and South Asians feel more integrated than many observers claim.'[24]

In fact, it has been argued that feelings of inequality among Muslims now tend to have little to do with personal socio-economic disadvantage at all. As observed by Slootman and Tillie in an analysis of their Amsterdam case study, 'individuals who do not belong to the lowest social groups could still feel deprived if their situation lags behind their efforts and expectations (relative deprivation): "The more an individual is oriented towards the majority society and wishes to integrate, the more sensitive they will be to cultural conflicts and expressions of exclusion."'[25] According to Wiktorowicz's study of Britain, feelings of frustration come about when an individual believes that 'they face a discriminatory system that prevents them from realizing their potential. They grew up in Britain but are not considered British by many in society.'[26] This is also reflected in Maxwell's study, which finds that South Asians and Muslims born in Britain are less likely to feel British than those born abroad.[27]

It is likely that this is because the conception of Britishness, *fraternité*, *hispanidad*, or nationality among first-generation immigrants entering a country is significantly different from that of people born into that nationality, knowing no other. Those who migrated from the colonial periphery came for opportunity and egalitarian values of the British governing power. Their children and grandchildren were born with it. This indicates that there has been a change of what Britishness (for example) is, across generations. Although nobody knows what today's Britishness is, one knows when one hasn't got it, when it is questioned, or when one is attacked as a national. In the same spirit, fraternal deprivation, disadvantage among those to whom the individual is affiliated, is also a cause of significant anger.[28] According to these studies, many Muslim individuals desire the space to form their own identity and they desire the same treatment that any other native of the West would receive.

This complicates our understanding of 'disadvantage' by directly challenging the socio-economic or class nature of it. However, it also confronts the above politico-theological contention that Muslims are not sufficiently familiar with the structure and means of democratic civic life in the West to be active, shrewd participants. In fact, it appears they are all too familiar.

Public Discourse Explanations

Social Discourse

Discourse-related explanations straightforwardly address young European Muslims' sensitivity to cultural conflicts and expressions of exclusion. While many young Muslims encounter discrimination, profiling and racism on an interpersonal basis, their treatment in mainstream Western discourse and news media can feel just as local and direct. As democracies become less direct, discourse and the public sphere become the primary points of access and mediation.[29] However, fulfilling news media consumers' need for quick reference and succinctness makes publications and broadcasts susceptible to gross generalization and un-nuanced explanations. And the need to sell papers and attract audiences makes sensationalist reporting that plays off public paranoia profitable. Abbas writes that 'where the media encompasses Muslims at one level, at another it spreads Islamophobia—not least by focusing on preachers from the wilder fringes of Islam rather than the more recognized authorities. News media also tend to focus on a range of international political events, many of which involve diplomatic efforts or conflicts pitting Western alliances against the Islamic world.[30] Other observers contend that the media are not only subject to the 'nature of the business', but actually culpable for presenting a one-sided view of Islam that exploits the ambiguities of images and terminology, and promotes stereotypical connections with violence and fanaticism that obscure all other aspects of the Muslim world.[31]

Interpretations of Islam that portray it as irreducible, impermeable, undifferentiated and immune to processes of change have long obscured the complexities of the historical experience of Muslims across different societies.[32] Today, these perceptions persist, overlooking the complicated process of acculturation and mutual adaptation by Muslims and the institutions of Western Europe. They ignore Islam's plasticity and diversity, and instead allow exaggerated misimages—stemming from exotica or invented in a narrow historical context and augmented by selective episodic details—to constitute Muslim history and tradition.[33] And by considering Islam as an undifferentiated whole, essentialist discourse is able to broad-brush Muslims as a threat to the equally undifferentiated, 'good' societies of the West.[34] In turn, Islamic radicals are then able to rotate the same simplistic dichotomy to instill the same monolithic perceptions in their followers—creating a tennis rally of generalizations that only heads downward.

A study by the Pew Research Center found that the biggest influence on non-Muslims' impressions of Muslims was what they heard and read in the news media. With regard to these impressions, Edward Said once wrote:

> It is only a slight overstatement to say that Moslems and Arabs are essentially seen as either oil suppliers or potential terrorists. Very little of the detail, the human density, the passion of Arab-Moslem life has entered the awareness of even those people whose profession it is to report the Arab world. What we have instead is a series of crude, essentialized caricatures of the Islamic world presented in such a way as to make that world vulnerable to military aggression.[35]

In a recent study by Sadaf Rizvi, she suggests that such news reporting about terrorism is a significant factor in instilling a sense of insecurity and vulnerability among British Muslims.[36] Culpable or not, media misrepresentations throw another log onto the fire of essentialist discourse suggesting that 'Islam is one, and Islam is dangerous', which has led to an equally reductive view of the West: 'The West is one, and the West is attacking.'[37]

While many young Muslims won't be quite so naïve, the exclusivist sentiment of public discourse in the West can reasonably alienate young Muslims from their societies, as the above sociopolitical explanations suggest. However, if all Muslims are aware of and are exposed to the ubiquitous reach of mass media and sociopolitical discourse, why are some young Muslims alienated and others quite engaged? The reach of the discourse argument does not explain individuals' responses to the broad phenomena discussed. One can only hypothesize that individual responses are greatly dependent on how such discourse is interpreted and what individuals believe to be the most effective means of reconciliation.

Foreign Policy Discourse

Some studies have argued that European Muslims' alienation from democratic political systems is the result of dissatisfaction about foreign policy in the Muslim world. The British think tank Demos published a 2006 report arguing that foreign policy (and domestic policy) since the 7 July 2005 terrorist attacks in London have 'driven a wedge' between Muslims and the wider British community, rather than isolate extremists.[38] The report said that government actions were fostering 'resentment and alienation' among Muslims and 'playing into the hands of the extremists'. It read, 'In the meeting rooms of Whitehall, ministers were assuring Muslim leaders of the need for partnership, but in press briefings they were talking of the need for Muslims to "get serious" about terrorism, spy on their children, and put up with inconveniences in the greater good of national security.' But even before the Demos study, according to the British cabinet's 'Draft Report on Young Muslims and Extremism', the British government was aware that its political actions—particularly abroad—have substantiated radicals' warnings that there is a war against Islam. The report acknowledges...

> ...a perception of 'double standards' in British foreign policy, where democracy is preached but oppression of the 'Ummah' (the one nation of believers) is practised or tolerated e.g. in Palestine, Iraq, Afghanistan, Kashmir, Chechnya... The following quote by a young British Muslim leader best demonstrates the link between extremism/terrorism amongst young British Muslims and foreign policy issues. 'What is needed is a debate about the root cause of terrorism, which is our country's foreign policy. As part of a truly globalised community, many young British Muslims carry the burden of struggles elsewhere.'[39]

A 2005 survey found that 83 per cent of British Muslim university students are unhappy with British foreign policy—particularly in Iraq, Afghanistan, Israel/Palestine and in Britain's alliance with the United States government.[40]

The argument here is that Western democracies' foreign policy choices that subject the people of Muslim countries to occupation and war alienate Muslims from the governments pursuing those efforts abroad, and perhaps suggest the government's wider disposition to all Muslims including those within their territory. While it appears clear that foreign policy is a contributing factor to young Muslims' disaffection from the state, for those disenchanted by foreign policy decisions, actions abroad seem only to confirm already-held suspicions or impressions of the government—impressions previously established by other factors. And indeed, many of those Muslims dissatisfied with foreign policy strategies have utilized democratic means of expressing their views and influencing future decision-making. Under such circumstances, their disagreement is actually a galvanizer of political engagement in the form of peaceful dissent. This explanation thus complicates our understanding of Muslim perspectives, but not Muslims' political alienation.

Identity Construction Explanations

Gender

Recent research suggests that a stronger Muslim identity frees young women from the constraints of their parents' culture and empowers young men against perceived stereotypes of weakness. In several studies of British Muslim women, respondents often viewed their mothers and grandmothers as limited by their ethnic traditions, and indicated that their Muslim identity qualified them to resist family prohibitions and discourses on appropriate behavior—enabling them greater choice in their decisions about marriage partners, higher education and fashion.[41]

It is likely that young men are also troubled by the constraints of their ethnic traditions. But as Louise Archer documents, for men Islam is also a way to resist stereotypes of weakness and passivity, by replacing it with an association with strength and power.[42] Based on interviews with teenage boys in the North of England, she finds that Muslim boys act out and challenge a range of identities, most of which are intimately connected to issues of masculinity. Talk of religiously inspired violence and martyrdom is a part of this interpretation of masculinity, performed in response to stereotypes of 'weak, passive Asians'.[43] The boys position the self and the Other to 'assert themselves in relation to white men' and rise above ethnic divisions between Pakistanis and Bangladeshis. According to a study by Marie Macey, a prominent aspect of the Muslim sense of masculinity is the maintenance of appropriate gender roles and familial authority, through which they can control the freedom of young women.[44] But young Muslim men of South Asian origin are experiencing a sense of dislocation because of the presence of aspirational and committed women—particularly those inside the South Asian community who are outperforming men educationally.[45]

Such gender-related explanations demonstrate not only how Islam serves as a vehicle for young Muslims to appeal to modern social norms without feeling as if they have forsaken their embattled cultural traditions, but also how an embrace of Islam's new-found notoriety compensates for Western society's undercutting of minority ethno-cultural norms. This is significantly revealing about the changing social dynamics of Muslim society. However, this stream of thought does little to explain sociopolitical alienation among Muslims from the democratic system and society. According to these studies of gender, young Muslims' relationship with the state is merely contextual. In fact, they suggest that the well-chronicled increase in identification with Islam is not related to an increase in religiosity or to the rise of Islamic fundamentalism against the civic identity of places like Britain, but becomes prominent, paradoxically, as young people become increasingly British.[46] The Britishness of their lives is not inhibiting a desire to be more Muslim. Instead, their community's ethno-cultural constraints are hindering their desire to be more British. In this light, the rise of Muslim identity among some young people works toward integration—albeit in a hybridized form.

The Social Psychological

Essentializing discourse among local non-Muslim communities is often countered with alternative, yet equally essentialist, Islamic identity constructions—some of which pertain to gender, but others to religion. In response to the monolithic images and representations of Muslim people and Islam in the public sphere, some Muslims have created a reactionary self-image that assumes a corresponding moral superiority and monopoly on truth. This promotes the idea that all Muslims have been universally victimized by Western hegemony and are free of any dissent within their own community—itself a monolithic construction.[47] Any monolithic identity construction is particularly contradictory in modern Western democracies, inside of which the societies demonstrate that being Muslim and being Western are not mutually exclusive components. There is, and has always been, a substantial 'middle ground' that creates the space for the vast majority of European Muslims and their diversity of identity preferences.[48]

Social boundary theorists suggest that examinations of this middle ground should focus particularly on the margins where one identity meets the next, because such boundaries are the points of distinction.[49] However, such lines of dichotomy are questionable because identity formation is not always manipulated at the elite level of communities, but has become increasingly decentralized and therefore less generalizable across individuals. Indeed, we must recognize that individuals tend to identify according to multiple social boundaries simultaneously, and with each boundary, individuals maintain different relationships.[50]

Principal socio-psychological arguments suggest that alienation is European Muslims' reaction to the manifold challenges posed by this middle ground. Straddling the line has indeed become more difficult. According to empirical work by Abdullah Sahin, young Pakistanis in Britain commonly experience British values of independence, civil rights, career-choice, liberal attitudes toward relationships. Yet at the same time, they are expected to show loyalty to an extended family, care for land in a supposed homeland, and look to the elders of the community for decisions.[51] Many young Muslims in the West see their parents' or grandparents' homelands and religious habits as geographically and culturally distant from their lives. The 'old country' is viewed as backward and they are often unable to relate to the customs, which appear foreign when juxtaposed to the social habits and ideas by which they have been conditioned in the Western educational system and society. Many people of older generations are known to suffer from what Margaret Pickles calls 'frozen clock syndrome' to describe those immigrants who live as if the culture clock stopped the moment they departed from their homeland.[52] As a result, according to Wiktorowicz, the older generations' understanding of Islam is viewed as 'archaic, backward and ill-informed' and too 'focused on issues of ritual and tradition devoid of political import'.[53] Many researchers have found that a compounding factor is that the younger generation is often unable to communicate in the language of their family's homeland, and subsequently loses touch with that country's traditions and culture as an aspect of their identity. The combined effect is a group of young Muslims less inclined to follow their parents' dismissal of Western culture, styles and customs, seeking guidance that is more attuned to a modern life outside the ethnic homeland.

Already disaffected from what is often viewed as an anachronistic cultural heritage, many young Muslims are also faced with a significant degree of social rejection by members of the national majority—whether by discursive means or via directly experienced discrimination. This creates a different dimension to the middle ground, one between the obsolete ethno-religious traditions and expectations of older generations of Muslims and the modern, liberal cultural norms of the fellow young people in the West who sometimes socially or discursively reject Muslims. Muslims' navigation through this middle ground is a matrix of different paths chosen as a result of social class, education, family pressures, ethnic ties, gender, piety and ideology.

Some social scientists argue that the embrace of Muslim identity among younger generations is an act of in-group solidarity in response to the public derision and scrutiny discussed earlier in this chapter,[54] and also in response to social rejection by the national majority.[55] Islam has become more significant than ethnic ties, argues Ballard, because it is that part of the younger generation's identity that is being maligned. In this manner, younger generations of Muslims are reclaiming the stigmatized identity and inverting it into a positive attribute.[56] Gardner and Shuker write that 'Islam provides both a positive identity, in which solidarity can be found, together with an escape from the oppressive tedium of being constantly identified in negative terms.'[57] For these individuals, the rediscovery of Islam acts as an authentic medium to 'out-Islamize' authorities in the Muslim community and divorce a Western society that rejected them first. As opposed to swinging more toward a Western alternative to the perceived anachronism of older Muslim customs and lifestyles, exclusivist ideologues use orthodox Islam as a way to handle the ambiguities, uncertainties and contradictions of the West with structure, amid circumstances over which young people feel they have no control.[58] The collective strength empowers young Muslims in the light of their feelings of helplessness resisting the onslaught of a perceived neo-imperial ideology and discriminatory society.[59]

While socio-psychological explanations of alienation illuminate the micro-level challenges confronting the individual, two elements of the argument remain unknown. First, the territory of the middle ground of Muslim identity is a vast space, and we are uncertain about why some individuals are able to hybridize their identity away from the extremes better than others. As a result, we can develop no criteria for identifying disengaged individuals, other than to say that disengagement is often a response to the sociopsychological difficulties encountered in the middle ground. Second, it remains questionable whether in-group solidarity harms or behooves political engagement in democracies. On the one hand, democratic politics is about coalition-building and special interests pooling their resources to assert influence; on the other hand, ethnicized coalitions do little to build social cohesion in diverse polities, and may do more to create cleavages between competing interests in the civic sphere. There is a significant amount of debate on this subject that is beyond the scope of this study.

Observable Implications

In summary, there are four primary streams of thought that seek to explain micro-level factors that affect Muslims' civic participation and the individual's relationship with the state (Chapters Four and Five will exhibit just how variable Islam and Muslim communities are):

The Politico-Theological stream explains alienation as a product of Islam's irreconcilability with Western identities or political behavior. These researchers argue that critical thinking and political judgment have traditionally been the exclusive privilege of political authority in Muslim polities, and that this legacy has disoriented and handicapped modern Muslims. If politico-theological hypotheses are accurate, individuals engaging in passive and active anti–system behavior will demonstrate less acclimatization and understanding of their country's political institutions and processes, while the democratic activists and the complacent will be adequately comfortable or knowledgeable.

The Socio-Economic stream contends that workplace discrimination, lower wages and the marginalization of European Muslims from the mainstream labor force all render them disinterested in the public sphere of a state in which they remain un-invested. If socio-economic hypotheses are accurate, it will be difficult to find subjects who are politically engaged within democratic channels of participation, because the case studies only examine working class communities.

The Public Discourse and Foreign Policy stream cites essentialist public discourse that constructs monolithic misimages of Muslims and instills a sense of insecurity and vulnerability. Some researchers refer specifically to Muslims' dissatisfaction about foreign policy in the Muslim world. Because of the ubiquitous and intangible nature of discourse, this causal factor is particularly difficult to operationalize. A proper examination would require greater time and a different set of resources. That said, if discursive hypotheses are accurate, it would be reasonable to expect that individuals engaging in passive and active anti–system behavior would reject public discourse, and perhaps shelter themselves from it.

The Identity Construction stream argues that alienation is a product of young Muslims' status in the middle ground of identity—between the values of the ethnic homeland and the modern liberal democracies, between the discursive constructions of Muslim and non-Muslim identities. Gender theorists contend that although a more Muslim identity can alienate some young people, it also frees young women from the constraints of their parents' culture and empowers young men against perceived stereotypes of weakness. If socio-psychological hypotheses about identity construction are accurate, individuals engaging in passive and active anti–system behavior will exhibit confusion about their self-image, while democratic activists and the complacent will feel greater security about their identity.

While each of these multidisciplinary causal factors reflects a different component of anti–system behavior among young Muslims in the West, I contend that each of them is insufficient to explain some ordinary Muslims' propensity to disengage from civic life and the process of democratic claims-making. The following section defines the apartism hypothesis that attempts to fill this void.

Testing Perceptions

Expectations and their Subjective Fulfillment

In the previous section, I reviewed a range of politico-theological, socio-economic, socio-psychological, discursive, and gender-related explanations of anti–system behavior among young Muslims living in Western democratic societies. From this list, we see that each offers a different background to the difficulties endured by contemporary Muslims, as Others in an increasingly securitized West. Indeed, from these ideas, we have a significantly better understanding of why there has been a tighter embrace of Islam in recent decades and what structural social challenges and inequities confront European Muslims. However, each explanation is insufficient to explain what causes some individuals to engage democratically and others to withdraw from civic life—even though all Muslims face reasonably similar structural challenges.

The newest generation of Muslims has been socialized in Western civic life and is keenly aware of their rights, routinely pushes the limits of their freedom, and is sensitized to conceptions of justice. As a result, they have a complicated understanding of 'disadvantage' that directly challenges its conventionally socio-economic tint. All young Muslims live amidst the sensationalized and divisive macro-discourse of global news media and popular opinion, and confront the East-West divide on a micro-level inside their homes and in the causeways of their communities. In short, many Western Muslims occupy the middle ground. So one can only speculate that individual responses to this set of commonly experienced circumstances are massively dependent on how their environment is interpreted and what individuals believe to be the most effective means of reconciliation. For these reasons, I hypothesize that anti–system behavior has an attitudinal basis—that the spectrum of individual Muslim engagement patterns within a common socio-political environment is associated with their diverse interpretations of that common socio-political environment.

This hypothesis fits neatly into the framework of engaged and anti–system behavior introduced in the previous chapter. Individuals' perceptions and attitudes change through their lifetimes, and this fluidity is facilitated in the model's gradient between activism and passivity, between engagement and anti–system behavior. To put it simply, anti–system behavior entails the belief that the democratic society and the referent individual no longer hold convergent interests—I call this belief 'apartism'. Like other concepts of alienation, this means apartism also has a counterfactual—the acknowledgment of the possibility of coming to a mutual understanding. Engagement thus entails perceiving a convergence of interest with fellow citizens and the democratic government. Convergence, of course, is highly dependent on the individual— both what he values and desires, and how he interprets the state of affairs in his local existence. To solicit these key perceptions, individual actors must be asked questions such as: 'What is your government and society interested in?' 'Do you believe that your government and society are interested in your welfare, and the welfare of people like you?' 'What changes do you want to see in your neighborhood or society?' 'Do you believe your society can change?' 'Can you and other people like you affect your society to create the changes you desire?' 'What do you owe your government and society?' 'What does your government and society owe you?' 'Does your government and society hold up its end of the bargain?' 'Do you feel indebted to your government or society?' 'Does your government or society hold the same basic values you do?'

In practice, this hypothesis and the questions it inspires place a high value on individuals' expectations of their political system, and their impressions of how well such standards are fulfilled. Both the level and nature of what individuals expect their political system to deliver or do, along with individuals' subsequent determination of how closely such expectations are met, are utterly contingent upon their perceptions. I anticipate that those individuals with greater discrepancies between their expectations and their perception of fulfillment will be more likely to exhibit active anti–system behavior. Meanwhile, those individuals with smaller discrepancies will be more likely to demonstrate engagement with, or at least complacent support for, the political system. Those individuals with very base expectations of the political system will withdraw from it, on the logic that the individual actor will neither disrupt nor engage a political system he expects nothing from in the first place (see Figure Two.)

ENGAGED	ANTI-SYSTEM
I. Active: Activity within the demo-cratic system:	II. Active: Activity within the democratic system intended to undermine, disrupt or overthrow the democratic system:
Small or no discrepancy between expectations of the political system and perceived levels of fulfillment.	Large discrepancy between expectations of the political system and perceived levels of fulfillment.
III. Passive: Inactivity within the system:	IV. Passive: Inactive modes of alienation outside the system:
Small or no discrepancy between expectations of the political system and perceived levels of fulfillment.	Extremely low expectations of the political system.

Figure Two: Hypothesis The four quadrants model the attitudes of different individuals who are anti–system or engaged, passively or actively—and also the nature of their expectations.

The salience of these ideas will ultimately depend on fieldwork, where their observable implications can be tested. If my hypothesis about the salience of individuals' expectations and perceptions is accurate, individuals engaging in active anti–system behavior will have high expectations of the political system to deliver certain levels of justice, equality and liberty but perceive low attainment. Meanwhile, individuals engaging in passive anti–system behavior will have very low expectations. Democratic activists and the complacent will have expectations that are either fulfilled or sufficiently met by the political system.

Of course, to emphasize expectations in this way is not to say that they are asocial. Expectations are shaped by the structural context of agents. As Anthony Giddens argued, agents are knowledgeable—reflexively constituting their respective realities—but ultimately always bound by structural conditions and unintended consequences.[60] My hypothesis emphasizes the underlying importance of agency and judgment, and individuals' subjectivity in how they reproduce their surrounding social circumstances. Structures are rarely 100 per cent determining.

This hypothesis and its relevance to the case studies led me to consult a 1970 examination of political violence by Ted Robert Gurr. In *Why Men Rebel,* Gurr contends that actors are disposed to violence when there is a discrepancy between the 'ought' and the 'is' of collective value satisfaction.[61] In Gurr's terminology, the discrepancy between individuals' 'value expectations' and 'value capabilities' produces a sense of 'relative deprivation' that drives them to employ violent tactics against opposing political groups or institutions.[62] Similarly concerned with perceptions, Gurr surmises that people may be subjectively deprived with reference to their expectations even though an objective observer does not judge them to be in need.[63] And alternatively, the existence of what an objective observer deems to be abject deprivation is not necessarily thought to be unjust by those who experience it.[64] This theory has yet to be applied in any detail to the communities of European Muslims, or to individuals' non-violent withdrawal from the political system.

The importance of perceptions was also suggested by the work of Sidney Verba and Norman Nie. Their Civic Voluntarism Model has remained one of the more prominent models of political participation since its initial publication in 1972. Though initially heavily focused on the resources of individuals, the model has over time evolved into a holistic approach, as it is applied by its creators, their collaborators, and other scholars to different cases. As Verba and Nie explain, it is derived by asking why people do not become political activists:

> Three answers come to mind: because they can't; because they don't want to; or because nobody asked. In other words, people may be inactive because they lack resources, because they lack psychological engagement with politics, or because they are outside the recruitment networks that bring people into politics.[65]

The first group, as described in an earlier section, lack the 'time, money and civic skills' to be properly engaged. The second group is defined by their sense of a lack of impact on the political system. And the third group is defined as 'requests for participation that come to individuals at work, in church, or in organizations—especially those that come from friends, relatives, or acquaintances'.[66] For my research objectives, 'activism' is merely one way in which individuals exhibit their commitment and trust in the just functioning of civic institutions and society. Still, it is the suggestion that (with the second group) activism is affected by people's perceptions of their personal efficacy that, in my mind, merits further examination—particularly in circumstances where disengagement is documented among those with strong social networks and without great resources.

This idea was also integrated into the policy recommendations of Marieke Slootman and Jean Tillie in their 2006 study of why some Amsterdam Muslims become radicalized.[67] The authors cite a Salafist religiosity and utopian political ideals as the major factors leading to radicalization, but argue that such outlooks are founded partially on waning social trust and confidence in Dutch governmental institutions, politics and society. While relating such apartist attitudes to extremism is beyond both the capacity and interests of my research, it seems reasonable to hypothesize that apartist worldviews could lead to more than the mere political disengagement I suggest, but form the basis of violent, ideological movements targeting the government and society from which apartist individuals feel disaffected.

However, extremist terrorism is an exception. It can be life-altering and its consequences are no doubt significant, but it does not shape democratic civic life and social cohesion; it only contextualizes it. While there is a fractional minority of Muslim extremists in Western societies, this study is more concerned that there are larger communities of ordinary, young Muslims who feel befuddled by their identity, rejected by both their ancestral in-group and their home society, disadvantaged by phenotypic characteristics beyond their control and lifestyles of their free choice, and skeptical of the national government and society's will to remedy all this. In this way, apartists are 'apart' in a manner that is much more rhetorical and political than it is physical, psychological or lived. In any case, apartists are liable to withdraw from or rebel against the civic sphere, leaving a lack of government accountability, a less representative political system and a widening social rift.

It is worth emphasizing that the introduction of anti–system behavior and apartism comes from a need to characterize and understand properly the behavior of democratic citizens—not only Muslims, but any citizens—who are disaffected from their political system to the extent that they withdraw or rebel against it. Alternative words are either ambiguous in meaning (alienated, marginalized, disaffected, estranged) or inaccurately descriptive (separatist, apathetic, atomized, unpatriotic). However, we must be careful not to similarly over-interpret these new concepts and apply them beyond their scope and intention, nor attribute any normative aspect to them. The terms label a form of political behavior and its attitudinal basis, and in equally objective fashion I observe that such political behavior is unsupportive of established democratic institutions because it circumvents them. The world does not require another adjective to patronize or criticize Muslims and other minorities. It simply requires a more precise vocabulary to classify, contextualize and understand their and other individuals' political behavior.

Case Studies and Methods

The next two chapters will test the outlined causal factors and their observable implications to derive a sequence of germane descriptive and causal inferences. They will also describe my attempt to understand, map and characterize this apartism empirically, in the light of young Muslim men's changing relationship with the state. This study is limited in its scope, as I set out to examine second-generation, working class Muslim men—as subjects of contemporary socio-political scrutiny. It is hoped that researchers with greater access and resources can examine young Muslim women, the affluent, and other ethnic communities in future research. (Indeed, this study suggests that the educated—and perhaps therefore those who are more affluent—may be more likely to exhibit active anti–system behavior. And as touched upon earlier in this chapter, previous investigations demonstrate that Muslim women and members of other Muslim ethnic minorities face similar disadvantages to the populations examined hereafter, and they respond to such challenges in ways that complicate my conclusions.) However, in the interest of limiting the effect of different variables, the case studies are limited in focus and follow a uniform structure.[68]

They first examine the social and political context of each neighborhood. To contextualize research findings and interview content, there is a close focus on the housing, lifestyle, institutions, history, culture, disadvantages, pressures, and the character of quotidian existence. The case studies then progress into an investigation of civic life in each venue. They document the formal and informal channels of participation and activism, while acknowledging local histories, power structures and political rifts that define civic life and individuals' choices of whether and how to engage.

After the social and civic landscape is established, a great deal of interview content is presented to understand the nature of local identity structures. Political choices are often related to the construction of the young men's self-image. But in the case of Muslim men, a great deal of self-expression and activism is spurred by a sense of collective injury, regulated by common paradigms of morality, and purportedly connected to a wider Islamic fraternity. To address questions about these young men's changing relationship with the state—and its effect on their choice of whether to be engaged or anti–system—it is therefore essential to develop a comprehensive understanding of the Muslim identity. The case studies examine the relationships that individuals have with three particular aspects of their identities: their British or Spanish nationality and residency; their country of family origin, Bangladesh or

Morocco; and their religion, Islam—components which, as Jorgen Nielsen writes, arise 'out of migration and settlement experiences into a new complex whole which functions more successfully in European, urban, industrial life'.[69] Other studies have also included a focus on subjects' 'Asian' or 'Arab' groupings, but such delineations are reproduced in practice to a limited extent. Olivier Roy further distinguishes the Muslim religious identity from the Muslim 'neo-ethnicity'.[70] Again, however, such a (conceptually useful) separation was not reflected in individuals' expressed conceptions, and is more of a normative suggestion.

Once the available structures of identity are grasped, the cases characterize the incidence—but not the extent—of anti–system behavior and apartism in the selected venues. These assessments are particularly concerned with apartists' reconciliation of the underscored identity complexity, along with the challenges of civic and social life. The findings are compiled and compared in Chapter Six, which will juxtapose evidence from London and Madrid in relation to the explanatory hypotheses and observable implications reviewed in this chapter. For those interested readers, a note on methods is located in the Appendix.

4

INTEGRATED YET APART

BANGLADESHIS IN LONDON'S EAST END

This chapter presents the results from an in-depth, qualitative case study of the Bangladeshi community of London's East End conducted using interviews and observation throughout the municipal borough of Tower Hamlets. Based on a set of thirty-nine interviews that includes twenty-seven with 18- to 28-year old Bangladeshi men and twelve with community leaders and imams, this chapter seeks to understand better the challenges and patterns of civic engagement and anti–system behavior among young Bangladeshi men from London's East End—and particularly why some individuals engage in anti–system behavior. Rather than profile a select few interviewees, this study solicits and analyzes a diversity of outlooks and behaviors within a substantial variety of individuals in the same community. This is done in order to trace the landscape of British Bangladeshi civic life and identity forms, and map participants' perceptions about these factors and the British political system with rough indicators of the weight of different groups in the sample. The next chapter compares and contrasts the findings from the East End with those from Southern Madrid.

The borough of Tower Hamlets and its shared spaces is a crossroads of influences that exhibits the diversity of London and the conflicting pressures felt by its young inhabitants. On Whitechapel Road, street market salesmen hawk *bhangra* CDs, leather coats and hardback Qurans. On Cannon Street pedestrians walk briskly, donned in everything from skimpy skirts to *burqas*, vintage t-shirts to headscarves. And in Mile End, the treble of hip hop music emitted from mobile phones mixes with the roar of passing buses and the cacophony of English, Bangladeshi *Shudoh*, and Somali Arabic.

Despite the threads of foreign civilizations woven through East End life, the collected information indicates that young Bangladeshis—the first of their families to be born and/or raised in Britain—are actually quite integrated into British society. In interviews, nearly all participants exhibited a strong sense of entitlement to their place in the United Kingdom and the provision of justice, liberty and representation that the democratic system affords. However, nearly all of them also possessed grave doubts about the capacity of the democratic system's civic institutions to deliver. And nearly all participants' insecurities about East End civic institutions were connected to their insecurities about the relationships they are struggling to maintain with one or all of the three principal forms of identity that underlie those civic institutions. Within the borough, young Bangladeshi men are confronted by the draw of three primary forms of identity: the national British, the ethno-cultural Bangladeshi, and the religious Muslim. Correspondingly, this chapter explores the roots and continued relevance of each construction, describes the concurrent social pressures each exerts, and classifies the corresponding civic manifestations of each identity form.

Acknowledging that each participant and every young Bangladeshi man in Tower Hamlets confronts similar circumstances, I investigate how and why the nature and levels of participants' civic engagement is variable. In the end, I find that, exposed to the same structures of identity and civic engagement and sharing a common sense of democratic entitlement, participants' different behavior is commonly attributable to their different perceptions of those structures of identity and democratic engagement. Many of those who perceive a democratic system and British society that—although imperfect—are ultimately interested in their welfare and affected by their individual activism engage in the institutions that promote such activism within the democratic system. The apartists don't tend to be characterized by the employment of an exclusivist Islamist moral paradigm that rejects all three forms of identity, including their local mosques, and retreats to an absolutist, closed-minded worldview that espouses the undermining of the very system of government that facilitates its public role.

To this end, the first section will introduce the nature of life and community for young Bangladeshis in the borough of Tower Hamlets with particular attention to the community's civic history and public life. The second section identifies the primary civic entities garnering activism and civic engagement in the borough. The third section reviews the three intersecting loci of identity for the study's subjects. And the fourth section examines the roots and basis of apartists's rhetorical rejection of all three forms of identity and their civic expression.

Borough Life

What is so paradoxical about young British Bangladeshi men in Tower Hamlets as a case study in socio-political alienation is that the British Bangladeshi population may be the most civically active and socially networked group of people in Great Britain. Seemingly every adult male is a member of several organizations at once—perhaps a community center, a mosque committee, a volunteer organization, a political effort in favor of a law or governmental ruling, a political party, an advocacy group, or if they are older, an association working for the benefit of a remote village (*bari*) in the tropical flats of Bangladesh. They are likely to have at least one entrepreneurial business venture that they tend 'on the side' of—or perhaps during—their primary occupation. Their extended families connect to many people they barely know, in places they may never have visited. And the call of Islam is rarely (and if so, carefully) turned down, whether it means attending a panel discussion, an event or a political function.

Indeed, at any given time outside of normal business hours, one can be relatively certain that the average British Bangladeshi in London's East End has a 'meeting' to attend. And due to the compact seven and a half square miles that Tower Hamlets covers, one can also be relatively certain that the meeting is not very far away. Many Bangladeshis execute a remarkably small—what Robert Putnam calls—civic 'triangle', or the area between the venues of home, work and social activities,[1] even as that triangle expands greatly for the majority of Britons commuting from expanding suburbs created by urban sprawl.

The triangle fostered within Tower Hamlets is framed by borders that are marked conspicuously by the shiny high-rises of Canary Wharf to the south and the towers of the City to the west—the beacons of London's lucrative and powerful international financial center. While the borough of Tower Hamlets boasts some of the highest salaries in the United Kingdom, it also has one of the country's largest communities of welfare recipients and highest unemployment rates. Indeed, the wealth that streams through during the day is taxied off each evening, leaving a community in socio-economic and socio-political despair behind. However, this is the same old story for London's East End—the proverbial backyard of the British Empire's naval waterfront, turned trading docks, turned industrial sector. It has always been the downstairs to

London's upstairs. And today, the untouchable symbols of London's affluence now taunt the 200,000 Tower Hamlets residents from the skyline.

According to a 2001 census, the 65,553 Bangladeshis in Tower Hamlets comprise a third of the borough's population and nearly a quarter of the entire population of 283,063 British Bangladeshis. About 54 per cent of the entire population live in the Greater London area, and nearly all those who are in Tower Hamlets have roots in the eastern Bangladeshi province of Sylhet. The first significant waves of Bangladeshi migrants to settle in the East End arrived in the 1960s and 1970s, before and after Bangladesh's war for independence from Pakistan. The compact civic triangle is easily derived from their original circumstances. The initial migrants usually worked long hours in automotive or textile factories, and sent much of their earnings back to their families in their *bari*. 'The older generation never complained about harsh times and conditions,' said Tayyib, an office clerk near Brick Lane. 'My father left for work in the dark and returned in the dark. Before we came, he lived in the same house with fifteen men from our village in Bangladesh, Purpushpal in Beanibazar. There was no *halal* meat or curry powder back then. So all they ate was vegetables or fish. They asked the Indian chemists for curry powder.'[2] These first migrants were often harassed or openly threatened on the streets of East London and formed extremely tight-knit communities in particular neighborhoods to rely on one another and protect themselves from racist gangs of British nationalists who would roam the streets of Stepney, Poplar and Mile End. Said Zubair:

> The roads in Britain were thought to be paved in gold. But every time I ask my father, he says it was very gloomy, dark and cold. The housing was rubbish. There was six of them and they lived in a one-bedroom flat. He was a tailor. He had stories about racism and being chased. He used to bring home fabric to sew and a lot of the time people would burn it on the way. It's one of the reasons why Bengali people are so tight now, from relying on each other. It was difficult but he was able to provide for the family. The benefits were financial, not anything else back then. There was the Naz Cinema where they would rotate two Bengali films each week. And the wrestling ring on Commercial Road.[3]

As the nationalist gangs have receded east towards Essex since the 1980s along with much of the white British population, greater numbers of Bangladeshis immigrated, and their tightly knit communities expanded to more council houses and neighborhoods in Tower Hamlets. Tower Hamlets now has the largest percentage of 20– to 34–year-olds of any local authority in Great Britain, at 57 per cent to the national average of 41 per cent.[4] Despite the greater safety in numbers, and probably due to the admonitions of elders,

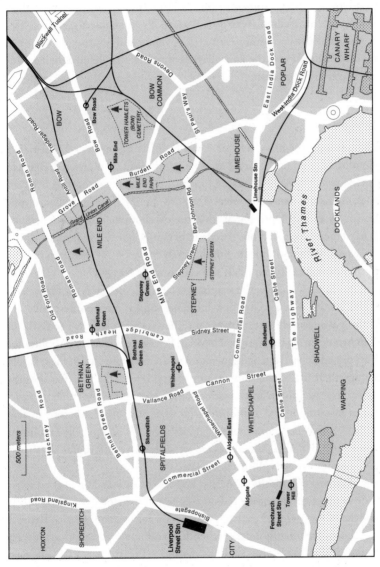

Figure Three: London's East End by Mina Moshkeri Upton, Design Unit, LSE

the majority of young Bangladeshis have still maintained a mentality and lifestyle that limits them to their local 'square mile'. Due to this compact triangle and well-networked social and civic life, few decisions are made without consulting—or affecting—someone else. So quite practically, the more than 65,000 British Bangladeshis who now reside in Tower Hamlets' council estates have recreated the community structures, values and—subsequently—the forms of identification of the *bari* village community that defined their grandparents' lives in Bangladesh.

Council Estates

The Bangladeshi neighborhoods of Tower Hamlets, like most in the East End, are dominated by council estates.[5] Massive, government-administered, concrete and brick structures of modernist architecture pack residents together between thin walls and few common areas. They are cramped, congested, with few green spaces and little privacy. Within the overhousing reside young adults who need their own space, but Bangladeshi family dynamics complicate matters. According to respondents, youths rarely move out of their parents' flat until they get married. The eldest son is ultimately responsible for caring for his parents in their old age. Once a sister is married, she leaves the family and flat. Her loyalty is first to her new husband and his family. These roles are something Bangladeshis accept over time, they say. Girls feel the need to be in the kitchen or caring for younger children. Boys accept the responsibility for parents passed down from one generation to the next, and within these family dynamics, there is a strong emphasis on 'marrying off'. The fact that the girls will one day leave is both an obligation for the parents to help facilitate and a factor in investing in the relationships between siblings. But before anyone gets married, two-bedroom council flats are regularly occupied by families of seven or nine. Bangladeshi families are typically large, and rooms are shared until the family can move into a larger space.

Such housing conditions mean that boys are often asked or allowed to go outside to the streets for space and privacy, resulting in less oversight. Exacerbating the lack of parental oversight is a significant language barrier. Reports from schools are often not comprehended, and many parents don't always understand Western social and cultural dynamics. In extreme cases, young men bully their parents and siblings. There are high levels of unreported domestic violence. Though cognizant of their gender roles, girls utilize advanced education as a vehicle to resist them. Schoolwork is a conventionally acceptable excuse for avoiding domestic duties and interacting with friends and learning. As a result, young women in the Bangladeshi community are statistically better-educated and higher-achieving than young men. Fadhil, an artist based in Tower Hamlets, said:

> There are no facilities for youngsters. They spend their time hanging about. They have nothing to occupy themselves with, so they're getting into fights and drugs. I used to use a lot of heroin, and it was because you had nothing better to do. It was God's miracle that I quit. When I was 18 years old, my older brother said to me, 'You're digging your own grave right now. And you might as well keep digging because the family is not going to help you out of this.' We weren't given opportunities outside the schools. Now you see drugs *in* the schools. They've got no way to occupy their thoughts.[6]

The rebellion against cultural norms extends into the economic sphere as well. The curry restaurants that have sustained so many families are perceived as the 'hard life' by many young people. Restaurant work isn't considered a position of value, but of desperation. Employees arrive at 11 a.m. to prepare for lunch, and some nights they do not leave until 1 a.m. Heavily drawn to the materialistic excesses of Western prosperity, many young Bangladeshis exhibit a fondness for chic clothes, fast cars and sparkling jewelry. The strongest influences are Hollywood, Bollywood, the 'bling' culture of hip hop and their idealized lives of affluence and airbrushed contentment. Stories about Canary Wharf bonuses travel like brushfires through the neighborhoods. But they are usually about white people from 'the Shire parts'. Feeling barred from such opportunities, many young men are influenced to 'go for the quick money' to 'retire early'. Though they certainly exist, genuinely successful Bangladeshis whose wealth is based on hard work are not very visible in the community. Drug dealers are very visible though. They have a new girl on their arm every day, and amplify music out of slick cars when they speed through the matt housing estates. 'Most Bengali kids want things, and they don't care about the means of obtaining it,' says Ridwan, a university student from Mile End. 'They just live their lives day-to-day.'[7]

Police officers also cruise these neighborhoods frequently, and the most problematic regions are patrolled by plain-clothed secret officers. For many young people, their only interactions with agencies of the British government and local institutions are with the police. In the Cannon Street corridor, the unmarked cars have passed through so often that the local youths have memorized their plate numbers. This instills a significant amount of distrust. Yasir, a 22–year-old sales clerk, says he films all interactions with police officers with his mobile phone.[8] Ridwan, the university student, says:

More police makes me feel watched all the time. Anything you do, you might be taken in for it. I can't act normally. This is where they get the wrong perspective about the government. They need to break down social barriers, but by expressing cultural preferences, they suggest that breaking down barriers is conditional on assimilation. The government doesn't like what's naturally on the other side of those barriers. So hatred builds in our hearts toward them. I'm an average citizen. Just because I have a beard shouldn't make me a suspect.[9]

And from the bulk of interview responses, there appears to be a strongly positive correlation between the level of police interaction and the perception of institutionalized racism, and a negative correlation between the level of police interaction and engagement with civic organizations.[10]

With the police and drug dealers, small gangs of teenagers also roam many parts of the borough. They are divided by social groups, which are generally tied to the council estates where members live. When something happens, they often wield a very long, sharp, Bangladeshi fish knife called a *boti* to 'cut someone up'. They are just starting to pick up on the fact that a three-inch pocket knife is just as effective, and can be concealed. Historically, gangs have merely been social groups that are irregularly mobilized for a 'cause'. Causes range from deterring one man's relationship with another's sister to revenge for 'nickin'' a doughnut'. They're called territorially based names like Cannon Street Massive, Brick Lane Massive, Stepney Terror Posse, or Shadwell Posse. Since the late '90s, the pecking order system of organized crime has broken down into more atomized form. Many kids became scared, were injured, their ambitions took over, and they became more individualistic. Gangs are now very local, and very personal.

Street Boys and House Boys

Depending on the parental restriction and housing arrangements of families, teenaged boys are easily dichotomized between those that are permitted to go outside after school hours without supervision and those who are not. This dichotomy is said to be closely linked to future dichotomies of class and educational attainment within the Bangladeshi community. Those who loiter together or 'cotch' in the streets, the council estate courtyards and building stairwells tend to join gangs, as much for a sense of belonging as for protection from other gangs. A 28–year-old youth worker from Newham says that 'many Bengali people tend to stay within their square mile because there is no culture of exploration. You're taught at a young age not to leave the flat unless you must.

This is built on the idea of safety in numbers from the 1970s, when Bangladeshi migrants were liable to be attacked on the streets. The community mentality has continued, even though time and the conditions have changed.'[11]

The gangs are generally territorial, keeping to and defending their local estate and neighborhood. When a known member leaves his region, he is at risk of violence at the hands of another gang in whatever area he happens to pass through—even if his trespassing is haphazard or innocuous. Members of the E3 gang (mundanely named for their postal code) decided to skip the Bangladeshi New Year festivities this past year, because at last year's festival they were attacked by the E1 Boys for straying too far to attend the celebrations. Tales of gun crimes and vicious violence endure in the minds of young people. Deterred by such stories and aware of territoriality, members of gangs are significantly less mobile than non-members in their youth. They remain exclusively in their ward, perhaps exclusively within a radius of mere street blocks—creating what could be referred to as a 'square mile mentality'.

Still, for many, life outside council flats is more desirable. 'The alternative to street wars is being inside,' one gang member said. And being inside is something that many associate with the discipline expected of girls, and with utter boredom. 'I don't have no homework, so there's nothing to do. I can't watch telly all day.' His friend chimes in: 'If I'm at home, my mum will be asking me to go to the market for something new every five minutes. I'm like, why not just put it all on a list at one time?'[12] Ridwan, a university media student who still lives in Mile End with his parents, says that the choice to be outside is also one of social image. 'These guys my age, they're just conforming to a subculture,' he says. 'It's a big subculture with lots of fights within, but they're all actually the same. Even within territories, there are divisions between estates. They're just seeking some way of claiming territory, when in reality there are no rigid boundaries. They idealize the lives of gangsters they see in movies about the Bronx.'[13] In an effort to limit gang association, local police officers more regularly confront those 'cotching' on benches or street corners. Non-Bangladeshi residents have also begun to contact authorities at the first glimpse of any small gathering of youths—leaving the young men with fewer and fewer options.

The experience of non-members is significantly different. They do not go out with as much freedom and tend to socialize in more structured environments at the mosque, family events and schools. They are often more studious and mobile as they get older. This provides a range of experiences beyond the local neighborhood, transcending any likelihood of a square-mile mentality.

'All of society's problems are due to a person's upbringing and environment,' says Tayyib.[14] 'In my house, my father emphasized education, education, education. If there was no studying, there would be no food on the table.' Similarly, Bilal says that his father always repeated the *Shudoh* phrase, *kholomar ago*, Sylhe i for 'From the tip of your pen...'—signifying that one should earn money via one's education and intellect.[15] For another non-gang member, his childhood was simpler: 'My parents were proper dominant in my life,' he says. 'They were constantly telling me what I should do, and I got so tired of hearing it that I just listened and did it.'[16]

The youths venturing beyond their square mile are exposed to opportunity, difference and a variety of lifestyles. Paradoxically, this means that they are also exposed to experiences with discrimination and Islamophobia. Tayyib says:

> Young people fear difference because they usually have no experience with it. Schools can create boundaries of territory like housing estates. And youth clubs don't solve this, because they do not transcend territorial divisions.... But those who do leave their square mile often encounter employer discrimination. With my marketing degree from Westminster, I wanted to get into banking and marketing. When I called an agency, they told me that I was too inexperienced. When I checked the profile of the ultimate hire, he was less experienced than me, but he was white.[17]

Another university graduate, Zamil, says:

> With higher-end jobs, some companies discriminate against people. It makes you question democracy.... There is a small minority of racists. Mile End is like a second Bangladesh. But say I was dressed like this in the City, I'm bound to get looks. People are thinking, 'What's he doing here? He doesn't belong.' But I'm going to do what I want to do. So they can think what they want. I don't give a crap.[18]

In his first excursion outside of London, one gang member joined a neighborhood youth group trip to a funfair in the country. But he said that when he and some friends arrived, white youths asked them collectively, 'Where's your bomb? Is it in your rucksack?'[19] Another participant says that he has even been harassed navigating through internet social networks such as Facebook. Once while playing online Texas hold'em poker under his Arabic username, another player made comments to him to suggest that he was a terrorist. 'What are you gonna blow up next?' he was prodded.[20]

Can't Forget the Ghetto

With the mixed consequences of leaving and staying within Tower Hamlets, there is an ongoing dialogue between those individuals who are trying to 'move on up' and others who claim they 'can't forget the ghetto'—a cultural monologue mimicking that of African Americans as heard in the hip hop songs that are regularly played on mobile phones and car stereo systems. On the one hand, participants described a sense of blissful ignorance that is enabled by leaving the conflicts that take place within the square mile. However, several participants criticized those who move out for trying to shirk obligations to their families, to their community, to their religion, and to their relatives in Bangladesh. Many of those interviewed blame the desire to leave on the insidious influence of Western social norms which dictate that children can move out of the parents' home at age 18, remain unmarried, and retain little obligation to their families or communities. That said, other participants said that they wish to move out of the borough precisely for the benefit of their loved ones. 'We've lived in the borough for twelve years now,' said Bilal, a medical student from Stepney. 'And I wouldn't want for my brothers and sisters to be living here for another twelve years, surrounded by drugs and other problems, and people who are happy with being mediocre in their lives.'[21]

For many, the greatest common denominator that keeps Bangladeshis in or near Tower Hamlets is the presence of the Bangladeshi–administered East London Mosque and the activities of its London Muslim Centre. So those who do move go eastward. From the east, it's easy to commute back and forth to go to the mosque and shop for food and clothing. Yusuf works steps from the mosque but lives outside the borough:

> My parents are 62–, 63–years-old. My dad is 50 per cent up for moving. My mom is 100 per cent for staying. She's made a lot of friends in the neighborhood and hears the call to prayer from their house on Parfett Street…They're used to a small colony, and they want to maintain the feeling of living in a *bari*…It's the next best thing to Bangladesh. It's a lot more difficult to adjust. Personally, I drive, I've got my car, and I can get used to new areas.

> But once you go to the east, it's not that easy to move back. The people who have moved out of Tower Hamlets are getting used to it. I guarantee you 100 per cent they are not moving back. Once they've got their own houses in a quiet, safe neighborhood with better schools, they don't want to come back to what's comparably a slum. The young kids today want to get out faster than previous generations. They want a big house, a nice car, that kind of life.

> It's been two years since I moved out to Wanstead, Redbridge, but I still come see my parents every day. Tower Hamlets is still the hub of the Bengali community—the place to connect to your community of Bangladeshis and to know what's going on. The people outside of Tower Hamlets, their day-to-day lives are still affected by what happens inside.[22]

Thus Tower Hamlets, and not Sylhet Town or Dhaka, endures as the true home-away-from-home for many British Bangladeshis—but increasingly so, as the memory of life in Bangladesh fades. Indeed, the young people who were the first in their family to be British-born or British-raised citizens (and are the subjects of this study) have a very different relationship with Bangladesh and Britain.

A Sense of Entitlement

Because they experienced the hardships of Bangladesh that motivated migration and the journey to Britain, the first generation's image of the British state is typically one of a provider—the government that bestowed great benefits on a people who had yet to contribute to the system. The second generation, the vast majority of whom did not experience their parents' journey, has a very different relationship with the British state. Quite simply, they feel entitled to the benefits that are afforded to other British citizens without question. Interview content reveals a very strong feeling of entitlement, rooted in their oft-denied personal feelings of Britishness. This feeling among participants transcends their differences in the nature and levels of civic engagement, and is a clear testament to the integration of study participants and the Bangladeshi community. As we see in the statements below, this sense of entitlement takes different forms, but the message is clear: Britain is my country as much as anyone else's.

To solicit feelings of indebtedness or entitlement, interviewees were asked if they felt indebted to their government and society. Several of those respondents who were democratically engaged acknowledged the stark differences between their approach to the British political system and that of their parents. Ridwan says,

> My parents came to Britain because they saw an opportunity for a better life. They were uneducated and worked in takeaway shops. They were migrants and they knew that if they messed with the government, there would be problems. ...They felt a little displaced. But I have the same rights as an MP [Member of Parliament]. Why should I conform like my parents? I feel the need to question them. That's my right. I've gone through assimilation by being brought up here. The way my parents didn't question, I will. Their mentality is from a different time. It's my duty as a citizen to question.[23]

Zaki portrays this mentality as a difference between his parents' sense of desperation and his civil rights. 'I don't feel indebted at all,' he says. 'I pay taxes. The only difference is my skin color. I don't think people should feel indebted to this country. Some parents might, because they fled to this country for a safer life. So maybe that generation would. And maybe some parents may feel like their children should feel indebted.'[24]

Such sentiments are similar to those of respondents who were not engaged in the political system at all, or are engaged in forms of participation that undermine the system. Zakaria, who is withdrawn, says,

> It's all about perceptions. My dad, he sees black and white. He sees the police, and says they're on the right side of the law. He respects institutions, and thinks the police would only bother you if you are a criminal. But I know better. I guess he does feel indebted, but I don't know why. He worked for it. I guess it's for the opportunity here. Yeah, obviously the UK gave me a school and stuff, but that's my right, 'cause I'm born in this country. There's a bare minimum that they owe me. It's like the way you aren't grateful because your mom gave you clothes when you were born. I expect that. Sometimes I tell the police, 'I'm paying your salaries with my taxes, and you're giving me shit.'

Like others, Zakaria distances himself from his parents. 'My father's pact is *his* pact,' he says. 'Not mine. It's like if my brother owes you ten pounds, that's your deal with him, not me.'[25] Non-participatory like Zakaria, Uqbah suggests that his sense of entitlement is a product of greater awareness of British law and his life experiences. 'My dad was a tailor, living in Brick Lane when it was just becoming Bengali,' he says. 'It was worth coming here just to get a better life, but they fear that the day will come when immigrants get kicked out. I don't fear that like they do.'[26] Ismail is a member of the anti–democratic group *Hizb-Ut-Tahrir*, but nevertheless acknowledges the salience of the social contract. 'I didn't choose to be born here,' he says. 'I appreciate the government. I may not vote, but I appreciate the benefits it provides. In return, I owe them my taxes. Doing your part, taking part in community activities to improve the neighborhood.'[27]

It is this near universal sense of entitlement that informs many of the trends this chapter will underscore—young Bangladeshis' activism, their feelings of rejection at the hands of British society, and their disappointment when this sense of entitlement is unfulfilled by civic institutions. Above it all, it reflects the extraordinary integration of this group into life in London and the United Kingdom. And as the following sections explain, it is this very integration into the community that makes certain individuals' alienation from it so profound.

Civic Life

History and Structure

Bangladeshis in the East End were not always so integrated in the United Kingdom. As the earliest generations of migrants in the 1960s and 1970s were mostly comprised of single men with families in South Asia, most civic organizations remained connected to the political events surrounding Bangladesh and its 1971 liberation from Pakistan, or inspired by them. Sarah Glynn has documented how developing community activism followed the progress of the new nation, and *probashi* (Bangladeshi emigrants) proclaimed their beliefs in the principles of socialism, secularism and democracy.[28] At the time, these principles echoed the 1971 movement organizing for Bangladeshi independence from the Islamist politics of (then) West Pakistan and the Bangladeshi *Jamaat-e-Islami* party. Most Bangladeshis sought a secular government that facilitated their cultural norms, which were more closely tied to those of the greater Bengal region spreading across borders with India. Many of the original migrants to the East End were businessmen, operating a clientele system and restricted to the political parties oriented to Bangladesh, mosques, the Bangladesh Welfare Association, and village-kin allegiances.[29]

After most family reunification had taken place in the 1980s and ties with Bangladesh faded with the purity of the independence movement, the first generation's leadership was challenged by a more Anglicized group of Bangladeshi–born youths, which forged effective alliances with radical activists in the Labour Party.[30] They criticized their elders for a pusillanimous response to racist attacks in the late 1970s and early 1980s.[31] Rather than act as peace-brokering intermediaries, the younger generation earned greater credibility for their resolute and aggressive action.[32] These individuals became active in an array of community organizations and government entities that remain relevant today, but continued their parents' tradition of socialist secularism. Their fortunes tied to those of the Labour Party, this group would decline in power when Labour ceded its council leadership and control of community development funding.[33] Today, they are being undermined by a generation of young, British-born activists inspired by the Islamism that their grandparents rebuffed in Bangladesh. This generation rejects the more formal town-hall politics of their elders, which has failed to emancipate them from the marginalization of the urban East End, and increasing numbers seek ideological guidance and inspiration from a revivalist sect of Islam.[34] As this heterogeneous political culture has been squeezed into a mere forty years, the civic manifestations of each trend endure and evolve.

In London, the structure of local governance is quite decentralized. The Mayor of London and the Greater London Authority oversee the metropolitan area, but with around twelve million people in the market, a significant amount of control and funding is administered and allocated through the city's twenty-six local boroughs and their councils. Councils sit atop the hierarchy of local government, but underneath their legislative decisions and leadership, there exists a honeycomb of bureaucrats that manage the day-to-day logistics of housing, youth services, health care, community support, crime prevention, parks and recreation, and other tasks. These bureaucrats make a large city feel significantly smaller and more accessible by diagnosing and responding to local needs, and also accommodating special requests and community projects. Council bureaucracies are asked to administer citywide, but also national policies and budgets. Their quiet executive decisions hold as much, if not more, power on the average East Ender than votes cast by the council members, who must sift through the quicksand of politics and debate.

Amidst the extraordinary cohesion and civic action within the Bangladeshi community, the vast majority of established movements and organizations administered by Bangladeshis remain *for* Bangladeshis. Because of this insularity, Bangladeshis hold little influence on the direction of policy and administration of borough politics in greater Tower Hamlets, despite their internal politicization. People of Bangladeshi origin hold thirty of the fifty-one seats on the council. However, many respondents (and council employees) said that the borough is effectively run by the bureaucracy of officers and managers who are mostly white and hail from 'the shires' of outer London. Some fault the infighting and incompetency of council members for leaving such a void of power. Indeed, several of the Bangladeshi representatives are not even literate in English, and struggle to communicate beyond their base of older Bangladeshi voters. But in any case, this widely perceived disconnection between the size of the Bangladeshi community and its continued subjection to the political will of others has frustrated young and old alike. In response, many Bangladeshis face a choice of either constructing non-governmental bodies of leadership or simply disengaging from British civic life completely by perhaps even joining gangs.

Either way, much of the civic engagement by second-generation British Bangladeshis is not actually affiliated with the national government or wider British society. Local political institutions must compete with alternative forms of informal power based on faith, family and frustration, which can only be called 'village politics'. Previous studies of East End political culture have illustrated a competition for support between the secular nationalists of the earliest generation of Bangladeshi migrants and the rising coalition of Islamists.[35] However, I find that there has been a pluralization of the public sphere in the East End and a mixture of civic entities have emerged, reflecting the complexity of political identities. Today's British Bangladeshis choose from a selection of socialist formal democratic institutions, the secularist capitalist *desi*–politics, the inclusive, territorialized Islamism of the mosques, and the exclusive global Islamism of apartist groups.

Council and British government represent only one form of leadership in the East End, though many young Bangladeshis do engage with such formal institutions. Other power brokers claim a significant degree of influence and sway. More mundanely, there are economic power brokers—capitalist, and often secular, business owners who can throw their money and weight around behind certain causes. Colloquially, they are referred to as *desi* politicians—meaning 'back home', playing the role of village elders who prefer muscle over the British political tradition of oratory and persuasion. A second power broker is the mosque. The East End is spotted with *masjids*, often in places one would least expect. But the London Muslim Centre and its East London Mosque remains the most powerful leader of the Islam-conscious in the borough. Its sponsorship or support is golden and influences the thousands who attend its *jummah* services each Friday afternoon. Its form of socialist Islamism suggests that Muslims' adherence to Islam should go beyond ritual prayer, and extend to inform private, individual decision-making. A third power broker is the anti–establishment Islamist group, *Hizb-Ut-Tahrir*, and its expanding reach among young Bangladeshis and other Muslims in Britain. Unlike the underground group, *Al-Muhajiroun*, which has advocated violence against the British state and society, *Hizb-Ut-Tahrir* remains legal. In frequent, passionate, well-scripted meetings around Tower Hamlets, high- and low-level members express forms of an ideology that condemns Western, liberal democracy as an un-divine, and thus ultimately flawed, system that works against the global interest of Islam and Muslims.

In Tower Hamlets, there is a fight for the minds of young Bangladeshis between the formal government and these three protagonists. But ultimately, from the perspective of civic engagement, they can be dichotomized by their outlooks: the *desi*-politicians, the mosque, and the local government complement the British state and society by working within it. The political group *Hizb-Ut-Tahrir* challenges the foundations supporting that society and state. This section examines each.

Desi-Politicians and Village Politics

Because of Tower Hamlets' compact geography and the sheer concentration of Bangladeshi people within its borders, the borough often feels like a village. As social and kinship networks, business markets, gossip and mosques follow suit, politics does too. 'The people running the show are unelected,' says Qadim, a former gang member turned keen political observer. 'It's a village mentality. It's the village elder who speaks the loudest, who knows the most people, who has the most sons, and is the most financially stable. Before, in the London communities, it was about the *desis'* honor and respect. Now it's all about their money and power.'[36] One political leader said that he cannot successfully govern by sequestering himself in Britain's formal political institutions:

> I feel like I've been bridging British and Bengali culture all my life. I'm not Bengal-izing the system; I'm trying to broker an understanding between young Bengalis and older Bengalis. The politics of Bangladesh is about muscle. It's more about hammers, guns, manpower and dynasty than it is about vision. The politics of Britain is still relatively intellectual. But that said, I'm certainly exposed to Brick Lane politics—screwing people over for power. You have to play your cards right. I wear a suit, but during the campaign I sit around eating betelenuts, drinking tea late at night, speaking in the language people know best. Politics in Tower Hamlets, you can't always do it by the book. There are village politics. Young people can either be put off by it, or be inspired by their affiliations with individuals or organizations. We haven't been motivated to engage them, and some of my elders don't want to.

Most politicians are not as adroit. The image of the council and local government is characterized by inaction, and the voids of power they leave. *Desi*-politicians take pride in filling the vacuum. In 2008, council administrators were going to cancel the annual carnival for the Bengali New Year—*Boishakhi Mela*—for what was called a lack of public funds, but suspected to be bureaucratic laziness. However, a group of *desi*-politicians contributed over £100,000 to force the council's hand. One member of the group said, 'The council bureaucracy thinks that Bangladeshis are too busy fighting over petty issues like *Boishakhi Mela*, and are missing the bigger picture. The councillors are dumbos who don't have the knowledge to fight the managers' reluctance to hold the festival in what's somehow known as "the festival borough".'[37] A similar group is also lobbying for the renaming of Shoreditch Underground Station to 'Banglatown.' Most *desi*-politicians live outside Tower Hamlets in Slough, Redbridge or East Finchley. Hearsay suggests that many are involved in heroin trafficking and sales between Bangladesh and Tower Hamlets. The borough is one of the cheapest places to purchase heroin in Europe. In 2008, it cost about

£3.50 for a tenth of a gram of very poor quality, unfiltered heroin from Bangladesh—inside the so-called 'Golden Triangle' of heroin production in southeastern Asia. 'There are two ways to make your mark here,' Qadim explains. 'Either you're a big man in fighting. Or you've got a lot of money. The *desis* do their fair bit of community work. It lends them credibility and shoulder-rubbing access to the right people.'[38]

However, the *desi*-politicians do not only try to out-maneuver the government in the interest of the wider Bangladeshi community. There is also significant infighting within the community for positions of power and influence. The 'golden chair' is the parliamentary seat representing Bethnal Green and Mile End. A Bangladeshi winner would be the first Bangladeshi person to serve in parliament outside of Bangladesh. 'It's a dream seat,' says Yusuf. 'The winner would be on the level of Baroness Pola Uddin, the only Bengali baroness.'[39] *Desi*-politicking is also one way for the older generation of Bangladeshis to maintain some relevance. Nearly each of the tiny governmental districts inside Bangladesh's Sylhet region has an association in the United Kingdom: those for Golabgoinj, Beanibazaar, Balagoinj, Bishnath, Jogonathpur, and the list continues. These organizations are based on who they know and their role in the Bangladeshi politics 'back home'.

The nature of the relationship between Bangladeshis in the UK and their country of origin has to be understood, therefore, according to different interconnected arenas (local, regional, national, transnational).[40] The first generation living in London might have kept a strong attachment with their ancestral villages through regular visits, the improvement of their family properties and regular remittances; but since the mid-1980s, this financial involvement has been institutionalized through the work of many 'development groups' (*Jonokollan Shomittee*) controlled by lineage leaders closely linked with the activities of Bangladeshi political parties in London, in particular the Awami League.[41] The creation of these groups coincided with a sub-regional decentralization of governance in Bangladesh which reinforced the role that *probashis* (emigrants) could play in local Sylheti politics.[42] The secularist *desi*–politicians thus promote the idea that Bangladeshi cultural heritage remains central to the greater integration of young people in Britain, by centering their sense of identity as part of a cohesive minority within wider society.[43] Though often subject to the consequences, young people tend to stay out of this fray—a dogfight about issues and places irrelevant to their British lives.

The Mosque and its Moral Paradigm

East End mosques and their committee members—historically a center of power in all Muslim communities—act as the socialist, Islamist balance to the *desi*-politicians' secular capitalism in Tower Hamlets. Religious practice in the East End was initially based around small prayer rooms in council flats or private commercial spaces. During the 1980s, several larger facilities became available in neighborhoods with large concentrations of Bangladeshis.[44] Many mosques converted synagogues, community centers and parking lots to accommodate growing congregations, as when the East London Mosque—Tower Hamlets' biggest—expanded to create the multi–purpose London Muslim Centre in recent years.[45] Today, such larger facilities are still complemented by a plethora of localized prayer rooms that often cater to a tightly related congregation and date back to the Bangladeshi community's early days in London.

Immediately after 11 September 2001, there were a string of attacks by non-Muslims on Muslims, but also by non-religious Muslims on religious Muslims, who were erroneously blamed for the rise of religious extremism and the British backlash. 'Now, my mum can't walk down the street without being harassed,' it was said. In response, the mosque's Young Muslim Organization began heavy recruiting to build bridges with the less religious people— particularly gang members on the streets of the East End. One former gang member says, 'It failed because, ultimately, we saw little in it for us. They wanted our protection, and we all knew that we didn't need to join a group to go to heaven. The Islamists weren't prepared to share power. Some of us were businessmen and [street leaders] and we knew they weren't sincere.' Still, among its thousands of members, the East London Mosque and others in the neighborhood wield significant power. After the 2003 commencement of the War in Iraq, Member of Parliament George Galloway received the tacit endorsement of the East London Mosque and opened an office on Brick Lane. 'Mosque endorsements have always been subtle and cautious,' Yusuf says. 'People began to understand that Galloway was the choice. The regulars got the vibes and spread it.'[46]

The strength of the mosque against the pragmatism of *desi*–politics resides in its employment of a compelling moral paradigm that counters that of the British government and the *desi*-politicians who allegedly 'play along'. Using the teachings of the Quran, Hadith and Sunna, this moral paradigm informs individual decision-making in rejecting Western society's expedient rationality that relegates morality as a secondary concern, and instead supports a falsely clear-cut morality of justice that examines the means as much as the ends. Perhaps obliviously, the British political system is actively competing with these values of Islamic faith, family and culture—which many in the East End perceive to be quite distinct from each other.

The vast majority of Islamists couch their adherence to this paradigm by referring to a principle from the Hadith of Said Al-Bukhari and Said Al-Muslim, which teaches that as long as government laws do not ask the individual to do something that is *haram* or sinful, then they should abide by them. But many perceived injustices straddle the border of good and evil in the minds of many young Bangladeshi men interviewed. Britain's participation in the Iraq and Afghanistan wars is foremost among them. There is a 'mentality of being victims', one British Muslim leader says. 'This could be a product of the little perceived difference of the two million person march against the war, and the continuous bigotry, hypocrisy of foreign policy. It is viewed as a moral issue—evidence of a deep spiritual malaise [in Britain]—where national interest is represented in greed, arrogance, hatred, and usurping others' rights. These are the major moral vices, which are destructive within us as individuals. When governments display this on a massive scale, there are consequences.'[47]

However, British *haram*, or sinfulness, extends beyond the national foreign policy in the eyes of many participants. Beyond the support for an unjust war, they say British society is culpable for its lifestyle. Several participants say they believe they fight the temptation of such sin everyday—in the form of the most mundane aspects of life in the West. Amjad, a strictly religious, unemployed 20–year-old who spends his days at the East London Mosque, says:

> They try to teach British values. I follow the values of my religion.... I follow the Quran like my rulebook, and look to it for guidance. Everything you see around you in society are temptations. Naturally, I'm tempted. I think the whole reason for having these things around us is to serve as a test. It's quite hard, like if you see a woman in front of you. If she's beautiful, naturally you want a second look. But Islam teaches you to lower your gaze. It's the same with waking up in the morning from your warm bed to go to the *masjid* for prayer. It's about fighting the *nafs* [desire]. You win, you lose, but there's always a chance to get back on the track. We learn from our mistakes.... I don't need to find out about temptations. If the Quran says don't drink, I know I'm not missing out.[48]

Viq, a 26–year-old business owner from Stepney, says, 'It's the culture and ideas in this country that is messing things up. It's the idea of freedom and secularism.... But the government [rhetorically establishes] that excess and materialism is okay; and that criminality in white collar crimes isn't wrong unless you get caught.'[49] In response to such value discrepancies, many of the study participants have morally divested themselves of the institutions of the state. As several stated, their sovereign is Allah.[50] 'Right now, the government is a religion itself,' says Ridwan. 'It runs our lives more than Islam runs our lives.... We're supposed to believe in it. But there is a lack of faith.'[51]

Local Politics and the British State

'Of all the Muslim ethnicities in the UK, the Bangladeshis are the most organized,' states Qadim with certainty. 'The Pakistanis, they're huge, but they're split into castes, villages, you know. So why in Tower Hamlets, if we're so organized and hold a majority of council seats, why do issues like overcrowding and unemployment go un-tackled?' Many young Bangladeshis interviewed asked similar questions, and the answer from council employees deters many from engagement in formal British politics.

Participants point fingers in various directions, but most led to the individuals on the council and the bureaucratic managers beneath them. One mid-level council employee says that several Tower Hamlets councilors 'are literally illiterate in English, and are elected essentially via village politics. They've occasionally come to a school to encourage degree attainment and learning, when they can't even boast the skills they're touting. The kids just laugh. They think, "these people can't possibly represent our interests".'[52] The effect of this image is significant as the council seems at best detached from British reality, and at worst irrelevant. 'The Tower Hamlets council has more Bangladeshi councilors than any other, but there's more infighting for power.... Most young, entrepreneurial Bangladeshis avoid political service, because of the damaging reputation of these people. Politics seems not as desirable.'[53] Another side believes that the council is really managed by career bureaucrats pushing paper beneath the Cabinet. They argue that this group of decision-makers is unreflective of Tower Hamlets and unaccountable. 'The politicians' inability to deliver leaves the real power to the non-Bengalis from the shires who run the council's bureaucracy,' says one *desi*-politician. 'But fewer than 100 council employees are Bengali. There is no Bengali management. The council doesn't represent the community, which gets a raw deal.'[54] One council employee says, 'There are no Bengalis in the top three tiers of the government's bureaucracy in Tower Hamlets' civil servant hierarchy, and most of them don't even live in Tower Hamlets. They live in the shires.'[55]

Levels of activism among young Bangladeshi study participants are quite high. However, perhaps because of the council's low profile and low standing, little activism is through government channels. At the national level, policy-makers have changed Muslim dialogue partners with great frequency, until finally in late 2007 the government quietly facilitated the creation of MINAB (the Mosques and Imams National Advisory Board) to oversee and regulate Muslim religious entities and attempt to unify the different Muslim communities of Britain.[56] Necessitating the cooperation of a disparate set of competing groups with competing agendas, MINAB has been largely unsuccessful for various reasons. Many Muslim communities are not satisfactorily persuaded that the Board is not just another instrument of government surveillance and control. The constitutive groups have had trouble reconciling their ideological and religious differences. And finally, without direct government funding, the Board has little financial backing.

Similar to the generations before them, those interviewed tend to associate themselves with organizations and groups that are either non-governmental or not directly overseen by the government. These include neighborhood groups, volunteer efforts, sports teams, school-related activities, mosque associations, and also gangs—which represent a deviant variety of associationism. However, in recent years, the Tower Hamlets council's youth services division has developed a set of evening youth clubs to appeal to Bangladeshi boys between 12 and 25 years old. Taking place in neighborhood community centers, these clubs are open any time from twice weekly to everyday and give young people a place to congregate after other venues have closed. They are usually run by other Bangladeshi members of the community who are slightly older, but young enough to offer relevant guidance. In the homogeneous atmosphere, there are discussions about East End and Bangladeshi politics and the community, which make use of a moral paradigm that is more Islamic than secular. The government ties are almost clandestine, and the effort has been relatively successful.

The government is simply not a credible entity in the eyes of many young people. However, if they are approached in the right way, previous successes show that they can be mobilized to participate. One local council member says:

> The boys here are much more politically active than boys in other boroughs, when you compare them to Afro-Caribbean boys. While some are active because they're genuinely interested, others are active because they're part of a youth organization or political culture. Then there are also the mass movements, like the one Galloway created. Young Tower Hamlets boys have been more politicized of late. A lot of credit goes to Galloway, as much as I hate to say it. But people are much more aware of political issues than they used to [be]. However, being active is something different.

But I still think that the vast majority don't understand what they are a part of. As a council, we put more money toward young people and more is done to bring them in, but I think that the truth is that the majority of them are simply not interested...

The kids are far more talented than we give them credit for. You don't have to be in the system to be politically active. The problem is that there are so many young ones who do not know that there is life outside of Tower Hamlets. They don't have any exposure to the outside world.

Many young people are confident enough to give police officers the lip, but not confident enough to speak out publicly. They have the talent to challenge authority, and that's raw talent that should be tapped. Instead, I think we tap those who are going to get involved anyway. It just makes the council officers' lives easier.[57]

Though a general lack of confidence in government efforts and efficacy is nearly ubiquitous, participants split over the next step in logic. While some still believe the system is the best available, others believe it is irreparably flawed. This manifests itself most conspicuously in the choice of whether or not to vote. 'In Islam,' Omar says, 'we believe in choosing the better of two evils.'[58] However, a growing movement of Islamists—particularly those from *Hizb-Ut-Tahrir*—is canvassing college campuses and street corners, arguing that voting is *haram*. 'If I voted, I'd be supporting a government that allows *haram* things,' says Naz. 'Islam is about black and white, *halal* and *haram*. The better of two evils is still evil.'[59] In this microcosmic dispute, the government is losing the fight to sway perception.

The Activist Apartism of *Hizb-Ut-Tahrir*

Reviewing the previously discussed civic institutions in the East End, we see that Bangladeshis' civic entities have traditionally remained within the Bangladeshi community, reluctant to build bridges to incorporate non-Bangladeshis or orient themselves for purposes that are not of specific interest to Bangladeshis. However, the younger generation of people under 30 years old has little use for political associations that look out for the interests of remote villages on the other side of the world, investment opportunities to build a hotel in Sylhet Town, or a mosque committee that conducts meetings in a foreign language. Their sphere is Britain. And given their expressed feelings of entitlement, the second generation feels empowered to end quietism and seclusion by expressing themselves, jettisoning certain Bangladeshi traditions, and joining wider British society as a recognized member. Many established civic entities do not attract or embrace this younger generation, and there are limited alternatives. While youth groups are sprouting around the East End, these groups tend to attract (and, some argue, babysit) the young people with video games, billiards and ping pong, rather than genuinely attempt to address the conflicts and issues in their lives. As a result, some young people engage in apartist groups that do, and others do not engage at all.

This illustrates two types of anti–system behavior and apartism. There is the passive apartism of a socio-politically withdrawn citizenry. This group would be characterized by nihilism or hopeless disenchantment with the democratic system, leading to marginalization from it and the other civic entities mentioned above. This is best exhibited by the scores of gang members encountered during the fieldwork, many of whom were not interested in giving interviews. However, among the Bangladeshis, the social cohesion and activist culture of the community suggest that many passive apartists are a recruitment effort away from becoming active.

After attending a variety of *Hizb-Ut-Tahrir* meetings in the East End over my fieldwork, it is clear that the transnational political party reflects and attempts to spread this actively manifested apartism. Although other activists lament the intransigence and ineffectiveness of the democratic state, they still find channels for participation and self-expression in informal or non-government groups, which complement the civic efforts of the government—even if this is done by confronting the government. Apartists, such as many members of *Hizb-Ut-Tahrir*, pin these informal and non-governmental groups with the same criticisms those groups make of the government. *Hizb-Ut-Tahrir* members believe that working within institutions of the government reinforces the power of an un-divine—and therefore inevitably failing—system. As a result, they believe that people must defect from that system, and seek an alternative—in this case, Islamic—system of governance.

Hizb-Ut-Tahrir ('Party of Liberation' in Arabic) is a transnational Islamist political party that directs its efforts to re-establishing the ummatic *khalifa* or caliphate that once covered much of the Eastern Hemisphere in the centuries following the Prophet Mohammed's death. They aim to undermine status quo political systems and build public support for Islamic rule—based on the idea that Islam is not merely a set of rituals or religious norms, but a complete system of governance over all aspects of life. In gradualist fashion, the group readily admits that the United Kingdom and other Western states are not their primary targets, but says that the West is their main source of ideas and strategy. 'In this country, all we can do is spread ideas,' says Viq, a member. 'A lot of ideas in the Muslim world start here. When a Muslim in the Muslim world sees Western Muslims—in our prosperity—desire *shari'a*, that's going to make them want it too.'[60]

It is important to note that, unlike the other Bangladeshi civic entities discussed thus far, *Hizb-Ut-Tahrir* (HT) does not extend organically from the Bangladeshi community. It is very much a transnational organization with a globalized leadership to complement its globalized ambitions. Branches function in various boroughs within the United Kingdom in different neighborhoods with different ethno-cultural compositions. The organization's local leadership is usually a reflection of its local constituency. So although the East End's local HT activists are Bangladeshi, the organization pre-dates their membership and is attempting to root itself in the fertile soil of Tower Hamlets. With other civic entities and gangs, HT competes for the membership and participation of young Bangladeshi men quite directly. Like two grocery stores on opposing street corners, HT has established youth clubs in the same neighborhood where mosque-sponsored and council-sponsored youth clubs meet. On Ponler Street in the Shadwell ward, HT gathers a weekly meeting in the same building as a council-sponsored youth club. Before Thursday meetings, the neighborhood's HT leaders will go into the council-sponsored club downstairs to recruit attendees for their discussion group upstairs. They offer free snacks and soda, along with a discussion about issues that are slightly more relevant and enlightening than the adolescents' game of billiards—Islam and British society. Moreover, the clubs offer a sense of belonging and community, all of it exclusivist.

The sessions provide extensive guidance about a very specific way of life, and usually involve a 'guest speaker' (invariably a member) who offers a lecture followed by questions (often planted), discussion, and then fried chicken and chips. 'Who wants to be a sheep when you can be the shepherd?' the youngest age group is prompted at one session. The kids are taught how to pray, shown clips of an Islamic comedian, they discuss school problems like bullying, and describe heaven. 'It's a place where you can eat all you want and not have to go to the toilet,' they are told. 'You have to be a good person to go to heaven.' One boy says that his heaven would boast a back door to Old Trafford—Manchester United's stadium. Another says that in heaven he would be given a Star Wars light saber, which he would use to cut green beans. These local groups complement higher level efforts, in which the group and its inscrutable hierarchy attracts dozens of professional, well-educated Muslims to monthly meetings where often news-relevant topics are discussed by panels.

Especially with the teenagers and young men, the sessions strive to relate Islam to their modern lives and challenges. Weekly meetings follow the same format, and aim to address the very questions and confusion faced by the individuals in attendance. The topics are often those that mosques will not address, but remain at the forefront of young people's minds—such as 'Citizenship in Islam', 'Obama's foreign policy', 'Is Islam confined to the mosque?' They also tap into young people's frustrations and anger. 'Sometimes I get very angry about injustice, and I just want to run around killing everybody, but I know better,' says Omar, who has dabbled in HT circles.[61] The withdrawn and alienated are attracted to HT, one Muslim leader says, 'because they speak the words which they are afraid to say'.

However, those words are directed at a specific constituency of young Bangladeshi men in the East End: the educated. Their leadership is reportedly composed of successful professionals, and their messages correspondingly represent advanced interpretations that question traditionalism and the status quo, as described above. Given the dichotomy of 'street boys' and 'house boys' in Tower Hamlets, HT recruits the latter. Their younger members appear to be striving for university educations, and the focused studiousness such aspirations require alienates some from larger, less studious social groups. HT offers 'house boys' a sense of belonging and new identity security to combat the same challenges facing their 'street boy' counterparts. One gang member interviewed said that he had joined HT after being persuaded by one of the group's leaders. The leader was deported a year ago, and the young man has not returned since. He said that the HT members were 'a cool lot', but it was clear he had difficulty relating. So while *Hizb-Ut-Tahrir*'s cause appeals to many young Bangladeshis struggling with questions of their identity and civic belonging, their message and social circle segregate Bangladeshis to comprise a distinctly educated group of dissidents. Calim, a local HT organizer, explains:

> I see a lot of anger. There's hatred for the sake of hatred. Some of those ghetto youths haven't got a job or education, so they fight in gangs. These guys may start to mellow out by coming to Islam. Others become angry Islamic bullies. They maintain that anger and Islamify it. The appeal of HT to these guys isn't there because we operate at a high level with advanced messages and a higher benchmark.

> Nationally we're trying to get the Muslim community to take some responsibility for themselves. We should be eradicating problems by returning to our moral values. At the moment, there's an identity crisis where neither are we following Islam, neither are we Bengali, neither do we feel part of the wider society in Britain. We're lost.[62]

It is their continued response to this continuing crisis that has sustained HT's appeal. However, their guidance involves a retreat that undermines the inclusiveness of British democratic society. So unlike the worlds of business, the mosque and the state, HT competes simultaneously with the first three civic entities *and* the overarching democratic system of governance that facilitates their activism.

Doubting Democracy

Regardless of whether interviewees participate in the first three civic organizations working within the democratic system, participate in the exclusivist activities of groups like *Hizb-Ut-Tahrir*, or do not participate at all, just about every interviewee acknowledged the ways in which government services and democratic processes provide services in the United Kingdom. Indeed, most young Bangladeshis have benefited from effective public housing, education, food subsidies, unemployment coverage and welfare payments—instilling the near ubiquitous sense of entitlement discussed in the previous section. However, equally ubiquitously, participants expressed significant doubts about the ability of the democratic system to deliver fully on the justice, liberty and representation it promises. In numbers that would probably be mirrored by a study of non-Bangladeshi young people, not a single respondent says that the democratic system is fully sound. Indeed, each participant acknowledged certain—and sometimes many—considerable imperfections and dysfunctions.

Those participants who were able to see themselves as part of an ultimately fair and efficacious—however imperfect—system that strives to improve and can be changed by its constituent citizens working in democratic institutions (the government, the mosque, or *desi* avenues) tend to be more engaged in democratic participation or activism. 'Gordon Brown wasn't even voted in by the people. How is that democracy?' asks Pir, who has written letters to his local member of Parliament and is a member of various organizations at his university. 'I think that every system has a flaw. Capitalist regimes work better than communist regimes. But they're not good for everyone. In the end, there are so many opinions. Still, democracy is better than other options, but only marginally. It works on paper, but not in practice.'[63] Amjad, an active congregant at the East London Mosque who has met with many civic leaders says, 'People in authority, we can send them letters and make demonstrations, but will it be implemented? It's all about who they consult. We can get into their positions.... I also don't see how [some people] reject their Britishness. They are protected by a British passport. If I were not British, then I should be asked to leave.'[64] Ridwan votes and closely follows political news. He expresses a sense of powerlessness intermingled with hope:[65]

People are disbelieving. They are losing faith in the government. We give our vote, but if they carry on in a manner we don't accept, then they lose our trust. This is a problem with the system. We think it's gonna work, we think our vote is gonna count. We, as Muslims, vote for the one who will create the least harm. But when that comes back in our face, we don't have the power to affect change. All we can do is create pressure groups and march. But we shouldn't have to take illegal or external means to speak to and access the government. As an individual, I don't have that kind of authority. They're just going to think of me as one individual. The local MPs don't represent all our views. They pick and choose what they want. Values should stem from those of the people. But [politicians] have created their own values. It's selfish, looking out for the good of the system and the people in charge, and not for the good of society.

Among those individuals who believe that the democratic system's imperfections corrupt any chance of efficacy, that the system was not ultimately interested in a fair outcome, and feel powerless to change it through democratic institutions (the government, the mosque, or *desi* avenues), they tend to be withdrawn or engaged in forms of participation that undermine the system— both are anti–system. Yet only a minority of this group actually indicts the entire system for not fully providing the justice, liberty and representation to which they feel entitled. 'I'm relatively satisfied with government services,' says Ebrahim, a university student withdrawn from the political system. 'They give me education, health coverage, housing for a family of nine. And I've been given a voice. But how loud is it?' He cites experiences with employer discrimination, police racism, and sensationalized press articles that demonize Muslims, but says he has seen no policy change despite protests. 'What can I do? I've seen other people try and they all fail. So why try?'[66] Similarly, Omar says, 'They don't care about me. What has the government done for me? The government's never done nothing for me.... I wouldn't go to a council meeting because they wouldn't listen to me. They'd treat me like a kid.'[67]

Those individuals engaged in forms of participation that undermine the democratic political system explained why they are unable to overcome their sense of doubt. 'British foreign policy says we're gonna engage the Muslim community, but after one million people marched against the Iraq War, they were ignored, and five years later, we see all the hypocrisy,' says Bilal, a member of *Hizb-Ut Tahrir*. 'You don't need to engage the government to affect politics in the community. I didn't vote in the mayoral elections. You need to take an active role in the community.... I don't have to take part in the government to do that.'[68] Bilal's counterpart, Viq, says, 'There is no way you can change the British or US governments. It's not going to happen. It's impossible to change the system by getting involved in the system. You can't run in an election if you don't believe in secularism or capitalism. For me, the things I'm doing won't improve the lives of people in this country, but it'll help the whole, the *ummah*. This country has never been a Muslim country."[69] In each of these examples, the interview content shows a substantial amount of doubt about the efficacy and responsiveness of the democratic system. The extent of this sentiment is of concern. However, there are nuanced differences in how each participant rationalizes the imperfections of the democratic system. Those who participate in the system have faith that it ultimately works, despite signs to the contrary.

Democratic Participation Promotes Faith in Democracy

Interviews suggest a strong correlation between those young people who participate in the first three civic entities described in this section and those who believe that the system of government normally works in their interest and should be entrusted with checked powers. These are people who participate in elections, activist movements, civic organizations, or interacted with government institutions in the past—even with relatively negative results, and even in the most limited way, or for the most self-serving reasons. Some may indeed participate because they already believe in the system. But in other cases, it seems clear that participation promotes belief in the efficacy or functionality of the system because participants either see themselves as invested in the potential results or because they have actually witnessed results. These groups include those who join the system and work within it, and activists who confront the system in peaceful ways facilitated by democratic institution and rule of law.

Correspondingly, interview content exhibits a similar correlation between those participants who participate in exclusivist organizations or not at all and those who perceive the system of government to be working against their most general interests. With *Hizb-Ut-Tahrir*, access is conditional upon the individual's submission to an ideology and its exclusivist outlook. If apartists participate in the civic sphere of the community, they do so in a way that weakens the democratic structures of engagement, or they do not participate at all. And by doing so, active and passive apartists damage the representativeness and responsiveness of the governing structure.

From this case study, the objective of democratic authorities is unequivocally clear: to promote inclusive democratic participation and faith in democracy. However this task is not a simple one in the East End. The first three civic entities—*desi*-business, the state and the mosque—that work within the democratic system are inseparably connected to specific forms of identity and their moral paradigms. As the next section explains, the civic entities are losing their relevance and credibility in the eyes of young Bangladeshi men precisely because the identity forms—of which they are civic manifestations—are losing their relevance and credibility first.

An 'Identity Crisis'

Between 18 and 28 years old, just about every second-generation British Bangladeshi in Tower Hamlets is grappling with some degree of what participants almost universally refer to as an 'identity crisis'. This crisis is created by young people's confusion about the definitions of, their grappling with the rigidities of, and their sense of judgment about three main sources of identification: their British nationality and surroundings, their Bangladeshi ethnicity and culture of kinship, and their increasingly deterritorialized Islamic religion. 'Sometimes I say I have five faces,' says Tayyib. 'Some friends think I'm religious. Some friends I go clubbing with. Some friends I talk politics with. Some friends I do community work with. And then I'm different with my family.'[70] One community elder who works with young people said, 'I see them all as zombies. They are juggling their faith, cultural ties and attention to modernity in the West all at once. Depending where they are, they are different people.'[71] The so-called identity crisis entails many individuals' simultaneously questioning their own nationality, culture or religion—each seeming to overlap and undermine the other.[72] Such simultaneous questioning is an evolution from the findings of earlier studies of young Bangladeshis, who noted their difficulty 'ranking' their multiple identity forms.[73] While many other Britons will also question their identity, this is typically a quiet and more personal struggle that is not given the public scrutiny and paranoid treatment that young Muslims are attracting from their schools and workplaces. Young Bangladeshis must therefore handle this traditionally private struggle very publicly, and their sensitivity to social judgment (by all parties) is especially acute.

In fact, nearly all the young Bangladeshis interviewed were indeed simultaneously questioning their nationality, ethnicity and religion. One council official says that the identity crisis among young men is leading to broken families, disobedient youth and domestic violence—both parents-on-kids and vice versa. He says children and parents are feeling demoralized because neither have fulfilled their roles or are accepted in society. 'From where I sit,' he says, 'confusion is very difficult. Until a person knows who they are, where they come from, they can't do anything. As human beings, we have a purpose in life. So whatever you are, remember that every action has a reaction. You choose what you want to do, not because that's what someone else tells you to do. It's your choice and your consequences. Many of them don't know the consequences or why, really why, they are doing it.'[74] In the case of most young British Muslims, the consequences of their private struggle are perceived to be in the public interest. As the British government and social discourse continue to base contemporary social divisions on religion, young Bangladeshi Muslims are unnecessarily forced to defend theirs.

Britishness

Nearly all the subjects of this study were born in Britain, attend or have attended British schools, and have absorbed years of British television, music and media content. English is their best and usually only language, as many speak very broken Sylheti, and little to no Arabic. They survive on a diet of curry when at home and *halal* fried chicken and chips on the streets. 'I do want to feel British,' says Ridwan, 'because then I'm not isolated. I don't want people to say that just because I'm Asian or Muslim, I'm not British.'[75] Similarly, Shahid says, 'I don't see myself as someone from outside this society. I'm British, and I am a product of this place.' At a Perfect Fried Chicken shop, Hanif was asked what British people think of him. 'I *am* British!' he chuckled, producing an outburst of laughter from his friends around the table.[76]

Indeed, despite this personal and private acquaintance with British culture and society, many participants found public acceptance of their Britishness laughable in the light of perceived double standards. A majority of respondents say they feel definitively rejected by British society. 'When I have kids, they may not even speak Bengali,' Qadim says. 'But in the UK, I've been forced to think I'm different because of my skin color and the shade of beard I keep. Everything I have is for this country. But I'm not allowed to feel a part of it.'[77] Naz, a 20–year-old university student from Stepney, asks:

What is British? Is it that I was born here? Or do I have to adopt the culture? Britain is multicultural. I know that. But there are certain things that I don't accept, that this society does. So people assume, 'Oh, he's not like us. He's radical.' All Muslims feel out of bounds. Because of secularism, individualism, materialism, many people put Islam second. Where is multiculturalism if Britain is going to treat people differently, and not British? I've faced it. I've been told to go back to my country by an older white lady when I was playing football as a kid. Yes, my parents aren't English. But I was born here. I went to the same schools.[78]

From news reports that cast South Asians and Muslims as dangerous, laws designed to profile them, personal and collective experiences with discrimination and racism, and negative informal social interactions, young Bangladeshis have become intensely insecure about their role in British society. Many young people feel singled out and subjected to unfair double-standards. 'I felt like I belonged before the Terrorism Act,' said Imran, an 18–year-old student from Shadwell. 'But now I'm scared I might do something wrong. People used to speak their mind without worrying about it. Now people think they're going to be put in prison.' Juxtaposed to the liberalness with which non-Muslims appear to express themselves, freedom of speech is perceived by many participants to be conditional.

Such double standards particularly undermine personal claims to Britishness. During the course of the case study in the East End, British Bangladeshi commentator Rizwan Hussain was beaten, interrogated and detained by police forces at Dhaka airport. Though followed closely by East End publications, this story never made it into a mainstream British newspaper. For such reasons, Jalil, an unemployed gang member from Tredegar, said he doesn't feel as if Bangladeshis are looked upon as equals, even if, personally, they feel as British as anyone else. 'I'm in the books as British,' he says, 'but if push comes to shove, it's a double standard, right? Look at Guantanamo Bay. If it were white Britons being tortured, they'd be out of there.'[79] As a result, Bangladeshis quite generally are actively questioning their belonging and acceptance in the only country in which they hold citizenship—the only country they know.

Out of pride, many participants denied their desire for recognition, but still expressed frustration with the standards of belonging. 'I feel like this is home,' said Zubair. 'This is my comfort zone. This is the system I grew up with. As a citizen I want to reap the benefits. The government provides me with a source of security. That said, just after 9/11, I once got stop-and-searched three times in a one hour and forty minute span, three minutes from my house. It made me feel very angry, undermined. I produced evidence that I'd been searched already, and the cops weren't having it.' Ultimately, it appears that a (repressed) desire to be recognized as British is what makes rejection subsequently affect them so strongly.

Bangladeshi Heritage

If they are not fully British, are they Bangladeshi? The answer from respondents—young and old—is a resounding 'No'. Depending on the age and class of the respondent, this response is for different reasons. Many of those who have earned enough money to leave the *bari* atmosphere of Tower Hamlets have begun to assimilate to British borough life. Within Tower Hamlets, elders believe the younger generation has abandoned their Sylheti cultural roots which once worked seamlessly with Islam to set them apart in an all-Muslim region carved from a Hindu subcontinent in 1947. While these elders have maintained points of reference from their rural lives in their new urban existence, the newest generation cannot make the same connection. One community elder says, 'People are diverting away from our way of life, our culture, and one day, they'll come back but it'll be too late. Bengalis are not given enough opportunities to keep our roots. Whose standard is community cohesion based on? It's about accepting people, not changing them. Our young people are disowning the very society they are from, and that is, in effect, genocide. They are changing their names, everything. There's an old Bengali saying, just because you change your behavior, doesn't mean you'll change your skin.'[80] However, young people who live in the Christian-secular modernity of Britain are identified exclusively by their Islam and find the culture of their parents to be out of context. Many respondents in the study and in several secondary source materials have expressed an utter disconnection with a Bangladeshi identity that they believe is 'backward'.

Interestingly, young British Bangladeshi men have been taught to isolate as ethno-cultural the social traditions which their parents and grandparents (and many Westerners) have linked with Islam. Norms like arranged marriage, restrictions on female behavior, clothing preferences and certain ceremonies have been identified as part of an antiquated Bangladeshi culture that has no place in modern British lives. Zakaria says:

> There's a lot of things that the Bengali community does that I'm like, 'You're not following Islamic culture, you're following Arab culture or Bengali culture.'...Most Muslim weddings in Tower Hamlets go by Bengali traditions, which are derived from Hinduism, not Islam. In Bangladesh, women had to stop studying to take care of the family. Here, they can keep going. A lot of Bengalis have twisted Islamic arranged marriage into forced marriage. Islam doesn't give the parents the final say.[81]

One explanation for this discrepancy is offered by Pnina Werbner, who argues that 'by contrast to South Asian popular culture, which is inclusive, absorbent, experimental, reflexively satirical and politically incorrect, the South Asian Muslim diaspora in Britain is represented by spokesmen as socially exclusive, high cultural, puritanical, politicized and utterly serious.'[82] Between the older generation's secular Bangladeshi cultural norms and the younger generation's Islamist image, Werbner identifies a middle ground of lucrative, hybridized culture that is palatable to British consumers, integrating many South Asians into British society without the demand that they abandon their South Asian transnational affiliations and orientations.[83]

One significant problem is that there is a great deal of uncertainty about what actually constitutes Bangladeshi. The second generation in Britain is far removed from Bangladesh, and few return with any frequency. In another conversation at a chicken and chips shop, I ask a young man to describe his ideal world. He responds by suggesting that it would resemble 'Bangladesh', as his friends giggled together. After an awkward pause, Zakaria said, 'Yeah, but that's not the right place either. They don't really understand us. In Sylhet, everyone thinks of us as *Londoni*.' Their accent in Sylheti is usually a 'dead giveaway'—if the spiked hair and baggy designer jeans are not. Sylhetis migrated mostly from rural farming villages amid the tea plantations in the tropical northeast of Bangladesh, with few resources to construct exportable cultural goods. Truly, the spicy curries, masalas, tikkas and naan bread that attract Londoners to the Bangladeshi–run balti houses on Brick Lane represent a Bangladeshi cuisine that is actually an assortment of influences from across South Asia. Bangladeshi film and television is dominated by Bollywood content. Bangladeshi fashion consists of a selection of Western trends and Indian sari gowns. Indeed, the 'dirty little truth', as one Bangladeshi business-owner and community leader called it, is that 'there really is no such thing as Bengali culture anyway'.[84] So even if there was a desire to engage a tangible Bangladeshi ethnicity among youths in the East End, it is evanescent at best.

Islam

The simultaneously perceived rejection by British society and alienation from their Bangladeshi roots has led to a significant and well-documented 'embrace' of a deterritorialized, ummatic Islam. However, the so-called 'embrace of Islam' appears to be significantly rhetorical and fitted for identity discourse. Lifestyle preferences among participants interviewed are influenced by British social norms, and—as with so many other people who live in secular democracies—Islam is woven in as a set of moral virtues, heritage and culture. The embrace of religious Islam is almost reluctant, as many youths appear very fond of the freedoms, liberalness and individuality of British life—despite the fact that many aspects such as drinking, dancing, music, and 'free-mixing' with the opposite sex are looked down upon in religious terms. Their embrace thus appears to be reactive to a securitized, polarized British social environment that undermines their claims to Britishness.[85] Islam is a way to respond, that also satisfies the desire of parents and other local community members to follow certain ethno-religious traditions. So while many young people are separating themselves from the restrictions and anachronism of Bangladeshi culture, Islam is a sufficient replacement for all involved. Still, in this light, many young 'cultural' Muslims who are indulging in questionable Western habits, temptations, and excesses seem to do so as a conscious choice. They are aware of the influence of British mass culture, and have chosen to engage with it. The question for them is not only, 'Do you feel British?' but also, 'Do you want to feel British?' The answer commonly appears to be 'yes'.

Nevertheless, for those British Bangladeshi participants sensing a degree of rejection by their white British peers, the idea of an identity that ignores borders and unifies like-minded people holds great relevance. 'Islam simplifies,' Mahir says. 'It's all about unification, and that's what we're getting away from. I am a Muslim. Not a Barelwi, Tablighi Jamaat, Salafi, Hanafi or whatever. I'm a Muslim. I'm not British or Bengali. I'm Muslim.'[86] Mahir did not seem to understand the differences among Islamic sects. However, his rejection reflects a common desire to move beyond differences to a universalist Islam that enables Muslims to transcend exclusive ties. Similarly, Ismail, a high school student, says, 'I don't feel an identity crisis, because I feel like I have a relationship with God and so I don't have any problem saying that I am a Muslim. I've put myself in a box, and eliminated my British and Bengali ties. Do I need to claim to be British? No, I don't need to. I have a British passport. And I've only been to Bangladesh once, when I was a child, and I was too young to remember any of it.'[87] Putting it quite simply, Pir says, 'Once I get to the mosque, I know who I am.'[88]

Given their social lives, which are generally limited to coteries of Bangladeshi friends, and their lifestyles, which are mostly British existences interrupted by Islamic obligations (not the other way around), participants' relationships with their British and Bangladeshi identities are simultaneously self-evident and impossible—as any individual's relations with larger identity forms are. Their relationship with Islam therefore becomes chosen (and thus more closely defended), rhetorical (and thus more volatile), and one of necessity, as the religious intersects with the ethnic and national.

Because it supplants a rhetorical national or ethnic identity which requires no exercises beyond discursive identification, Islam as an identity doesn't necessarily suggest practice or even accurate knowledge. 'Without Islam, I have no identity,' Ebrahim, a student at Queen Mary University, says. 'My practice is weak, yeah. I have little time in life for Islam. But it's still my base. When I have nothing else, it'll always be there.'[89] One particularly zealous participant, Jalil, says that his ideal is embodied by 'the peace of Islam. Everyone should read the scripture and they would be at peace.'[90] Interestingly he admittedly does not, and instead he relies on elaborately colorful and fantastic stories about the roots of human civilization that sharply dichotomize good and evil. His ideas about good and evil are firm, clean-cut, and without any attention to nuance or grayscale. His knowledge of Islam is at best anecdotal, and at worst downright apocryphal. He confesses to engaging in the *haram*—sexual desire, encounters with women, violence and deception. But he says he does so for the 'pleasure', which he views as the result of hedonism. All participants who discussed their dabbling in the *haram* say that they will return to the 'right path' later in life. Islam is therefore an entity that—unlike Britishness and Bangladeshi culture—is perceived to be most flexible and enduring. It is not withheld because of third-party disapproval, nor is it evanescent with increasing time and distance. Indeed, Islam is perceived to be more subject to personal interpretation than either British nationality or Bangladeshi heritage—even if this is erroneous.

Irrelevant to individuals' depth of practice or knowledge, Islamic identity simplifies the divisive networks of Muslim sects and ethnic groups that compete for power, and enables some degree of felt unity against their collective vilification in the West. 'Up against violence, drugs, poverty and bad housing, what holds this community together is religion,' says Tayyib. 'Everyone has been told the difference between *halal* and *haram*. Those boundaries are always there. And the sense of brotherhood encourages help and feelings of solidarity.'[91] Islam also provides an unequivocal answer to young people's identity crisis. Omar, an unemployed former gang member in Tredegar, said:

> Things in my life were rough—family issues, girls, school, money—everything. So I turned to Islam, began reading several books. I grew out my beard to emulate the Prophet, which makes me look older, forcing people to take me more seriously.... The Quran is my way of life.... I don't need counsel because I can always look at the book. Everything I need is here. I don't adapt the Quran to British citizenship. British citizenship is adapted to the Quran.[92]

Demonstrating his inherent insecurity about the thoughts he offered so confidently, after his interview, the same young man quite humbly texted, 'It was nyc talking 2 u geeza. I dnt knw wat u fout ov me. Hw was I at arguing, or putin ma point acros ratha?' Indeed, he was quite convincing and charismatic. Many other youths become more religious or at least project a more Islamic identity in response to significant events in their lives. Much like people of other faiths, several participants said they relied upon Islam after a family member died, a friend was stabbed, a near-death encounter with narcotics, some simply because they encountered racism.

Many respondents described their embrace of Islam as much as a reaction against their rejected Britishness as a way to re-center their morals and values against a public sphere filled with Western temptation and vice. Many participants fingered the creeping influence of contemporary 'Western culture' and its malicious allure as the primary impediment to a more Islamic life. The temptation of mixed gender relations, alcohol, drugs, music, secularism and individualism was regularly blamed for the perceived deterioration of moral values among Bangladeshis in Tower Hamlets and the waning ethno-civic solidarity within the community. 'We are so bloody gullible,' says Calim, a 25–year-old schoolteacher from Stepney. 'Look at the kids with the low, baggy trousers. They'll follow anything. And as the generations go by, they're getting spoiled and they're throwing it all away.... The situation has gotten so bad, and it's going to get worse and worse. The hip hop culture is so damaging. These kids live for that life of guns, drugs, cash...'[93] In a similar vein, Bilal says, 'We still have the nuclear family structure here among Bengalis, but these kids are taking 50 Cent as their role model. The community is slowly becoming, you hate to say it, ghetto.'[94]

Indeed, by providing a transnational source of community to supplant the problematic local, the *ummah* not only facilitates claims to collective pride, loyalty, but also to collective injury. And like a culture, followers of an Islamic identity tend to apply Islamic teachings as a complete way of life—as opposed to the way some of their parents have treated Islam, as a set of rituals to perform and repeat. However, this becomes problematic for many young people in Tower Hamlets because religious teachings and norms often clash with other more embedded aspects of their non-Islamic identity. 'Religion clashes with the style of the subculture,' Ridwan says. 'I feel bad if I go to mosque when I style up my hair, so I wear a hat. I feel weird, self-conscious when I wear my ripped jeans.'[95] Other youths are perplexed by the competing priorities of a demanding faith and demanding career ambitions. 'I'm busy,' says Faisal, 'but Islam says that Islam is always first.'[96] Shahid asks, 'How can we stick close to the text, and yet stay in the modern world? ...I mean, if I had a job interview, I wouldn't be wearing [a prayer gown and a cap]. A *hijab* similarly doesn't go in our society. We are living in the West. It's about conforming to local society.'

In the light of similar statements, Olivier Roy contends that the term 'Muslim' is now used as a 'neo-ethnicity', with no reference to faith or genuine religious practice.[97] He writes, '"neo" means that the culture of origin is no longer relevant, and 'ethnicity' that religion is not seen as faith but as a set of cultural patterns that are inherited and not related to a person's spiritual life.' Indeed, I concur with his argument that 'British Muslims have constructed a new ethnic group, which did not previously exist as such, through a limited set of differential patterns isolated from a more complex and diverse cultural background.' However, this ethnic group is used more rhetorically in the socio-political sphere. In practice, young Bangladeshis' neo-ethnicity has quite a British and post-Bangladeshi tint to it. They tend to socialize in insular groups of British Bangladeshis (often excluding non-Bangladeshi Muslims, and even non-Sylheti Bangladeshis) and relate as much to their shared experiences in the British public sphere as they do commiserating (often in jest) over their shared household customs. As a result, I believe their Muslim identity is not nearly as deterritorialized as some leaders claim. Though influenced by the words of sheikhs and individuals from beyond their countries and sensitized to the plight of Muslims worldwide, the young Bangladeshi men interviewed apply such messages to a distinctly post-Bangladeshi, British life. Indeed, the Muslims to whom they might feel connected elsewhere tend also to remain quite culturally rooted to the traditions and norms of their native Morocco, Indonesia and Iran—where they can also hardly relate to a British life of modern conveniences, luxuries, and the means to stage ideological revolutions.

Ubiquitous Social Judgment

For the young British Bangladeshi in the East End, judgment is simply ubiquitous—by community elders, by prospective employers, by imams, by police, by parents, by peers. This feeling of being judged by people in the community is a form of projected identification (or the confusion thereof). Indeed, the individual's insecurities are often most candidly expressed through their specific concerns about judgment or compensatory fixation on one aspect of their persona. What further complicates these insecurities is the existence and implementation of more than one criterion based on the different identity constructions present.

With their impatience for Bangladeshi cultural traditions and felt social rejection by white British society, many British Bangladeshis who are not religiously inclined claim to employ a moral criterion connected to a distinctly restricted Islamic lifestyle. As explained earlier in this chapter, Islam dictates that food must be *halal* at all times; alcohol, drugs and any other intoxicants are banned; cross-gender 'free-mixing' is not permitted; and depending on interpretation, non-Islamic music, iconography, charging interest on loans, and certain feminine fashion is frowned upon. Many of these are very public choices. In interviews, however, the same men who claim a Muslim identity often admit to consuming alcoholic beverages, frequenting night clubs, listening to hip hop music on their mobile phone, and dating women casually. Without the foundation of a secure (hybridized) identity, these choices proved to foster strong feelings of guilt and weakness that affect their confidence and ability to assert themselves, participate in inter-ethnic activities, or join social spheres of other Bangladeshis who purportedly avoid *haram* activities. Calim says that before he became strictly religious, 'My perception of Islam was a sensible, stable thing that grown-ups do. There was a certain amount of guilt, and I didn't want to feel that guilt of getting punished and displeasing.'[98] Many others say that they do not feel comfortable speaking to even slightly older Bangladeshis about taboo issues—particularly sex and 'Western' temptations—which subsequently build up in their minds and lead many to keep secrets that estrange relationships between generations. 'I would never even speak to my brother about a girl,' said Yusuf. 'The British lifestyle is still not generally acceptable, and young people are still scared about judgment.... As a result, they're still not able to do what other British kids do. So they still stick mostly to other Bengali boys, and real assimilation and change hasn't happened.'[99]

Perhaps the most basic criterion for judgment—of which a young Bangladeshi male is cognizant since childhood—is that of marriage suitability. This is a criterion rooted in Bangladeshi culture. And outside of exceptional circumstances, no matter how backward a boy finds Bangladeshi culture, if he wishes to marry within the Bangladeshi community he must navigate a minefield of social judgment. Drawn from an overview of participants' statements, this involves an elaborate dance to adhere to etiquette and heed Islamic restrictions. Because casual dating and romance are barred, this is usually secretive. When a relationship based on text messages, encounters in the street, and going out in separate groups is ripe, the male must approach his non-girlfriend's father to request the commencement of wooing. Permission is based on what is already known about the young man, and the prospect of such an ultimate

Judgment Day resides in the back of his mind at all times within a community where reputations reach all corners. If permission is granted, thus commences a period in which the male is invited to his non-girlfriend's home for a series of dinners and other family gatherings—during all of which he will be scrutinized. The consequences are manifold. Many secretly enduring 'love' relationships are deemed improper when they are found out. Many marriages take place before a male has had much interaction with women, or without the persuaded interest of the bride. And more than anything, young Bangladeshi men can almost never feel truly free from the community's judgment. 'A lot of things in the Bangladeshi community are about what others think of you,' Yusuf says. 'One bad reputation for the family ends their chances of marrying off their children. So if the kids are taking drugs or doing bad things, the family can become socially isolated or they may just shut off communication with the community. The son is a reflection of the family.'[100]

While there is significant overlap between Bangladeshi marriage and Islamic criteria, a third criterion of judgment—that of greater British social acceptance—can seem quite conflictive. British youth social spheres are perceived to be—and occasionally are—significantly based on drinking alcohol, casual dating, listening to diverse types of music, and clubbing. And young Bangladeshi men are confronted with this social model by newspaper reports about household-name celebrities, television content and, increasingly, online personal profiles on sites like Facebook, MySpace and HighFive. In this manner, a drastically different lifestyle is showcased and many participants said that they are either attracted to it, or feel pressured to accommodate it in the interest of social acceptance (perhaps both). They say social pressures are manifested in school, at work, and during social interactions with non-Bangladeshis. The three criteria of judgment make for existential conflict, but parents and elders are showing some signs of flexibility. Zubair says:

> It's like you have an oxygen mask on, and the air is slowly depleting. Things are getting tight. Our hierarchy of needs is changing.... The *bari* culture, it's not something that we can carry over to this country. My parents and their generation can. But London is like a machine, a clock that ticks non-stop. But I think people here are changing. I think Bengali people are very happy for their daughter or son to go to uni, in a free mixed environment. My mum now learns English, she swims in the sea in a sari, attends a women's club. She carries a diary now. This is just in the past three years, and it's empowering. The women, they're moving much faster than the men. They're the ones who are progressing. I think people are embracing Western culture and lifestyles. But some things, of course, won't change.[101]

Qadim explains that meeting the three criteria makes for a hybridized individual:

> The sisters want what I call a 'bad boy brother': someone who is attractive and respected by the boys, but presentable to the family. So I say '*insha'allah*' and keep this thin beard. But even your beard is thicker than mine. I don't pray, and I'm gonna want to shag every chance I get. The embrace of Islam is huge and it's become mainstream now. H&M is selling Palestinian checkered scarves. If I claim to be practising, I get a support system. It's for protection.[102]

The individual's management of these three criteria of social judgment contributes to the definition of their civic life. Indeed, the more security with which they can go about their affairs, the more likely they may be to lead or participate publicly and bridge ethno-religious differences. The question is, can individuals find a substantive base for this security despite their overlapping and intersecting identities? In practice, those youths with greater apprehension about reconciling their manifold identities are more susceptible to the clarifying exclusivist doctrine of *Hizb-Ut-Tahrir*, or more likely to become socio-politically marginalized. Indeed, few participants were surer of themselves than the members of HT.

Apartist Rejectionism

Hizb-Ut-Tahrir's East End activists and recruiters recognize that young Bangladeshis feel excluded from British society and have retreated into a tentative, defensive embrace of their embattled Muslim faith without actually accepting its traditional moral paradigm. Though they represent a small minority of people, the group opportunistically exploits young Bangladeshis' perceptions by filling the voids created by these circumstances—an uncertain nationality and an uncertain moral paradigm. HT attempts to replace Britain as young Bangladeshis' nation-state by connecting them to an invisible, global, ummatic nation governed by the resurrected structures of the extinct *khalifa*. It welds this nation together by their segmented religion, but more strongly by a false moral paradigm that claims to supersede the 'petty divisions' and 'irrelevant' rituals of their parents and relatives. In doing so, all three principal pillars of the young British Bangladeshi Muslim's identity are abandoned in favor of one which simultaneously encompasses all of them and none at all.

In this study of young Bangladeshis, apartism in the East End is limited to those individuals who are withdrawn from the British civic sphere (mostly gang members and drug traffickers) and members of *Hizb-Ut-Tahrir*. While the British government continues to investigate cells of *Al-Muhajiroun* and Al-Qaeda, these groups were not encountered in the fieldwork and therefore not interviewed or observed. However, from secondary sources, it is clear that each doctrine promotes the same deterritorialized Muslim culture and state that challenges the foundations of local Islam, local ethnicity and local democratic government.

Rejection of Britishness

A general rejection of the British democratic government is underpinned by the argument that the West fosters hatred for Islam, uses an undivine system of governance, and provides freedoms which promote the *haram*. *Hizb-Ut-Tahrir* showcases democracy's imperfections and attempts to exhibit a global agenda against Islam to demonstrate that it is a system not fit to govern Muslims anywhere. It highlights the system's obvious weaknesses that require the representative 'leap of faith' shown to be necessary for active civic engagement in the institutions of democracy. At a May 2008 meeting in Toynbee Hall, the lead speaker said:

> The Western governments have achieved backwardness, corruption, and the oppression of the masses based on a policy of secularism and Western values. There is an utter loss of confidence in our rulers, and utter loss of confidence in our system of government.

> While Muslims in the West hate our rulers, rulers like [Afghanistan's Hamid] Karzai are treated like heroes when they [make state visits to other countries, because they are propping each other up]. The West relies upon them for access to resources and markets. We should replace these useless states with one that will protect unity, honor Islam, and rob the West of what it's been stealing.

> Today, if you want forces out of Iraq, *shari'a* law, Islamic economics, then you are extremists. If you accept [oppression, invasion and inequality], then you are moderates, and have been accepted into Western Islam.

> The West needs hatred for Islam to support its interventions in the Muslim world. They want us to be afraid enough to accept Western Islam, because our Islam is scaring them and making them lose sleep.[103]

The leader of the Stepney group organized a month-long series on citizenship in Islam, in which weekly dialogue condemned democracy and encouraged attendees who wished to 'get involved' to do so by circumventing the vehicles of activism provided by the state. In one discussion, he employed a deceptive account of democracy's 'lies':

It is explained to us that democracy is the only system. But democracy is a system based on lies and myths; just like the myth of British prosperity for a Bangladeshi immigrant, who comes here and ends up cutting onions in a restaurant.

The first lie is that the government is going to look after us. Members of the government are just looking out for themselves. Just last month, MPs in the House of Commons were debating about whether to give themselves a pay rise to £60,000. That's more money than we'll ever make.

The second lie is accountability. The Brown tax breaks only went to the middle class, but not to the guys who work at Sainsbury's [supermarkets].

The third lie is that political parties actually care about Muslims. The terrorism laws are passed by MPs who are arguing about how long to put you in prison. These people looking after your interests are trying to get rid of habeas corpus so that they can throw you away without evidence. ...These laws are aimed at Muslims.

People say there are no politics in Islam. But there are so many verses. [He recites a sequence of Arabic excerpts that few attendees understand.] Who is worse: the ones who want to imprison you for twenty days under anti–terrorist laws, or the BNP [British National Party]? They're going to send you back home [to Bangladesh].

So how do Muslims get involved in politics, when we don't believe in democracy? Politics is simple. It's about looking out for people's needs. Islam can do that too. Allah gave us clear rules and laws for doing that. Allah provided us with a system. Allah chose for us the Islamic system and way of life because we didn't need democracy.[104]

Shortly after the meeting, Ismail, an 18–year-old from Stepney, says he is persuaded not to support a democratic system. 'At any moment,' he says, 'maybe 70 per cent of the population doesn't want the government in power. It has its mistakes. But that's because it's man's law, and man is fallible. That's not something we can live by when we've been given divine texts. Here, someone with money gets a bigger say. Poor people are usually underrepresented. Democracy entails capitalism which requires inequality in the world.'[105] Another attendee says, 'Democracy is a man-made system, so of course it is going to fail. We are not averse to believing that people have power. It's the source of where the problem lies. The will of the people isn't being acted on. The system isn't anything like the system claims to be. The choices are always limited to those which are secular and Western-oriented. It's just a tool to serve the interests of the superpowers. People genuinely want to live by the *shari'a*.'[106] HT activists point to their own success in the East End as evidence that the state is not necessary to build community strength. Viq says:

I spend more of my money on this community project, but I have a greater effect in my volunteer work than any committee or councilor ever would. The councilors know we control a lot of youths, and they've even approached us for votes...

Our community, we've had many councilors, many different governments, and nothing has changed. Until we established the club. No councilor can solve our problems. He can write a speech, but he's not on the ground. There were these two boys who approached in the midst of a serious, threatening argument over a drug deal in which one purportedly owed the other fifty pounds. So I just gave one of them fifty pounds, and asked if life is really worth killing each other over.[107]

Such deceptively clear solutions also underpin HT's response to the social rejection their young members are encountering from their non-Muslim British peers. They claim that the freedom of British society is un-Islamic in its enablement of temptation, and that the culture of individualism undermines the solidarity of the Muslim minority. 'We live in a society where everyone wants to think they are free,' said a HT leader at a meeting in Shadwell. 'So they think they are also free from God's restrictions. They want to get out and enjoy themselves. We're not free. We are slaves to Allah. And if so, we need to follow Allah. And it's not just Muslims. We have got the solution for the whole of society. We have to give up freedom.'[108] At another meeting in Toynbee Hall, a speaker says, 'Freedom of speech is a licence to attack Islam. There was culture, science, discovery in the old *khalifah*. It didn't need freedom of speech to make people think. The Quran addressed them in a rational way that made people think.'[109] In spreading this *da'wa*, or message, the Shadwell group leader compared the social rejection experienced by its members to the disbelief and condemnation experienced by the Prophet:

In every town, when prophets are sent, they are always mocked. Like when Mohammed walked in Makkah. Sometimes they are even threatened with death. This is the same thing you see today. You want to go speak to someone about Islam. They say, 'Hey, those preachers are coming. Let's have some fun with them' or 'Oh, here goes that ninja girl' or 'Here goes Bin Laden'. Our duty is to convey the message. If the prophets were ridiculed, then surely we should expect that people will ridicule us. Wherever we go, Islam is being attacked. The media, everywhere. In this situation, our obligation is to tell people about Islam.

'Forget about talking about politics,' we're told, 'because if you talk about the government, they'll close down our ministry.' When the Prophet told people not to cheat in the market, not to bury unwanted babies alive, they said, 'you are a troublemaker'. People want to remain comfortable. The same goes here. People are on the streets smoking a spliff with a bottle of alcohol, going after girls. These are people that are comfortable. If you tell them to stop, you become a troublemaker.

> When people can't win an argument, they will resort to making fun of your funny beard or long gown. When we call out the British government for killing innocent people, they make legislation. Now if you criticize the war, they'll put you in prison. If you join a certain group, they'll put you in prison. But this is nothing new.[110]

HT members' attempts to separate themselves from British society are undermined by their integration and upbringing in British life. They are very much consumers and products of the British society that facilitates their self-expression and has informed their tastes and lifestyles. Many HT members remain quite unfamiliar with the alternative regime and society that they aspire to install.

Rejecting Bangladeshi Heritage

Hizb-Ut-Tahrir rejects the cultural ties of East End Muslims to their decreasingly relevant Bangladeshi heritage, calling it Hindu-ized, backward and *haram*. This echoes the thoughts of many young Bangladeshis who grow impatient with the seemingly misplaced traditionalism of their parents. HT's stand against the embrace of Bangladeshi culture was applied strongly during the East End's *Boishakhi Mela* new year's festival. On a local club's website, an author wrote:

> With many Muslims attending the *Boishaki Mela*, an event which was a sad day for Muslims in London. Ask yourself; why are the Muslim youth so blind that they proudly wear the flag of Bangladesh when Bangladesh has legalised prostitution and in itself is a mela of corruption? So then why do Muslim youth celebrate nationalistic pride (*kufr*)? That day was truly a sign of the days of *Jahiliyyah* (ignorance) that our beloved Prophet (*pbuh*) faced before. So, like then we need the mercy of Islam again, and its isn't just growing a beard, praying, and wearing Islamic clothing—as these types also attended the mela! What does it mean to feel the true mercy of living under the shade of the Quran? Will we enter the shade of the Quran during this hot summer weather and abstain from un-Islamic behavior, thus avoiding the searing heat of *Jahannam*?
>
> The prophet (*swa*) warned against imitating those ignorant people who think they're free. Muhammad (*pbuh*) said:
>
> 'Do not be a mere imitator with no firm determination. You say, "I am with the people. Should people do good, so do I. And if they do evil, so do I." But school yourselves. If people do good so should you. But if they do evil shun their evil deeds.'[111]

Such a statement reflects the organization's argument that Muslims must operate according to a pan-Islamic moral paradigm—in all aspects of their lives, in full. They reprimand Muslims who limit Islam's role and follow Islamic norms halfway, leading to a chastising critique of Bangladeshi mosques for tolerating such malpractice:

Islam is a complete way of life; it is unlike any other religion. We do not believe in secularism as it is a separation of church from state i.e. Deen from Dunya. We believe that Allah (*swt*) has blessed us with a complete Deen which solves problems in ALL aspects of life. We do not believe like the Christians do, 'render unto ceasar what is ceasars' [*sic*], render unto God what is Gods' as in Islam everything that belongs to ceasar belongs to God as well as all creation.

So if we reject secular values, why do Muslim youths act the way they do? Is it because by being brought up in a secular country we have adopted secular values without knowing?

If you think Muslims don't think in a secular way, why does the following happen, and why is it justified by some Muslim 'scholars, community leaders, councilors, parents, older brother etc.:

Muslims pray on Friday Jummah, but not any other fard prayer (kind of like going Church on Sundays)

Fasting in the first few months of Ramadhan and then 'allowing it' for the remainder... mosques are so packed, people are praying on the pavements... Fifteen days into Ramadhan and the Masjid is half full.

Why is it that Muslims dress up in 'Islamic clothing' and go to the Mosque on Lailatul Qadr (night of power) and cry their eyes out in dua, and then the next day, continue with the *haram* (interest based) mortgages, vote for non-Muslims who implement other than Islam. Isn't that render unto ceasar what is ceasars...?

Why do restaurant owners who have fully licensed (serving pints and fine wines) go to Hajj every year with their Alcohol money? Do we accept as a Muslim that it's ok because it's legal in the UK or is it the same as drug dealing according to Islam?

We see Muslims boasting about how many restaurants and takeaways they have, and how many houses they've bought with interest based loans (*riba*). If this is sinful and shameful why are they viewed as 'successful Muslims' in the UK?

Why do some of our elders wear a *fanjabi* and a waistcoat and a cap and walk into Ladbrokes? Why can't they see the contradiction?

Why do some parents say, that '*namaz* is *fard*' (=obligatory) and yet when the exam time clashes with the Salah, they say you should miss the Salah and go to the exam. How can a Muslim youth grow up to be practising and fear in Allah, when he/she is told to only fear Allah in the Masjid and not in the exam hall?

Why do some Muslim youths who pray and fast because it's *fard* but won't do Dawa and won't do 'politics' even though it *fard* [*sic*].

How come the 'Masjid committees' say 'no politics in the mosque' yet they work with MPs and councilors and have old traditional divisions over 'party' lines of BNP, Jamaat & Awami league.

If the Khutbas are meant to be a vital opportunity to speak to the community about anti–terror laws, the Iraq war, difficulties Muslims are facing in the UK and abroad, then why are the Khutbas always providing the government message? Like 'spy on your Muslim brothers...or Shari'a is for the individual and not for life's affairs'. So every government's message is explained in plain English, and everything else is said in a language we don't understand.

Why do some scholars say to seek 'the lesser of two evils'? It sounds like enjoining the evil and forbidding the good to us!

Has the disease set in? Pray to Allah (*swa*) for Hidayaat (guidance) gain *Ilm* (knowledge) about the Deen and discuss your issues so that we can filter out the good ideas from the bad.[112]

Despite this rejection of Bangladeshi culture and ties, HT meetings maintain the cellular structure that characterizes most British Muslim communities' organization. Despite the cohesion provided by Islamic fellowship, most British Muslim communities tend to associate within their own ethnic group— Somalis with Somalis, Lebanese with Lebanese, Pakistanis with Pakistanis, and more specifically Sylheti Bangladeshis with Sylheti Bangladeshis. The occasional non-Bangladeshi attending an East End HT gathering marks an exception, not the embodiment of the group's ummatic spirit.

Embracing Global Islam, Rejecting Local Islam

In response to what it portrays as a war on Islam by Western governments, HT advises its members to take refuge in the solidarity of a global transnational *ummah*. Facilitated by 'the tools of globalization'[113] that make the *ummah* feel more real than imagined, HT attempts to blend the local ethnic, tribalist and nationalist affiliations into a homogeneous Islamic populace. The group produced a slickly made eight-minute film, with graphics and a full soundtrack. It explains how non-Muslims perceive the Quran. There are images of a hand getting chopped off, of graphic Quran-burning demonstrations. Yet it remains unspecific about which non-Muslims hate the Quran and how many. In response, it shows a force of millions of non-descript pilgrims making *hajj* to Mecca to demonstrate Islam's strength in numbers outside the Western world. It shows images of women in prominent career positions as doctors and scholars. A tint spreads across a map of North Africa into the

Middle East and South Asia. It calls for the *ummah* to stand for Islam, to stand for the *khalifa*. After showing the film at one East End meeting, Furdoz reads a passage in Arabic and translates, 'Take no friends but yourselves, they will do nothing but harm.'[114]

This message extends to exclude other East End Muslims—both the aforementioned enablers in mosques, the 'halfway' Muslims, and the terrorists who have rendered Islam its negative reputation in the West. The criticism not only estranges youths from their mosque communities, but also from their parents and an older generation. A HT blogger wrote:

> Every Jummah, I want to scream and shout out: Tell them how they, the parents, tear our lives apart. Tell them how the parents have become strangers to their own sons and daughters. How we don't eat together any more and there is no laughter at home. Tell them to stop forcing us to be someone else and be proud of who we are. Tell them to stop bribing us with their politics and their love to look so good in front of the community. Say to the rest of these people that it's time we find out what the youth need. Tell them that we can run, laugh, play, fight in a mosque. Tell them, this mosque is our home, our identity, our foundation to build our community.

> Every Jummah, my heart starts pounding, the sweat starts to touch my brow and I am consumed into silence. I then sit and stare at the Imam and listen to words that don't inspire me. I see that same robotic expression and hear that same burst of shouting and that same movement of lips from people, which is drowned by insincerity. I look around at some of the community leaders who promised so much to each other and still, years have gone by and everything is still the same. No, I lie. It has gone backwards.

> The man on that pulpit keeps talking and I reflect on how we, the youths, have become nothing but ghosts, a dowry, a graduated photograph, a status, a symbol for recognition, a cry of acceptance for adults to obtain from the world. We've become numbers on a government file or outputs for a college. We've even become competition for banks who want to loan us money and get us into debt. As if we haven't got enough problems. The greatest one of all is—many don't know the meaning of the Holy Qur'an when they rock to and fro and some don't even read it in its own language—Arabic. And we expect to solve the issues of the world and make it happen? They must be kidding. I must be kidding myself too because I don't know the meaning of the verses I read. Now, that is one twisted way to live a way of life called Islam, isn't it? Yes, it is![115]

In this scenario, the political party and its 'real' Islam also stands in for its members' schoolteachers, imams and fathers—leaving believers alienated from all three support structures of their identity and fully dependent on the ideology of *Hizb-Ut-Tahrir*. They advertise this ideology as a 'real', purist Islam that is as true today for the modern world as it was for the Prophet and his followers in the seventh century. They make (often flawed) analogies between today's challenges and those of biblical and Quranic figures to demonstrate Islam's adroit ability—and the secular, Western, democratic system's incapacity—to resolve their most pressing problems with simple (and exclusivist) black-and-white answers. Such ideology attempts to fill a void created by a severe lack of faith in the competence of the democratic system, its complementary institutions and, quite counter-intuitively, local mosques.

A common denominator shared by all HT activists interviewed for this study was their estrangement from their local mosque. It is this estrangement—often for different reasons—which both inspires their affiliation with HT and also enables their persuasion, due to a lack of proper Islamic education. Yusuf, the community leader, says, 'With the extremist groups, the deal-breaker is teaching. Who taught them Islam? Their viewpoints are the product of not having teaching at an early age. And just because you're academically smart doesn't mean that, Islamically, you'll pick the best option. Bit by bit, you're attracted by what seems like the truth. And you're not knowledgeable to know the difference. After regular attendance at their meetings, it's just a matter of time. My madrassas taught me to read Arabic without telling me what the words mean. Most mosques are like this.'[116]

Independent of their levels of Islamic education, participants expressed different reasons for their mosque disaffection. Calim, a local *Hizb-Ut-Tahrir* leader says, 'You'd go in the mosque and they'd send you to the back of the line. The committee, they'd be older guys, and it was as if you were a nuisance in their private club. So I decided to just step out and relax. It was the same in all the local mosques. The imams couldn't speak any English. Not there. No guidance. We used to go for Arabic prayers, and they were just angry old men.'[117] Bilal, medical student and member of the Stepney group, similarly points to a generational divide. 'Where were the older people addressing us at the mosque?' he asks. 'There is a large age gap, but where was the family feeling? I feel welcome at the youth club. I didn't feel that way walking into the mosque. I never talked to elders about the Iraq War and the things that affect Muslims. You go, you pray, and bish bash bosh, you leave. The only announcement they ever made that affected youth specifically was a warning from authorities to drive safely on Eid. The imams, they'd never talk to me about the world. Just 'salaam', 'how's your family?' It's not that I wasn't comfortable talking to them. It's that they don't feel comfortable talking to me. Young people bring change, and yet, every single time, we are ignored.'[118] Another Stepney affiliate, Ismail blames mosques for what he believes is government-imposed quietism. 'The mosques and their sermons are influenced by the government. They're not speaking about 42–day detention laws, human rights, et cetera. They're speaking about ablution before prayer. Even the prophet didn't do that. He talked about things that mattered.'[119]

The key themes that emerge are twofold. First, many young people do not feel comfortable or welcome in mosques. Youth organizers say that youth clubs are remedies for that void. 'The mosque, as it was 1400 years ago, was a vibrant place,' says Qadim. 'It was social, you could wrestle with other boys. There was a café and marketplace. Now if you go into a mosque, shhh, it's like a library. You want to attract young people? Put in a luxury leather sofa and a Playstation. We wanted the mosque to be open, without limitations, for 24 hours.'[120] Ghalib says, 'Most mosques don't want to engage the younger people. Their committees are usually run by the elders, and they don't understand that young people don't want to go to mosques just to pray like the elders. They want a place to talk, laugh, learn, socialize and network.'[121]

Second, imams are failing to communicate in an appealing or relevant way. This spectacular failure is made all the more significant with Bangladeshi youths' embrace of an Islamic identity. Quite simply, their primary point of reference for this identity construction is incapable of explaining its meaning and its proper role in non-Muslim society. Viq says:

> I'm not happy with the mosques. After the War in Iraq started, people went to the East London Mosque for a response. They did a talk on the benefits of honey. When I was young, I remember I wanted to get rid of the mosque and start one in the basement. Now I know better. Because so much is government-funded, it's hard for the masjid to be anti–establishment. They have to play ball. But because of terrorism, the mosques that have always wanted to remain depoliticized were all brought into the politics. I mean the East London Mosque asked people to spy on fellow Muslims. Imams are supposed to share their knowledge. They aren't doing this. They're just following the government line. They teach Islam in the wrong way. They teach young people to be individualistic by making Islam look like a bunch of rituals, rather than a complete way of life. The mosque doesn't view itself as a place to discuss worldly issues. But if you need a marriage, funeral or blessing, they're there for you.[122]

Naz argues that imams are simply unaware of the role they should play. 'Imams are the people who are meant to give you guidance,' he says. 'But they only come in for prayer and then lock you out. If they're there to help, why don't they say what's best for you? And they speak in Arabic, but 95 per cent of people can't speak Arabic. [My imam] taught me how to pray, how to wash myself. At a young age, you're with your parents. But from 10 to 16, the imam taught me. After that, I thought, Islam can't just be about prayer. There are so many other obligations. There are so many other problems that Islam can fix. Imams are the people we look up to, but don't tell me that it's only about prayer.'[123] Subsequent interviews with several imams exhibit a conscientious and well-meaning group of Islamic guides, who readily acknowledge their inability to connect with young people. Each imam interviewed for this study required an interpreter. One imam in Shadwell says, 'Because of the communication gap, I can't always communicate with youth. I refer them to the madrassa teacher who speaks English. I see all the problems among young people, and I wish I could handle them all, but it's just not possible. It's mostly Bengalis I see, and they know they should act better. With young people, we need to get them to the mosque to be taught. There is a gap between older and younger people. Each thinks that the other doesn't know anything.' The greater part of UK mosques 'import' imams after training or experience abroad, because many British seminaries lack legitimacy among local mosque leaders and many communities prefer imams with specific ethnic ties. Inside the UK, there are only twenty local, independent and often small institutions of Islamic scholarship—or *dar al-uloom* (houses of knowledge)—where they can train to become imams and lead mosques. 'These places are doing a great job trying to produce people who aspire to a very frugal, simple and devoted lifestyle,' Zaki said. 'Of course, that doesn't fit into our materialistic, consumerist society. At the end of the day, they are producing people with a simple outlook on life. But our society is much more complicated, and these people are inadequate to deal with that.'[124] Many smaller and even medium-sized mosques import imams from the home villages of their congregation and committee members. While this fosters comfort with the older generation, it does little to comfort youths.

Such a gaping void in guidance is being filled by other sources of information. HT members and non-HT members say that they receive information about Islam from a variety of sources including books, sheikhs, pamphlets and especially the internet—none of which are distributed with any accountability. Only three participants say that they go to their imam for advice. It is the same imam—Sheikh Abdul Qayyum of the East London Mosque, who is fluent in Arabic, Bangladeshi and most importantly English.

Spectrum of Identity Construction

In sum, we see that *Hizb-Ut-Tahrir* does not merely reject British nationality and its cultural norms and values. It also rejects the equally fundamental identity components of Bangladeshi heritage and local Islam, in the interest of promoting a singular—simultaneously purist and revisionist—identity: its own. This completes the spectrum of identity construction for young Muslims in the East End. One group of individuals is able to accept all components of their identity (in all their conflicting complexity) as part of a postmodern existence. In this group, we can include those individuals who are culturally Islamic, whereby Islam is the individual's heritage but it does not necessarily dictate private or public life. We can also include ethnically Islamic people, for whom Islam defines a private sense of identity, but it is one factor among many that influence lifestyle choices. And we can include secularists, for whom Islam exists powerfully in the private sphere of prayer and custom, without it being imposed on other people's choices more publicly.

In the middle reside those who are confused by all of their competing identity components, a significant proportion of young Bangladeshis in London's East End that this qualitative study could not measure. And on the other side of the spectrum are non-exclusivist Islamists and *Hizb-Ut-Tahrir*, an organization which advocates accepting none of those identity components at all. For the non-exclusivist Islamist, Islam is a complete lifestyle that informs all private decisions and daily choices, personal and political. While such individuals believe they should spread *da'wa* and advocate Islamically sanctioned choices and public policies, others may respectfully disagree. Finally for the exclusivist Islamist, Islam is a complete way of life that not only dominates personal and political choices, but should also be adopted as a divinely created politico-legal system. Anything else is flawed and should be rejected.

Conclusion: Integrated yet Apart

At its beginning, this chapter set out to understand better the challenges and patterns of civic engagement among young Bangladeshi men from London's East End. From this case study, we discover a tripartite paradigm of identity and moral judgment that complicates nearly all participants' private decisions within and statements about what is a remarkably active and cohesive public sector. This tripartite paradigm is sharply broken down into the nationally British, the ethno-culturally Bangladeshi, and the religiously Islamic (see Figure Four). Yet civically participants exhibited that they are all identities at once—transcending such man-made, ideological boundaries. However, this convenient rationalization conceals the reality that participants are extremely cognizant of the corresponding moral criteria produced by this paradigm and

| | Democratic Sphere | | | |
	British	Bangladeshi	Islamic	Apartist
Identity Form	National	Ethno-cultural	Religious	All at once, and none at all.
Moral Paradigm of Judgment	Rationalist—Secularist, Universalist	Traditionalist—Culturalist	Quranic—Islamist, Ecclesiastical	Quranic—Fundamentalist, *Khalifa*-based
Civic Manifestation	State Government and Institutions, Social Activism	*Desi*-politics and Transnational Associationalism	Mosque-based affiliation and organizations	HT and other anti–democratic groups

Figure Four: Identity and Politics. This chapter outlines three forms of East End Bangladeshi identity construction, their corresponding criteria of social judgment, and their corresponding civic manifestations.

employed to judge their public behavior; the common realization that one will be unable or unwilling to satisfy fully all of the criteria from each aspect of their identity, which inspires as much personal dynamism as it inspires remorse and disappointment.

Among apartists in particular, these private feelings are exacerbated by perceived public rejection from 'British society'. Participants experience this via interpersonal interactions, discriminatory public discourse, or collective injury from a peer's negative experience. British citizenship is rhetorically advertised to be a flexible identity that embraces a spectrum of difference into a common, open political arena, but many participants believe recognition of Britishness is dispensed on a highly conditional basis, riddled with double standards and discrimination against Muslims. In interviews, participants show a sensitive awareness of their rights under a democracy (more than of their obligations) and are subsequently acutely sensitive toward their non-fulfillment. While some participants acknowledge such democratic flaws as features of an imperfect but ultimately effective political system, apartists suggest that the flaws are reflective of a system that is ultimately not interested in the welfare, equality or future of British Muslims. This case study thus suggests that such variability is strongly correlated with participants' perceptions of the structural environment that they share in common.

Apartists' perception of a breach in British citizenship terms produces intense feelings of socio-political alienation and a reluctance to express themselves or participate in the mainstream institutions of British civic life. Their response reflects an important truth that emerged from the case study: active apartism—as much as ideal normative democratic activism—is related to successful political integration into the state and society. Indeed, a sense of entitlement about civil liberties, individual rights, representative institutions and responsive governance can only emerge from political integration and an understanding of the democratic system of governance. Therefore, it would be erroneous to argue, as many government authorities have, that 'better integration' of religious or ethnic minorities is essential to combat political alienation. In fact, the former appears necessary for the latter to occur.

In some ways, the best hope for many young British Bangladeshis to reconcile their 'identity crisis' of belonging is through membership in a state which actually does accept all comers on the basis of a civic contract that is blind to the disparities and contradictions of ethnicity, culture and religion. This is not to say that private lifestyle choices about levels of piety and traditionalism would be resolved. They would not. However, the public manifestation of such private dilemmas would be limited and the state would not be implicated—just as the state is neither involved in a Buddhist family's debate about the spirituality of their children nor a Chinese family's discussion about speaking Mandarin in the house. Indeed, in all democratic countries with large communities of ethnic or religious minorities of migrant origin, individuals face questions about how much they assimilate into their family's new home country—often the only home country that later generations know. Indeed, in all democratic countries, citizens must grapple with the necessary truth of democracy that some people will simply not get their way. Representative democracies and their independent politicians rely on the perception that individual voices matter, and that all are equal under common law despite the inequity that pervades daily life. Unable or unwilling to make either democratic leap of faith, apartists defect from the system or place their faith in a competing system of government. Importantly, the Islamic alternative promises nothing more than its democratic counterpart—equality and protection for all. While the Islamic system's ability to deliver is highly debatable, apartists are certain that they would not be discriminated against or treated as an underclass in the ways they feel currently. And that is appealing to them.

While this qualitative study is unable to permit generalization about the extent of the discovered trends, we are better able to comprehend the nature of the phenomena discussed. Among the minority of young Bangladeshis who subscribe to the apartist outlook detailed above, we see that their path is only slightly divergent from their non-apartist peers in the East End. Nearly all study participants demonstrated a strong sense of entitlement to the democratic provisions of justice, liberty and representation. Nearly all participants expressed severe doubts about the democratic system's capacity to deliver. And nearly all participants' insecurities about East End democratic institutions are connected to their insecurities about the relationships they are struggling to maintain with one or all of the three principal forms of identity that underlie those civic institutions. While the democrats and activists who invest and sustain faith in the democracy can overlook its inherent imperfections, apartists—in the light of their sense of entitlement—seem consumed by these imperfections, perceiving them to be symptomatic of a society and a state that do not have their interests in mind.

What is clear then is that there are doubts in the East End's community of young Bangladeshis about the democratic state's ability and interest in delivering equality and protection to British Muslims. While such doubts are common in any democratic community of people, many participants in this study believe that the state's inefficacy is targeted and some are seeking to undermine the system's channels for reform in order to foster the change they desire: equal protection—a change that doesn't actually seem so impossible to deliver.

5

ON THE INSIDE LOOKING OUT

MOROCCANS IN SOUTHERN MADRID

This chapter presents the results from an in-depth, qualitative case study of the Moroccan community of Madrid's southern neighborhoods conducted using interviews and observation, focused especially on the *barrio* of Lavapiés. Based on a set of fifty interviews that includes thirty-three with 18- to 28-year-old Moroccans and seventeen with community leaders, observers, first generation migrants and imams, this chapter seeks to understand better the patterns of civic engagement and alienation among young Moroccan men from Lavapiés and the surrounding area called Madrid Sur—and particularly why some individuals become apartist. As with the previous chapter, rather than profile a select few interviewees, this study solicits and analyzes a diversity of outlooks and behaviors within a substantial variety of individuals in the same community. This is done in order to trace the landscape of Spanish Moroccan civic life and identity forms, and map participants' perceptions about these factors and the Spanish political system with rough indicators of the weight of different groups in the sample. The next chapter compares and contrasts the findings from Madrid Sur with those from the East End.

The true second generation of Moroccans in Spain is in its nascence. The first Moroccan migrants came from the northern, Spanish-influenced port cities of the country in the mid and late 1980s. Their Spanish-born children are now no older than 25 years old, and there are few of them. However, beginning in the 1990s, greater numbers of Moroccans began crossing Spanish borders, and family reunification rules permitted more and more children and women to join their fathers and husbands in Europe. As a result, there is a sizeable number of young Moroccans in Spain today who were born in Morocco; many even spent their childhood in Morocco, but their mature lives in Spain. They are members of Generation 1.5. Their adolescence—a more independent time of identity and opinion formation—has been strongly influenced by their lives in Spanish society amid Spanish culture. The subjects of interviews belong to these two groups, but overwhelmingly the latter.

In interviews, first-generation immigrants showed themselves to be thick-skinned and unsentimental. They are able to prevent their feelings about Spanish society affecting their opinion about life within it. They also have an ability to prevent their disputes and frustrations with Spaniards being taken personally. Their mentality centers on the bottom line. They are in Spain to do a job, to pursue a goal—a better, richer, more stable life. The surrounding society and its ills are irrelevant, as long as they do not affect that bottom line. It is an attitude that in any case reflects a certain degree of detachment, as much as it reflects resilience. This shoulder-shrugging is sometimes manifested as forgiveness and other times spiteful ignorance. The emerging question is whether the children of these immigrants will maintain this detachment in later generations, or whether they—entrenched as nationals in Spanish society—will begin to recognize a future and stake in Spanish democracy and Spanish society. While answers are predictably mixed, a significant proportion of those participants interviewed demonstrated disturbing indications of extraordinarily passive apartism.

To understand the nature of socio-political alienation among the second generation of Moroccan immigrants, this chapter evaluates the civic structures available to the young men interviewed and finds a very green, discriminatory Spanish democracy that is struggling to establish a culture of activism and associationalism among Spaniards, let alone Muslim migrants. Interview content also exhibits exceptionally low engagement in a weak and dispersed array of Moroccan associations and mosques in Madrid and much of Spain. Many second-generation Spanish Moroccans interviewed, some of whom have lived under a democracy about as long as any Spaniard, have not only maintained their parents' detachment from Spanish society, but cling tightly to an enduringly relevant Moroccan ethno-religious identity. Interviews suggest that, for a variety of reasons, young people continue to clutch a lingering 'myth of return' that prevents them from investing in a future in Spain. Many participants perceived their Moroccan identity to be irreconcilable with not only the ethno-religious Spanish identity, but also the *civic* Spanish identity. In analyzing Spain's ability to win their engagement, interviews point to a variety of obstacles to organizing Moroccan activism and a remarkably flawed structure of representative governance in Spain—leaving an expanding community of apartist Moroccan-origin people withdrawn from the civic sphere of their country with little expectation of change.

Life in the Streets

Lavapiés is a small neighborhood encompassing much of the Embajadores district in the south-central part of Madrid, occupying a downward slope that descends from the plateau of Madrid's commercial hub (see Figure Five). The southern and eastern border is a channel to the southern suburbs of the Spanish capital, connected by Metro tunnels running through the Arganzuela region and Atocha train station toward scores of low-rise neighborhoods settled on the outer arid flatlands. To the west of Lavapiés and Embajadores runs Calle de Toledo, near where the enormous, animated *Rastro* Sunday market takes place. The northern limit sees Madrid's dramatic plazas, grand avenues and tree-lined grids cascade and collapse into the narrow, sloping passageways and crooked corridors of Lavapiés—the city's Jewish neighborhood before their 1492 expulsion by the region's Muslim community. The neighborhood gets its name, which literally means 'wash feet', from the medieval denizens who washed their feet before entering the houses of worship. Since then, it has generally remained a low-rent slum of Madrid for centuries before Moroccan immigrants moved in during the late 1970s and early 1980s and took control of the streets.

In London, the streets are a venue for transit and functionality. Loitering is not tolerated unless it is in a designated location. When young Bangladeshis chat on street corners—even within their own residential neighborhoods—police officers are regularly called to break them up. A threat is suggested. In Madrid, and especially Lavapiés, the streets and many plazas are venues for communal social life. Loitering is a cultural norm, as the streets serve as a shared social space. Especially when the summer sun descends and shadows extend from sidewalk to sidewalk, street life responds to the temperate weather. Footballs are kicked around, elderly people are perched on benches chirping like birds on a wire, dogs bark, and there is incessant haggling and gossiping from people leaning on the windows of corner stores and the railings of their balconies. A symphony of languages, music and mobile phone tones ring through the alleyways of the neighborhood.

There is less of a need for the 'youth clubs' found in the East End, which attract young people needing a social space outside of their family's cramped two-bedroom council flat. The clubs offer more privacy and things to do, keeping young people of 14–24 years old occupied, out of gang activity (even though they usually maintain affiliations), and 'off the streets'. However, in Madrid, the absence of structured street gangs and the different mentality about social space makes these clubs less necessary from the perspective of general peace and security. 'Look at this old man sitting outside on the bench,' says Hasan, a Spanish Moroccan who works in the central *barrio* of Lavapiés. 'Every bench is occupied here. Everyone is in the streets. We don't need clubs to get kids off the streets. They're on the streets with everyone else. They share that space.... There are hundreds of pairs of eyes on them, people share the same community.'[1] Instead, clubs would be useful to foster skill-attainment and social mobility. Indeed, from a security perspective, the streets are a good place for young people to be in Spain—in the vigilance of the public eye, mixing with people of other ages and ethno-religious backgrounds. However, the streets do little to develop the minds and abilities of the growing children of labor migrants and teach them about the opportunities and politico-economic structure of Spanish society. While the streets are safe beyond the occasional pickpocket, young adults lack a center where they can be trained, seek employment and be notified about educational opportunities. The few of these centers that do exist are usually privately administered and are offices more than they are social spaces. For this reason, young Moroccans would only go to such venues for very specific reasons—to visit a lawyer or consult someone for assistance. They would not go to *pasar tiempo*, or hang out.

The streets' role as a social space also makes ethno-religious and cultural differences very evident. Different people and their activities are in plain view, and residents of neighborhoods are confronted with the composition of their society every minute. Fights and disputes take place outdoors, the smell of food is in the air, garage alcoves serve as urinals, benches serve as kiosks for hashish dealers, and some Muslims occasionally pray in local plazas. This significantly blends the public and private spheres, as a polity of Spaniards—still adapting to the presence of foreigners—is confronted with difference head-on. Alfonso, a forty–year resident of Amparo Street in Lavapiés, offers his summary of this metamorphosis:

> This was a marvelous neighborhood once. All the doors were left open. The neighbors were always talking to each other. In about 1978, the novelties store across the street was opened by a family of Moroccans, and they were fine. They made good money.

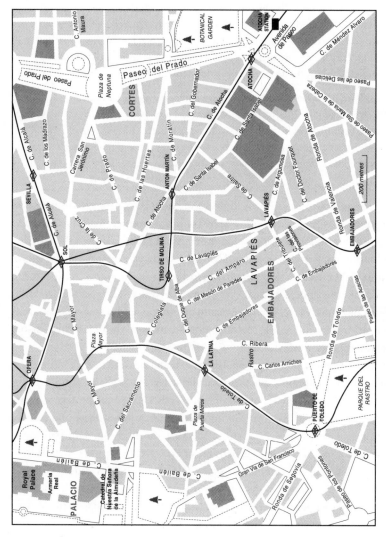

Figure Five: Lavapiés district of Madrid by Mina Moshkeri Upton, Design Unit, LSE

But more and more came. And they began to attack and mug people on the streets. Soon came the Chinese. Then, after them was the brown people, wherever they're from [Bangladesh, actually]. Later came the blacks. They're not bad actually. But they do get into fights with the *Moros*. The doors weren't open any more. All the entryways got shut. The immigrants would open little shops selling specific things: wine, milk. The Moroccans would soon start opening their barber shops that you see everywhere now. Some of them have even opened restaurants. But it's all Arab food. They were mostly well received. There were some who didn't pay their rent and acted badly. But the actions of those people gave the rest a bad reputation…

I still wouldn't rent a flat to them. They're very individualized, and don't get along well with people. They're dirty. They get in a lot of fights in the streets with neighbors. Spanish people don't like them. They just aren't looked upon well. When *Moros* start frequenting a bar, the bar will lose its clientele. You know, they take off their shoes in there. No one wants to be there any more. They're out late until 4 a.m. Not like the Chinese. The Chinese go to work, and go home.[2]

Such an oral history, most importantly, reflects an appreciation of new migrants' inconspicuousness—a 'seen not heard' perspective. As some of the first people migrating to Spain after the cushioned fall of Franco's dictatorship and the opening of the economy, Moroccans were viewed through the lens of Spanish labor needs.[3] They were in Madrid to work, and were not expected to affect any other sphere. Since the Moroccans' arrival, residents in the neighborhoods of Embajadores—a historically bustling neighborhood of transient diversity in Madrid's south-central region—witnessed the genesis of a further metamorphosis: gentrification.

Flats in the *barrio*'s antique buildings are being renovated, air-conditioned, and sold at double and triple the price of the flats inside the unkempt edifices next door, as a new generation of bohemian artists and young professionals are taking advantage of the neighborhood's centrality, atmosphere and relative cheapness. Complaints about street noise are slowly rising. And as Alfonso explained, over the past decade, families of Ecuadorian, Chinese, Bangladeshi and Sub-Saharan African migrants have joined the yuppies, diminishing the proportion of Moroccans. The newer migrants work in a more cooperative fashion and their more reserved, private nature has contrasted with the Moroccan community's brash public presence.

In the immediate aftermath of the 11 March 2004 train bombings, several young Moroccan, Algerian and Syrian suspects were arrested in the corridors of Tribulete Street in Lavapiés, where the mobile phones that detonated the bombs were purchased. And ultimately, eighteen of the twenty-six men identified by police as participants in the attacks at the time were Moroccan, most from Tangiers and the neighboring former colonial outpost of Tetuán.[4] Suddenly, Arab migrants were no longer people to be tolerated, but a threat to be managed. Since then, a bolstered presence of police officers who patrol the plazas and alleys by car, moto and horseback interrogate people regularly, demanding immigration and identification papers. 'The 11 March bombs really changed things a lot,' says Majid. 'And it was by Moroccans. We really just fucked ourselves. The behavior of Spaniards changed. When you're in the streets, they treat you differently, they look at you differently.'[5]

Increasingly outnumbered, shushed and interrogated, the Moroccan community is steadily moving to the peripheries of Madrileña society. Neighborhoods of Moroccans are gradually growing in the outer suburbs, particularly in the southern, working-class *barrios* of Villaverde, Rivas, Fuenlabrada, Getafe, Móstoles and Leganés, a region generally referred to as Madrid Sur. There is more space and cheaper housing available for families of Moroccans which, since the 1990s, have been reuniting in Spain.[6] In a study of such trends from 1992 to 2000, Bernabé López García finds that 50 per cent more new migrants are settling in the periphery of Madrid than within the capital itself.[7] Nevertheless, Lavapiés has maintained its distinction as a cultural hub for the Moroccan community, where several thousand still live and thousands more make regular journeys to visit the *halal* butchers, shop in Moroccan markets, chat over Moroccan tea, play football, and get their hair cut. 'Lavapiés is an exaggeration,' says Idris, a charismatic 23–year-old who just left Lavapiés for a flat in Móstoles. 'Everything is moving. It's never calm. I have a lot of memories here, and a lot of things that I'm accustomed to. But there are also a lot of people selling drugs, it's still dirty, and there are a lot of drunken people on the streets.' A 2006 tally recorded about 70,000 people of Moroccan origin in Madrid, nearly five times the number present ten years before—and more than any other of Spain's autonomous *comunidades* besides the larger regions of Cataluña and Andalucía. National surveys estimate anywhere between 400,000 and 700,000 people of Moroccan origin currently residing in Spain, with hundreds of thousands more unauthorized people unaccounted for[8]—one of the largest national minorities in a rapidly diversifying democratic polity.

Moroccan Exclusion from the Spanish Civic Sphere

Observers of Spain's Moroccan community discuss their political alienation as a matter of nature versus nurture. On the one hand, Moroccans have limited experience of democracy and have been reluctant (and generally unin-vited) to participate in Spanish politics, as later sections will discuss. However, Spanish democracy is hardly fertile ground for a new minority to engage with civically.

A Green Democracy

Civic institutions in Madrid are weak. And they are almost as weak at motivat-ing the activism of Spaniards as they are at motivating the inclusion and activ-ism of migrants—particularly people of Moroccan origin. Installed in 1978 after the parachuted departure of General Francisco Franco's thirty-eight–year authoritarian regime and King Juan Carlos' monarchical transition period, the Spanish democracy and open market are hardly 30 years old. As recently as 1982, the King was still involved in politics. As a result, only the most recent generation of Spanish adults have lived their entire lives in a free, democratic society. A survey by the *Centro de Investigaciones Sociológicas* in November 2006 reflects a significantly disengaged Spanish population, which is more mobilized for civil disobedience against the state than it is for civic participa-tion within state, community, or civic institutions.[9] About 20 per cent of those surveyed said they had participated in a protest or sit-in at least once in the past. About 19 per cent said they had signed a petition at least once in the past. No other forms of civic participation—in non-profit organizations (6%), news media self-expression (9%), public associations (10%), internet chat rooms (2%), political parties (4%), contact with government personnel (15%) or official representatives (7%)—had higher rates of interaction before 2006. More than 40 per cent of the 3,900 respondents said they had never partici-pated in any of the listed civic activities in their lifetimes. Among the inactive, 44 per cent cited complacency, 25 per cent lack of interest, and 13 per cent did not believe their action would have any effect—perhaps in part a legacy of authoritarianism. To support such a hypothesis, in almost all the mentioned outlets of civic participation, people under the age of 45 were about as active in their shorter lifetime—if not more—as those over 45 years old. The rates of associationalism and activism are higher across the board among those under 45 years old, with the exception of neighborhood and geriatric associations, consumer groups and political parties.

Corresponding to Spain's short history of open democracy, the country's experience with immigration is also quite recent. Before the 1980s, the coun-try's encounters with migration almost exclusively entailed Spaniards *emigrat-ing* to other Western European countries, Latin America, and even North

Africa.[10] That chapter of Spain's history has been nearly disregarded in a relatively unsentimental and divisive debate about the presence and role of migrants in the Spanish polity, to which there is still no political consensus or real effort for conciliation. Before 1985, there was no official immigration policy in Spain, nor any legislation detailing the rights of foreigners in Spanish territory.[11] This would change with Spain's signing of the Schengen Agreement, which dismantled the internal borders it shared with France and correspondingly Belgium, Germany, Luxembourg, and the Netherlands. Days after the agreement's enactment, the Spanish Parliament passed the *Ley Orgánica sobre Derechos y Libertades de los Extranjeros en España* (Organic Law on Rights and Liberties of Foreigners in Spain), which came into effect on 1 July 1985. The law would create the category of 'legal' immigrant and, accordingly, 'illegal' immigrant based on the principle of *jus sanguinis* rather than *jus soli*. Indeed, unless an individual has 'Spanish blood', the law made it difficult to attain citizenship. Children born on Spanish soil to illegal migrant parents were not recognized, nor were spouses married to Spaniards. However, such standards have been compromised by the reluctance of the Spanish economy to deport unauthorized or un-contracted workers, who provide cheap labor to a market that has only started to level off since about 2007. As a result, the Spanish government has 'regularized' illegal migrants on numerous occasions since 1985. The first occurred with the *Ley Orgánica* in 1985 and 1986, then a larger amnesty program in 1991, and a smaller one in 1996. There were further opportunities with guest-worker transitions in 1993 and temporary worker transitions in 1999. For many unauthorized migrants, regularization in Spain was just a matter of time—confounding interpretations and enforcement of the law.[12]

Symbolic of this ambivalence, after four decades of propaganda about the 'divine' ascendance of Franco to leadership for the good of the Spanish nation in children's textbooks, new editions still do not address the role of immigrants in Spain.[13] 'Foreigners are conventionally seen as people with special needs in Spanish society, but not as equals,' says one observer who has worked with government policy-makers. 'It's not a product of ignorance. People are conscious of racist sentiment. It's political ambiguity.... And the question remains: Is Spanish identity based on blood or law?'[14] One high-ranking government official on the matter responds:

> The codes dictating nationality go by blood. They were made previous to the trend of immigration to Spain. It was during a time of emigration *from* Spain. For that reason, we wanted to still be able to call a Spaniard in Germany a Spaniard. In the

beginning, we weren't as much of a destination country as we were a bridge to the rest of Europe. So it was all viewed as temporary. Why worry? They're just going to go to France or the United Kingdom. Whatever. So today's permanent migration was unplanned. We thought, 'What could we possibly need to give them?' That still exists in parts of our society.

I think the communities of Spain are working on policies of immigration that are now directed at permanency. But these policies of integration are very basic in their elements. That is to say that they only thought of social services and coexistence. That meant health, jobs, education, language. And with that, that's integration. But we need to do more. We need to make immigrants into citizens. The problem is that they're not treated like citizens. For the first generation, that's okay. But it's not enough for the second generation.

They don't want to be viewed as second-class citizens. They were born here. This is a problem of identity, and the second generation looks at it with different eyes.[15]

The second-class status of many migrants is clearly reflected in the statements by Alfonso on Amparo Street in Lavapiés. 'It's the fault of the democracy that we opened our doors like this,' he says. 'The freedoms of the democracy are good, but there's a disadvantage because we've had to take in bad people.... The Moroccans shouldn't get to vote here. They can vote in their own country. Maybe they can vote if they were born here.... I think that Spain will have to change for them.' Asked what he is willing to change, Alfonso says, 'Oh, I don't know. I really don't know.... If they behave well, they're welcome. But they're not Spaniards.'[16] This perspective is not lost upon immigrants themselves, especially the second generation which has hardly lived elsewhere. 'The government doesn't give a shit about us,' says Walid, who moved from Tetuán, Morocco to the Tetuán *barrio* of Madrid in his youth. 'Not just Moroccans, but all foreigners. They don't care about anything with us that doesn't have to do with labor. There are a lot of people sleeping on the streets, and the government doesn't offer much help.'[17]

While migrants are treated and generally thought to be unequal to Spaniards, Moroccan migrants are treated and generally thought to be unequal to migrants from other countries—most poignantly, under Spanish law. The most glaring double standards regard the rendering of Spanish nationality. While citizens of other former Spanish colonies (including the Philippines, Latin America and Equatorial Guinea) only need two to five years of Spanish residence before being able to apply for Spanish nationality, Moroccans must be full-time, uninterrupted residents for ten years. Also, unlike other former Spanish colonies, dual nationality is not recognized with Morocco. Any Moroccan applying for Spanish nationality must officially renounce their Moroccan nationality, and nullify their Moroccan passport. (Many do so rhetorically, but evade official renouncement in the eyes of the Moroccan government. The Moroccan state purposely maintains strong links with its diaspora.) There is also a different standard for Moroccan Sephardic Jews, who can receive residency in Morocco without needing a contract.[18] 'Unlike what the law says, we're not all equal here. Blacks, Arabs and Latinos are all the same to Spaniards,' says Gamal, a 20–year-old from the *pueblo* of Brunete, who was visiting Lavapiés to buy food for the approaching Eid holiday. 'But to get nationality, it takes Latinos two years and Moroccans ten years. It's because we're Arabs and they hate us. Especially after the terrorist attacks.'[19] Even residency cards which prove migrants' legal status still print the word *Extranjero* or 'Foreigner' and their country of origin: *Marruecos*.

In order to match labor supply with demand, Moroccans who come to Spain are only permitted if they have been offered a *contrato* or proof of employment. Once one contract expires or is terminated, another one must be obtained to maintain legal residence, unless nationality is given. Because Moroccans can only apply for nationality after ten years, and the application process can take several more years, several young adults interviewed who have lived no longer than five years of their childhood outside of Spain still do not have Spanish nationality.

Older migrants who were schooled in Morocco find that Moroccan education credentials are also not recognized in Spain, nor are many rulings by Moroccan law—such as with regard to divorce. A recent immigrant who works as a groundskeeper in Madrid's large park, Casa del Campo, says, 'I have a bachelor's degree and two diplomas in industrial electronics and information technology. That's why it's such a shame. I have spent so many years of my life trying to become qualified. And now I'm working with shit, literally, as a gardener.' The Spanish government also recruits what are called *contingentes* to fill labor demand in certain industries identified by a government economic institution. However, the Spanish government chooses where to make the appeal for workers, and this is rarely if ever done in Morocco.

Unfacilitated Engagement

Feeling unrecognized—socially and/or legally—as an enduring part of Spanish society, many second-generation Moroccans interviewed expressed disinterest or skepticism about civic participation. Mainstream civic institutions do not make it easy to get involved anyway. One young Moroccan man from Al

Hoceima interviewed in Victor Morales Lezcano's study of Moroccan associationalism said:

> The mechanisms that regulate the possible associationalism among Moroccan immigrants are simply a facade or a process of masking what little liberty that, in theory, exists here in Spain... I think that the official organisms can't prohibit associations because the Constitution permits association among immigrants. But it's practically always impossible to associate ourselves when it involves Moroccans.[20]

One Spanish-born Moroccan union activist based in Barcelona says:

> We need to normalize the participation of those who are ethnically diverse. For a Spanish politician to not have a Spanish name would be absolutely impossible. But it's also difficult to participate as a member of a minority, mostly because most Spanish civic organizations don't have any plan or strategy to mobilize minority participation. They haven't reflected on how to incorporate. The Spanish organization of Boy Scouts has, but only in the last five years.... The Socialist Party [which separates target constituencies into industrial groups like] justice, education and banking, [has a group] called 'Arabs'.[21]

Such a crude categorization reflects the perception that 'Arabs' do not belong to any group that might be industrial or issue-related. A significant reason is that the profile of a Moroccan person in Spain is not one of someone interested in participating in the political process, says Mohamed, a Moroccan journalist in Madrid. 'In the last election, 10 per cent of those Muslims who were eligible to vote actually did,' he says. 'That's not an attractive rate for politicians.'[22] A recent survey of only Moroccans in Spain found that only 2.4 per cent of all respondents had *ever* voted.[23] Without a bilateral treaty that grants mutual municipal voting rights between Spain and Morocco, Moroccan people without citizenship cannot vote locally either. One Moroccan man in his mid-40s, who canvasses for the Socialist Party in Valdebernardo, makes the party's view unequivocal: 'Expecting [Moroccans] to engage in Spain is throwing them in to the wolf's mouth. If you don't have nationality here, you're essentially nobody. They do me no good. So I don't even bother. I go and work with the Latinos.'

The only civic elections in which Moroccans can vote are union elections. However, very few Moroccans are members of unions, which are few in Spain and only occasionally powerful. Unions also mix Spaniards together with Moroccans, and this has proven to be a significant impediment to organizers. The union activist in Barcelona says that his group attempted to unionize Ryanair baggage handlers at Girona International Airport—80 per cent of whom are Moroccan—but were impeded by the minority of Spanish workers who resisted 'because they thought a Moroccan representative would only defend Moroccan interests. The perception is that anything that helps Moroccans can't possibly help me. ...The second generation of Moroccans knows who we are by knowing who we are not.'

With few opportunities to vote, opportunities for civic participation that are not through organizations established by Moroccans for Moroccans (which normally have little interaction with the government or non-Moroccan society) are slim. In Madrid, the structure of local governance is very centralized. The *ayuntamiento* (mayor's office) oversees the entire city, which is divided into twenty-one *distritos*. Each district is overseen by a *concejal presidente*, or district chairman who works out of a local administrative office and is appointed by the *ayuntamiento*. Each *concejal* has administrative obligations delegated specifically by the city assembly or mayor. These functions include transportation, urban planning, licenses and permits, youth policy, social services, parks, public works, security, administrative sanctions and wedding licenses—each overseen by a specific *jefe del servicio* or service chief. Within the district, a *Junta Municipal del Distrito* (District Governing Council) is appointed according to the proportion of party representation in the city assembly, and not elected directly locally. These *juntas* are also attended by *vocales vecinos*—unelected individuals appointed by the *alcalde* (mayor) at the request of political groups. Local politics therefore always run through the central administration of the city, where Moroccans (and many migrant minority groups) are mostly unrepresented—hindering effective grassroots mobilization.

Lavapiés is in the southern portion of the *Distrito Centro*, or Central District encompassing the *barrios* of Palacio, Embajadores, Cortes, Justicia, Universidad, and Sol. If a Moroccan person wishes to participate in district politics, there are two primary channels. First, each district convenes a *Foro Convivencia*, or Co-habitation Forum, which can be attended by local organizations, NGOs, and associations, but not individual actors. Second, each district also convenes *Mesas Diálogos*, or Dialogue Tables, open to visits from individual residents. While residents who wish to consult the Tables do not have to be citizens, they must prove their residence in the district with proper documentation (rent contract or bank statement)—a step that intimidates some Moroccans fearful of deportation, even when they are legal. Not a single respondent once mentioned any of the aforementioned institutional structures when prompted about their political involvement or the structures of involvement in their local community. A representative who works for a Moroccan advocacy organization in Lavapiés says that many Moroccans do not have the time to accommodate the specific requirements of participation, and most do not even know such channels exist.

For the purposes of this study, these structures of representation and engagement (and the lack thereof) suggest a variety of reasons which prohibit young Moroccans from perceiving a congruence of interests with Spanish government and society, and investing in it. From interviews, many of the study participants who said they desired Spanish nationality said they wanted it so that they could then move freely elsewhere in the European Union to a place in which they would feel more comfortable, rather than for any advantages it brings within Spain.

(Mis)Representation

Moroccans' lack of representation in Spanish structures of governance is not merely a perception to be taken into consideration. Moroccans literally have no form of representation at any high or even intermediary level of authority in Spain today. A government minister who asked to remain unnamed in this study acknowledged this truth. '[Moroccans] are not represented,' he said plainly. 'Not here [in this ministry]. Not generally. But the first generation doesn't care about that. They just want their basic needs met. They want a better house than they had before. The parties know that. The second generation does care. We need to create causes for the second generation to participate in. There are few causes right now.'[24] Indeed, other than a deputy in Cataluña's *Parlament*, there is not a single other Moroccan member of any provincial or national legislative body in mainland Spain. Without even token representation that purports to look out for Moroccans' interests, few Moroccans are persuaded that the Spanish state understands their point of view or is acting for their benefit. Many people do not even know that Muslim Spaniards have an officially recognized body of governance, the Comisión Islámica de España (CIE). In a 2004 survey of Muslims in Spain, only 12.7 per cent of respondents said there was an official Muslim Council representing the interests of practising Muslims in Spain. Of those who acknowledged the council, only 11.5 per cent said that they believe their interests were well-represented by this council.

However, the CIE—the main representative body for Muslim interests in Spain, which serves as the Muslim community's exclusive interlocutor—is very much part of the problem. Spain's institutional agreements with its different religious groups happened before the large-scale arrival of Moroccans. Spain passed the first law allowing Muslims to organize in 1967, paving the way for the 1971 founding of the Association of Muslims in Spain (AME), the first national association, which would work under the Statutory Law of Religious Freedom. In 1992—the 500th anniversary of Columbus' discovery of the New World, and of the expulsion of Muslims and Jews from Spain—to resolve the country's 'dark' history of relations with minorities, the government extended an arm to its religious groups. They gave seats at the table to each religion at the Directorate of Religious Affairs. At the time, there was still only a small community of Moroccans in Spain. However, there was a group of influential Syrians at the time, supported by other Middle Eastern Arabs and a group of influential ethnically Spanish Muslims. At that time, Moroccan leaders thought that their interests would be taken more seriously if they were represented by the Spanish Muslims. More than fifteen years later, the same structure remains in place, though the size of the Moroccan community has exploded. CIE is directed by two constituent organizations which officially represent 394 of Spain's 607 local Muslim religious groups. While the other 213 independent Muslim groups are atomized, the vast majority yield to the Board of Directors of UCIDE, the Union of Islamic Communities in Spain—an organization made up of Middle Eastern Arabs—and FEERI, the Spanish Federation of Islamic Religious Entities—an organization administered and made up of ethnically Spanish or converted Muslims, mostly from Andalucía, Ceuta and Melilla.

The problem is that today's Moroccans in Spain make up approximately 700,000 of the 1,000,000 Muslims whom CIE claims to represent. Indeed, of the 340 organizations represented by UCIDE, 300 are directed by Moroccans. Yet there is only one Moroccan individual on the Board of Directors of either UCIDE or FEERI. Meanwhile the 213 independent groups essentially have no influence over the commission's actions. According to interviews with staff from the Directorate of Religious Affairs, many local directors do not even realize they are partners in CIE. Of those who do, many do not realize they have a say. Both UCIDE and FEERI are extremely dispersed and, as the following section will describe, are made up of associations that are intensely personal and unaccountable. In the 2004 survey of Moroccans in Spain, only 2.9 per cent of respondents said they have a 'great deal of trust' in Moroccan organizations. Only 10.2 per cent said they have 'some trust' in them. Recently, one group called Junta Islámica split off from FEERI simply because Mansur Escudero, its director, lost the election for the FEERI presidency. The Spanish government stays out of what one staff member called such 'internal problems'.

'It's a private matter,' the staff member says. 'I'm not the Pope or the boss of any religion. And Moroccans aren't a sect of Islam. They're a nationality.'[25]

In response, several politically savvy religious organizations call themselves 'cultural groups' to avoid the umbrella of CIE and work for Moroccan interests independently. The most promising contemporary effort is a coalition of forty-three cultural groups called the Federation of Catalán Cultural Entities of Moroccan Origin (FECCOM). Administered by the only Moroccan parliamentary deputy in Spain—Mohamed Chaib of the Catalan *Parlament*—the organization is anchored by the organization he founded, *Ibn Batuta*, which celebrates Moroccans' cultural roots while facilitating integration in Spain. Chaib is often consulted by the Moroccan monarchy of Mohammed VI, and his federation is subsequently geared to counterbalance the influence held by (non-Moroccan) CIE and (anti–monarchy) ATIME in Madrid. So ultimately there is a scramble between very powerless organizations and leaders for what is a sliver of influence on Spanish governance.

According to the interviewed minister, the government is quite unconcerned about the lack of representation. Policy-makers simply want a unitary interlocutor with Spain's Muslim and Moroccan population, and cannot be bothered with petty infighting. The Minister says:

> It's a question of time here. The leaders of these organizations have been here for thirty or forty years. The oldest Moroccans have been here twenty-five.

> The Moroccans have no idea, no vision, of where they want to direct their people. What status or posts do Moroccans occupy in their own communities? Syrians are doctors! Engineers! Moroccans who are working 12–hour days don't have the time for this stuff.

> [Mohammed] Chaib's dynamic is as a citizen of this country. He is a member of the second generation. The parents can't be bothered with participation. [Besides him,] there are zero Moroccan organizations in the hands of the second generation of Moroccans in Spain. They're not even active or socialized in the civic communities of their own locality: the mosques. They need to be leaders.[26]

However, the Spanish government has also not acted to remedy the problem the Minister cites. Law-makers are extremely reluctant to address the dilapidated condition of religious facilities, despite their great potential as hubs for integration, civic engagement and learning. The Minister says:

> We have a Catholic history. And while I know other countries are similar, like the UK has an Anglican history, Catholicism is different. We've only been a democracy for thirty years, and the separation of church and state is only that old. And our

model is the French model of *laicité*. So we don't finance religious schools, religious buildings or organizations. So how do you explain that the government can't build any cathedrals, but mosques? Sure! You can't do that.[27]

Interestingly, one of the policy recommendations listed by Spain's post-11 March 2004 Commission was for the CIE to 'facilitate the Muslim religion and those who practise Islam in dignified, open spaces for the community'; to 'permit the economic support of Islamic organizations'; and to 'support imams or representatives of the Islamic community to isolate terrorists'.[28] The Minister says that the government is aware of the long-term risks of not representing Moroccans in the structures of governance and not facilitating their civic integration properly. But he says that the immediate risk of political backlash against the accommodation of Muslims is scarier to most politicians:

We've done work on this. We know that the roots of radicalization are in marginalization. But it is difficult to pull off a solution politically. The challenge is doing it without raising fears in society. We will pay a price for fear.

We've created the foundation. The government knows all these things [about the role of the mosque and their shortcomings in Spain]. We know it's just a little money. But the point of a political party is to win. This issue plays out in the future. Political parties do not.

We're talking about twenty years from now. It's difficult to explain these things in Spain—that it's not just services, education, jobs and health care that integrate immigrants. It's difficult to explain that we need to establish mechanisms of participation.

The party doesn't want to play like that. It's a problem of perception; perspective. People need to understand, immigrants' first three contacts with Spain are the following: the police when their *patera* hits the beach, then the Red Cross, and then the mosque. The weird thing is that Spaniards were no different fifty years ago. They were *emigrating* to other countries, and their first point of contact was the cathedral. Churches were the first things we built in our colonies. They were the instruments of supporting immigration.

We're talking about the country! Not the party, not the government. The state! And this isn't about religion, about Muslims. This is about people! This isn't about Islam in Europe. This is about Europeans! That's my opinion. But not the people here.[29]

Moroccans sense this subordinate position. Indeed, it is manifest in Moroccan quotidian life from the restrictions placed on non-citizens to the discourse of security and fear, from limited political opportunities to the discrimination of employers, police and fellow Madrileños. This social positionality (discursively and logistically) informs the nature and restrains the extent of Moroccans' associationalism.

Moroccan Associationalism

Contrary to the expectations produced by the underdeveloped nature of Spanish democratic activism, Moroccan-specific organizations have grown in the sunny southern half of Spain like Iberian olive trees, with about as many varieties and equally autonomously. In fact, a 2004 La Caixa *Muslims in Europe* survey of 200 Moroccans in Madrid found participants to be just about as active (and inactive) as the low bar set by the overall Spanish population surveyed in the aforementioned *Centro de Investigaciones Sociológicas* poll from November 2006. Among the Moroccans, 17 per cent said they participated regularly in the activities of a mosque or religious organization, 22 per cent in a sports or recreational organization, 18 per cent in a Moroccan cultural organization, and 20 per cent in a student organization or union.[30] In total, 22 per cent participated in more than one organization, 13 per cent in one organization, and 66 per cent did not participate at all.

Heterogeneity and Instability

According to Sonia Varedas Muñoz, there are two principal characteristics of the Moroccan associative movement in Spain: heterogeneity and instability.[31] Most associations are intensely personal groups of friends or neighbors following a charismatic leadership. They lack any offices or facilities. They hold few events. They are utterly disconnected from any national institutions. And their contact information usually leads to a mobile phone and a 'director' who answers from his living room with the clamor of his children's voices in the background.

Almost entirely depoliticized, Moroccan associations are usually cultural organizations that were established to provide services to their most local communities or as a reaction to the stigmatization of the Moroccan Muslim identity. Many provide services such as legal aid, literacy, instruction in Arabic or the Quran for children, marriage preparation, women's groups, conflict mediation, and liaising with Morocco. They are usually structurally diluted and heavily dependent on the availability of members.[32] A few organizations based in Madrid began in the early 1990s as political organizations that promoted human rights or sought to foster government relationships for social services and funding.[33] But the majority of Moroccan associations in Spain, and nearly all organizations outside the capital, reflect the diversity of their members' needs and cultural identities, and remain utterly isolated from nationally representative bodies.

Participants who were engaged in non-Moroccan specific political organizations say that the Moroccan community must create a culture of participation and activism. 'There's no legacy, no example, no influences right now,' says the coordinator of a Moroccan youth organization. 'The young people who attended the recent protest of the *Ley de Extranjeros* [Foreigners' Law] went as a result of the influence of the adults around them. That encouragement is not usually there.'[34] Mohamed, the Moroccan journalist, says, 'The Moroccan model of new associations here is simply what they already see in Spain—which isn't much. The Moroccan political associations that have existed over the years have lost their credibility because they were intensely personal and corrupt. Also 'Moroccans,' whether by nature or education, are not preoccupied by such things.'[35]

Making matters worse, there is significant competition over who will define the Moroccans within their community and externally to the rest of Spain, fomenting atomization among those who are civically inclined. There are no major Moroccan politicians, businessmen, power brokers—partially due to a lack of social cohesion, but also due to the absence of high-level Moroccan individuals in Spanish society. And as a result, there are no real role models or tracks to success for younger generations to follow. 'There is no interlocutor that connects democratic agencies and people in the public sphere,' says Jordí Moreras. 'It is all very individualistic, with a great dispersion of interests and voices.'[36] And without a strong voice or nationality, it is difficult to combat externally created images of the Moroccan Other, which increasingly focuses on their Muslimness and erases the other dimensions of their needs.

Around a third of all study participants acknowledge the existence of Moroccan associations, but nearly all of them say that they are powerless or useless. 'No foreigners here feel represented,' says Rafiq, a 30–year-old first-generation migrant who has lived in Spain for thirteen years and has been denied nationality thus far. 'There are a lot of organizations and associations that try to be represented but they are ignored. Here, foreigners are being shut into closed collectives rather than being freed like the ethnic minorities in other countries. We are laborers and nothing more.'[37] Tariq, an unemployed construction worker who has lived in Carabanchel for twelve years and now has a 9–month-old son, says:

> The solution to the racism is to show the face we're hiding. We need to start a campaign showing the real Muslims. The associations out there don't have the means, or

are just shit because they're often run by Arab governments.... The Spanish government doesn't care about the opinions of Moroccans. It's very difficult to get our way because we don't have a voice or enough weight behind us. They always listen to groups with strength and a lot of people behind them. Moroccan organizations here speak, but no one listens. We're not united. It's not like the UK. Muslims there have a voice. The government may still not respond, but at least they have weight.[38]

Such expectations seem to influence significantly the micro-level civic action (or inaction) of many study participants. Many of those interviewed who expressed a lack of interest in nationality say that it is because they don't believe a change in status will affect their social or political subordination.

Perhaps as a result, most organizations that are in existence do not lobby or even really interact with government bodies beyond basic registration. 'Here, the associations you see in other European countries don't exist,' says Sadik, a 21–year-old unemployed computer technician who has lived in Madrid since the age of 4. 'In Spain, organizations aren't founded to raise money for causes or take action. They are built to defend us. They don't build structures, they just protect what little we have. ...You need a lawyer to explain your rights or the government will take advantage of you.'[39] Young people are further predisposed to the defensive because of their pervasive fear of Spanish immigration officers and undercover Moroccan intelligence agents (DEST), who are known to roam Spain with the approval of Spanish counter-terrorism police. 'Young people here are scared to talk,' says Omar. 'They think they'll say one small thing and get thrown into prison. They're scared to make any religious statements which might frighten other people.'[40] The Moroccan monarchy is wary of Moroccans educated in Europe who may work to oppose King Mohammad VI's power. [Indeed, ATIME, one of the largest Moroccan civic organizations in Spain was founded upon its opposition to the late King Hasan II.] 'Spaniards can then imprison a threatening activist, under the false pretense of terrorist charges,' says the youth coordinator. 'When you are at the border, you are often quizzed about the nature of your affiliations. This fear then spreads to other groups that are not political in nature, but more cultural or social.'[41]

Though several Moroccan leaders argue 'that which is cultural is also civic', this argument is less tenable in light of the utter absence of social cohesion within the community. The discussed distrust (of Moroccans as much as Spaniards) contributes to further atomization. Though most Moroccans are said to be primarily concerned about sustaining themselves in Spain, many choose to do it on their own—rather than bond together communally like other groups of immigrants. 'No one can help me with my problems,' says Gamal from Brunete. 'The system of support among Moroccans is very weak. All I really have is my family, and that's enough. ...I handle my problems alone.'[42] Many study participants lamented this tendency to 'go it alone', particularly after being confronted with the unity and cooperation demonstrated by communities of Chinese, Senegalese and Bangladeshi immigrants in Lavapiés. 'It's no one's fault but our own,' says Omar, an unemployed 23–year-old technician who lives in Lavapiés. 'Everyone has a mind of their own. They are independent to make choices. All of these people are living in the same place. But not together. They are not united. Everyone is out to make money.'[43] 'All Moroccans are trying to survive, so no one wants to help each other,' says Sadik. 'Because of that, there's not a lot of trust. We're not as good of a community as the Chinese.'[44] Indeed, the Chinese might make the opposite argument with the same logic: All Chinese are trying to survive, so everyone helps each other. Because of that, there's a lot of trust. 'The Moroccan community is united, not for economic reasons, but for religious purposes,' says a Moroccan contractor from Fuenlabrada, who has lived in Spain for twenty-five years. 'Everyone looks out for themselves. But we all share the same religion.'[45] However, as the next section shows, shared religion produces even less civic activism than cultural links.

Garages

As Jordí Moreras writes, mosques occupy the space of cultural expression for Spanish Moroccans. As the mosque shares convivial references with other organizations, local prayers become expressions of collective will where modest resources can be spread around. The mosque is converted into an institution of tradition and orthodoxy, in which the opening of prayers coincides with the reunification of families and different generations from their dispersal.[46] Considering this central role in the communal life of Moroccans, it is shocking that in all of Madrid there are only two purpose-built mosques. All other facilities are comparable to—as one community leader says—garages.

In Lavapiés, Madrid's hub of Moroccan culture and society, there are three *masjids*. One is a semi–subterranean, storage basement with very low ceilings and a few windows that look out to the contiguous Peña de Francia Street at sidewalk level. Another is on the ground floor of a large, south-facing apartment complex in Plaza Agustín Lara. With rugs laid down in converted office space next to a municipal women's aid center, the mosque can squeeze in around ninety people for prayer, cheek-to-cheek. It is separated from the plaza by iron gates that protect the entrance to the apartment entryways. Finally, the third mosque is actually free-standing on Provisiones Street. It contains a pillared prayer chamber and an office in the attic. Like the others, it is shut when there are no prayers. Like the others, there is no full-time staff. Like the others, the imam is simply a dedicated community member. Like the others, there is no dedicated space (and so no space at all) for female visitors. And like the others, there are no Moroccans among the administrators. Though each *masjid* welcomes all comers, the first and third mosques are Bangladeshi–run, and the second is Pakistani–run. There was once a Moroccan-run mosque in Plaza Tirso de Molina, but it was shut down for lack of funding, and was otherwise no different in its capacities than the others.

Says one self-described secular Moroccan in Lavapiés, 'The mosque only functions during Ramadan. It's a spiritual organization, not a place you go to for information or political strength. It doesn't function in the everyday lives of the people. It's a place to pray and be spiritual. So citizenship and social questions are outside of its realm and influence.'[47] The physical plants of mosques further reinforce this one-dimensionality. But given their centrality to the lives of many Moroccans, a lot of potential for civic activism and social cohesion is left unfacilitated by the condition of most spaces. The aforementioned community leader says this is unacceptable:

> The mosque can never be only a place for prayer. It has to be a social place to speak about everything, a voice for all questions. Here in Spain, they are garages. It's all very precarious. If you have one next to a salon, a café, a library, you can have activities. And it's not a matter of funds. It's a matter of the will and support of the state. They need to change the model.

> The Saudis don't want to fund more mosques. Today there are people with money in many different parts of the world who will donate funds transparently to structures. We don't want Saudi mosques. We want a foundation built here, by Moroccan people from here.

> In a big mosque, you pay people for accountability. It's hard to do anything with these garages. They are often run by fundamentalists, so you can't control the process. When your traditions and religious beliefs place you against others who believe differently, I consider them to be fundamentalist—and they are advancing in many mosque committees. In garages, imams are in charge but who is going to pay them? The community is diverse, as people come from many different countries and sects of Islam, and each one wants their path to be followed.[48]

Similar to cultural associations, mosques tend to be intensely personalized operations—run by a few active administrators for a small community of people. Exclusivist, first-generation Moroccan elderly men are normally in charge, and each wants their path to be followed. These men typically have little acquaintance with Spain and a modern Spanish lifestyle. Leaders are also unacquainted with the democratic structure of Spanish government, representation, and the importance of participation. Many members of these organizations do not know how to assert themselves more publicly or lobby the government, and they generally disregard any forms of accountability. There is almost no participation or influence held by women or young people. Outside Lavapiés in the more segregated suburbs, some mosques only hold about thirty people. So they can hardly scratch the cultural or civic life of their members in the way a larger, multifaceted center might.

This is partially related to the recent historical legacy of mosques in Morocco. The regime has repressed Islamist dissidents, and correspondingly the influence of religious institutions has waned—leaving Islam reduced to privatized tradition and rituals. As a result, migrant families are not accustomed to mosques occupying space in the civic sphere, and are ill-prepared to build such multi–purpose institutions where it is now legally possible. 'I have read the Quran, but you can't discuss religion over there [Morocco],' said a young man from Tetuán interviewed by Lezcano. 'I wanted to learn Islam for myself but no one taught me.... The Muslim religion would not let me [understand or translate] it: Allah has said this, full stop. And so I see a religion of mandate, not thought, founded in ancient times and unchanged from people in the desert.'[49] This obviously also leaves similar individuals vulnerable to radical Islamists who may engage the inquisitive and preach fundamentalist interpretations of the Quran and Hadith, made relevant for a modern existence.

Among the two purpose-built mosques in Madrid, the famous Mezquita M30 (named for its juxtaposition to a main motorway in the east-central part of the city) is the most conspicuous. Built and backed by Saudis, it is a striking Arabesque structure apparent to all passersby. With conference facilities, a school, restaurants and recreational spaces, the mosque and its large full-time staff are the main Islamic reference point for Madrid. It is frequented by as many as a thousand Muslims for Friday afternoon *jummah* prayers—the majority of whom are Moroccan—and packs in even more during Ramadan festivities. All members of the administrative staff are Middle Eastern Arabs, with only two mid-level Moroccans who fill what some believe to be a quota. The other main mosque is in Tetuán and run by a group of Syrians. Significantly smaller and less prominent than the M30, the mosque still has several communal spaces and offices, filled mostly by leaders of the Union of Islamic Communities of Spain (UCIDE), a group representing Middle Eastern Arab migrants. Like the M30 Mosque, most congregants are Moroccan. And like the M30, Moroccans go mostly unrepresented and uninvolved.

Apartist Organization

As the previous chapters have described, I argue that apartism may correlate to both active and passive anti–system behavior. In Madrid, the only expression encountered was indeed passive. Moroccans possess neither the social capital nor the natural activism to exhibit any form of active apartism, like the Bangladeshis in London. Accordingly, the presence of such apartist organizations in Madrid is almost negligible. Quite generally in Spain, organizations that actively undermine the democratic system are limited to the very few Al Qaeda operatives who work under the radar of the state (let alone researchers) infamously recruiting the marginalized into violent extremism, and very few *Hizb-Ut-Tahrir* ideologues. Neither were found in Lavapiés or the other southern *barrios* of Madrid, and the only mentioning of *Hizb-Ut-Tahrir* was one participant's recollection of a HT activist shouting down a politician at a speech in Barcelona's Gracia neighborhood in early 2008. Instead, without exception, apartist sentiment inspired participants to withdraw totally from the Spanish civic sphere. Participation was non-existent in any formal associative or expressive activity, and their interaction with institutions of the state was down to a minimum.

While active apartism runs the severe risk of organized action undermining the state and democratic system, passive apartism initiates a cycle in which alienation leads to low participation, which leads to a lack of legislative and social service-oriented responsiveness to citizens' needs, which leads to institutionalized disadvantage, which fosters further passive anti–system behavior (see Figure Six). This cycle has already begun in the streets of Lavapiés and Southern Madrid. And simply because the alienated are passive at the moment does not ensure that they will not one day become active. Indeed, sharing the same perceptions as active apartists, passive apartists could be shy of motivation (derived from unmet expectations) that might otherwise catalyze action against the Spanish state or society. It is clear that many young Moroccans would be interested in associations that appealed to their interests and needs. The Spanish state has yet to fill that void, and another more dangerous group still may.

There is one association in Spain with a substantial Moroccan following that undermines state power—but not that of the Spanish state. *Justicia y Spiritualidad* (Justice and Spirituality, or *mouvement Justice et Spiritualité* as it is known in Morocco) is an organization of Sufi Islamists whose primary objective is to overthrow the Moroccan regime. Banned in Morocco and known as ONDA (National Organization for Dialogue and Participation) in Spain, members refuse to acknowledge ties with the Moroccan sister organization

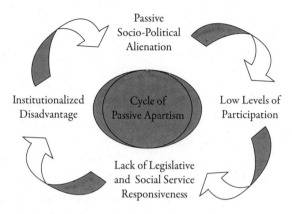

Figure Six: Cycle of Passive Apartism. Passive apartism initiates a self-reinforcing cycle of low participation and disadvantage.

and instead emphasize their objective of promoting integration and activism in Spain. Indeed, ONDA's activism does promote integration, but it is telling that such an effort is contextualized by the group's transnational loyalties. In any case, ONDA is actually a case study in how to mobilize the Moroccan second generation for civic purposes. Unlike any other group encountered in Madrid, ONDA has shown a unique capacity to engage groups of otherwise disaffected youth in their neighborhood associations throughout Madrid Sur and Andalucía.[50] According to one of the leaders from Getafe:

> We give young people a big role in our organization. We have held camps in Cuenca, Valencia, and other places. It's a success because they leave happy after our activities, which are creative and foster friendship. They work in our local associations in their communities.

> Our activities respond to the needs of the lads. They need to clarify and develop their identity. So we promote their Spanish identity and cultural investment in Spain. They are underachieving in school and are not advancing to the university level of education for career development. So we emphasize finishing university and entering a profession. There is a great deal of family conflict. The house is still a part of the Moroccan world, and the parents want to sustain that, in light of children getting accustomed to Spanish ways. The father often isn't bringing in enough income, or there may be issues of divorce. Sometimes parents want to go back to Morocco because of the lack of opportunity here, and the children want to stay. Our message goes to the parents more than the kids here. We try to orient them and their mentality.[51]

The comments made here were not made by any representatives from the other organizations or civic institutions examined in the previous sections. Their secret appears to be similar to that of *Hizb-Ut-Tahrir*. They use Islam as a paradigm to address the issues most pertinent in the lives of young people, and empower them to express themselves. They listen and mold their activities and message to the relevant concerns of their members. Rather than shy away from the tension surrounding religion and religiousness in Spain, ONDA takes the issue head-on, working to contextualize Islam in Spain and acclimatize their participants to the idea of integrating piety in a non-Muslim country:

> Islam is key in their private life. The public life is free, but the youths must have their beliefs. This is as true for the kids as it is for their parents. Sufism is gaining popularity because in a world that is increasingly materialistic and ideological, people want something more spiritual. The ideological world is filled with clashes and conflict. Sufism is a rejection of that, and the discourse of eliminating other options. We diverge with other groups over issues like violence, including verbal violence.[52]

ONDA appears to have a finger on the pulse of the Moroccan second generation. And even if it operates with an agenda, that agenda does not undermine the priorities of the Spanish state. Instead, ONDA recognizes the roots of apartism, and is counteracting them:

> In Spain, young people don't have political rights. There is no organization to represent their preferences about living, education, etc. They have an interest. We need to engage them and their interests. Young people have a more modern vision. So when mosques don't give them a big role, and national organizations don't work from the ground up, who is listening to them?

> It's hard to convince some of them that they are Spanish, because they haven't been treated in a way that makes them feel Spanish. The ones who are born here, they don't see any other home. The problem is that none of them sees a place for them to express themselves. Kids who have a stable family, in school, it's difficult for them not to feel Spanish.[53]

Any state action to ameliorate relations with young Moroccans should examine the nature of this small group's extraordinary success. Their achievement underscores the remarkable deficiency of all other forms of engagement in Madrid and Spain more generally.

This section has detailed the deficient civic structures of a very green Spanish democratic society, which does little to fertilize the civic sphere occupied by Moroccan people. There are a significant number of small organizations that nevertheless sprout amidst the adversity, like plants in the Sahara. But much like desert flora, these groups mostly struggle to subsist defensively in compact spaces, focusing on very local and personal objectives. For the most part, the remarkably underdeveloped and inactive Spanish civil sphere matches the limited participatory inclinations of the Moroccan minority. This is of course the inverse reaction of London's East End Bangladeshi community, which confronted a similar socio-discursive environment. Indeed, like the Bangladeshis interviewed in London, the majority of study participants sense that they are not being treated as 'people', but as 'Moros' or 'Muslims'—a secondary class.

However, facing similar political channels and disadvantages, the fledgling communities of first-generation Bangladeshi, Pakistani, and Equatorial Guinean people and the second generation of Middle Eastern Arabs in Madrid have proactively developed structures of community and civic relations. As one community leader said, 'When you want to organize a meeting with Pakistanis and Bangladeshis, all you need to do is tell them how many people you want to be there.' Problematically, a sizeable group of second-generation, Moroccan respondents without nationality say that if they were granted citizenship, they would not vote in elections or engage in the civic sphere. This suggests that passive apartist withdrawal from the state is not merely a product of not being invited. Usman, a 23-year-old architectural engineering student who has lived in Spain since he was 9 years old, says:

> Democracy doesn't exist in any country. If you're not famous or rich enough to bribe, you don't count. We all want justice and security, but how it is applied is a different question. The government doesn't think about anyone...let alone a woman with a veil who wants to work. ...If I had the chance to vote, I still wouldn't. No one represents my views here. Islam says that you should choose the better of two evils. But here, the choices are all equally evil.[54]

So while we can conclude that the Spanish state has still not taken proper measures to integrate or engage its growing Moroccan population civically, we cannot solely point to such opportunity structures as culpable. Indeed, the issue is not just that nationality is difficult to attain and participation is not facilitated, but that many Moroccans are not interested in investing in a future in the Spanish polity—even as recognized members of the polity.

The following sections will now examine why their reaction has been to withdraw from, rather than confront or undermine, this seemingly inhospitable society and its political system. As the next section explains, like East End Bangladeshis, Moroccans' socio-political alienation is also attributable to the nature of Moroccans' identity construction and the perception among many that the culture and requirements of their new home are irreconcilable with those of their not-so-distant homeland.

The Enduring Relevance of Moroccan Identity

A major reason that many members of the second generation of Moroccans in Spain remain socio-politically alienated from the state and society of their country is that, quite simply, they don't perceive Spain to *be* their country. 'It's all about their perceptions,' says the union activist. 'It doesn't matter what the reality is. If they don't have the sense that this is their country and that they have social responsibility here, there will be problems. And as long as they have lived, they've been Moroccan.'[55] It is also not a matter of whether their Moroccanness or Spanishness comes first. Indeed, many Spaniards may consider themselves Catalán, Catholic or European first, the way many Britons consider themselves first to be English, Western or an Arsenal football supporter. Instead, many young Moroccans do not believe that Spanishness occupies *any* part of their identity, that they have no stake in the future of Spain, and worse, that the norms of Catholic Spain and Islamic Morocco are either irreconcilable or in a zero-sum relationship. Several participants believe that a person is, quite simply, one or the other—culturally and civically.

As this section explains, interview content suggests significant differences between the identity construction of British Bangladeshis and Spanish Moroccans. Unlike the Bangladeshis, Moroccans maintain a potent nostalgia for their homeland that endures in the second generation. Unlike later generations of Bangladeshis, many Moroccans interviewed view Islam as an inherent part of their Moroccan ethno-cultural make-up. Unlike Bangladeshi participants who impugn British society for its divergent worldview and customs, many Moroccans interviewed acknowledge and respect Spanish norms and perspectives in their difference. And unlike many of their British counterparts who have striven to reconcile their differences, most Moroccan participants say that the two identities are utterly irreconcilable.

A Lingering 'Myth of Return'

'Every person who leaves Morocco for Spain thinks he'll be back soon,' says Karim, a 35–year-old Moroccan man who owns and manages a barber shop on Mesón de Paredes. He has lived in Spain for eleven years. '"It's just for five years," they'll say to themselves. "I'll make some money and I'll be back." But it never happens. Nobody ever goes back. It's just a dream. Nobody is happy here. At least Spain has a social system that doesn't leave you on the streets. Why do I stay here? It's not that I have roots here. Why don't *you* drop everything in *your* life to move somewhere else? I have a career here.' Termed the 'myth of return', Karim's experience is typical of first-generation migrants everywhere. Across Europe and North America, the myth is usually sustained until families bear children in the new country, and prefer to raise them with the higher salaries and advanced care of the developed world. Once children reach adolescence and become more independent, few are inclined to return to their parents' homeland, and the parents acquiesce. Such a narrative has become pedestrian, producing the adage that 'nothing is as permanent as a guest worker'. However, according to interviews, the myth of return appears to linger indefinitely in the psyche of the Moroccan second generation, and profoundly so.

One factor that separates Spain from other European migration recipient countries is the proximity of one sending counterpart. While Britain's Muslim population came from South Asia, France's came from Algeria and Morocco, Germany's came from Turkey, and Sweden's came from Iraq and Turkey, the Moroccan community in Spain essentially shares a border with their homeland. Many Moroccans return to see family in the south frequently. Some involved in imports and trade conduct business monthly. 'The proximity of Morocco makes it so that it's never a problem to go back,' says an official from ATIME, the largest Moroccan advocacy group in Madrid. 'That's different from France or Holland. Part of their heart is still in Morocco. We're in an age when it doesn't matter where you are, but rather what you want to do.'[56] As a result, neither parents nor their children are integrating into Spanish culture as quickly as Latin American migrants in Spain and other migrant populations elsewhere in Spain and Europe. 'Some parents live like they're still in Morocco,' the ATIME official adds. 'At the mosque all day, watching Al-Jazeera, without adopting anything of Spanish life. There is a role for organizations like ours to bring them into the social life.'[57] 'They don't see the Strait of Gibraltar as a border,' says a researcher who works with Spanish government policy-makers. 'They are Spanish when they want to be Spanish, and Moroccan when it serves them better.'[58] Several participants' parents who are nearing retirement age have already purchased property and six–bedroom houses in Morocco for their children to join them.

For many members of the second generation, Morocco is seen through a rose-colored lens. Life there is idealized—an impression derived from airbrushed Moroccan media forms and occasional visits, during which the young men are treated like royalty by relatives and community members who seek to share their wealth or are simply happy to see them. The idealized mirage of life in Morocco thus endures despite the continuing stream of migrants desperately seeking life in Spain. 'They're very hospitable to me [in Morocco],' says Sadik, who is unemployed in Spain. 'But that's because they want me to share. They think I'm from Hollywood or something. Because I have more money, they flatter me and invite me back.'[59] Morocco (and its economic growth potential) is also perceived to be a land of opportunity after some time in Spain. It's cheaper, underdeveloped, and void of products that can be easily exported from Spain. The Moroccan government also facilitates the return and business from members of the diaspora, primarily by ignoring people who maintain both a Spanish and Moroccan passport—illegal for Spanish nationality. Still, ultimately most of the six–bedroom houses are left empty. Despite their connection with their country of origin, many young Moroccans appear ultimately to follow their parents' logic all over again. They wish to remain in Spain in search of their own prosperity, even if that means adapting publicly until their own myth of return can be fulfilled.

However, their private life is often precisely what they are being judged on by their Spanish community members. While living parallel lives can be stimulating and convenient, it is dangerous for a laborer without resources to separate himself from the society on which he depends. Ultimately, the second generation will be asked to answer questions about their preferences in Spain. They will ultimately be asked to invest or remain on the margins. And the reality is that almost none of the individuals interviewed for this study could offer any sort of timeline for their return, any real role model to follow, or any set of defined goals in Spain. The objective is simply marginal improvement on the life they had. And without a measuring stick or standard of achievement, how can one know when one has advanced far enough to merit returning to Morocco? Without a terminal ideal, the myth of return lingers. There is thus a significant amount of self-generated insecurity and uncertainty, compounding that created by Spanish laws and discrimination.

These circumstances are very different from those of the cosmopolitan, educated Arabs who migrated to Spain from Egypt and Syria in the 1970s and 1980s, hailing from places like Cairo and Damascus with grand ambitions. This is also very different from the circumstances of early Moroccan guest workers in the 1970s who first entered the Spanish labor market to help harvest seasonal crops in the Andalusian orchards for a set amount of time, and then return to Morocco with their yearly salary. Their goals were concrete in Spain. The proximity of Morocco changes everything for the later arrivals and the second generation. With Spain's granting of family reunification across the southern border, there was no longer any immediate need to return to Morocco, and the prospect of any return became utterly indefinite. The myth of return thus lingers longer in popular imagination—making Morocco a tempting security blanket, and Moroccans in Spain hesitant to invest in a future in the North.

The enduring myth of return and sluggish integration of Moroccans (in tandem with the discrimination of citizenship law) perpetuates the population's status as 'foreign'—even for those who have been in Spain since the fall of the Franquista autocracy. The Spanish collective memory has rooted the figure of the 'Moro' in the national imagination to the point that the image of the existential Other supersedes the facts of reality, writes Gema Martín-Muñoz:

> The construction of the Other is a universal phenomenon that is conformed to agree with cultural, historical and social facts of the society that recreate it, always keeping the great relevance of the geographical element. In the case of the Muslim Arab, that geographical factor holds particular force that has not only been related to vicinity, but to eight centuries of living together that has united us against Islam, against the *Moro*... Spanish life remained dominated by the counter position between the Christians and the Moro. The latter is simultaneously Muslim and foreign, in agreement with the recreation of the relationship held by the Catholic Kings of Spain: the understanding that unity is through cultural and religious homogeneity.[60]

Indeed, Moroccans were the first large group of migrants to enter Spain in the nascence of its market opening, and yet are often regarded as ephemeral, opportunistic transients. In self-perpetuating fashion, this negative public image further disadvantages Moroccans who have lived their entire lives in Spain, as much as it disadvantages recent arrivals. 'There are Muslims who don't pray,' says one recent arrival. 'We drink. Some Moroccans are atheists. My girlfriend is a Protestant Finn. Some Muslim women wear mini–skirts. At the minimum, we speak two languages. But Spanish society broad-brushes us as all the same.'[61] 'The majority of people don't understand us,' says Idris, a 23–year-old Moroccan who appears Spanish. 'I studied Spanish culture and geography. The knowledge and image of Moroccans is very low. They are very distrustful. One dead fish in the kitchen makes the whole house stink.... This is a politics that goes much deeper than the politics of [terrorism]. A lot of people don't think that I'm Moroccan, so the treatment changes.'[62]

Discrimination is subsequently common in various contexts. Alonso on Amparo Street swore he wouldn't rent a flat to a Moroccan family. Kalid, a 24–year-old construction worker, reports, 'I've called phone numbers advertising job openings in the newspaper many times. And almost always, the first question they ask me is, "Where are you from?" Then, "Oh, this job is not open to foreigners."'[63] Says Amir, 'At a local bar down the street, they didn't want me there because I'm Moroccan. I've worked five different jobs as a waiter, and I've never rejected a customer. They've probably seen other Moroccans who steal, fight or sell drugs.'[64] From the perspective of civic engagement, the discriminatory treatment and perpetual 'foreign' status discourages Moroccans from applying for Spanish nationality, because a Spanish passport does not protect a visible minority in casual interactions. 'I don't want nationality,' says Kalid, who will be eligible in eighteen months. 'I'm still going to be a foreigner even with citizenship. It's just a sheet of paper. I'll still have my roots. And in effect, even with nationality, I still won't have the same rights as Spaniards. Once you get nationality, you don't lose the way you talk or look.'[65] According to one review of different surveys and investigations, Spanish public opinion established a hierarchical order among foreigners, in which Moroccans and Africans are classified at the bottom: 'Moroccans are still the group that suffers the most ethno-cultural prejudices and stereotypes.'[66]

With uncertain status, an uncertain plan, and a complicated process of integration, many Moroccans cling tightly to their Moroccan identity which robustly endures in Spain. This persistence is a product of an enduring myth of return, which reduces the incentive to invest in a future in Spain. But it also appears to be because Spaniards are in denial about the changing composition of their society. As the next two sections show, the enduring Moroccan identity has recently been altered and strengthened by being tethered to an increasingly relevant Islamic faith and the perception of its irreconcilability with Spanish life.

Built-in Islam

For those who assume a Moroccan identity, which almost every participant did, it is a sort of 'pre-packaged identity'. Whereas concepts of postmodern identity conjure up a salad bar of options to toss liberally into an individual tray, the Moroccan identity comes like a pre-packaged Caesar salad. Part of being Moroccan is the Islamic faith, Arabic ethnicity, a *halal* diet and lifestyle, and one side of the age-old conflict across Gibraltar. These elements are simply inseparable into *à la carte* options. Whereas many British Muslims feel the need to embrace their Islamic faith more closely in the light of their integration into a post-Christian secular British society, such an 'embrace' would be redundant for Moroccans in Spain. While many British participants in London's East End only felt as Islamic as the last time they prayed—those British Bangladeshis who had lapsed spoke of Islam with shame or regret—this was rarely the case with Moroccan participants. As Moroccans, they are quite naturally Muslim, and feel little need to re-assert this or 'prove' it. Mahmud is 20 years old and has not returned to Morocco since his parents moved to Madrid ten years ago:

> I respect the customs, but I never have and never will feel Spanish. Morocco is my country. The land is in my blood. I will always feel this way. In the future, I will return. I don't want Spanish citizenship.... The problem isn't the Spanish identity. It's the Spanish people.... They think they are superior.

> My mother says, 'Pray, pray.' But I say that I will when I'm ready. Right now, I don't have the time. You aren't a Muslim because your parents tell you to be, or because you're scared of God. You're a Muslim because you feel it in your heart. It has to be there [gesturing inward].[67]

In this way, Islam is learned to be an inextricable, built-in part of being ethnically and holistically Moroccan.

Because there is less need to assert one's Islam among Moroccans, practice and faith tend to be inward, private, and a more mundane aspect of life for many of the participants interviewed. Indeed, many who were interviewed did not bring up their faith until prompted. Even statistically, in Metroscopia's survey of first generation Spanish Muslims, respondents on average ranked the importance of religion below that of 'family' and 'work' and just barely above 'friends.'[68] Interestingly, politics and associative activities ranked last, far behind all the other parts of life. In the same survey, 50 per cent of all respondents said they do not practise Islam or do so irregularly.[69] In explaining the more relaxed approach Moroccans take with their faith, several of the more pious participants suggested that their outlooks are derived from the Moroccan monarchy's aversion to opposition groups, many of which are Islamist. At the beginning of 2008, King Mohammed VI dissolved one of those parties because its leadership was implicated in an alleged terrorist network.[70] 'The religious are not free [in Morocco],' says Nasir, a 19–year-old from Lavapiés. 'The regime says that the religious are dangerous, blaming them for all the bombs. It's not a Muslim country any more. None of the Arab countries are any more. I think the whole world thinks Muslims are terrorists now.'

The privatization of Islam also reduces the role of the mosque and its administrators. Many participants say their Islam is self-sufficient, some because they were taught well, others because mosques provide so little. 'I know where the mosque is, but I haven't visited yet,' said one recent immigrant. 'We pray in the house. [He points to Mecca and a rug on the floor.] I have a copy of the Quran, and when I read it, life is good. I read it on my way back from work on the Metro, and everything gets better. We serve as our own imams. When I have a question about Islam, I go on to Google in French or Arabic. But my family has taught me almost everything I need to know.'[71] Says Sadik, 'When I have questions about Islam, I go to my father. If not, I'll usually go to a friend or the internet. I don't see the imam for those things because they are too important to bother them with small questions.'[72] Usman, a 23–year-old architectural engineering student who works at the airport managing security cameras, says, 'The difference between [a place like] Cairo and [Spain] is that yes, the politicians are disgusting, but there are at least a lot of imams providing leadership. Here in Spain, we have almost no imams of any depth or strength. They lack the studies, the knowledge. When I have doubts, I use the internet or consult books.'[73]

The inextricability of Islam from the Moroccan identity has only been reinforced by the discursive tendencies of the Spanish state and society, which regularly refers to Moroccans as 'Muslims' and, more crudely, as *Moros*—a derogatory term that literally means *Moor*, the anachronistic classification of the Maghrebi existential foe and Other on the Iberian peninsula. Attacks and struggles against Turks and 'Moros' through the centuries constructed images of Muslims as an invading threat, writes Gema Martín Muñoz, citing associations with words like 'savage', 'threatening', 'fanatic' and 'enemy'.[74] In later conflicts during the twentieth century, these negative images of Morocco were reinforced, as contested lands, political ambiguities and tensions over natural resources renewed the confrontational relationship.[75] Such discourse positions Islam within the individualist and privatizing framework of Spanish secularism, which converts Islam into a matter of personal belief or an integral product of family heritage—something more festive and cultural than it is spiritual or sacred. Referring to Moroccans as Musulmanes or *Moros* pairs Moroccan identity with Islam, and also reflects the non-neutral perception of the majority population that these people do not think or behave the same way as 'us'.[76] As a result, even those participants who were quite assimilated into Spanish culture, and looked upon Moroccan customs and norms as relics, identified with the very lifestyle they rebuff. Zahir, a 20–year-old from Fuenlabrada, was born and raised in Madrid:

I don't feel Moroccan or Spanish. I'm somewhere in the middle. But I'm mostly Moroccan. Moroccans are more closed. They are in another century. They're very traditional. You can't go out at night, you can't have sex before marriage, you can't wear short clothes. I don't feel obligated. I was taught things, but you take the path you want. That's what my parents taught me, but Islam is more strict. In the future, I will also be a strict practitioner of Islam. And I'm certain that my wife will be Islamic. My ideal is to find a Spanish woman and convert her.[77]

Reading his statements in other parts of the interview contextualize this reluctance to embrace the Islamic aspect of his Moroccan identity:

The image of Islam in Spain is that it is closed. That women are dominated. They have reason. It is closed. Women are undervalued. They're supposed to have kids and no more. I've lived in Spain a long time and I've been influenced by the society here. I think we need to integrate. If we were in an Arab country, it would be fine. Our values are not incorrect objectively. They're just incorrect for living in Spain...

I go out in Madrid. But there are a lot of places there that won't let me in because I'm Moroccan. It's because the real Moroccans, the ones who recently immigrated, get into a lot of trouble. They fight, they cause problems.

The racism affects me because all of my friends are Spanish and I get singled out. And you know, they joke around about it. I don't hang out with Moroccans. The Moroccans often make fun of me too for being Spanish. You know, things like 'He's a shit Spaniard'? My old group of Moroccan friends dissolved because they didn't want to stay together. They had problems expressing themselves to Spaniards, like a lot of Moroccan people. They can't explain themselves and why they left Morocco, so they often get aggressive.[78]

Clearly, Zahir's attempts to have it both ways are futile. He is Islamic simply because he is Moroccan, but not necessarily because he wants to be. He feels the pairing is socially forced upon him.

The War in Iraq and the 11 March 2004 terrorist attacks in Madrid raised the profile of Islam, and shifted social tension from the Spanish versus the Moroccan to one of Christian-secular Europe versus Moorish Islam. Says the journalist Mohamed, 'Before the war against Iraq, conflict with Moroccans in Spain was viewed in more ethnic or cultural terms, and Spain actually held a good image in the Arab World—outside of Morocco, but that [tension] is always there... Since the war, the conflict is perceived as a war against Islam. And everything is placed in the context of religion.'[79] As Moreras writes, today, the Spanish public sector employs the same deterministic charge once used in reference to cultural differences with Moroccans to justify a conflict with Muslims. This, he writes, is based on three mistaken assumptions: 1) that of the immutable transplant, 2) that of the internal homogeneity of Moroccan collectives, and 3) the centrality of culture (and now religion) in the construction of identities.[80] Such assumptions suggest that Moroccans express a higher degree of religiosity than their Spanish counterparts in a country where religion has become more privatized.[81] With such visibility, Islam is acquiring a greater public relevance associated with a group of people for whom religion was almost never the exclusive point of identity reference.

Irreconcilability with Spain

Unlike culture, which is increasingly adaptable and easily shared in a globalizing world of mixing influences, norms of religion are (albeit erroneously) conventionally perceived to be rigidly based on unchanging 'truths'. Because of this, the aforementioned shift of the axis of difference from ethnicity to religion holds major implications for social cohesion, as religious differences are simply not as easily reconciled. In fact, a significant number of participants who were asked to identify certain lifestyle choices as Spanish selected only those choices which are distinctly prohibited by Islam. Spanish choices of music, sport and or media content were never mentioned. Instead, the Spanish lifestyle is characterized by that which Islam is not. 'For me,' says Usman, 'coexistence is about doing what you have to do to live peacefully with other people. It's not a matter of integrating. I can't eat pork or drink alcohol. I can't go out to clubs and find girls. Those are rules. But going out to clubs, getting drunk and getting with women are *like* rules for young people here.'[82] Says Qasim, 'Islam and Spanish society don't go together. This is a Christian society, they don't go to the mosque. They drink, they eat ham. Here, God is Jesus.'[83] The perception is that in order to integrate or adopt an acceptable Spanish lifestyle, the Moroccan must break one set of rules and acquiesce to another. Says Walid:

> A lot of Spaniards are racist, not just against Moroccans, all immigrants. To integrate with those types of people is difficult. We don't drink. We don't eat pork. We don't party. We don't go to dance clubs. Spaniards in my area, when they see an immigrant, they just start yelling at them on the street. ...People here are scared of some kind of re-conquest of Spain by Muslims. This is a centuries-old rift...

> You have to be here for many years to learn and understand Spanish culture. And I finally have. But I'm Arab, I'm Muslim. I guess I feel like a Spanish Muslim. I don't really care if I'm accepted as a part of the society. My roots are still in Morocco. When the Moroccan national football team plays, I get really excited. When they play the national anthem before the match, the hairs on my arm stand up. I don't even know

the words to the Spanish national anthem. Every religion has its rules and beliefs. I can't change my religion. And I won't change in order to integrate.[84]

Such sentiments, widely echoed among study participants, suggest that the Spanish civic identity is viewed as if it were a religious identity—rigid. Many participants plainly believe that Christianity is a presupposed characteristic of being civically Spanish, the way Christianity characterizes Spanish cultural identity.

Moroccans' unwillingness to change and be more Spanish is complemented by the reciprocal expectation that Spanish society will not change to accommodate Moroccan preferences. From interviews, this appears to be derived from participants' reluctance to identify Spain as *their* land, despite their time living there. Amir, a 19–year-old retail worker, says:

> Some religious customs affect others. During Islamic festivals, people kill lambs and sometimes pray in the street. Spaniards don't look upon it very well, and neither do I. It's not that praying in the street is [inherently] bad. It's just that it's a bad idea here because they will upset others.

> Spaniards are better at holding up their end of the deal, because they keep their business private. They have a right to drink in the streets and build dance clubs next to mosques, but I wouldn't want to. It's their choice.

> I think that Muslims have a responsibility to not upset Spaniards and others, and Spaniards have a responsibility to not upset immigrants. But it's the Spaniards' country initially, so we need to yield to their customs more than they need to respect ours.[85]

Rather than reflecting a willingness to blend preferences and mutually accommodate, such passiveness reinforces the feeling that Moroccans are mere guests in Spanish society, when they are actually a constituent part of its composition. Tiptoeing around one another will only institutionalize parallel living and corroborate perceptions about the irreconcilability of Spanish and Moroccan identities.

Many second-generation Moroccan men interviewed already believe that gaining Spanish nationality would entail changing who they are, particularly religiously. 'I don't want nationality. I'm not going to change,' says Gamal. 'I'm Moroccan until I die. I want rights, but I don't want to change who I am. Nationality would change my religion. What if they turned me against my family? That's what might happen in my imagination.'[86] Omar is an unemployed technician whose parents have lived in Mallorca for twenty-five years. Nevertheless, he perceives naturalized Spaniards as apostates. 'There are a lot of Muslims with nationality,' he says. 'But I'm Moroccan and nothing more. I'm not going to take the flag here and cross myself. To feel Spanish would mean entering another religion. And if you don't change your religion, you won't be accepted by Spaniards. A Spaniard can be a Muslim. But a Muslim cannot be a Christian.'[87] Anwar sells DVDs on the black market after losing his job as a plumber. He has grandparents in France and parents in Spain, and insists that, he nor his children will integrate. 'I don't feel Spanish. It's the religion,' he says. 'They're of a different religion. I can't be a Spaniard. My daughter isn't going to be a Spaniard either. She won't drink or bring home a boyfriend. That's not our identity.'[88] In his article about Muslims as an irreducible Spanish alter ego, Fernando Bravo López explains that Spaniards commonly employ a culturalist approach that schematizes politics according to a bipolarity between Islam and the West, thus exaggerating differences and distorting the true nature of the Other.[89] For Ricard Zapata-Barrero, it is not exactly racism or Islamophobia that exists in Spain, but what he calls 'Maurophobia', a phobia of the Moors.[90] It is clearly reciprocated.

This is as much a reflection of Spanish ignorance as it is a reflection of the interwoven histories of these two groups of people. It is familiarity that has bred division. Spain remains the only Western European country to have belonged to the Islamic sphere of influence and control. For over eight centuries (711 to 1492), the southern region of the Iberian peninsula was ruled by Muslim Arabs. Their expulsion by the *Reyes Católicos* (Catholic Kings) Fernando and Isabela continues to be one of the most prominent images in Spanish history, but the subtle yet ubiquitous legacy of Moorish cultural influence has haunted Spanish traditions in art, architecture and language. Spanish–Moroccan relations since the *Reconquista* deteriorated with the persistent raids of Spanish ships and port cities by Moroccan corsairs, who often took Christian captives as slaves. The rivalry spawned stereotypes of Moroccans as satanic, and would eventually spark Spanish involvement in the African War of 1860, during which Zapata-Barrero writes the Moroccans were painted as 'vile, lewd monkeys, dogs, gangsters, etc.'[91] Once Spain gained shared control of Morocco after the 1906 Conference of Aljeciras with France, Moroccans became the object of mockery, 'simple savages'. The northernmost regions of Morocco were a Spanish Protectorate from 1912 to 1956, when Spain surrendered the territory to the new Moroccan regime, with the exception of outposts Ceuta and Melilla and the Western Sahara region. It was during this era that the idea of *hispanidad* (Spanishness) was developed to counterweigh the loss of the last colonies in the Americas during the Spanish–American War of 1898, and later recycled by the Franco regime to refer to a group of people linked according to linguistic and religious criteria—the two pillars of the Spanish discourse of exclusion.[92] Barrero thus derives the enduring enmity with Muslims from the 'permanent conflict' with Morocco, which has fostered the stereotype of 'the Moor' as somebody suspicious, physically dirty and pestilential, ugly and potentially criminal.[93] Since the 11 September 2001 terrorist attacks in the United States, Moroccans have been increasingly associated by their religion rather than their Moorish ethno-cultural heritage, as migration policies have begun to favor Latin Americans and Eastern Europeans. One Spanish government official was sensitive to this discourse:

> What messages are we sending? Moroccans are thinking, 'What am I?' They're not seen as Spanish or European. They're Muslims. That's the big worry.

> Before, in the newspapers, articles wrote about Algerians, Tunisians, Syrians, Moroccans and Egyptians. Now they're all just called Muslims. 'A group of Muslims are entering the country.' When Latin Americans arrive, they are not Catholics or Protestants. They're Ecuadorians, Colombians or Argentines. That is dangerous. [Why?] Because, if they're Muslim, that means they're not Spanish.

> Three generations later in France, they're still called Muslims, and not French. They are citizens! Spain is on the same path. And we are going to repeat the history of other countries.[94]

Strong images of opposition endure in Spanish society today, none more striking than the legend and celebrated legacy of *Santiago Matamoros*, literally St James Moor-slayer, the patron saint of Spain. James was one of Jesus' apostles who is said to have been buried in the northwest of Spain at Santiago Compostela in Galicia—the third holiest site in Catholicism after Jerusalem and Rome. Traditionally depicted wearing armor and a pilgrim's hat, Santiago is said to have materialized to fight for the Christian army during the battle of Clavijo during the *Reconquista*. Santiago has since been etched in the public psyche, occupying lines in the Spanish army's battle cry and Cervantes' *Don Quixote*.

Perceptions of irreconcilability are also buttressed by third-party rejection encountered in some participants' interactions with white Spaniards. When Ali was a child, he says he felt welcomed by his Spanish neighbors who invited him into their homes. However, once he began to work, he became a stranger in his community.[95] Wasam tells the story of his father: 'Many Spaniards don't like to hear the Quran recited. My father is an electrician, and while on a job one time, his mobile ringtone played a recital. His client, an elderly Spanish woman, heard it and began to cry and asked him to turn it off. So he did.'[96] 'There's an image of us as robbers, terrorists and *machistas*,' says Akil. 'Television constantly reinforced that image, and some people feel estranged from us as soon as they ask us where we are from. But I don't care...unless it's a girl I like.'[97] Bombarded by adverse discourse, social interactions and folklore, many of those participants who did not have Spanish citizenship expressed an interest in obtaining it. No participant who indicated a perceived irreconcilability between their Moroccan Muslim identity and Spanish nationality planned to apply. The sample number of respondents is not generalizable, but it remains suggestive.

Reconciling Difference

The few participants who chose to identify with the Spanish identity and wanted nationality cited cultural reasons over civic reasons and found ways to blend their identities. Amir works casually at a store run by his Spanish partner:[98]

> I have a Spanish girlfriend, a Spanish daughter. I've been back to Morocco two times in my life. I have tattoos and an earring. I'm Spanish. I'm not Moroccan. But I'm not accepted in Madrid. I always felt accepted in [my hometown] Bascara. They treated me as if I was Spanish like anyone else. My father looks Spanish. He served in the Spanish military and lived here for twenty years. He just moved back to Morocco after retiring. As soon as I am eligible, I will immediately apply for nationality. That way, if I ever have a problem, there's never a threat of being sent back to Morocco. ...I would vote. I want to do what other Spaniards are doing.... My daughter makes me feel more Spanish. She represents my roots here. Now I would never leave.

Amir's desire to gain Spanish nationality is strongly connected to his relationship. On the other hand, Yusuf's interactions with Spaniards has been characterized by rejection. So rather than a sense of acceptance, occasional trips to Morocco confirm his belonging in Spain:[99]

> I've lived here for more time than in Morocco [twenty years], so it feels more comfortable. I think it's just as hard to find a job if you're Moroccan as if you're Spanish. I think people are comfortable with me here, as I am with them. My beard attracts attention and some distrust. People make fun of it and stare in the Metro. And I think people are more controlled when I go out, for fear that I'll harass them or rob them. I feel more Spanish than Moroccan. I've lived here for more time, I studied here, and I only go to Morocco for two weeks every year. And for those two weeks, I feel like an immigrant. Here I feel at home, like a new Spaniard, especially with my new nationality. I feel very integrated, but I've had more time here. But I

haven't changed that much. I still practise my religion freely. To say that Islam and democracy don't work together is a lie.

Others who desired or held Spanish nationality exhibited a many-faced public persona, which accepted a range of identity characteristics as compatible with their own. Akil, a plumber interviewed at the M30 Mosque says:

> My girlfriend is Romanian, but the family doesn't know we're together. They wouldn't be happy about that. So I don't say anything out of respect for them and my religion. They also don't know that I go out and party sometimes. There's a small conflict of values sometimes, and I have to live both ways. I have two faces. In the moment, I enjoy it. But in my heart, inside, I know it's not right. So in the future, I'll follow just one path.[100]

Though not nearly as common, this is reminiscent of the identity confusion described by British Bangladeshis in the last chapter. In a similar spirit, Abbas says, 'I feel equally Spanish and Muslim. My parents are Moroccan. Morocco is my roots, my heritage. It doesn't really hold relevance in my life. My friends are Spanish, and they respect who I am. The only relevance for my Moroccan roots is my Islam—my belief in God. Culturally, I eat *patatas bravas*, I listen to rock, house, funk. I'm very Spanish. I feel sincerely accepted here: at work, when I was in school; in all places, I've felt valued'.[101] Separating the private and public realms, Kalid says, 'In the house, I live my life the Arabic way. On the street, I do what is Spanish. It's two different lives. And usually my life in society wins over my life at home. I feel Moroccan, but I have Spanish culture. Mostly, I feel accepted.'[102] While exhibiting this comfort with different identity characteristics and roots, these respondents also fall back on social acceptance to justify their claim to a successful blended identity. This is threaded through their responses.

Not surprisingly then, from the statements of other individuals, perceptions of irreconcilability were most commonly overridden by strong personal relationships. The participants who were open to Spanish nationality pointed to such relationships specifically. For Abdullah, the connector is his Spanish girlfriend. 'I love her, because she's given me a hand,' he says. 'I help out with some food and some things. And she doesn't buy any wine or pork because Ramadan is coming. Islam and Spain can coexist. I'm with a woman who doesn't believe in God and we work fine together. Every religion is about respecting other people. Nobody tells me what to do, and I don't tell anyone else what to do.'[103] Hakim shares an apartment with a Columbian woman and her father near Atocha Station. 'In our country, we don't usually move out of the house until we get married. And we certainly don't share a flat with a woman. At first I thought I wouldn't like living with Spaniards or Colombians, but it's been fine actually.'[104] Majid has several friends who are Spanish, which has complicated his social identity. 'I could have two nationalities,' he says. 'It's normal to be both Spanish and Moroccan. What is a Spaniard anyway? We're all equal. It's just paper. There are still some Arabs with Spanish blood after living here for 800 years. When I'm with my Spanish friends [he has a substantial number], I definitely feel Spanish. But walking around this neighborhood, have you looked around? I don't just feel Moroccan. I feel like I'm in Morocco.'[105]

Schools also possess great potential for dominant perceptions of irreconcilability. Many of the younger participants described important relationships with friends and teachers that were built in schools. Sadik, who was one of only five migrant children in his school as a child, says that 'integrating is a matter of time. Older people aren't going to accept us. But after growing up with Moroccans, the next generation of Spaniards will accept us. The children now are growing up together. If you never went to school with punk rockers, you wouldn't understand them and why they do what they do. The same goes for understanding Muslims and their traditions.'[106] One participant says that the only reason he would like to acquire Spanish nationality is because his football coach at school emphasized its importance—demonstrating one way the most minimal associational engagement fosters more. On the other hand, one of the study's most despairingly alienated participants dropped out of school at the age of 13. 'I feel like I live in a different world—a country that's not mine,' he says. 'I feel like the world is watching me and saying things about me. I always feel suspected.... Here in Spain, I have the right to be freely religious, but I don't feel comfortable. In Morocco, I feel comfortable, but I have no rights.'[107]

In the light of this personal catch-22, the Moroccan identity in Spain is very much a variant that has been informed (however inadvertently) by Spanish ways, despite the discussed rhetorical claims otherwise. As with Muslim identity in Britain, many of the participants who made such claims concede that they do not feel fully comfortable on trips back to Morocco. Like the ethnicized Islam of British Bangladeshis, Moroccan identity has become relatively hybridized in the natural process of adaptation, and defensive in response to the vilification. If perceptions about identity irreconcilability are to be surmounted, young Moroccans must first recognize and accept this hybridization before they will be able to envision a future and vested interest in Spain.

Currently, hybridization remains much less common than in the United Kingdom. Interestingly, Spain is not incriminated for its cultural differences.

Instead, Moroccans interviewed seem to accept Spanish life as part of 'another way' to exist (whereas many Bangladeshis suggested that any other 'way' was wrong or indicative of a flawed British moral character). Moroccans' brushes with the *haram* tend to be explained in terms of their own poor choices rather than a culpable society that enables such activities. While this attitude is not exclusivist, it does not go very far to bridge Moroccans' disagreements with their Spanish countrymen. And without bridging such differences, further apartist withdrawal from the Spanish social and political sphere is likely.

Faith in Change

As detailed in previous sections, the channels for engagement in the Spanish state are lacking. Given the discriminatory treatment of the minority of immigrant-origin Moroccans by both politico-legal institutions and in casual interpersonal relations, Moroccans are not well-enabled to participate in the Spanish civic sphere. Nearly all Spanish Moroccans are subject to such structural obstacles. Nearly all the participants also described the proximal security blanket of their Moroccan identity, and their difficulty adapting to Spanish cultural norms and gaining social acceptance. However, despite such shared disadvantages, around a third of the participants interviewed for this study reported political disengagement in passive apartist fashion.

In my attempts to explain this variability, I have found that, for some of those apartists, their detachment from the Spanish state and society can be related to a perception that Moroccan and Spanish identities are simply irreconcilable—culturally and civically. Such a perception is corroborated by a lingering myth of return and the enduring salience of a discursively Islamized Moroccan identity. In this section, I present collected information that suggests that anti–system behavior can also be related to the perception that Spain lacks the capacity to change in the future. Participants holding this outlook lack the civic sense of entitlement that fuels British Bangladeshi claim-making in London's East End. Instead, the perceptions of many anti–system Moroccans interviewed are informed by the distracted and corrupt structure of governance back in Morocco and tinted by the corresponding expectations of negligent leadership. This appears to dis-incentivize participation significantly.

Entitlement

The active anti–system behavior identified among the young British Bangladeshi men examined in the previous chapter is often related to their fervent

	Bangladeshis in London %	Moroccans in Madrid %
Do you have relatives living in your neighborhood?		
Yes.	75	19
No.	25	81
Do you have relatives living in other areas of London/Madrid?		
Yes.	80	64
No.	20	36

	Bangladeshis in London %	Moroccans in Madrid %
In the last month, how often have you spent time with Bangladeshi/Moroccan friends?		
More than three times.	66	28
One to three times.	32	30
Never.	2	42

Figure Seven: Muslims in Europe Survey. British Bangladeshis maintain tight physical and communal cohesion with their family and friends in their destination country, unlike Moroccans who are less physically or socially close, despite and perhaps because of the proximity of their home country, which allows many to return or disperse.[108] Indeed whereas Moroccans inhabit many different regions from Madrid to Andalucía to Cataluña, half of the British Bangladeshi population is in the Greater London area. This suggests that integration is aided by the comfort provided by family reunification and social cohesion—which many Moroccans lack in Madrid.

sense of entitlement to the equal rights, freedoms and resources of the British state. And it was the profound dissatisfaction of that sense of entitlement and its accompanying expectations that, in some, produced an impression that democracy's flaws are reflective of a system that is ultimately not interested in the welfare, equality or future of Muslims. While Moroccans were disappointed by similar encounters with discrimination and exclusion, they did not say that they believed they were 'owed' anything different. Such undesirable circumstances were simply a part of being the minority. Analogously, a sense of entitlement was almost completely absent from the commentary of those Moroccans interviewed in Madrid.

This is telling for two reasons. First, a sense of entitlement first exhibits that the referent individual feels a sense of belonging to the society which renders the rights, freedoms and resources in question. It suggests that the individual perceives that he or she is on equal footing with the rest of the citizenry. This is clearly not true for the vast majority of the Moroccans interviewed for this study. However, British Bangladeshis are also grappling with the confusion of *de jure* equality and *de facto* subordination. Second, making claims to a sense of entitlement in the light of one's disadvantages also exhibits the individual's expectation that their legal standing will become equal to their social standing—that the society and state can change to balance the discrepancy.

Few participants in Madrid exhibited this understanding about democracy's inherent dynamism, let alone awareness of the channels for social change. For most participants, the state was something to be avoided and often feared, rather than an entity to be confronted and engaged as an instrument and advocate of the people's benefit. Corresponding low levels of civic engagement and isolation among many of the same respondents suggest a potential correlation: the more integrated and entitled an individual feels, the more likely he or she will actively undermine (but in most circumstances, engage) the state if those expectations are unfulfilled. Similarly, the more isolated and uninvolved an individual feels, the more likely he or she will politically withdraw from a state or society perceived to be unjust.

Such a potential correlation portrays integration as something that leads to both democratic and anti-system behavior, according to how the individual perceives his or her disadvantage. It portrays a lack of integration as leading to a belief that neither engagement nor disengagement will have much of an effect at all. Interview content from Madrid suggests that this latter status may strongly pertain to Moroccans' very fresh experience with the structure of Moroccan governance.

You Can Take the Man Out of Morocco...

A variety of circumstances hinders civic participation and organization among Moroccans, and this chapter has already touched on several. First, the acquisition of nationality is a long and discriminatory process that leaves many Moroccans without the legal status to participate in civic activities fully. Second, many Moroccans who are consumed with obtaining and maintaining work say they lack the free time to engage in activist causes. And third, many Moroccans have low levels of social trust—with regard to one another, because of the atomized scramble for survival, but also with regard to Moroccan associations which are commonly perceived to be corrupt and self-serving.

Beyond these important explanations, many participants related such skepticism and disinclination to Moroccans' learned civic habits in Morocco—which are few. 'Moroccans were not just dropped into Spain from heaven,' says the ATIME official. 'They came from a place of origin, and that is an obstacle for civic participation.'[109] Another political leader explains further. 'Moroccans are not coming from a country with a history of democracy,' he says. 'So when the government hands you a piece of paper and requires you to pay a tax or fee, they have had no experience with that. To understand Spanish society, it's simply a matter of its history with the Maghreb. There is no experience with associationalism in Morocco. It is prohibited most of the time. So how can we expect it to emerge in among Moroccans in Spain?'[110] This point is echoed by a first generation migrant. 'We're not accustomed to associations,' he says. 'There is no democratic culture in Morocco. There's no voting. So I'm not a member of any group or party here. I have no affiliations with Spanish government. I can express myself on the street, but that's about it.'[111] A compounding factor is that since the early stages of Moroccan migration to Spain in the late 1980s and early 1990s, most arrivals have come from more rural and underdeveloped regions. So even while Moroccan civil society has been gradually expanding with the spread of globalizing technologies, new organizational activity and social movements remain primarily based in the more metropolitan cities of Casablanca, Rabat and Fès—and away from the regions sending a growing number of migrants to Spain.

The overall democratic deficit of the Moroccan monarchy has a split effect. While some Moroccan migrants—of the first and second generation—value Spanish institutions for their fairness in comparison with those of Morocco, others are jaded by the corruption and injustice in Morocco and transfer similar expectations to their impressions of Spanish government. 'Rarely does the democracy work,' says Mahmud. 'The law is not worth anything. The people making laws are not trying to help.... The interest of the state is to make money and make people work. They don't want to lose money. They should be interested in equality for all. Our general welfare is not a concern for politicians. I don't trust any politicians here or in my country. The majority are thieves and corrupt. And the police are in the same group. If the government has the power to change this system, and they don't, then the system is not going to change because I do something.'[112] Moroccans' loyalty to their Moroccan identities (as discussed earlier) is complicated further by such rebukes of the Moroccan government. Their loyalty is evidently to the land but not the state, suggesting a degree of comfort with being impervious to seemingly uncontrollable government actions over the territory they occupy. This outlook can only foster complacency and a general reluctance to invest socio-politically in Morocco, let alone doing so in Spain where there is barely any attachment to the land either. Such feelings appear only more entrenched given the aforementioned strength of identity constructions and cultural norms from Morocco, thanks to its proximity and Spain's inability (and unwillingness) to engage the newcomers.

This all reveals a severe lack of faith—in the representation of Moroccan interests within government and therefore a severe lack of faith in the system to generate change itself, but also in the structure of organizational activism and therefore the capacity of individuals to affect change individually. According to the interviews, along with perceptions of identity irreconcilability, civic engagement often hangs on this question of faith. Each participant who reported high levels of participation also believed in Spain's capacity to change—whether by confrontation and protest or by internal reform. Saad is involved in several protest movements and a squatters' cooperative. He says:[113]

> We'll move up in society and out of closed pens, but it will require a fight to do it. We need to find a system to make our voices heard, and exercise our rights. If the fight is not a political fight, it won't work. Breaking glass and burning cars doesn't do it. We need results. Other groups in Europe have done it. Right now, I'm not in that fight. Before, I used to lend a hand to migrants to educate them. Now, I'd like to find a group of like-minded people to form a cooperative. We're planning it now. The way to do it is with demonstrations.

Abbas is a 26–year-old graphic designer and member of a football organization. He says he is generally politically apathetic but he takes part in protests against certain government policies. He explains, 'The democracy works in all senses. Spain evolved from a repressive dictatorship, where you couldn't give your ideas. Now you can protest and communicate your ideas. I feel like those ideas are listened to. Ultimately the government will disagree with some of those ideas, and they won't go along with it. But that is natural with any government.'[114]

Accordingly, individuals who believed the disadvantages and discrimination of the democratic system were entrenched exhibited little civic participation. Walid is politically withdrawn and he expresses no confidence in the Spanish political system. 'I wouldn't vote, even if I had the chance. Nothing would change,' he says. 'At the end of the day, all governments are the same. All politicians are the same. My salary and my position in the work force aren't going to change with my vote. I can't do anything to change things here. A Muslim woman with a veil can't even get work. What does that mean for a Muslim man who has a beard and wants to change society?'[115] Chakir elaborates on this sense of powerlessness. 'When someone lives somewhere but doesn't feel a part of it, they must understand that the country is critically changing in composition and nature,' he says. 'There is no trust that the change will occur. And as long as society is segregated, there will be no basis for that trust. They need to participate in organizations and associations that are not only identity based.'[116] Under circumstances which leave many migrant-origin Moroccans dissatisfied, the question of a democratic system's capacity to change is little different from the definitive question of apartism: Do my most general interests converge with those of the state and society? Indeed, if the system is static, there can be no ultimate convergence in the future.

Among the study participants in Madrid, apartism was exclusively passive in its behavioral manifestation with one-third of all individuals interviewed simply withdrawn from civic life. Because of this withdrawn detachment from Spain as a country, culture and home, fewer demands were made of it. Even those participants who acknowledged Spanish identity or nationality did not necessarily express higher expectations of the state and society, or a sense of entitlement to certain rights—as demonstrated *en masse* by the British Bangladeshis interviewed. While many complained about the efficacy of the democracy, almost no participants stated that they were owed something better. Says one young community leader: 'When you consider something to be a right, you'll fight for it. For many, the right to participate or vote is seen as a benefit or privilege.'[117] This analysis suggests that with greater integration come greater demands of the state. Indeed, the dissatisfaction with government that motivates the active anti–system behavior we see elsewhere can only come from an understanding of what is owed to the citizen. Therefore, quite counter-intuitively, integration is actually an inherent feature of active apartism, while an orientation to inactivity seems to produce the withdrawal of passive apartism. Either way, both reactions are underpinned by perceptions that the state and society are ultimately too different, too discriminatory, or too indifferent possibly to act in the interest of the given individual.

Conclusion: On the Inside Looking Out

For the second generation of Moroccans in Madrid, their choice to remain in Spain is a Lockean decision that is constantly reflected upon, and re-decided each day, for as long as they stay. It is consistent with the theory of instrumental citizenship. Immigrants may implicitly or explicitly accept a tacit social contract, but their civic bond is extremely weak because of this instrumentalist orientation. Thus, participation does not necessarily accompany the Lockean decision to stay, nor does recognized membership—whether it is *de jure* (actual) or *de facto* (felt).

The lack of social cohesion among young Spanish Moroccans is reinforced by the nature of the social milieus re-established in the streets of Madrileña society. The streets are a less institutionalized, less formal way of associating, and the identity of the Moroccan in Spain leads to an outsider–insider dialectic in Spanish society, as felt by the migrant. Indeed, the relationship specified by democratic theory assures membership via the congruent relationship between decision-makers and decision-takers. Contract theory in particular discusses this relationship with a premise that the state is bounded. However, even though migrants are *de jure* 'insiders', they can feel like (and in many circumstances are) *de facto* 'outsiders'. In the light of this contradiction, Spain and its relationship with the Moroccan minority feature a series of mismatches. Among them are:

– Migrants with defined needs, but undefined goals.
– Laws that reunify families and promote rooting without facilitating citizenship.
– A society that has opened itself and its market to a group of people exceptionally reluctant to relinquish their homeland identity, without desiring the consequences of diversification on national culture and identity.

Comparing the Spanish Moroccans with the East End's Bengali community, who feels more like an outsider? One way to approach the question is to assume that the more that immigrants feel as if they have assimilated and changed to accommodate the new society's way of life, the more acute their sense of hurt will be if they are subsequently rejected. Those who subsequently feel accepted are the most committed. With Moroccans, most have not assimilated enough to feel any actual sense of a wasted moral investment. However, many young Bengalis in the British second generation have indeed made that moral investment; therefore many feel as if that was betrayed by their public vilification after the 11 September 2001 terrorist attacks.

Terrorist attacks had strong impacts on both Spain and Britain at the same time, but took place at very different stages in the development of the countries' respective Muslim minorities. Moroccans' relationship with Spanish society barely had a chance to evolve (fewer than fifteen years for 90 per cent of the Moroccan community). However, in 2001, the UK's relationship with Bangladeshi Muslims was the product of around thirty years of coexistence. Racial tension began to emerge between South Asians and white individuals beforehand with the riots in Bradford, Oldham and Burnley that summer. So the subsequent scrutiny of Bangladeshis (and hundreds of thousands of Pakistanis, Indians and Arabs) pulled the rug out from underneath an imperfect but well-founded relationship. The deeper roots of Muslims' presence in Britain produced a greater sense of betrayal by British government and society. For most young Moroccans, it is nearly impossible to imagine a relationship with Spaniards that is not already characterized by severe distrust and cynicism.

As this chapter illustrates, the channels for engagement in the Spanish state and society are terribly deficient, and those that are in place are openly discriminatory and evidently uninterested in mobilizing Moroccans' participation within the civic sphere. Among the individuals interviewed for this study, one-third expressed apartist sentiment that was manifested passively. For those individuals, their detachment from the Spanish state and society can be related to two primary (and sometimes coincidental) perceptions. The first perceives the structures of Moroccan and Spanish identities to be irreconcilable—culturally *and* civically. This perception is corroborated by a lingering myth of return and the enduring salience of a discursively Islamized Moroccan identity. The second perceives a static Spanish polity that neither represents Moroccan interests nor facilitates the individual expression of those interests at a local or national level. In this light, civic participation seems abortive. The result is pervasive civic isolation.

While active apartism runs the severe risk of organized action undermining the state and democratic system, passive apartism initiates a cycle in which alienation leads to low participation, which leads to a lack of legislative and social service-oriented responsiveness to citizens' needs, which leads to institutionalized disadvantage, which fosters further apartism. This cycle has already begun in the streets of Lavapiés and Southern Madrid. We should remind ourselves that several young Moroccans in this study indicated their ultimate interest in joining civic organizations. Ignoring them, and limiting their engagement with the democracy, only leaves them susceptible to the lure of alternative forms of engagement which may undermine the very democracy that welcomed their arrival a short thirty years ago.

6

STRUCTURE AND PERCEPTION

COMPARING THE LONDON AND MADRID CASES

The case studies presented in this book set out to reach an understanding of the patterns of political behavior and interpretation between different Muslim migrant minorities in different European countries. The communities selected were chosen for their similar democratic contexts, their positioning as the objects of socio-political scrutiny, and their contrasting patterns of social cohesion and political activity, in the interest of reaching a clearer understanding of what cross-national factors cause anti–system behavior and what factors lead to greater engagement. In comparing the cases, we encounter a selection of engaged and disaffected individuals. In Madrid, many young Moroccan men demonstrated increased levels of distrust, socio-political atomization and passive apartism. In London's East End, many young Bangladeshi men exhibited exceptionally tight social cohesion and civic engagement, but also heightened levels of resentment and apartism. This leaves us to address the primary research question of this study: what differentiates alienated young Muslims in Western democracies—in all their different circumstances and expressions—from their more democratically engaged peers?

The literature addressing socio-political alienation among Western Muslims underscores four primary causal factors to help explain the causes of alienation, as discussed in Chapter Three:

a) Politico-theological factors
b) Socio-economic status

c) The impact of national public discourse and foreign policy
d) Identity construction

This chapter compares the nature of these four structural variables in the two case studies, and their potential for explaining the discovered nature of anti–system behavior and apartism—evaluating the relevance of the literature correspondingly. It then examines what common threads are woven through these distinct cases, and whether or not they reflect the observed implications outlined in Chapter Three. While this study is not representative of the extent of the identified trends, we are able to map the diversity of political behavior and draw conclusions about what explanatory factors appear necessary, sufficient, or unsupported.

In the end, I find that the young Muslims interviewed are significantly exposed to the structural disadvantages outlined above. However, in trying to differentiate why some young Muslims engage in the democratic system despite these conditions and others do not, I find that the four streams of causal explanation are of limited empirical use. Examining participants' responses to structural disadvantages distinguishes passive anti–system behavior from active anti–system behavior and democratic activism—which of course ignores the latter two's opposing means of engagement. Instead, I find that what distinguishes democratic activists from both forms of anti–system behavior is the nature of their individual expectations and perceptions about shared sociopolitical realities.

Political Disorientation

One set of researchers argues that Muslim migrants in the West are sociopolitically disoriented by the changes in the public sphere from their land of origin to their destination.[1] This could refer to the changing role of religion in the public sphere in the destination country (theocratic versus mixed institutions versus secularist), the structure of its political and participatory institutions (participatory versus repressive versus oligarchic), or the general political culture (protest versus associational versus autocratic). The changes in the social, political, economic and cultural environment present a challenge that impedes political engagement. This, the argument concludes, leaves migrants less able to navigate new social and political systems and negotiate a place for claims-making in civil society. While evidence from both cases address this hypothesis, Madrid's juxtaposition of first- and second-generation migrants is particularly telling.

Madrid

This argument holds a great deal of value in describing the obstacles to participation among the earliest generations of migrants to Western democracies. Indeed, the disorientation argument was nearly universally true among first-generation Moroccan migrants in Madrid. The case of Hakim, a 25–year-old immigrant who lives near Atocha train station in Lavapiés, is a key exemple. He and his best friend Monsif came to Spain together, following in the footsteps of their older brothers who migrated several years earlier. At the urging of their older brothers, who boasted of connections to contracted work in Madrid, Hakim and Monsif left their families, girlfriends, social lives and comfort in the town of Khouribga to pursue more money in Spain. They left behind what Hakim calls a 'crisis' of difficulty in getting a job, and their subsequent inability to 'enjoy life'. Now in Spain, the two are a downtrodden pair, leaning on each other for comfort, strength, and a source of motivation and commiseration as they confront the realities of life as immigrants. Hakim explained that the Spanish public sphere was still foreign to him, and he said that he believed Morocco was dependent on its King for its well-being:[2]

> I don't understand government policy well [in Spain] because of my difficulty with the language. In Morocco, we cannot speak about the King in a critical manner publicly, but we can privately. Spain is different like that. But...we need a King to live. It's the same way we need an imam to lead prayers in a mosque. The [current] King [Mohammed VI] is close to the people. He's already visited our city three times on tours around the country. He has built hotels and invested in the city. But the city's mayor is a thief who was not elected legitimately. The elections were corrupt.... My brother told me that, in a democracy, everyone is equal. The problem is that I don't feel equal. My brother says that I have to wait. He says the first years are hard, and I need to have patience.

Without experience in the Spanish democratic system and public sphere, Hakim's worldview is only informed by his understanding of Morocco. As a result, his encounters and challenges are interpreted without a full awareness of alternative frameworks. Abdullah, a shopkeeper in an *al por mayor* (wholesale) store in Lavapiés, is similarly situated but draws different conclusions. He also left his wife and young children to pursue a better wage in Madrid. He arrived on a fraudulent contract that he paid €3,000 to receive. In an all-too-common set of circumstances, Abdullah purchased the contract without a job attached to it, and was forced to find work on his own. His employer now exploits his desperation by paying him below the minimum wage and overworking him. Unfamiliar with Spanish governance structures and migrant protections, Abdullah is scared to report the situation for fear of being deported. From his statements, this fear is translated from his understanding of the Moroccan public sphere:[3]

> If you live your life straight—mosque, home, work—it's fine. So I stay away from trouble. The police are always doing right [in Spain]. They just want the truth. If you're calm, they won't do anything. They're much worse in Morocco, where they're corrupt and always want money. Society here is easy. Nobody cares about you. You're just free. In Morocco, you're always worried about being thrown in jail.

Like Abdullah, some Moroccans interviewed appreciated Spanish governance and laws more because of their enduring acquaintance with Moroccan public life, which looks authoritarian and corrupt when juxtaposed. This makes the benefits of the Spanish system more obvious. Indeed, the earliest generations of Moroccan migrants from the 1970s and 1980s left Morocco precisely for such reasons: Yasir has spent the last eighteen years in Madrid:

> The government in Spain treats foreigners well. They don't bother you, and if they do, they treat you properly. If they want to see your identification and you don't have it, they let you go get it. I can go out at night freely. All Moroccans that live here should favor the Spanish government. Here they can work, be free, and be protected. All of that is not true in Morocco, where you are constantly questioned. There are a lot of problems and one small problem can get you in prison for five years. In Spain, if you need the police, they come. There are offices that help you find work. There are kitchens to feed older people. If you don't work like me, there are unemployment benefits. I have them for three months. You can just sit in a park like this without being harassed.[4]

Yasir's standards are quite low. With greater integration and understanding of the capacity of the democratic public sphere, expectations can be expected to rise. Indeed, if the Moroccan government continues to set the standard, the Spanish government will not be asked to provide Moroccan migrants with more than the bare democratic minimum of human rights and justice.

Respondents who moved to Spain at early ages demonstrated better political orientation than more recent migrants and individuals who migrated later in life—both of whom continued to clutch strong connections and identity affiliations with Morocco and Moroccan public life. Rashid, Tariq, Abbas and Saad each exhibit such orientation, grounded in their experience with Spanish public life. 'My parents didn't always understand Spain,' says Rashid, a 25–year-old man who moved to Spain with his parents as an infant. 'They didn't have time to change. I speak much better Spanish than they do, because they couldn't learn it quickly.'[5] Similarly, Tariq feels he is better oriented and therefore more discretionary than his parents:

> My parents vote. They're less critical than I am. But I have more information. We know more, because they're older and we know more about the world. They know their neighborhood. They were living in Arab dictatorships, without the access to information, without access to the truth. The government had control over the minds of the people and kept them ignorant.[6]

Abbas, a graphic designer who was born in Lavapiés, recognizes the evolution of Spanish democracy and the individuals joining it from his family's country:[7]

> People from Morocco have a different mentality. The issue is the way they think and relate to other people. They tend to stay with people similar to them. It's mostly just fear. They're in a new country. They won't change but I think their kids will. The democracy works in all senses. Spain evolved from a repressive dictatorship, where you couldn't give your ideas. Now you can protest and communicate your ideas. I feel like those ideas are listened to. Ultimately the government will disagree with some of those ideas, and they won't go along with it. But that is natural with any government.

Saad moved to Spain at 17 years old without his parents. And after thirteen years in Spain, this first-generation migrant still seeking citizenship is oriented enough to feel empowered to plan democratic demonstrations against discriminatory policies of the Spanish government:[8]

> We'll move up in society and out of closed pens, but it will require a fight to do it. We need to find a system to make our voices heard, and exercise our rights. If the fight is not a political fight, it won't work. Breaking glass and burning cars doesn't do it. We need results. Other groups in Europe have done it. Right now, I'm not in that fight. Before, I used to lend a hand to migrants to educate them. Now, I'd like to find a group of like-minded people to form a cooperative. We're planning it now. The way to do it is with demonstrations.

This group represents a minority of the Moroccans interviewed. Indeed, the interview content presented in the previous chapter documents Moroccans' enduring acquaintance with their country of origin and its political, cultural and social norms—prominently manifested in the persistence of Moroccan identity structures. However, if Moroccans follow the path of British Bangladeshis, it is likely that an increasing number of Moroccans will soon boast fluency with the Spanish system of governance and an interest in participating.

London

The enduring relevance of homeland identity and norms is limited among Bangladeshis in London's East End. The political disorientation of recent Moroccan migrants and the enduring Moroccan identity among later generations is only paralleled by the sentiments of older Bangladeshis, who moved to London as adults. Yusuf's parents live near the heart of Banglatown in Whitechapel, while he has moved with his wife and children east to Redbridge:[9]

> The elders never got a chance to understand the UK and its lifestyle and culture.... The elders came from farms in a third world country to a modern city in a first world country.... Our parents never had TVs or any exposure to real culture on their farms.... The first, older generation of men are holding on to any association and relationships with Bangladesh. They simply maintain the same lifestyle—transplanted.... For them to change their ways is a very big deal. They still hang onto that part very tightly.

As the interview content exhibits and illustrates, the younger generation of Bangladeshis is well-oriented in British public life. They are conscious practitioners of norms and cultural habits. While appreciating and occasionally honoring their ethnic roots, they have distinctly British preferences, accents, hobbies and culture. And even if they choose not to participate in the British political system, there was generally an awareness of the opportunity structures of the system. The political system of Bangladesh is irrelevant, and, if it is even known, it is typically perceived as backward or corrupt.

Synthesis

The political integration and orientation of Bangladeshi respondents and the political evolution of Moroccan participants exhibit the limited application of explanations of alienation that point to political disorientation. Across the diversity of respondents and their different civic activities, Bangladeshi participants exhibited great fluency with British institutions and governance, to the extent that many are able to circumvent them or exploit their vulnerabilities with ease. Indeed, the hypotheses of scholars underscoring the significance of political disorientation in political marginalization are only useful to explain disengagement among the generations of migrants who migrated to the United Kingdom later in life. Participants who were born in Britain tend to be as politically oriented as any other British-born person.

In a recent study, Ronald Inglehart and Pippa Norris find that the basic socio-political values of Muslim migrants in European countries fall about midway between those prevailing in their country of origin and their country of destination—leaving them well placed to integrate and engage themselves in the new public sphere.[10] And yet, still, many migrants—even once oriented—do not. The information from the two previous chapters demonstrates that, even among the second and third generations of migrants who are better oriented in the political system and society of the destination state, a significant number are alienated. In fact, some of the most actively anti–system individuals were among those with the most fluent understanding of the destination country's political system. They tended to boast the greatest fluency with institutions and structures of governance. This is especially true in the East End. But even in Madrid, Tariq—who spoke about his parents' inferior acquaintance with the government—says that his fluency is what enables him to determine that Spanish democracy is 'false':

> Even when I get the chance, I still won't vote. Nothing is going to change. They promise a lot, but they don't do anything. The democracy is false. They fool the people with elections.

> I've become more religious lately. The beard is relatively new, one year. I used to be bad, but I've found the truth. I had an arch. I started off empty with drugs and girls. But I was sadder like that. But with Allah as my guide, I'm not alone. Divine law is easier to follow than the law of man. If Spaniards knew that law, but it wasn't called *shari'ah* or Islamic, people would like it. But you can't impose Islamic law on people who don't accept it.

His ideas are remarkably reminiscent of those encountered among Bangladeshi apartists in London, suggesting that as generations of Muslim migrants assimilate and feel a greater sense of socio-political entitlement, they are more likely to reject or re-interpret those homeland ethno-religious cultures and traditions. While this opens the door to assimilation and adaptation, this also opens the door to apartist reinterpretations and outlooks.

Socio-economic Status

Some social scientists point to the entrenchment of minority Muslim communities in a socio-economic underclass as a main reason for alienation.[11] They contend that workplace discrimination and the marginalization of Muslims from the mainstream labor force discourage their interest in the public sphere of a state in which they remain underinvested. And at a more basic level, the argument suggests that the better educated, the wealthier and the more financially stable people become, the more likely they are to engage.[12] Other scholars point to the coincidence of the cutback of social programs and the mass population influx of Muslim immigrants and their children. This, the argument goes, has fostered further resentment from poor nationals, and enhanced polarization between ethno-religious groups with a common social gripe.

London

In the selection of neighborhoods for this study, socio-economic status was effectively limited to members of the working classes. Bangladeshis in Tower Hamlets are almost uniformly a working-class community. Average income among the borough's Bangladeshis is £182 per week, and 45 per cent of the Bangladeshi community have no educational qualifications.[13] According to the Greater London Authority, the greater Bangladeshi community has the highest levels of unemployment, poorest housing, and lowest levels of educational attainment and health in the United Kingdom.[14] They acknowledge that 20% of Bangladeshis live in seriously overcrowded housing, and 80% have an income below the national average.[15] Among all of England's local authorities, Tower Hamlets is the second most deprived. With a quarter of the borough's households earning an income below £15,000, Tower Hamlets is the eighth most income-deprived, and the thirty-second most employment-deprived.[16]

Among these young respondents from working-class families, there was a spectrum of educational attainment levels. However, as study participants ranged between 18 and 28 years old, nearly all the more educated respondents were still in school, living with their parents, and/or not old enough to have accumulated much money. Customarily, Bangladeshi young men and women continue living with their parents until they get married and begin to support themselves. For this reason, educational attainment was also an inadequate way to differentiate socio-economic status.

Nevertheless, if socio-economically referenced explanations for socio-political alienation are correct, political engagement would be very low among East End Bangladeshis. However, this is simply not the case. Within the generally similar social status among the study's Muslim respondents in both venues, there were great differences in levels and patterns of engagement, inactivity and anti-system behavior. And indeed, as the case study shows, the Bangladeshi respondents are a remarkably civically active group. This suggests that socio-economic variability does not have a directly causal relationship with the levels and nature of engagement.

If anything, several pieces of evidence from the East End case study show that many of the individuals engaging in active anti–system behavior are among some of the most educated respondents in the sample. The earlier chapter on the East End observes a possible correlation between Bangladeshi young men's educational attainment and childhoods supervised by their parents in households. This facilitates better study habits, and it enables youths to venture beyond the boundaries of their local 'square mile' without fears of gang violence; but it can also lead to in-group social rejection by the Bangladeshi 'street boys' who dominate the available default social life around council estates. Indeed, in several instances, interview content suggests that active anti–system behavior is often preceded by experiences with social rejection or isolation due to 'house boy' childhoods.

For young men with intellectual capital and experiences with such social isolation, the spontaneous and organic associationalism of late adolescence provides an organized means of belonging beyond the home. Such alternatives include sports teams, special interest societies and music bands—but also apartist groups. Bilal, a medical student at Kings College and an active *Hizb-Ut-Tahrir* member, says:

> Before [I joined *Hizb-Ut-Tahrir*], I was a bit of a study geek, tossing around in my books. I was around in my community but I didn't take on a helping role. It may have been a lack of maturity, plus I thought that such helping was for older people. I would play snooker or football, but otherwise I was just sitting at home, lazing around.[17]

While his 'house boy' peers may have been satisfied to join a youth club or artists' cooperative, Bilal was more socially conscious, and interested in political activism:

> We've lived in the borough for twelve years now. And I wouldn't want for my brothers and sisters to be living there for another twelve years, surrounded by drugs and other problems and people who are happy with being mediocre in their lives. I met [my local *Hizb-Ut-Tahrir* leader] in the neighborhood when I was 17. He said he wanted to do something for the community.... [He] said to me, 'What are you gonna do with your life? Are you just going to be mediocre?'
>
> ...*Hizb-Ut-Tahrir* is made up of people that think. People that question the status quo. People who are conscious. Other people who think similarly but actually engage the government to create change aren't doing as much for the Muslim community.[18]

Similarly, Viq is a promising small business owner, who also leads a local *Hizb-Ut-Tahrir* division. Skilled with information technology, he also acknowledged a sense of social displacement.

> I guess I'm different from the [other] Stepney kids, I went to all-white schools while they were with Bengali kids here.... When I was 12 years old, I went through *Ahma-*

didat books, *Ikhwat* books, and debated. From that time, I would go to HT events when they were held at the Royal London Hospital.... There's no community feeling here. I'm not happy. I feel out of place with the government.[19]

For those with such social and political awareness, apartist organizations like *Hizb-Ut-Tahrir* resolve many moral and existential questions—often by appealing not to young people's base levels of frustration, but to their intellect. This is a strategy that attracts higher achievers by design. Calim, a school teacher and local organizer for *Hizb-Ut-Tahrir* in Stepney, says that this is part of an overall strategy:

> We [*Hizb-Ut-Tahrir*] operate at a high level with advanced messages and a higher benchmark.... I came to Islam because some of the guys I hang around wanted to. In our estate, a lot of the guys were getting heavily into drugs and violence, and a bunch of us—the sharper bunch—decided we didn't want that. I lost a lot of friends there. After that, I had a buckle with a girl who wanted to get serious at 17–years-old and caused me a lot of emotional problems. And I thought, 'I'm not going to go down this road. I'm not living this kind of life.' Then I decided to dedicate myself to getting serious, and getting the qualifications I needed. I ended up having to break a lot of ties with friends because those ties would have taken me down.[20]

Madrid

In Madrid, the vast majority of Moroccan respondents were not only socio-economically disadvantaged, but also had lower levels of educational attainment. In the most recent count, fewer than 5 per cent of all Moroccan men in Spain worked in professional, technical or director-level jobs. About 80 per cent worked in agriculture, mining, transport, construction labor or domestic services.[21] Statistics specific to Moroccans in Madrid Sur were not available due to the dispersed nature of the population and the fact that the region's concentration of Moroccans spans across different municipal districts. However, over 40 per cent of all Moroccan men in Spain are illiterate and about 95 per cent hold only a high school education or lower.[22] Moroccans also make up a greatly disproportionate segment of the unemployed in Spain, and 14 per cent of all unemployed Moroccans reside in Madrid.[23] As in London, because of this near universal low income and educational qualifications in the case study venue, it was not possible to differentiate between respondents of significantly different socio-economic status in Madrid either.

Synthesis

Taken in scope, the evidence suggests that active anti–system individuals may actually be disproportionately well-educated and socially conscious—the same characteristics of individuals whom previous research identified to be predictably engaged in mainstream society. In East London, the pertinent individuals are indeed engaged, but in an effort that rejects democratic society. And they are also working class. It is possible that wealthier Bangladeshis and Moroccans are disproportionately active in the British public sphere, but this study cannot comment, due to its focus on the working-class neighborhoods of Tower Hamlets and Madrid Sur. The conclusions here do not necessarily mean that socioeconomic status is relevant; it simply suggests that there are clearly other factors in operation.

From the evidence documented in the previous two chapters, we also see a tendency among both Muslim minority groups to avoid discussing socioeconomic discrepancies when framing their sense of injustice within or alienation from the political system. Indeed, interviewees rarely bring up poverty and class status, and when they do, it is usually in reference to their family's or another person's starting position after migration from the country of origin. This is despite the fact that British Bangladeshis and Spanish Moroccans are among the poorest ethnic minorities in their respective countries. Instead, sentiment tends to be expressed about discrepancies of interpersonal treatment and political clout. The examined communities do not appear to believe that these inequalities are related to parallel socio-economic inequality, but are more based on disregard and discrimination among the established political class and endemic in the political system. Empirically, this means that the situation might be different 'if I weren't Muslim [or Moroccan]' rather than 'if I weren't poor'. It is precisely one's potential (and in later generations, the expectation of equal opportunity) to earn more money, become better educated, and rise within the social class system which galvanized many migrant communities' initial pilgrimage and justifies their continuing residence. Further research would be useful to pursue the relationship between class and anti–system behavior.

Public Discourse

Explanations pointing to public discourse argue that many young Muslims encounter discrimination, profiling and racism on an interpersonal basis, but their treatment in mainstream Western discourse and news media can feel just as local and direct.[24] If anything, it feels distinctly uncontrollable. They cite that as democracies become less direct in access, discourse and the public sphere become the points of access and mediation. Within this sphere of mediation and exchange, there is an abundance of sensationalized, monolithic representations of Islam and Muslims that ignore Islam's plasticity and diversity, and instead allow exaggerated mis-images (stemming from exotica or invented in a narrow historical context and augmented by selective episodic details) to constitute Muslim history and tradition.[25] Increasingly, commentators and government officials have argued that the playing field of these mis-images and misrepresentations is foreign policy, particularly that which pits Western states against Muslim organizations or governments. Some studies have argued that alienation from democratic political systems is the result of dissatisfaction about such foreign policy and its accompanying discourse, fostering resentment among naturalized Muslim citizens. Further literature suggests that this discourse leads many Muslims to rotate the same simplistic dichotomy to instill the same monolithic perceptions of the West and Westerners—creating a race to the bottom. Continuing this logic, these scholars argue that such an uncontrollable discursive environment in a public sphere dominated by non-Muslims discourages some Muslims from engaging in it.

London

In the United Kingdom, public discourse about Bangladeshis is roped into a sensationalized, national discourse about Muslims. According to a recent study by the Cardiff School of Journalism, between 2000 and 2008, four of the five most common British newspaper story threads associated Islam and/or Muslims with 'threats' or 'problems' and dissociated them with 'dominant British values', while only 2 per cent of these stories suggested 'that Muslims supported dominant moral values'.[26] The same study finds that coverage of British Muslims was shown to have increased significantly since the 11 September 2001 attacks, and by 2006 had reached a level twelve times higher than that in 2000.[27] In the same content analysis, the most common nouns employed in relation to Islam or Muslims were 'terrorist' or 'extremist', while the most widely used adjectives included 'fanatical', 'fundamentalist', 'radical' and 'militant'. In all, references to radical Muslims outnumbered references to moderate Muslims, seventeen to one.[28] This report exhibits the continuation of a trend that began in the 1990s in the UK. An earlier study of news coverage of Islam between 1994 and 1996 underscored a discursive environment in which Islam had been presented as a threat to British society and its national values—a prism through which Muslims were perceived as deviant, irrational, different and unable to fit in with British society.[29] A further study finds that while arrests of Muslims on terrorist charges receive significant news coverage, the conviction of non-Muslims is not widely reported, leaving the audiences with the impression that the criminal justice system is successfully prosecuting Muslim terrorists in Britain: 'The reality is that large numbers of Muslims are being arrested, questioned and released while the majority of those actually convicted in an open criminal trial are non-Muslims.'[30] In an examination of British television, film and literature, a 2007 report by the Islamic Human Rights Commission finds institutionalized prejudice 'so embedded that anti–Muslim prejudice did not need to be maliciously motivated or intentional as it was structural'.[31] This stinging set of evaluations only establishes more scientifically a predisposition which many British Muslims have alleged over the last decade.

This alleged predisposition was also noted by numerous respondents. Omar, an unemployed gang member from Tredegar, says, 'Three white girls harassed and assaulted a young Muslim sister in Bethnal Green because she was wearing a *hijab*, a couple of weeks ago. Did you see it in the newspapers? If it were the other way around, it'd be front page.'[32] Other individuals highlighted stereotypes of Muslims they feel they have to hurdle each day. Fadhil is an artist from Limehouse:

> When we wear a traditional *thoubb* [gown], we get locked up; when you step into the bus; especially people next to you in the Tube. Hey, it's just an outfit. It makes me feel bad. These people have stored images of these fanatics and they place it on any Muslim they see.[33]

Nearly all respondents cited their disapproval of British foreign policy in Iraq, Palestine or Afghanistan. Six of the participants specifically cited their frustration with the British news media and public discourse. Of the six, two are actively anti–system, and the other four are exceptionally active engagers in the public sphere. In discussing essentialist public discourse, the two active apartists make particularly pro-active statements. 'Maybe we need to put destiny in the hands of Muslims,' says Calim. 'That's something we need to speak to others about. We need to reverse that bogeyman perception of Islam. Guys like Abu Hamza, and the Taliban, they've done a lot of harm to our image. And the British media has jumped on it. Now, you can't blame people for having perceptions like that. It's the responsibility of the Muslims to show that we are credible.'[34] A fellow member of *Hizb-Ut-Tahrir*, Imran, says, 'Since 9/11, Muslims are being attacked. It's a minority that are terrorists, and the government has over-generalized it to all Muslims. Unless they know you, all the non-Muslims think that Muslims are terrorists. I wouldn't want to talk to Muslims either if I was influenced by the media like that.'[35] The preponderance of active apartists concerned with public discourse indicates that inflammatory public discourse is a double-edged blade that can inspire participation and activism—not only marginalization.

Madrid

The Spanish media comprises fewer right-wing tabloids, and views itself more as a vanguard against a regression to fascist Franquista policies. That said, it has also shown itself to be susceptible to extensive stereotyping and monolithic imagery of Muslims. A 2007 study of racism in the Spanish press finds that while most of the national press is less openly xenophobic, right-wing papers such as *ABC* and *La Razón* often feature anti–immigration opinions.[36] Regional newspapers, especially in the south, where Moroccan workers 'are most conspicuous in intensive agriculture, might in this case be even more blatantly racist, typically so in more detailed coverage of "foreign" crime, or their defense of xenophobic local politicians, for instance in the *Voz de Almería*.[37] The report continues:

> The most conspicuous contributions to prevailing stereotypes and prejudices are undoubtedly the dominant topics of the coverage, such as the alarmist emphasis on border control and the 'invasion' of *'pateras'* from North Africa, immigration mafia, and as we have seen in the coverage of the 'assault' on Melilla, the repeated attempts of African youth to enter the country. The same is true for the extensive coverage of immigration policies, immigration laws, regularization, and so on—emphasizing the general opinion that immigrants and immigration are a serious problem, and not a boon for the country. Secondly, the emphasis on *'papeles'* conveys a dominant picture of immigrants who are not only *'sin-papeles'*, but also 'illegal'—that is, one step removed from being criminal, while breaking the law. On the other hand, unlike the rest of the European press, there is—as yet—little emphasis on 'ethnic crime'. Thirdly, less prominently, but no doubt increasing are the stories about the actual presence of immigrants among 'us', and especially about their cultural differences and threats (typically religion, Islam, head scarves, etc.).

These trends were also highlighted by a Spanish civil servant. In an interview, he blames Spanish news media for a shift in treatment of Muslims since the 11 March 2004 terrorist attacks: 'Before, in the newspapers, articles wrote about Algerians, Tunisians, Syrians, Moroccans and Egyptians. Now they're all just called "Muslims". "A group of Muslims are entering the country." When Latin Americans arrive, they are not Catholics or Protestants. They're Ecuadorians, Colombians or Argentines. That is dangerous... because, if they're Muslim, that means they're not Spanish.'[38]

In Madrid, as the previous chapter described, a small percentage of Moroccan-origin individuals have citizenship. Fewer actually vote. And even fewer are participants in public discourse. Very few respondents mentioned the Spanish news media. There is a sense of a lack of control over the nature of public discourse, and subsequent indifference about its content. However, underlying this ostensible indifference is fear and a severe lack of exposure. There is a pervasive fear of Spanish immigration officers and undercover Moroccan intelligence agents (DEST), who roam Spain in collusion with Spanish counter-terrorism police. 'Young people here are scared to talk,' says Omar. 'They think they'll say one small thing and get thrown into prison. They're scared to make any religious statements which might frighten other people.'[39] 'Spaniards can then imprison a threatening activist, under the false pretense of terrorist charges,' says one youth coordinator in Madrid. 'When you are at the border, you are often quizzed about the nature of your affiliations. This fear then spreads to other groups that are not political in nature, but more cultural or social.'[40] The securitization of the Moroccan community is clearly inspiring this reticence, which extends from Spanish public discourse to intra-communal distrust.

Fear aside, the vast majority of Moroccans choose not to participate or concern themselves with Spanish public discourse. Three respondents addressed this vacancy, and all three were active engagers. 'The solution to the racism is to show the face we're hiding,' says Tariq. 'We need to start a campaign showing the real Muslims. The associations out there don't have the means, or are just shit because they're often run by Arab governments.'[41] Abdel, the Socialist Party recruiter says, 'We [Moroccans] are not communicating. There's a lack of discourse. Society has an absolutely false image of Muslims. If we don't talk, if you don't get to know me, you're never going to understand. Spaniards don't want to make the first step. They don't want to break the ice.'[42] 'To fix the social rejection that I've experienced, I need to talk to people more and clarify myself,' says Amir. 'The problem is that it usually leads to a fight. So what can you do?'[43] Considering the trends that emerge from the London study, it is not surprising that a preponderance of passive apartists were encountered among a group with little concern for public discourse.

Synthesis

From this comparison of the two cases, the interview content suggests that those who were more concerned with (evidently discriminatory) public discourse were actually more likely to be actively engaged in the public sphere—either democratically or via anti–system means. Consequently, this suggests that negative public discourse does not necessarily alienate people from engagement, as some explanatory arguments have contended. As generations of Muslim migrants assimilate and feel a greater sense of socio-political entitlement, they may be more likely to pay increased attention to national public discourse, feel involved in policy-making, and seek out opportunities to affect change or express themselves. The act of engaging discursively—whether fulfilling or frustrating—produces both persistent activists (win-or-lose), but also frustrated failures with still a lot of political capital left to employ. This yields the question, what determines whether a concerned individual engages using democratic means, or means that disrupt, circumvent or undermine the democratic system?

The British government has recently made statements suggesting that opposition to British foreign policy is the cause of Muslim radicalization.[44] However, as this chapter demonstrated earlier, many Muslims are perfectly capable of and accustomed to expressing their opposition in non-violent ways with the expectation that they will be acknowledged. Instead, it is when the institutional means of self-expression and claims-making are perceived to be inconsequential that alternative tactics are considered. There is no doubt that foreign affairs pitting Western democracies against states with Muslim majorities have struck a sensitive chord among European Muslims, including those interviewed. However, participants were equally disappointed with specific domestic policies as well. Alienation will not end with the conclusion of wars in Iraq and Afghanistan. It will endure as long as there is a perception that Muslims' voices go unheard in the forums of public discourse.

Identity Construction

Finally, another group of social scientists argue that alienation from the public sphere can also be derived from a tighter embrace of Muslim identity or a more conflicting sense of identity.[45] This, proponents contend, comes in response to aforementioned discursive derision and social rejection from the indigenous community, and also in response to estrangement from ethnic heritage. Scholars like Roger Ballard explain that this 'embrace' of Islam has become more significant than ethnic ties—which are more commonly seen as backwards traditions—because it is the Muslim part of the younger generation's public identity that is being maligned. In this manner, younger generations of Muslims are reclaiming the stigmatized identity and inverting it into a positive civic attribute.[46] As opposed to swinging more toward a Western alternative to the perceived anachronism of older Muslim customs and lifestyles, some use exclusivist Islam as a way to handle the ambiguities, uncertainties and contradictions of the West with structure, amid circumstances over which they feel they have no control.[47]

The case studies suggest that the search for a civic identity is not particularly politically alienating. Indeed, most young people of any religion, ethno-cultural background or nationality tend to experience existential self-questioning. Instead, the cases indicate that anti–system behavior—passive and active—is more closely related to the individual's relationship with the national identity of the destination country. To understand how these identity configurations facilitated engagement or disengagement, we must examine the clear delineation between *de jure* identity structures (citizenship) and *de facto* identity structures (belonging) in both venues.

London

In the United Kingdom, British civic identity (formal citizenship) is attainable through extended residence in and tested knowledge of Great Britain. The British ethno-cultural identity (informal Britishness) is propagated as equally inclusive—forged with shared 'core values', rather than a common genealogy, religion or ethnicity. It is projected as open to newcomers, and Bangladeshis have sought to reconcile their ethno-religious identity within the scope of British lifestyles and customs accordingly. Among the sample of young Bangladeshi men in London's East End, we find a community that is actually well integrated into British norms, culture, behaviors and preferences. Participants demonstrated that they were actually post-Bangladeshi—at a point of identity construction where their roots in Bangladesh informed their ideas and social habits, but did not dictate them. It was a form of distinguishing heritage, shared customs and common upbringing that bonded the members of the community in a diverse British polity. Indeed, many respondents maintained a clear conception of their own Britishness—separated (irreversibly, they felt) from their country and culture of origin. Given the nature of a values-based, ethno-cultural British identity that is available to all in conjunction with the national civic identity, there is thus a greater expectation of flexibility and equal respect from British society. However, this leads to greater impugnation of that society if those expectations are unfulfilled.

Among study participants, those sensing a greater rejection by British society (often framed as an 'attack on Islam') were more likely to be passively or actively anti–system. Viq senses extensive discrimination and an agenda against the Muslim community in Britain:

> It's the culture and ideas in this country that is messing things up…. The more the government stops us from thinking, the more we are going to hate…. The social separation is because of the government. People don't understand us. In the Hadith, the thoughts and practices of the government get passed onto the people. So if the government is thinking we're all terrorists, then I don't blame these Englishmen who suspect smells of fish curry to be chemical weapons. [48]

Interestingly, Viq separates the British government from the British society. It is possible that that this is attributable to *Hizb-Ut-Tahrir*'s principal agenda—that of replacing the democracy with divine law. However, fellow HT member Ismail believes that the democracy is reflective of the outlook of its constituents from whom he claims to have separated himself. Rather than reacting against a discriminatory Britishness, Ismail, aged eighteen, rejects Britishness before it can reject him:

> My parents would expect me to integrate into British society by getting a good job, but I know that I wouldn't work for a bank or law firm. In school I have to take bogus citizenship classes, created to show us opportunities and equality. They're trying to integrate members of Muslim society who don't want to integrate. Beyond that, we don't need to integrate. They want us to believe in freedom, but I don't believe in freedom because I'm a Muslim. For me to integrate, it means that I have to accept things that my religion rejects…. I don't feel an identity crisis, because I feel like I have a relationship with God and so I don't have any problem saying that I am a Muslim. I've put myself in a box, and eliminated my British and Bengali ties. Do I need to claim to be British? No, I have a British passport…. I didn't choose to be born here. [49]

Ismail's rejection of all things British and Bangladeshi is unsupported by his upbringing and acculturation in British society, and the manner in which he generally restricts himself to Bangladeshi friendships. Indeed, his Islam is grounded in a particularly British Bangladeshi existence—the only existence he knows. Amjad is a very devout 20–year-old man who identifies with Muslim values, 'not British values'. He finds Britain to be full of temptations and vice that are contrary to Muslim lifestyles. However, he does not translate these moral disputes into social rejection. Instead, he says the same freedom that permits such temptations also permits his uninhibited religious worship:

> I've been for *hajj* to Saudi Arabia, and I've travelled to Bangladesh, Syria and France. And I've found Britain to be the safest place to live. So for that reason I feel British. Other places, you say something about the king or the PM [Prime Minister] and you're off. Here, you're alright.... My identity, my religion teaches me how to be a good person and respect people. That's my true identity. They try to teach British values. I follow the values of my religion. The government makes it easy for Muslims to stay in this country. We are protected.[50]

Amjad's relationship with Britishness emphasizes its inclusion and protections. Ismail's underscores its rigid judgment. And Viq's reacts to its purported ignorance. Their engagement levels followed accordingly. While Viq and Ismail were active *Hizb-Ut-Tahrir* members, Amjad has interacted extensively with councilors, soldiers, policemen and the Mayor of London through associational memberships and volunteer projects. However, they all are interested in claiming the geographic and social space where their British, Bangladeshi and Muslim identities overlap.

Madrid

In Spain, the Spanish civic identity (formal citizenship) is attainable via Spanish heritage or extensive residence in Spain or in the Spanish post-colonial world. The ethno-cultural identity (*hispanidad*) is projected as exclusively attainable via Spanish lineage or 'blood'. This alters the nature of newcomers' expectations. Because Moroccans are ineligible to attain the ethno-cultural Spanish identity and belonging, Spanish and Moroccan identities tend to be perceived as separate and irreconcilable. This also works with many Moroccans' expressed perception that a Spaniard could never adopt the Moroccan ethno-cultural identity—which would entail Arab lineage and Muslim religion. So there is little expectation of malleability from Spanish society, and hence little impugnation of it for any divergence from Islamic outlooks or any reluctance to change with the composition of its citizenry. Consequently, Moroccan participants were not struggling to reconcile multifaceted identities, as were their more integrated British Bangladeshi counterparts (see Figure Eight[51]). While British Bangladeshis' third-party rejection by white Britons was particularly disheartening and fostered a search for belonging elsewhere, Spanish Moroccans were less bothered but also significantly less engaged.

As the previous chapter details, the Moroccans interviewed reject Spanish identity in the same manner that Spaniards reject Moroccanness, so the feeling appears to be mutual. Among the Moroccans interviewed in the sample, Spain is rarely incriminated for its cultural differences. Instead, the Moroccans interviewed seem to accept Spanish life as part of 'another way' to exist (whereas many Bangladeshis suggested that any other 'way' was wrong or indicative of a flawed British moral character). This suggests Moroccans' ability to separate themselves from Spanish culture. (The Bangladeshis interviewed are more critical of a British culture to which they more closely identify.) Moroccans' brushes with the *haram* tend to be explained in terms of their own poor choices rather than a culpable society that enables such activities. While this attitude is not exclusivist, it does not go very far to bridge Moroccans' disagreements with their Spanish countrymen. And without bridging such differences, further withdrawal from the Spanish social and political sphere is likely.

However, without intending to, some Moroccans are evolving as Spaniards as a result of unalterable normative circumstances and cultural environments. Therefore, while Bangladeshi participants battle for the social space to express their Muslim faith and Bangladeshi heritage in conjunction with their British

	Bangladeshis in London %	Moroccans in Madrid %
I Feel Bangladeshi/Moroccan.		
I strongly agree.	25	64
I agree.	72	32
I disagree or strongly disagree.	3	4
I Feel British/Spanish.		
I strongly agree.	35	8
I agree.	56	25
I disagree or strongly disagree.	9	67
Proud to be Bangladeshi/Moroccan.		
I strongly agree.	27	62
I agree.	72	35
I disagree or strongly disagree.	1	4

Figure Eight: Muslims in Europe Survey. The difference between British Bangladeshis' and Spanish Moroccans' ability to reconcile their multiple identities is extraordinarily stark. British Bangladeshis' claim over their Bangladeshi identity is not as strong, though nearly all still recognize it. However, they are equally able to recognize their ties to their European country—which the Moroccans surveyed are clearly not.

nationality, Moroccans are drifting into an interstitial position. It is almost certain that, with time and investment, Moroccans will defend their equal Spanish civic status. Whether they will ultimately seek *de facto* acceptance on cultural terms will mostly depend on their capacity to transcend their Moroccan identity in the manner exhibited by British Bangladeshis.

Synthesis

Put together, the interview content enables us to map a comparative landscape of identity construction for members of the two examined communities. In Figure Nine, we see how young Bangladeshis maintain a tripartite identity structure that includes their embrace of Muslim British identity—both civically as entitled citizens (*de jure*), and ethno-culturally as equal, recognized consumers of British lifestyles and products (*de facto*). This Britishness is overlapped by the individuals' sense of Bangladeshi norms that pervade East End life, and the increasingly relevant pull of a deterritorialized Islamic faith that renders a sense of belonging in the light of social or discursive rejection encountered in British society. Many young Bangladeshis interviewed place themselves in the middle ground of this overlap of post-modern identification. This represents a social and physical space, the legitimacy of which many young Muslims are struggling to establish and maintain in the public sphere.

In the second part of Figure Nine, Spanish identity is split between its ethno-cultural and civic attributes, only the latter of which is *de facto* available to Moroccans. Among the Moroccans, their ethno-cultural (and national) Moroccan identity is substantially overlapped by the inherent presence of their Islamic faith. As represented by the two nearly congruent circles, for most Moroccans these two identity constructions are inseparable from each other, with the exception of secular nationalists and Islamist dissidents. Importantly, the figure illustrates the limited overlap between this 'pre-packaged' Moroccan identity and its Spanish counterpart. Note that there is no overlap with the ethno-cultural Spanish identity. This reflects how Moroccans are generally not recognized as ethno-cultural Spaniards, nor do many of them self-identify as ethno-cultural Spaniards. Many participants were content to maintain an instrumentalist relationship with the Spanish civic nationality, while others did not desire a Spanish identity in any sense at all—even legally.

This information and its analysis demonstrates that the search for identity is not as determinant of alienation as the nature of individuals' relationships with the ethno-cultural identity of the destination society. It also exhibits the role of

United Kingdom Identity Overlap

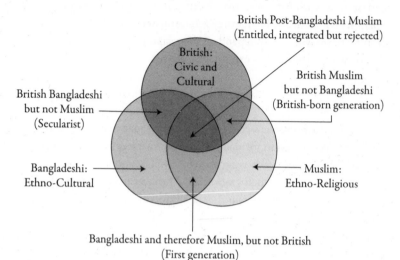

British Post-Bangladeshi Muslim
(Entitled, integrated but rejected)

British:
Civic and
Cultural

British Muslim
but not Bangladeshi
(British-born generation)

British Bangladeshi
but not Muslim
(Secularist)

Bangladeshi:
Ethno-Cultural

Muslim:
Ethno-Religious

Bangladeshi and therefore Muslim, but not British
(First generation)

Spain Identity Overlap

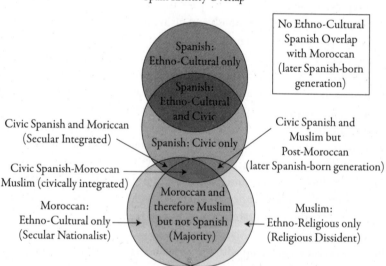

Spanish:
Ethno-Cultural only

No Ethno-Cultural
Spanish Overlap
with Moroccan
(later Spanish-born
generation)

Spanish:
Ethno-Cultural
and Civic

Civic Spanish and Moriccan
(Secular Integrated)

Spanish: Civic only

Civic Spanish and
Muslim but
Post-Moroccan
(later Spanish-born generation)

Civic Spanish-Moroccan
Muslim (civically integrated)

Moroccan:
Ethno-Cultural only
(Secular Nationalist)

Moroccan and
therefore Muslim
but not Spanish
(Majority)

Muslim:
Ethno-Religious only
(Religious Dissident)

Figure Nine: Identity Overlaps. The identity overlaps of British Bangladeshis and Spanish Moroccans are defined by Spain's unattainable ethno-cultural civic identity of belonging, and Moroccans integrated Muslim faith.

the structure of national citizenship ideals. In Spain, where citizenship is defined with ethno-religious factors in mind, it endures in conventional conceptualizations of belonging. In Britain, where ethno-religious factors are segregated from considerations of citizenship, belonging is more a matter of politico-legal factors such as passports and residence. This marks an important intersection of structure and agency. Across the cases, third-party rejection appears to inspire some active anti–system behavior—as alternative identities are constructed to compensate for the sense of associational disorientation—while mutual rejection appears to foster some passive anti–system behavior based on shared (rather than one-sided) perceptions of irreconcilability. However, as interviews show, rejection and irreconcilability are subject to individual interpretation.

The Power of Perceptions

Experience with Structural Disadvantage

Thus far, a comparative examination of the four primary variables suggests that variability in structural circumstances and disadvantage helps us greatly to contextualize political alienation. We see that the four principal causal factors are not mutually exclusive as they often overlap. And we have seen that they do indeed relate to individuals' estrangement from their government and society, as the sources of disadvantage or social rejection. However, these variables do not enable us to differentiate between (and therefore characterize) anti–system activists and democratic activists. Instead, juxtaposing the primary structural variables (see Figure Ten) suggests that active anti–system activists and active democrats are not actually all that structurally different. Instead, their common activism (albeit by very different means) exhibits structural similarities that defy the observable implications of the hypotheses as they were laid out at the end of Chapter Three.

Political Disorientation Hypothesis: If politico-theological hypotheses are accurate, passive and active anti–system individuals will demonstrate less acclimatization and understanding of their country's political institutions and processes, while the democratic activists and the complacent will be adequately comfortable or knowledgeable.

Observation: Democratic activists and active anti–system participants were among those with the most fluent understanding of the destination country's political system.

	Political Engagement	Diasporic Disorientation	Structures of Socio-economic Disadvantage	Discriminatory Discourse	Identity Confusion
Passive Anti-System	Disengage-ment (Withdrawal)	Disorientation or Disinterest	Mixed Class and Education	Disengagement w/Public Sphere	Mutual or Third Party Rejection
Active Anti-System	Engagement (Exclusivist)	Well-Oriented	Mixed Class and Education	Engagement w/ Public Sphere	Third Party Rejection
Democratic Activism	Engagement (Inclusive)	Well-Oriented	Mixed Class and Education	Engagement w/ Public Sphere	Third Party Rejection or Acceptance

Figure Ten: Responding to Structure. Passive anti–system individuals, active anti–system individuals and democratic activists have different responses to common structural conditions. However, active anti-system individuals and democratic activists respond similarly, but with different means.

Socio-economic Disadvantage Hypothesis: If socio-economic hypotheses are accurate, it will be difficult to find subjects who are politically engaged within democratic channels of participation, because the case studies have little variation in socio-economic status.

Observation: With little socio-economic variability, there were great differences in levels and patterns of engagement, anti–system behavior and apartism among participants—indicating that socio-economic deprivation produces passive anti–system behavior, active anti–system behavior and democratic activists. While I cannot comment on whether socio-economic deprivation is necessary, it is clearly not sufficient. That said, subjects engaged in active anti–system behavior tended to be university-educated.

Discriminatory Discourse Hypothesis: If discursive hypotheses are accurate, passive and active anti–system individuals will reject public discourse, and perhaps shelter themselves from it.

Observation: Those participants who were more cognizant of discourse were more likely to be actively engaged in the public sphere—democratically or via anti–system means.

Identity Construction Hypothesis: If socio-psychological hypotheses about identity construction are accurate, passive and active anti–system individuals will exhibit confusion about their self-image, while democratic activists and the complacent will feel more security about their identity.

Observation: The search for identity is not as determinant of alienation as the nature of individuals' relationships with the national identity of the destination society. And many of those respondents with a conflicting sense of identity were actually quite democratically engaged.

The empirical literature attempting to explain socio-political alienation is aiming to differentiate the disaffected (active and passive anti–system individuals) from democratic activists. Indeed, the primary research question of this examination asks what causes some young Muslims to engage democratically and others to withdraw from the state or engage in activities that disrupt the political system. A sole focus on structural factors enables us to distinguish those who are active engagers in the public sphere—but muddles active individuals who employ opposing means. Working outside the system, active anti–system individuals act to destabilize the democracy and disrupt the social cohesion that makes majoritarian democracies and the welfare state work. Any criterion that cannot distinguish such actors from those who volunteer in inclusive associations, participate in non-violent protest and petitioning, attend public meetings, and correspond with representatives, is not ideal.

The two case studies suggest that a more accurate determinant of whether an individual is alienated from the political system may be derived from his set of expectations about the political system—expectations about the provision of politico-theological rights, about the protection of equal socio-economic opportunity, about due acknowledgment in the discursive sphere, and expectations of socio-cultural acceptance. The examination of Bangladeshis in London's East End documented a generally accentuated sense of entitlement among the young men interviewed—a perception that the political system and British public sphere owed them certain rights, liberties, benefits and treatment that were all afforded by law and precedent.

Subjective Expectations and Attainment

Those participants who exhibited active anti–system tendencies typically asserted that such provisions were in some way undelivered by the British democracy, while those who participated in the political system or otherwise demonstrated complacency typically said that their expectations were sufficiently met. The few passive anti–system individuals who withdrew from the public sphere in the East End expected less of the political system, which they regarded as discriminatory, dysfunctional, perplexing or insignificant. With Moroccans in Madrid Sur, a sense of entitlement was absent among many of the men interviewed. Passive anti–system behavior was more prevalent, and of those demonstrating a withdrawal from the public sphere, expectations of the political system were either basic or characterized by fear. Higher expectations of the Spanish political system were only expressed by those who were somehow actively engaged with it.

So in both cases, we see the significance of individuals' expectations with regard to the political system's capacity to protect and provide for its citizens. But we also witness the critical role of individuals' perceptions of the fulfillment of their expectations—what I will henceforward refer to as their 'attainment'. Active apartists tend to perceive a significant discrepancy between expectation and attainment, while activists engaged in the political system perceive relative congruence. Equally importantly, passive apartists' expectations appear drastically low, suggesting a logic that the individual actor will neither disrupt nor engage with a political system it expects nothing from in the first place. These trends are mapped in Figure Eleven. The level of an indi-

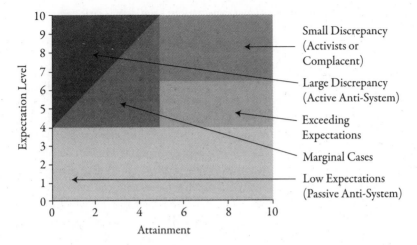

Figure Eleven: Mapping Expectations. A cross-referential graph of individual expectation levels and their perceptions of relative attainment. The shadings are hypothetical manners of classifying responses, but subjectivity will determine actual individual reactions.

vidual's expectations is measured on the y-axis, while their attainment is measured along the x-axis. This enables us to plot possible 'ought' values and 'is' values on a graph. The color shadings are potential manners of classifying responses, but as I will discuss later, subjectivity will determine whether the marginal discrepancies lead to activism, complacency, rebellion or withdrawal. For a model of exhibiting the necessary relationship between active anti–system behavior and a large expectation-attainment discrepancy and the necessary relationship between passive anti–system behavior and low expectations, see Figure Thirteen in the methods appendix.

These conclusions are relevant to those of the earlier referenced study of political violence by Ted Robert Gurr. In *Why Men Rebel*, Gurr contends that actors are disposed to violence when there is a discrepancy between the 'ought' and the 'is' of collective value satisfaction.[52] Reiterating Gurr's terminology, the discrepancy between individuals' 'value expectations' and 'value capabilities' produces a sense of 'relative deprivation' that drives them to employ violent tactics against opposing political groups or institutions.[53] Gurr's work does not extend such conclusions about the role of expectations beyond their relationship to violent action. This was not his intention. However, the evidence displayed in the earlier two case studies suggests that the level of individuals' expectations affects the nature of individual activism more generally—beyond violence—to dispose the choice also of withdrawal (low expectations), complacency (met expectations) and democratic engagement (met expectations).

Importantly, Gurr makes it clear that he makes no assumptions about the sources of individuals' values that inform their expectations. Instead, he categorizes the possible sources into three groups: 1) welfare values, which contribute directly to physical well-being and self-realization; 2) power values, which determine the extent to which individuals can influence the actions of other individuals and avoid interference by others in their own actions; and 3) interpersonal values, which provide the psychological satisfaction individuals seek in their interactions with other individuals.[54] From the preceding chapters and the earlier discussion of the structural disadvantages facing the European Muslims examined, their value expectations are diversified. But that which appears to disappoint individuals the most was the dissatisfaction of their so-called 'power values' and 'interpersonal values'. Despite their relative poverty, very few of the Muslim men interviewed referred to their socio-economic status. In fact, most were still pursuing their expectations of moving up in class status and out of their current neighborhood, whether it was Madrid Sur or London's East End. However, those interviewed expressed definitive concern that they were politically powerless. Across both cases, the young men interviewed shared grave concerns that the political system exercised double standards and lacked the capacity to reform according to their collective will. Those interviewed also displayed a clear sensitivity to social judgment experienced at the hands of their peers or their British/Spanish countrymen. Despite their shared norms, the Spanish Moroccans interviewed were sometimes as atomized from one another as they were from indigenous Spaniards allegedly exercising discrimination. Similarly, British Bangladeshis interviewed emphasized a tripartite paradigm of rigid social appraisal—carried out by indigenous British countrymen, Bangladeshi family members and Muslim peers.

Perceptions as a Causal Mechanism

As similar structural disadvantages were noted by nearly all respondents, there is a significant amount of space for interpretation about which disadvantages qualify fulfillment or failure. For this reason, the causal mechanism that appears to trigger expectation-attainment discrepancy or congruence is individual perception. Indeed, as Gurr noted, people may be subjectively deprived with reference to their expectations even though an objective observer may not judge them to be in need.[55] This is often the case with second-generation European Muslims examined through the eyes of their parents (and other members of society). Alternatively, the existence of what an objective observer deems to be abject deprivation is not necessarily thought to be unjust by those who experience it.[56] This is often the case with first-generation migrants through the eyes of their children (and other members of society). The interplay between subjective expectations and individuals' variable perceptions of their fulfillment is therefore crucial. This study was not positioned to determine which life experiences, conditions or personal characteristics were correlated with which tints of perception. However, this certainly appears to be a most promising direction for future quantitative investigation.

Targeted questions that solicit individuals' interpretations of the structural variables reveal a clear division between those of individuals engaged in anti–system behavior and those of democratic activists (see Figure Twelve). Passive and active anti–system individuals appear to share similar worldviews, but engage differently. This shows that the way agents reflectively monitor and constitute their personal realities is to some extent *sui generis*. Differences in perception and worldview are not about whether or not the participant agrees or disagrees with state policy or societal norms. Indeed, many respondents in both cases sustained various grievances and objections and still found cause to engage. Differences in perception and worldview pertain more closely to whether or not there is good reason to partake in the activities and institutions of the democratic system. Those who choose not to participate and those who choose to undermine the system believe that the social, economic and political disadvantages they experience are suggestive about the greater credibility and legitimacy of the democratic system. Indeed, the active apartists who answer 'No' to the questions listed in Figure Twelve genuinely believe that the answer should be 'Yes'. Those who choose to engage with the democratic system are otherwise able to reconcile the disadvantages of the system, and any dissatisfaction they encounter.

This chart also enables us to distinguish between individuals engaged in active and passive anti–system behavior. Indeed, despite their common interpretations of structural disadvantages, active anti–system individuals still believe they can affect their society's public sphere—albeit by disrupting it—while passive anti–system individuals lack this confidence. This is exhibited in Figure Twelve's left-most column. By understanding this final distinction, we can make three key distinctions:[57]

1) Individuals' experiences with structural disadvantages appear to distinguish the active from the passive.
2) Individuals' perceptions of structural disadvantages appear to distinguish democratic activists from those engaged in anti–system behavior.

| | Perceptions of | | | | |
	Political Engagement	*Diasporic Disorientation*	*Socioeconomic Disadvantage*	*Discriminatory Discourse*	*Identity Confusion*
	Can you affect the public sphere, through democratic means or otherwise?	Do government institutions offer you the capacity to impact on society?	Does your status in society have the capacity to change?	Does your society generally treat you equally to others?	Are the identities of your origin and destination countries reconcilable?
Passive Anti-System	No.	No.	No.	No.	No.
Active Anti-System	Yes.	No.	No.	No.	No.
Activist	Yes.	Yes or No or Maybe.	Yes.	Yes.	Yes.

Figure Twelve: Interpreting Shared Experiences. Passive and active anti–system individuals have similar perceptions of common structural conditions.

3) Individuals' confidence in their capacity to affect the public sphere appears to distinguish those engaged in active anti–system behavior from those engaged in passive anti–system behavior.

The interview content therefore suggests that many active anti–system individuals were once—and could one day be—able to reconcile their grievances and channel their political capital into democratic institutions. Particularly in the East End (where there is a small preponderance of active anti–system individuals), individuals' strong sense of entitlement and their lives in an exceptionally active community make young people already inclined to engage in associational life and claims-making. It is a socio-cultural norm among Bangladeshis there, particularly in order to access the public goods upon which many families are dependent. Bangladeshis must fill in housing application forms to be given larger flats by the council to make space for families of seven, nine and sometimes eleven people. They must address the government for enrolment in state-funded education, and for loans to pay for university tuition. They must appeal to the National Health Service for access to healthcare. And many are often savvy enough to write to Members of Parliament, contact council representatives, and visit bureaucrats to expedite action or gain special exceptions for their needs.

Their sense of entitlement (and need) emboldens young Bangladeshis to make demands of the state, which are regularly met in the provision of public goods. This sets a precedent for the equal treatment of claims-making, which young people expect to be followed in the provision of equal rights, liberties, and protections. When these expectations are unfulfilled and replaced with state-sanctioned double standards that appear to entrench their disadvantage, young people lose faith in the efficacy of the democratic system and seek alternative means of making claims.

From the interview set, resentment is mostly directed toward the national government—not local institutions, which are championed for their blind provision of public goods and representative councils. In Tower Hamlets, while the bureaucracy of civil servants is mostly white British, fifty-one of the fifty-one council members are Bangladeshi. On the other hand, the national government is associated with anti–terrorism policies that ostensibly target Muslim citizens and foreign policy that supports wars in Muslim countries. While most participants accept that they will not always 'get their way' in a majoritarian system, many respondents believe that government action in these two regards impugns the integrity of the greater democracy by undermining the right to equal treatment. These individuals interpret such policy action to be indicative of a greater agenda against Islam and Muslim people. It is interesting to note that as no respondent claimed any family members or friends in Iraq, Palestine or Afghanistan, much of their resentment is expressed in terms of collective injury.

Absence of Social Authority

The individual perceptions that differentiate passive anti–system behavior from active anti–system behavior from democratic activists are mediated by individuals' engagement with different manifestations of social authority—legitimate, illegitimate, or a lack thereof. In Islam, there is no Vatican equivalent. So it is often very difficult for anyone—Muslim or non-Muslim—to distinguish a random priest from the Pope. As part of Islam's egalitarianism, there is no spiritual hierarchy as all are equal under God. This is why Muslims prostrate themselves to pray, irrespective of social class or age. In the same spirit, while madrassas train imams, any individual from the community can lead a prayer session. And any individual can be called a *sheikh*—a term of reverence for their wisdom and teaching. This absence of a consolidated referential body that may address different social questions (or certify legitimate commentators) with a degree of superseding legitimacy enables individuals' perceptions and interpretations of the public sphere to go unchecked.[58]

The young people interviewed report that they form their opinions from a variety of sources—very few of which are certified or accountable. Because few Western Muslims read and comprehend Arabic, there is substantial demand for Quranic commentary and guidance among individuals who read the scripture but do not understand it. This demand is being met by a proliferating group of 'web preachers' who write commentary on internet weblogs. While some of these 'scholars' are actually quite well read and advocate peaceful, inclusive and balanced outlooks that work within democratic systems, others promulgate political agendas and hateful interpretations. The influence of both types is noteworthy, as several have gained a great deal of fame, but the internet is clearly a double-edged instrument that cuts both ways. Some young people say they rely on friends, neighbors and even 'playground debates' at school or university. Others read books or simply reflect. Very few actually refer to their local imams. And in London, very few British Bangladeshis cited guidance from their family members.

Within the United Kingdom, there is a broad selection of people claiming to hold social authority, but no one who actually possesses it in a centralized and consolidated way. The British Muslim community is extraordinarily heterogeneous—comprised of nationalities from Morocco to Indonesia, ethnicities from Arab to African, and sects of Sufis, Shia, and many divisions of Sunnis. Currently, no organization has been able to consolidate Muslim leadership across the different groups at the national level or even locally in the Bangladeshi East End. Consequently, myriad voices claim to represent 'true' Islam or the 'community of British Muslims' in all of its diversity, and they create a dissonance of institutions and individuals declaring social authority within the Muslim community. While this means that the government is uncertain about whom they should approach about policy, this also means that individual Muslims are equally uncertain about whom they should consult about life's difficult questions. Extremists and soapbox preachers have become prominent in response to young people's expressed search for 'true' Islam. As this book has underscored, they are skeptical of their parents' ethno-cultural traditions, estranged from their mosques' aloofness, and confused by the cacophony of voices and claims in the public sphere. The easy, clear-cut answers provided by groups like *Al-Muhajiroun*, *Hizb-Ut-Tahrir* and Al-Qaeda affiliates are attractive, but they are often terribly misinformed, exploitative, and rely on Islamic references taken out of context.

As discussed in the London case study, many British mosques—which are positioned well to combat extremist religious opinions—lack the awareness and the credibility among young people to counterbalance extremism. They are only occasionally purpose-built religious spaces, and most are small buildings with few facilities to attract young people. Imams typically cannot communicate well in English, and are ill-equipped to satisfy the counseling needs of young people. Mosques are therefore rarely the dynamic, multifaceted community centers that many young people require. Instead they are places for few things other than ritual prayer, dominated by traditionally minded elderly men. The government and leading Muslim groups have attempted to resolve the deficiency in oversight by creating a Mosques and Imams National Advisory Board (MINAB) that is tasked with setting certain baseline standards across the diverse array of religious groups and sectarianism. If this is successful, it will be a significant first step toward consolidating central Islamic authority in Britain.

In Spain, there is quite simply an absence of institutions with any crosscutting recognition, and the government is not prepared to facilitate such organizations itself. Social authority appears to emerge from the home and local mosques, despite severe limitations. For now, this may be satisfactory as most of the young people interviewed expressed their understanding of Islam in confident terms, with fewer questions and less confusion in the public sphere. However, in the event of any confusion, there is little authoritative guidance available. As the previous chapter discussed, Spanish mosques are mostly 'garages'—makeshift religious spaces often in converted commercial offices, stores or apartments. Imams are volunteers who open the mosque for prayer and are otherwise unavailable in their religious capacity. The government convenes the CIE (Islamic Commission of Spain) through the General Directorate of Religious Affairs. However, inside, the CIE is dominated by non-Moroccan Arabs who are divided between competing groups more concerned with power than actual leadership. On the ground, such structures are essentially irrelevant anyway, as nearly every Moroccan in the target interview group was unaware of their existence.

As in Britain, this general absence of clear social authority permits a range of different perceptions—projecting Islam and impressions of democratic participation purely in the eye of the beholder. Future research must continue to solicit these opinions rather than settle for documentation and analysis of structural circumstances, which are likely to be interpreted and experienced in different ways. And future government action must work to consolidate and strengthen bodies of social authority, but in the interim, work to engage young people on the ground—at the level where their perceptions are formed.

Conclusion: Structure and Perception

After this comparison of the London-based and Madrid-based case studies, three principal conclusions emerge:

1) The way agents reflectively monitor and constitute their personal realities is to some extent *sui generis*. In social constructivist fashion, perceptions are critical.
2) Individuals' perceptions are mediated by their engagement with different manifestations of social authority, or a lack thereof.
3) The tint of individuals' perceptions and interpretations to some extent determines the nature of their social and political behavior.

These observations headline two disparate case studies with distinct challenges, but related roots. British Bangladeshis' sense of entitlement to democratic liberties and protection along with their tight social cohesion produces high levels of diverse engagement and activism. While much of this activism is democratic, a significant plurality is anti–system. This is both promising for British democracy and troublesome. On the one hand, active anti–system activists aren't that different from democratic activists, and simply need to be persuaded to redirect their immense political capital. On the other hand, inversely, democratic activists are susceptible to the same discouragement, resentment and let-down of active anti–system individuals—and they too can redirect their political capital elsewhere. The key therefore appears to be the ability of British government and society to sway the perceptions and interpretations of young Bangladeshis to act within the structures of British democracy and not create reconstructions of Islamic identities that oppose the British state and society.

In Spain, there is a lack of active anti–system behavior, but also a deficiency in democratic participation among Moroccan individuals. In the short term, the discriminatory legal structure of the Spanish state and its public sphere's reluctance to accept their societal 'Other' has actually fostered a Moroccan community that, unlike their British Bangladeshi counterparts, is quite conveniently a) less likely to react against their failure to affect change in what is already perceived to be a discriminatory society; b) less likely to take third-party social or political rejection personally, or as a violation of their rights; and c) less likely to build fundamentalist reconstructions of their homeland ethno-religious identity; because, quite problematically, they are correspondingly: a) less likely to enter the public sphere; b) less likely to feel a sense of social or political entitlement to justice, rights or benefits; and c) less likely to break away from their homeland identity and habits to assimilate.

The process of assimilation is delayed by the Spanish government's elongated naturalization process, the extended period of immigration, and the endurance of Moroccan identity and culture in Spain—whether due to its proximity, the transferability of cultural landmarks, or Moroccans' reluctance to adapt. Either way, this will most likely break down over the next generation. Unless the Spanish government acts to persuade Moroccans to participate in the structures of governance and associational life, Spain will soon confront a sizeable minority of Moroccan-origin citizens who are disengaged just when they begin to feel a sense of social and political entitlement.

7

CONCLUSION

DEMOCRACY'S OPPORTUNITY

At the beginning of this study, we were confronted with the question of who exactly is alienated from whom—Western Muslims from their societies of citizenship, or vice versa? While in Europe we have seen that the short answer is 'a little of both', America poses an interesting application of our findings. There has been a developing 'consensus'[1] that the problem of Muslims' alienation and 'home-grown terrorism' is an exclusively European problem—that a country like America is immune by virtue of its immigrant history and inclusive identity. This chapter addresses this 'consensus' and what the findings of this book mean for future public policy in the United States, Europe and other democracies. It then concludes this study by addressing the principal debates outlined in the introduction.

Americans Apart?

The United States' population of Muslims has been predominantly characterized as 'middle class, mostly mainstream, assimilated, happy with their lives and moderate on many of the issues that have divided Muslims and Westerners around the world'.[2] Despite the criticism that the United States has endured from Muslim individuals and organizations internationally for its foreign and anti–terrorism policies, Muslims living within American borders appear quite integrated because of a variety of factors that reinforce a sense of belonging and identity. Perhaps the most significant factors are 1) the ideological foundation (not ethno-cultural heritage) of American identity and democracy, 2) higher levels of conventional religiousness (in all religions) in the United States, 3) higher incomes and 4) the great dispersion and diversity amongst Muslim-Americans that hinders a solidarist consciousness.[3]

However, following the conclusions of comparative fieldwork in Europe, we see that integration is quite paradoxically a feature of active anti–system behavior among the young Muslim men examined—as much as it may otherwise promote their active participation in the democracy. The logic is that integration fosters a sense of entitlement that predisposes the integrated to expect a more complete set of rights and liberties than the less integrated. The sense of injustice is therefore significantly more sensitive and disappointment more poignant among those with greater expectations, with a stronger sense of rejected national identity, but without much faith in the democratic system to remedy the inequity.

Accordingly, Pew's optimistic findings above were accompanied by an admonition that younger Muslim-Americans are more religiously observant, more self-identifying as Muslims than older Muslims, and are more likely to rationalize political violence.[4] Indeed, many young American Muslims experienced 11 September as a defining moment. Portes and Rumbaut introduced the concept of 'reactive ethnicity' to describe the rise of defensive identities and solidarities to counter confrontations with an adverse native disposition.[5] Since the 11 September terrorist attacks, American Muslim political organizations are reversing earlier tendencies to narrow the boundaries of the community at the expense of the *ummah*, and to emphasize foreign policy issues at the expense of domestic ones.[6] In a study of Muslim-Americans, Ayers and Hofstetter find that piety is negatively associated with political participation, while political resources and measures of political awareness, specifically feelings of anxiety following the 11 September 2001 attacks, are positively associated with participation.[7] These findings portray a community of Muslim-American youths that is not all that distinct from their European counterparts.

Following the findings in this book, American Muslims' relative wealth, education and geographic dispersion are all quite beside the point. Anti–system behavior appears to exist independent of any specific structural cause, and more as a product of the discrepancy between individuals' expectations about their political entitlements and their perceived levels of attainment. This does not mean that America's relatively integrated communities of Muslim individuals are naturally susceptible to apartism. It simply means that United States society cannot make the assumption that, by virtue of their history and demography, they need not concern themselves with the equal treatment of their Muslim minorities. As in Europe, and as with any other group of democratic citizens, Muslim Americans can be expected to hold their democracy to certain standards of equality and justice—particularly amid the sensitivity of the American security agenda. The violation of these standards is just as likely to cause withdrawal from or rebellion against the political system.

If this empirically based conceptual argument is not persuasive enough, the purported 'consensus' has been questioned by the revelation of an increasing number of alleged 'home-grown' plots of political violence. A *Washington Post* compilation exhibits an increasing frequency of charges and convictions in the United States:[8]

7 December 2009: David C. Headley is charged in Chicago in a terrorism plot against a Danish newspaper. The indictment also alleged that he conducted extensive surveillance of targets in Mumbai for more than two years preceding the November 2008 terrorist attack in India.

November 2009: Fourteen people are charged in Minneapolis, Minnesota with recruiting youths from U.S. communities to train with or fight on behalf of terrorism groups in Somalia.

5 November 2009: Maj. Nidal M. Hasan, a U.S. Army psychiatrist of Palestinian descent, kills thirteen people on the Fort Hood, Tex., military post and injures dozens.

21 October 2009: Tarek Mehanna is arrested in Boston and charged with plotting to bomb shopping malls and conspiring to kill politicians.

23 September 2009: Najibullah Zazi, an Afghan-born Colorado resident, is charged with planning a bombing attack in the United States.

27 July 2009: Daniel Patrick Boyd, a North Carolina resident, and six others are charged with conspiring to provide material support to terrorists. Boyd allegedly had spent time training at terrorist camps in Pakistan and Afghanistan. He was also charged with conspiring to recruit young American men and help them travel overseas in order to kill or maim.

June 2007: The FBI disrupts an ideologically inspired terrorism plot to allegedly destroy fuel supplies and pipelines at John F. Kennedy International Airport in New York.

8 May 2007: A plot to bomb the Fort Dix military base in New Jersey is thwarted. Dritan Duka, Shain Duka, Eljvir Duka, Mohamad Ibrahim Shnewer, Serdar Tatar and Agron Abdullahu are arrested. On 22 December, 2008, they were found guilty of conspiracy to harm military personnel.

13 February 2007: Daniel Maldonado, a former Houston resident, is indicted on charges of conspiring to train with al-Qaeda in Somalia. He is deported from Kenya to the United States. He was convicted of receiving training from a foreign terrorist organization and was sentenced to ten years in prison.

23 June 2006: Seven men are charged in Miami with plotting to bomb the Sears Tower in Chicago and a federal building in Miami. [After two mistrials, five suspects were convicted on 12 May, 2009.]

August 2005: Kevin James, an inmate in a California state prison, and three others are charged with forming a domestic terrorist group that planned to attack U.S. military installations, 'infidels,' and Israeli and Jewish facilities in the Los Angeles area. [James was sentenced to sixteen years in prison on 6 March, 2009.]

8 May 2002: Jose Padilla is arrested at Chicago O'Hare International Airport on a material witness warrant. At the time, he was alleged to have been plotting a radiological 'dirty bomb' attack. He was later alleged to have conspired with al-Qaeda to blow up apartment buildings with natural gas. He was convicted (with two co-defendants) in January 2008 of 'conspiracy to murder, maim or kidnap.' He was sentenced to seventeen years in prison.

The greater concern of this study is whether these headlines are the bellicose manifestations of a much larger number of Muslim American individuals who are increasingly withdrawn from their political system. This would be a much greater systemic threat to American democracy than the physical threat posed by violent individuals.

Learning from Experience

The United States is well-equipped and well-positioned to prevent the degree of social division concerning its European counterparts. The structure and public understanding of American civic identity is perhaps the country's most useful instrument for promoting belonging. America defines its identity as ever-changing with the composition of its polity, and historically set against the rigid, heritage-based, imperialist identities of Europe and other parts of the world. This flexibility and historical positioning have rendered the United States a significant amount of slack in the assimilationist demands it makes of its migrants. Indeed, while migrants are given a significant amount of freedom to maintain ethno-religious habits and customs, these are often commoditized in a way that integrates them into an American market of converted cultural goods. Such a market for culture-specific tastes and products reflects an associational political system that promotes claims-making by interest groups. In all of this (occasionally bizarre) communal and individual diversity, ethno-cultural difference can quietly reside under the radar of any sense of 'American' conformity—particularly around urban centers.

In the past, however, this marketplace has demonstrated paradoxical propensities to embrace and exclude. A historical asylum of diverse religious evangelicals, American society seems to seek new civic adherents similarly—extolling and marveling at newcomers like converts. The Chinese professional basketball player, the Indian American conservative state governor, and Latinos preaching the virtue of the proverbial 'American dream' are all absorbed as welcome members. However, the embrace of 'problematic' minorities is often only achieved after long struggles with exclusion and prejudice. As much as America touts its exceptional capacity to elect a dark-skinned president, secure homes for a plethora of religious minorities like Ba'hais, and maintain a state with a Latino plurality and an Austrian-born governor, the same country has turned a blind eye to anti–Semitic policies in the 1920s and 30s, interned its Japanese population during World War II, pursued a communist witch hunt during the 1950s and 60s, and continued a legacy of institutionalized discrimination against black people late into the twentieth century. 'With us' and 'against us' have been separated by a very thin line indeed.

Current fears about the allegiances of Muslim citizens provide America with a real test of the diversity and inclusion on which it hangs its exceptionalism. In the two democratic societies on which this study focuses, laws and policies have been implemented that betray the rights and liberties that the government purports to afford equally. Consider the extension of detention times for suspects held without a charge in the United Kingdom, and the roaming paper-checking round-ups in Moroccan *barrios* of Spain. Policies which restrict rights and liberties selectively (rather than universally) bypass the normal checks and balances of the democratic system, because most of the public will be exempted.[9] Such a double standard may very well lead Muslim individuals to question their expectations of equal belonging to the state, and thus their expectations of equal standing in participating in the public sphere.

We have already witnessed the commencement of similar government responses in the United States. In September 2009, an imam in Brooklyn sued the government, claiming that the F.B.I. had threatened to interfere with his application for naturalization unless he agreed to spy on foreign relatives—echoing similar claims made in recent court cases in California, Florida and Massachusetts.[10] In 2007, it was revealed that the F.B.I. was using informants to infiltrate mosques and collect information about congregation members. In a case from Orange County, California, a personal trainer informant described to the Los Angeles Times how the F.B.I. supplied him with a car key operating as a recording device to document conversations he had with hundreds of Muslim men over gym sessions:[11]

> [The informant] Monteilh said the agent would ask him to write down the name of the person in each photo, the mosque they attended, their nationality and the names of their associates. He estimated that he identified several hundred men, the majority of them between the ages of 18 and 50. Many were professionals, including doctors and lawyers, he said. Most were students.
>
> Monteilh said he broached the topic of racial profiling, but was rebuffed.
>
> 'White little old ladies aren't blowing up buildings and planes,' Monteilh quoted one agent as saying. 'We're looking at these people based on the fact that there's a terrorist threat in the Islamic community ... there's no other way.'
>
> ...Monteilh was reported to the FBI in June 2007 after members of the Islamic Center of Irvine alleged that he was promoting terrorist plots and trying to recruit others to join him.
>
> Monteilh denies being a terrorist and said anything he said or did at the mosque was in his capacity as an informant for the FBI. He said he was given permission by authorities to engage in terrorist rhetoric, planning and 'pretty much anything short of an actual attack' as part of his assignment.

Consequently, in the past year, many American mosques have begun to compile databases of complaints about infiltration and interrogation by counterterrorism investigators. Most concerning, a national coalition of two dozen Islamic organizations has vowed to cease cooperating with the government unless agencies stop infiltrating mosques and using 'agents provocateurs to trap unsuspecting Muslim youth'.[12]

Such tactics threaten to corrode the trust and engagement that many American Muslims maintain with their government and civil society—one of America's greatest comparative advantages relative to Europe. The federal government has promoted significant outreach into Muslim communities, and has been cautious in its approach to domestic counterterrorism—which may explain a preference for clandestine operations, rather than overt policy measures that target the Muslim community, as in Europe. Public figures have chosen their words carefully. After the revelation that several Americans were complicit in the November 2008 Mumbai attacks, President Barack Obama was sure to praise 'the extraordinary contributions of the Muslim-American community'.[13] F.B.I. representatives noted that several Northern Virginia families 'alerted their community and the authorities immediately when they knew there was something wrong with their sons. That is a very positive step.'[14]

However, the effect of infiltration operations without specific targets other than 'the Islamic community' may influence Muslims' perceptions about the fairness and openness of their American democracy. This is a slippery slope. In the United Kingdom, many organizations that cooperate with government investigations have lost the faith of their members and cease to be effective liaisons. In Spain, Moroccans generally do not join such associational bodies. The United States government would be well advised to manage their precious relationship with Muslim organizations and individuals with care. As in Europe, the American public and state's capacity to discipline their fear and govern with reason, empathy and equality could determine the future of both their external image and internal social harmony.

Profiling and Mosques

Given the findings of this book, the American government's focus on 1) profiling and 2) mosques is already problematic—certainly from the perspective of Muslim relations, but also from the perspective of counterterrorism. First, based on this book's contention that perceptions are a key determinative factor leading to passive and active anti–system behavior, we can conclude that threat profiling is only as useful as perceptions are visible. Indeed, from the results of this study, we see that the best way to predict the political behavior of individuals is to understand the way they interpret the world and its challenges. And worldviews are simply not demarcated physically. In fact, it is arguable that physical profiling does significantly more harm than good.

The trade-off between enhanced security policies and civil liberties has been well documented. However, this study suggests that there is also a trade-off between current anti–terrorism security policies (particularly those of profiling and surveillance) and the level of young Muslims' sense of belonging. If these policies are truly the most effective security measures (and I am not positioned to contest such an argument), then societies must determine what is actually the greater risk—vulnerability to an isolated terrorist attack, or a growing population of the alienated and the gradual dysfunction of democracy? Indeed in the medium and long term, the best cohesion policy may be the best security policy. We should measure what would be the security effect of eliminating or mitigating those policies that most damage Muslim citizens' faith in the political system. It is possible that the marginal increase in vulnerability is microscopic if other more effective policies are left subtly in place.

Many governments have been relatively frank about their 'need' to profile potential terrorists in clandestine operations and in police officers' semi–random searches of individuals entering public transportation networks and other determined targets. However, given the publicity of such profiles (beards, backpacks, etc.), appearance is easily alterable. A side effect has been that many Muslims feel as if they are considered guilty until proven innocent—default suspects. Recently, there was a row in the United Kingdom over whether, in order to randomize properly and provide 'racial balance' to such searches, white non-Muslim individuals should also be questioned by police. A government report cited cases where people were stopped by officers 'even though there was no evidence or suspicion against them'.[15] The report said that police were carrying out 'self-evidently unmerited searches' which were an invasion of civil liberties and 'almost certainly unlawful'. However, the question is whether it becomes self-evidently merited to search an individual simply because he or she appears to be a Muslim? Indeed, wouldn't such randomness make it that much harder for a criminal to hide?[16]

Second, mosques remain most Muslims' primary source of religious authority and fellowship. While this role may make them susceptible to influences spreading political violence and anti–democratic ideas, it also means that mosques have the most frequent and powerful opportunities to preach authentic Islam, connect faith to wider society, and persuade congregants to be active democratic citizens. It is therefore imperative that governments protect mosques' place as havens for the Muslim community and liaisons to sociopolitical relationships. They must be wary to maintain bonds of trust between congregants and their mosque administrators, and between mosque administrators and the civic sphere of governance and associationalism. These are crucial bonds of accountability, familiarity and reciprocity that the governments of neither the United Kingdom nor Spain have available to them. In the East End, many young people interviewed felt uncomfortable and unwelcome in mosques, and found that they were often one-dimensional spaces for ritual, rather than communal engagement. Furthermore, British Muslim leaders face a seemingly zero-sum relationship between sustaining their constituents' confidence and working with the British government. In Madrid, mosques were described as 'garages'—makeshift prayer rooms with few facilities at all. Interviews suggested that Spanish Moroccans were quite atomized anyway and unreachable by a distanced state. Juxtaposed to circumstances in the United States, Americans have an extraordinary opportunity to ensure that mosques and Muslim leaders act as the government's educational and civic partners.

Bolstering the capacity and public integration of local mosques will provide the government with non-clandestine oversight and empower mosques as sources of Islamic social authority. As this book has emphasized, Islam is interpreted in innumerable ways (like most faiths), its followers are remarkably heterogeneous, and its tenets have been indistinguishably intermingled with the norms of different cultural traditions. While this makes the creation of a representative, centralized religious authority (in different states) a complicated and thorny task, Muslim communities in all democracies must realize that it is more in their interest to make the necessary compromises and achieve some consolidation than it is in the state's interest to facilitate it. (Indeed, relations between European governments and Muslim communities have deteriorated to the point that the state's involvement is often undesirable anyway.) Doing so would not only institutionalize a 'seat at the table' for consultation by the government. It would also help legitimately clarify the practicable answers to certain key Islamic questions that perplex Muslim youths and their application of their faith in quotidian life.

In Madrid, the Islamic Commission of Spain (CIE) serves as such a 'seat at the table'. However, for the reasons described in Chapter Five, the Moroccan community is essentially excluded. Furthermore, the CIE holds no authority as a religious body. In the United Kingdom, there are a multitude of national Muslim organizations, each of which claims its purported political representativeness baselessly.[17] Frustrated, British policy-makers have changed dialogue partners with great frequency, until finally in late 2007 the government facilitated the creation of MINAB (Mosques and Imams National Advisory Board) to oversee and regulate Muslim religious entities and attempt to unify the different Muslim communities of Britain.[18] Necessitating the cooperation of a disparate set of competing groups with competing agendas, MINAB has been largely unsuccessful at persuading Muslim communities that the Board is not just another instrument of government surveillance and control. The capacity of European Muslim communities to settle petty disagreements and serve as representative bodies of religious and civic authority will significantly determine their future capacity to influence state policy and hold power in the public sphere.

As demonstrated in the East End, the risk is that the gaping void of social authority is filled by an unqualified leader. It is little coincidence that the two groups who appear to be the most effective at motivating the activism of young Muslims in London and Madrid are adept at relating religious teachings to real world challenges. *Hizb-Ut-Tahrir* in the East End and ONDA in Spain galvanize young Muslims' interest in socio-political affairs by connecting professed Islamic teaching with their practical application. This application ranges from coping with family dilemmas to public policy. Even though ONDA promotes Moroccans' integration in Spain and HT seeks to undermine British democracy, their tactics are the same and are transferable to other civic endeavors. They each effectively fill the void of Muslim social authority and confront the difficult questions that many mosques avoid or are otherwise not trusted to address. While the creation of ONDA-template groups is an option for governments and Muslim communities, mosques exist as institutionalized alternatives that can function in a similarly constructive capacity.

Adapting to Modernity

Addressing Alienation

In contributing the new typologies of passive and active anti–system behavior and apartism, this study renders a new way to conceive the spectrum of political behavior more generally that, by considering individual perceptions, recognizes the fluidity of political capital. As Chapter Six demonstrates, in many ways, active democrats who invest in the political system are not all that different from active anti–system individuals who undermine or disrupt it. They share a competent understanding of the democracy, a sensitive awareness of social discourse, and faith that their individual actions can exert an impact on the public sphere and political process. These two groups diverge according to individuals' choice to locate their activism within the designated institutions and means of dissent that reinforce the system, or outside the system in ways that circumvent or disrupt it. The findings of this study show that the flow of political capital one way or another is heavily influenced by the nature of individual perceptions about the political system's capacity for genuine reform and its ultimate concern for individuals' welfare.

For this reason, it is imperative that governments and agencies of the state endeavour to cultivate and harvest the bounty of political capital in their societies. Governments must recognize that the democratic system is in a struggle to demonstrate its enduring value as a source of civic fellowship and its expedience compared to other systems of collective organization. They must continue their efforts to instill democratic norms and create an awareness of those benefits which make the democratic system practical. Individuals must therefore be persuaded to feel significant, cared for, and heard. If left on the vine, individuals' capacity for participation and action will either decay or be plucked by those promoting an adversarial relationship with the state and local society. This study has underscored the importance of new means of communication that empower young Muslims' self-expression and self-definition. While many of these modes have been employed as a ballast to the formal power of state institutions, the government can easily acknowledge the virtue of weblogs, video conferencing, online petitions, text message mobilization and campaigning websites that compete for space in the public sphere, and also fashion their own channels of new communication that exploit these tools of participation.

Assimilation is Contingent

In embracing such tools, governments would merely be catching up with individuals' near ubiquitous employment of these instruments to sustain connections with alternative cultures, norms and behaviors. And perhaps this will finally make governments realize that it is increasingly fanciful to expect migrants and other minorities to fully assimilate to the native identity—particularly with any alacrity. To put it plainly, contemporary citizens are less subject to the constraints of the state than in the past. While assimilation is necessary in terms of people's adherence to laws and their respect for legally mandated rights, identity assimilation is not crucial to migrants' effective functioning in their destination society anyway. And indeed, other forms of assimilation (e.g. to business culture, accepted social behavior, tastes and preferences) are aided by market incentives and unlegislated social conditioning. Assimilation policies are increasingly unlikely to be effective, and more likely to offend or galvanize backlash toward the very identity the democratic government might like to instill. In Madrid, many individuals interviewed expressed a desire ultimately to 'return' to Morocco, even though they had only visited the country of their family's origin a couple of times—if at all. This is certainly somewhat related to the rigid concept of Spanishness maintained by the Spanish public sphere. Indeed, it is not necessarily clear that Spaniards even wish to instill Spanish norms and behaviors in Moroccan minorities—not out of tolerance, but out of disqualification.

This challenges democratic governments to foster the bonds of civic fellowship on the basis of something other than shared identity or ethno-cultural lineage. I identify two legitimate and practical sources of cross-cutting fellowship. The first source comes from citizens' mutual benefit from the success of their society. Societies are partnerships that require shared duties and sacrifices (not shared values)—such as jury duty, voting, and payments to the welfare state—which provide all citizens with certain social safety nets and a variety of public goods (education, healthcare, transportation infrastructure, bank deposit insurance, etc.). As Durkheim emphasized, the interdependency of this partnership promotes a certain normative agreement. Of course, Durkheim believed such interdependency to be ultimately insufficient. A second source of fellowship, however, derives from agreement on the basic rights and liberties the democratic system affords. Particularly in the British case study, it is clear that governments continue to have success instilling citizens' expectation of (or sense of entitlement to) these rights and liberties (and thus an awareness of the corresponding sacrifices). It is then left to the state actually to deliver them, and to migrants to fulfill their obligations.

The Role of the Citizen

Adaptation is not a one-way street. As democracies diversify and expand, the market and new technologies simultaneously condition individuals to demand greater personal accommodation—by goods, services, and also governance. This creates an ever-changing proliferation of self-entitlement that is unmanageable by governments. Citizens must learn to temper their expectations of governance and recognize the individual sacrifice that political fellowship entails. Disagreement, offense and losing are all part of democratic life, and should not be easily construed as indicative of a political system without regard for justice, equality and liberty. It is little surprise that levels of political alienation seem to be rising with perceptions of self-entitlement. Democracies must comfortably concede their imperfection, and citizens must recognize (and be invited to realize) their individual role in the process of reform. This should not be a hard sell.

Implications for Future Research

Populations of Muslims from a variety of Asian and African countries, cultures and sects are growing across Europe today. Turks in Germany, Iraqis in Sweden, Moroccans in Holland, Algerians in France, Pakistanis in Britain, Tunisians in Italy—the phenomenon of Muslim individuals' political alienation is transcendent across a vast number of cases, communities and circumstances. This development exhibits the salience of this issue, but also the difficulty of making broad generalizations. Of course, this was never my objective. Across previous case studies and surveys of Muslims in Europe, scholars have been challenged to address the phenomena they observe without the precise conceptual vocabulary and modeling to characterize the disaffection they document beyond its empirical description. My research offers a typology and framework of understanding to aid future investigations and commentary. Indeed, to pursue a more profound, personal understanding of European Muslims, the study's methods facilitated more specific examination of individuals and their changing relationship with the state. It was hoped that the resulting characterizations will enable other researchers and observers to typify political behaviors and understand their roots and contexts.

In particular, a future step would be to pursue a better understanding about how the discussed perceptions are formed, and whether different individuals share similar experiences or social, economic or political conditions. This study was not positioned to determine which life experiences, conditions or personal characteristics were correlated with which tints of perception. However, this certainly appears to be a most promising direction for future quantitative investigation. As it is derived from two specific cases, this study also cannot claim to be substantiated in all other venues or among all other Muslim minorities around Europe. For this reason, it is my hope that this study will equip future attempts to understand political behavior among different minorities of European Muslims and other communities with a high or low incidence of alienation. I also hope that the typologies and arguments generated by this investigation lend themselves to quantitative research that measures the extent of the trends identified and tests for causation on a wider scale.

Principal Debates

Despite this study's limitations in scope, the findings and their implications described above nevertheless change the way we consider the principal debates underlying the experiences of Muslim communities and their place in European democracies today.

(How) Are Muslims intrinsically different from other minority groups in Europe?

In every historical era, societies have found new reasons to believe foreigners were 'different' from the previous group of newcomers. Today's 'exceptional' dilemmas are hardly different. Controversies have erupted across Europe over Muslim apparel, religious instruction in state schools, accommodation for prayers, legal structures for divorce, family conflict and finance, construction permits for mosques, the observation of religious holidays, the provision of *halal* food, and animal rights pertaining to ritual slaughter. A new community has thus expressed a new set of needs, and many observers doubt society's capacity to adapt—even though the hallmarks of Europe's history of accommodating earlier migrants endure. Returning to the London case study, we see a city that has absorbed generations of Francophone Huguenots, Irish Catholics, Eastern European Jews, Afro-Caribbean blacks over the past five centuries. Today, in London, a potpourri of French phrases is interwoven into English figurative language; Catholic churches ring bells to announce the time or events; British Airways offers kosher in-flight meals; and the London transport system makes alternative arrangements to accommodate the Notting Hill Caribbean carnival each August. Communities whose foreignness were once considered to be too different have therefore not only adapted to the standards of their new societies; the societies have adapted to them as well.

The attributes which make European Muslims truly different are not intrinsic at all. They comprise an ethnic, cultural, religious and, in some cases, an ideological minority, like many of their predecessors. And like earlier occupants of London's East End and Madrid's southern *barrios*, they face casual and formal discrimination, inflammatory discourse, and selective government policy enforcement.[19] However, this study contends that unlike earlier generations of migrants, today's European Muslims possess the capacity to resist assimilationist policies, express individual dissent with greater ease and amplification, and connect with what were previously only imaginary communities. These new means have enabled Muslim individuals and collectives to convene transnational movements and spark individual resistance very much in line with the actions of earlier generations, but with greater extensity and immediacy. The 1936 Battle of Cable Street in London's East End, which pitted police-protected fascists against Irish and Jewish anti-fascists and communists, attracted anti-fascists' support with paper leaflets reading: 'Against fascism... the enemy of the people abroad and at home.' This slogan could only hope to attract local backing and garner local attention. But their modern-day counterparts have the advantage of websites, satellite television and mobile phones—not to mention more powerful weapons. This is exceptional.

Today's Muslim demonstrations not only link arms with their non-Muslim migrant predecessors; they also stretch the threads woven through a broader tapestry of youth movements in the West. Often emerging from the suburbs, these anti-establishment sub-cultures are inspired by hip hop, not just Quranic hymns. They feature bandanas, not only *hijabs*. Renegades rebel against the social exclusion of youth, the irresponsibility of parents, and the ignorance of a disconnected government—all of which has very little to do with Islam, yet sustains extraordinary appeal amongst today's European-born or European-raised Muslims. Indeed, as this study exhibits, the young Muslims examined are undergoing rather pedestrian identity crises, as they attempt to negotiate their traditional ethnic roots, their contested European nationality, and their polemicized religion. Like the children of non-Muslims, their orientation in the West is driving a wedge between them and their traditionalist parents. The politicization of their communities is inspiring activism that goes unacknowledged. And most perplexingly, this otherwise private struggle to understand themselves and their place in European society has been rendered unsolicited public relevance by processes, discourses and events beyond their personal control. These external factors and young Muslims' capacity for bold, public and occasionally volatile reactions are fuelling the erroneous perception that, this time, this newest group of migrants really is more different than the last. Yet again.

In response to migrants' new capacity to resist and express themselves, states like Spain and the United Kingdom are combating this reclamation by reconstructing a national identity of their own.[20] Behind government regalia, maladroitly sculpted images of history and tradition attempt to authenticate an immaculate and unwavering national character that can compete directly with the amplified expressions of difference in the domestic public sphere. Such demonstrations fly in the face of the European Union's attempt to harmonize the differences between state components. They also defy the nationalities' ability to absorb difference and progress as they did after the arrival of previous waves of migrants. No European democracy possesses a distilled identity or a history cleansed of external influence, and so current attempts to sterilize current multicultural compositions with references to finite *hispanidad* and a value-oriented Britishness also contradict these countries' earlier adaptations—the very adaptations that have enabled such identities to carry on in this modern era.

Contrary to the cries of nationalists, the alternative to assimilation is not social division or the dilution of a unified national identity. It is hybridity, and it has (perhaps subconsciously) defined the formation of national identities for centuries. Today's identities are hybrids of earlier constructions, as the exposure to new technology, diversity and innovations of each era bring change to what was once considered to be the unwavering status quo. It is because of this adaptability that the myths, traditions and images which nationalists hold dear

227

persist as popular anachronisms. Those that remain rigid in the face of an evolving environment risk losing adherents as such identity constructions grow irrelevant. Darwinistically then, adaptation appears to be the key to identity forms' endurance.

What is the role of Islam in shaping European Muslims' reconstructed identities?

This study demonstrates that European Muslims' embrace and employment of their revitalized Islamic identity are not characterized by the coordination suggested by authors like Gilles Kepel and Tariq Ramadan. Instead, the reformation and revival of Islam are a product of very local circumstances and very personal decision-making. After one or two generations of immersion in Europe, the activists behind such a movement are no longer mere 'foreigners,' divorced from their countries of origin as much as they are divorced from their country of settlement. Indeed, European Muslims are Danish, Dutch, British, French, Swedish and Spanish. In many cases, they are also Parisian, Catalan and Scottish. So their relationship with Islam is as affected by their relationship with their European culture and society as their grandparents' relationship with Islam was conditioned by their relationship with the culture and society of Bangladesh, Iran, Turkey, Egypt, Algeria or Morocco.

This study finds that the European Muslims examined have indeed reconstructed Islamic identities that are somewhat disconnected to previous ethnic or national ties. However, the reformed Islam that is so widely referenced is reclaimed and interpreted according to localized needs, and then expressed in terms that are intelligible to local countrymen—often in direct response to events and encounters experienced both personally and collectively. In fact, European Islam may have been deterritorialized from its original societies, but it has re-embedded itself in its new societies. This is what makes it ill-equipped for any functional global organization, as there are literally no universally acknowledged social, cultural or political coordinates that might otherwise synchronize such a movement. Instead, there is a scramble of organizations and individuals competing for such recognition—only to be unsatisfactorily representative of a group of diversely integrated constituents.

In the securitized environment of the post-9/11 era in Europe, Muslims are repeatedly provoked to redefine a maligned identity in the light of its purported difference from 'the West'. For many individuals in the Muslim communities examined, this process of identity formation does not necessarily require a religious foundation of any kind, so long as it accommodates local cultural understandings, satisfies government frameworks, or addresses their personal challenges. As Olivier Roy notes, 'We are witnessing an Endeavour by many Muslim community leaders in the West, as well as reformist theologians, to express the difference between Islam and the West in terms compatible with and/or acceptable by the other (a Western non-Muslim)...which by definition insists on the legitimacy of recognizing differences. But it contradicts the very definition of Islam as a universal true religion.'[21]

In this way, the so-called embrace of Islam in many ways represents Muslims' counter-solidarity to their local vilification and alienation. Unattracted to many of the traditions of their family's homeland and contested citizens of their European societies, Islam (as a faith or as a cultural identity structure) renders European-born and European-raised Muslims a source of strength and recognition. In practice though, these multi–layered ethnic and cultural histories are never really cast aside in favor of one dimension. Instead, they intermingle and produce newly constructed matrices of identification that are unique for each individual and relevant to his or her personal environment.

What is the impact of different regimes on Muslims' choice to engage in the public sphere?

From this chapter's discussion of findings and their implications, we see that current social policies and counter-terrorism agendas in the two European states examined tend to be constructed without recognizing that Muslim citizens form and will continue to form an enduring segment of their population. They are constructed without regard for citizens' perceptions, which pivotally influence the nature of their political behavior. Rather than acknowledge the centrality of individual impressions and the ultimate alteration of their society's composition, many of these policies are clinging to maintain an erroneously pristine national culture and identity or acting in ways that marginalize Muslim individuals from the societal mainstream. For their part, many Muslim individuals are independently reclaiming their Islamic identity—the aspect of their self-definition which is troubling for their countrymen to reconcile, and around which it is difficult for Muslim communities to organize coherently. While individuals are increasingly able to express their ideas and organize in the public sphere, the interpretative diversity of Islam is creating a dissonance that hinders national-level cooperation and claims-making.

Many commentators, including those evaluating the efficacy of different integration regimes, are seeking a group or policy to blame. However, it is clear that the preponderance of alienation in separate European Muslim communities is a product of various factors and actors. Just as it is the duty of governments to show regard for the welfare of different constituencies and facilitate equal opportunity to succeed, it is also the responsibility of Muslim individuals to fulfill the conditions of their membership and adapt as necessary in order to receive the benefit of state protections. However, states are increasingly subject to a set of transnational standards that ensure these protections, and individuals are increasingly able to straddle the line between pursuing their personal will and submitting to the determinations of their representative bodies. Citizens appear to feel entitled to the same societal benefits and protections without making the same sacrifices that earlier generations made in earlier eras.

As institutions that are tasked to be responsive to the changing attitudes and composition of their societies, democratic governments are supposed to be flexible, adaptive organizations. This is what separates them from the indifferent rigidity of autocratic and authoritarian regimes. However, democratic political systems (perhaps following the cue of some nationalist groups) are dragging their feet while their societies continue to evolve. Attempts to reassert a monopoly in the public sphere of different European countries represent a dilemma cross-nationally. While counter-arguments cite citizens' enduring responsibility to adapt, the instruments of governance that might facilitate this assimilation restrict individual liberties and rights in ways that are antithetical to democratic systems. Indeed, with societies diversifying so rapidly—even among what are often considered to be monolithic 'white' communities—it is increasingly unclear to which standard citizens should be adapting.

As this study finds, Islam in Europe is indeed detached from its cultural foundations in the Muslim world. However, it does not exist in Europe as a deterritorialized faith, filtered of cultural impurities. It is reattaching itself to the cultural coordinates—and standards—of Muslims' new local societies. These new environments create the context-specific needs that religion is called upon to meet, the cultural preferences that religion is asked to respect, and the specific personal challenges that religion helps individuals to overcome. Independent of its universal scope, religion has always, everywhere been interpreted to meet local challenges and fit local standards. From the perspective of integration in Europe, this is the most promising development of all.

In this way, this study's conclusions render some hope: integration and a sense of entitlement to state protections is fomenting alienation among disappointed individuals who feel as if they are subjected to double standards and an adversarial political system that is denying them their afforded rights. Islam in Europe is better described as European Islam, or more accurately British Islam and Spanish Islam, as it is interpreted to address local circumstances and needs. The 'identity crises' reported are the product of young people who identify with their country of residence, but feel rejected because they also identify with a different religion or 'civilization' too. Those who are acting to undermine national political systems do so because they feel that conventional channels are closed to them or are ineffective. Put simply, after a substantial amount of time in Europe, many of the Muslim individuals examined feel European or want to be treated as such. For the betterment of their democracies and the greater cohesion of their societies, European states—in partnership with the growing community of European Muslims—still have an extraordinary opportunity to make this happen.

APPENDIX

NOTE ON METHODS

Design

Based on the research in this volume, the working hypothesis was that individual actors' habits of political participation (as explained below) is based to some extent on the way in which they perceive the political system and its inherent disadvantages as experienced by the actor. In other words, the spectrum of individual Muslim engagement patterns within a common socio-political environment is associated with their diverse interpretations of that common socio-political environment. As described in Chapter Three, this hypothesis places a high value on individuals' expectations of their political system, and their impressions of how well such standards are fulfilled. I anticipate that those individuals with greater discrepancies between their expectations and their perception of fulfillment will be more likely to exhibit active anti–system behavior. Meanwhile, those individuals with smaller discrepancies will be more likely to demonstrate engagement with, or at least complacent support for, the political system. And those individuals with very base expectations of the political system will withdraw from it, on the logic that the individual actor will neither disrupt nor engage a political system he expects nothing from in the first place.

I test this hypothesis with a research design based on the framework proposed by David Collier, Henry Brady and Jason Seawright for evaluating necessary and sufficient conditions in qualitative research.[1] In response to Gary King, Robert Keohane and Sidney Verba's probabilistic concept of causation, Collier et al. support a more deterministic approach. Collier et al. explain that 'deterministic causation' refers to models of necessary and/or sufficient causation. The design they propose rules out necessary and/or sufficient causation by utilizing a design concerned with observation, rather than frequency or proportion. If a single case deviates from the hypothesized causal pattern, this finding casts doubt on the hypothesis—rendering a single variable a distinctive causal impact.[2]

This is demonstrated in Figure Thirteen, which separates the individuals interviewed according to their political behavior, their expectations of the political system, and their perceived levels of attainment. The dependent variable in Figure Thirteen is political behavior. In this study, I classify political behavior in four ways and coded respondents accordingly (see Chapter 2). The first category is composed of those individuals who participate in the political system through its democratic institutions and channels. These individuals may vote; be a member of a political party; be a member of a commune, union or cooperative; act as part of an advocacy group or an NGO; engage in non-violent protest or strikes; correspond with an elected official; attend civic meetings; serve or run for political office; volunteer in their community; or participate in social capital-building activities or others that reproduce or reinforce the democratic system. The second category is composed of those who currently (at the time of the interview) engaged in any activity that intended to undermine, disrupt or overthrow the democratic system. This might entail membership in an exclusivist or revolutionary organization, participation in violence for political purposes, or activity that persuades others to defect from activism in the democracy. Any respondent that acknowledged their engagement in such activity were placed in the second category, even if they also participated in political activity within democratic system. This was done because this study is concerned with those who circumvent the political system. It is to be expected that such activists initially (and perhaps continuously) try to affect change within the system, before or while they attempt to affect change by circumventing the system. However, the choice to do so classifies them as 'anti–system' because their violence, exclusivism or disruptiveness indicates their lack of faith in the democratic system to facilitate such political change. The third category is composed of those individuals who do not participate in the democratic political system in any way because, they say, they are satisfied with the system and see no reason to be active. These individuals may also define their inactivity in terms of complacency or laziness, but otherwise do not frame their non-participation as the result of a dysfunctional political system. Indeed, these individuals express their willingness to participate if the need arises. The fourth category is composed of those individuals who do not participate in the democratic political system and do not intend to do so. Their non-participation is framed as a withdrawal from a political system that is ineffective or disinterested in their views. These modeled categories were constructed to be mutually exclusive to facilitate the deterministic research design employed.

In Figure Thirteen, the observable implications pertain to interviewees' expectations of the political system and their perceived levels of attainment. Study participants were asked what they expect from the government or democracy. As this question was left open-ended, responses ranged from grand monologues about ideals of liberty and justice to specific statements about local needs to absolutely nothing. Responses which referred to the government or democracy as a paragon of equality, fairness and freedom were deemed to reflect high expectations, along with those which specified public services that were beyond the reasonable capacity of political systems (e.g. to stop drunkenness, to prevent a pub from opening next door, to ensure equal treatment of Muslims by people in the streets, to enact shariah law). Those who said they expected very little or nothing were deemed to hold low expectations. And those who expected certain provisions that were more specific in nature or expressed their demands in less ideal terms were deemed to hold expectations of a moderate level. Most relevant to this study's hypothesis, this question was followed by one that inquired about how closely such expectations were met—the discrepancy. Any response that suggested that a good portion of their expectations were satisfied (e.g. 'mostly', 'some', 'pretty much', 'mixed', 'half') were deemed to perceive relatively congruent levels of attainment, and therefore exhibit a small discrepancy. Responses indicating that 'few', 'a couple' or 'none' of their expectations were met were deemed to perceive low levels of attainment, and therefore exhibit a 'large' discrepancy.

In order for someone to be actively anti–system, my research suggests that it is necessary that he or she perceive a large discrepancy between their expectations of the political system and its actual functioning. However, a large discrepancy is not sufficient to determine that someone is actively anti–system. Similarly, in order for someone to be passively anti–system, it is necessary that he or she maintain very low expectations of the political system. However, such low expectations are not sufficient to determine that someone is actively anti–system. (Chapter six evaluates these proposed causal factors in relation to observed behavior, albeit without Figure Thirteen.) In Figure Thirteen, the cases providing the test for a necessary relationship are those in which the outcome actually occurs (A and B in Figure Thirteen), while those which provide the test for sufficient correlation are those in which the hypothesized cause occurs (A and C).[3] The same framework tests alternative hypotheses. From Figure Thirteen, we can see that participant responses suggest that there may be a necessary relationship between individual actors' expectation-attainment discrepancy (or their very low expectations) and their choices of political engagement.

Dependent Variable:	A)	B)
Active Anti-System Behavior	6 Cases Observed (10%, and positive)	No Cases Observed (0%, and negative)
	C)	D)
Democratic Engagement	3 Cases Observed (3.3%, and positive)	33 Cases Observed (55%, and positive)
Observable Implications:	Large Discrepancy Between Expectations and Perceived Attainment	Congruence Between Expectations and Perceived Attainment

Dependent Variable:	A)	B)
Passive Anti-Sytem Behaviour	12 Cases Observed (20%, and positive)	No Cases Observed (0%, and negative)
	C)	D)
Democratic Engagement	5 Cases Observed (8.3%, and positive)	33 Cases Observed (55%, and positive)
Observable Implications:	Low Expectations of Political System	Congruence Between Expectations and Perceived Attainment

Note: There were sixty total interviews of target subjects. Two respondents (3.3 per cent) exhibited passive anti-system behavior and a large expectation-attainment discrepancy (uncharted).

Figure Thirteen: Testing for Necessary and Sufficient Relationships. Research designs of my two primary hypothesized causal factors—1) discrepancy between high expectations of the political system and low attainment, 2) low expectations of the political system. These frameworks are based on the work of Collier, Brady and Seawright.

To solicit these expectations and further perceptions, interviewees were asked questions such as: 'What is your government and society interested in?' 'Do you believe that your government and society are interested in your welfare, and the welfare of people like you?' 'What changes do you want to see in your neighborhood or society?' 'Do you believe your society can change?' 'Can you and other people like you affect your society to create the changes you desire?' 'What do you owe your government and society?' 'What does your government and society owe you?' 'Does your government and society hold up its end of the bargain?' 'Do you feel indebted to your government or society?' 'Does your government or society hold the same basic values you do?' Subjects were subsequently asked to explain their answers.

As this research is interested in distinguishing the structures of civic engagement and developing a typology of behavior and perceptions among the subjects, a small-n case study was deemed to be most pragmatic. While I would embrace the need for research that addresses questions of frequency, correlation and probability on a larger scale, I identify a distinct deficiency of useful qualitative distinctions that characterize the nature of engagement and disengagement—particularly among young Muslims in Western democracies. For this reason, a small-n approach enabled the intensive observation necessary to construct the accurate typologies and characterizations that will inform future quantitative and qualitative endeavors. To operationalize the causal factors[4], this study uses in-depth case study interviews conducted by the author. The study's subject matter targets a homogeneous sample of individuals with respect to factors including gender, age range, religion, ethnicity, migrant generation, class, and neighborhood of residence so that variation across these factors do not have the potential to explain the observed variation in political participation.

Case Selection

To encounter actors in relevant socio-political environments, this research required two cases that share a) the same systems of government, and b) a significant Muslim minority group in a comparable social position. As this research is interested in examining comparative cases, the selected population groups in their locality exhibited variable political behavior.

Given the remarkable diversity of Muslim groups in Western democracies today, it is difficult to find a sizeable community in one country that occupies similar social and demographic strata in another country. In other Muslim communities elsewhere in the West, the Muslim minority was not sufficiently large, concentrated, homogeneous or rooted enough to examine and compare reliably. For example, Moroccans do not occupy the same space in the British political sphere as they do in Spain. And indeed, Bangladeshis are hardly even known in Spain, let alone in the Spanish political sphere. It is therefore important to acknowledge the similarities that validate this case selection, and differences that must be considered.

The similarities between the governments and societies of Britain and Spain are substantial. Both countries are parliamentary monarchies (though the UK is often called a constitutional monarchy), their GDP per capita is nearly identical (it is $35,200 in the UK and $33,700 in Spain as of 2009), and they have similarly aged (15 to 65 represent 67 per cent of each population), similarly urban (77 per cent in Spain and 90 per cent in the UK), and similarly indigenous (85 per cent of the UK population are of 'British ethnicity' and 88 per cent of Spain's population are of 'Spanish ethnicity') populations.[5] Both countries also feature:

1) Culturally specific ethno-religious minorities, with sufficiently large populations for empirically significant results—specifically a Muslim minority that is concentrated and homogeneous in most social strata categories.[6]

2) A liberal democratic government that has undergone the devolution of several territories within the nation-state, and mandates (in principle) equal protection—despite discourse surrounding a historic, national identity that is purportedly under threat.[7]

3) Large cities which have recently experienced a significant terrorist attack carried out by 'home-grown' Islamist terrorists, and the corresponding securitization.[8]

4) Immigration policies that have opened national borders for economic reasons particularly to former colonial subjects, and commonly grants citizenship to migrants within a single generation.[9]

5) National social policies grappling with the merits of a more inclusive multiculturalist outlook that embraces difference and an outlook of secularist assimilation (or ethnic segregation).

In addition, since the aforementioned terrorist attacks on Madrid's Atocha train station (11 March 2004) and the London transport system (7 July 2005), Moroccans in Spain and Bangladeshis (along with other South Asian Muslim groups) in Britain have been increasingly scrutinized as the subjects of police investigations and anti–extremist policies in both countries. This targeted status and social position is very much shared by both groups, in a way that few other groups can understand in European democracies. Indeed, Muslim minorities in other countries understand exclusion and suspicion, but their societies have not endured an experience with violent extremism at the hands of isolated members of these prominent European Muslim groups.

Several variables exist and must be acknowledged as potential reasons for varying levels of political participation between cases. First, Muslim minorities in Spain and Britain come from places with very different political, religious, cultural, social and civic traditions and histories. (Chapters Four and Five) Second, each host country has a distinct history with immigration and with the countries from which Muslim migrants come. Most Moroccans in Madrid have also been in Europe for slightly less time than their British Bangladeshi counterparts. Third, the local governments in Madrid and London (and their affiliated agencies) are structured differently, as described in the case study chapters. (Chapters Four and Five) I acknowledge these variables, keeping in mind that case studies are undertaken to explain differences in levels of political participation between comparable cases, and therefore conditional on any other factors that might also have an effect on political participation.

Subject Selection

Muslim populations in many Western democracies exhibit a remarkable degree of ethnic and sectarian heterogeneity. For example, Britain is composed of thousands of Pakistanis, Bangladeshis, Afghanis, Arabs, Somalis, Turks, Sunnis, Shias, Sufis, Ismailis, Barelwis, Wahhabis, etc. As a result, cross-national representative sampling was not feasible or desirable. Instead, I entered the field and interviewed about 100 total subjects whose responses varied substantially across the dependent variable.[10] As explained earlier, this research is interested in distinguishing the structures of political behavior and developing a typology of behavior and perceptions among the subjects before any measured frequency, correlation or probability can be attributed to the discovered trends. This is an exercise in producing useful qualitative distinctions that better equip social scientists and observers to comprehend the nature of engagement and disengagement among young Muslims in Western democracies, and perhaps one day be complimented by a greater, quantitative examination of one of Europe's most polemical and fastest growing constituencies. Instead, the local representativeness for which I strive is sufficient to encounter the spectrum of socio-political behavior—from democratic activism to complacency, from active to passive anti–system behavior—none of which fails to exist outside the selected cases.

Unit Homogeneity

One immediate challenge to constructing a research design was the common difficulty presented by the corpus-theoretical paradox.[11] I used pilot investigations and secondary source research to identify the range of outcome variation—the different forms of democratic and anti–system behavior. In both London's East End and Madrid Sur, the subject population was narrowly defined in order to 'hold constant' other potentially intervening factors or alternative explanations for the observed variation in political behavior. I then interviewed young (18–28 year-old), second-generation, migrant-origin, Moroccan or Bangladeshi, Muslim men living in the same regional neighborhood of a Western democracy. (Future studies would help provide a more complete understanding of Western Muslim communities if they expanded this sample to include the significant voices of women, the affluent, and people of other ethnicities.) The sample population is defined in the table below.

Young:	18–28 years old
Second-generation:	born in the Western country or has lived the majority of their life (perhaps with their parents) in the Western country
Migrant-origin:	parents or grandparents were not born in the Western country
Moroccan/Bangladeshi:	parents or grandparents were born in Morocco (in Spain) or Bangladesh (in Britain)
Muslim:	declared followers of Islam—no matter how fastidiously or properly
Western democracy:	respective country of residence is also that of the fieldwork, and is a state governed by a liberal democracy

In terms of socio-economic status, all Moroccans interviewed in Madrid Sur are labor migrants, who arrived in Spain poor and have taken up contracts in predominantly working-class professions. Many respondents were living off the welfare earned from their time employed. Similarly, the vast majority of Bangladeshis in the East End are working class, as many of those earning more money have moved to more suburban regions of London. Education levels are more variable, and I solicited opinions from subjects with a variety of educational qualifications. As no subject was over 28–years-old, high educational levels did not affect the lack of variation on socioeconomic status. In fact, nearly all of the most educated respondents (particularly the unmarried) still live with their parents in public housing estates. However, as Chapter Four discussed, British Bangladeshi interviewees engaged in active anti–system behavior tended to be disproportionately more educated. So known social strata were mostly controlled for, enabling me to examine the unknown representation variables that emerged after I selected preliminarily and analyzed the distribution.

Respondents who met the narrow selection criteria demonstrated a range of different political behavior across the four categories of the active democrat, the complacent, the actively anti–system, and the passively anti–system (See Chapter Two). To capture the diversity, I continued to interview subjects until I deemed there to be sufficient 'saturation'.[12] According to Bauer and Gaskell, saturation occurs when the addition of further demographic or social strata adds nothing new to the representational variety of the phenomenon studied—following the law of diminishing returns.

As all the subjects and topics were examined in the present (even if informed by experiences or influences from the past), the materials for the two case studies were synchronous (though not simultaneous) and considered in a continuous eight-month period in 2008—first in London, then Madrid. In both locations, subjects were examined using complementary in-depth interviews and observation. Even in youth clubs and mosques, attendees and officials were notified that I was present for the purpose of research and observation. Before each interview, participants were reminded of this and I explained that all statements would remain unattributed to them. All target subjects' names used in the study are aliases.

Interviews of Subjects

Though kept informal, subject interviews were quite focused, to solicit systematically explanatory answers that address the causal factors and their observable implications, outlined in Chapter Three. Interviews were structured according to a topic guide, built to discipline the collection of pertinent data required to make descriptive and correlative inferences. The structure of interviews was kept consistent across units, and across venues, to produce two congruent examinations. Repetition of questions was followed to ensure the reliability of the procedure.[13] That said, questions were asked in variable sequences and fashions, tailored to the respondent's interests, insecurities and capacities. This fostered the most outwardly casual approach, and permitted further inquiry about certain fruitful threads of discussion.

In London, I utilized youth clubs as a hub for social interaction among 18–28 year-old men. I attended clubs coordinated by the local council at Caxton Hall, the neighborhood's Young Muslims Organization's Ponler Street Youth Club, a local Christian church on Burdett Road, and the Islamist group *Hizb-Ut-Tahrir*'s at Toynbee Hall, John Knox Church and Ponler Street. Participants were interviewed at PFC and other 'chicken and chips' shops on Burdett Road, Mile End Road and Whitechapel Road, 'Ala Pizza' on Mile End Road, parks and corners in the Eric Estate and Berner Estate, the Skylight Cafe on Commercial Street, Altab Ali Park, Stepney Green, Mile End Park, London Muslim Centre cafe, the Dar Ul Ummah Mosque on Bigland Street in Shadwell, the Ishaatul Islam Mosque in Ford Square, the Mazahirul Uloom Mosque on Mile End Road, Queen Mary University, the Idea Store on Whitechapel Road, and the Mayberry Place council building.

In Madrid, there were few youth clubs, only those for young children before they reach adolescence. The opportunity to encounter qualified respondents was made even more difficult by the extraordinary lack of social cohesion within the Moroccan community and their noteworthy distrust of Moroccans and non-Moroccans alike. For this reason, subjects were sought in a variety of environments. I met participants on a local asphalt football and basketball pitch in a park along Embajadores Street, in front of an internet cafe on Calle del Mesón de Paredes, *al por mayor* shops on Calle Caravaca, the *carnecería* on Calle Tribulete, barber shops on Calle Sombrerete, and on the benches of Plaza Agustin Lara. I met other participants around prayer times at the M30 Mosque in the Carmen *barrio* and the Tetuán Mosque. Other subjects were encountered in public spaces in some of the working-class neighborhoods south and south-east of Lavapiés, like Villaverde, San Cristóbal, Rivas, Valdebernardo and Cañada Real. As nearly all subjects were uncomfortable even going to a *cafetería* to chat, most interviews—even some that continued longer than ninety minutes—were conducted on street corners, or public plazas and parks.

Data from both case studies were recorded by hand, in the interest of placing subjects at ease with regard to their anonymity in discussing what was otherwise very controversial subject matter. Interviewee responses regularly touched on racism, drugs, politics, sex, religion, money and family issues. It was feared that audio recorders would stimulate certain subconscious and conscious defense mechanisms, and mitigate subjects' candidness. In London, no interpreters were used except during interviews with imams who only spoke Bengali *Shudoh* or Arabic. In Madrid, a guide was occasionally used to maneuver through several of the peripheral regions of the southern *barrios* and interpret subjects with particularly dense Arabic accents.

In the case of Lavapiés, I lived in the neighborhood for the summer on Calle Amparo. Accurate observations were helped by integrating myself in local life. In the East End, this entailed 'cotching' on street corners and against the fences of council estates, playing ping-pong in youth clubs, sitting in on *jummah* (Friday prayers) at various neighborhood mosques, attending the *Boishakhi Mela* festival, and eating a lot of chicken and chips. In Lavapiés, this entailed playing basketball and football in the park, loitering in plazas, participating in *Eid* celebrations, attending *jummah* at various local mosques, visiting cultural centers, strolling through the Sunday *Rastro* street market and summer *feria*, befriending the local *halal* butcher, and drinking a lot of mint tea. I chose these locations because they represented a variety of Bangladeshi and Moroccan lifestyles in the East End and Lavapiés—that of the student, the unemployed, the gang member, the drug dealer, the religious, the employed and contracted, the businessman, the activist, the Islamist, etc.

Replication

The replication of this study is not as simple as with quantitative research, nor as straightforward as qualitative research focusing on targeted elites.[14] However, it is nevertheless reasonable to expect that a similarly structured study would encounter similar results. There are three principal impediments to precise replication. First, while the target group of subjects was selected systematically, individuals were often encountered randomly. Second, nearly all participants were ensured anonymity (non-attribution) due to the sensitive nature of the subject matter, and the extraordinary level of some individuals' distrust and suspicion. Only a few British youths accused me of working for the United States C.I.A. or Britain's MI5 or MI6 (the mere suggestion was remarkable considering my American accent). However, many Moroccans actively questioned me about my motives and relationship to either Spanish police, immigration authorities (occasionally even showing me their legal documents), or Moroccan secret police. Participants with such suspicions were not interviewed any further to protect against the inclusion of false responses said in the interest of avoiding self-incrimination. Anonymity was also granted to political and community leaders, to facilitate their free speech without concern for electoral or popular backlash after publication. It is difficult to imagine that participants' exceptional candidness could have been elicited without the assurance of such protection.

NOTES

1. INTRODUCTION: DEMOCRACY'S CHALLENGE

1. Open Society Institute, http://www.eumap.org/topics/minority/reports/eumuslims/index, EUMAP Programme, accessed 20 July 2009.
2. Don Melvin, 'Europe works to assimilate Muslims', *Atlanta Journal Constitution*, 17 December 2004.
3. Omer Taspinar, 'Europe's Muslim Street', Brookings Institution, March 2003.
4. Esther Pan, 'Europe: Integrating Islam', Council on Foreign Relations, 13 July 2005.
5. Tariq Modood, 'British Muslims and the politics of multiculturalism', in Tariq Modood et al., *Multiculturalism, Muslims and Citizenship* (Oxford: Routledge, 2006), pp. 41–2.
6. Associated Press, 'EU Sees Wide Discrimination Against Muslims', *The Guardian*, 28 May 2009.
7. Katrin Elger, Ansbert Kneip and Merlind Theile, 'Survey Shows Alarming Lack of Integration in Germany', *Der Spiegel*, 26 January 2009.
8. Thomas Hüetlin, 'Muslims in Britain: Feeling Foreign At Home', *Der Spiegel*, 14 August 2006.
9. Ibid.
10. Cahal Milmo, 'Muslims feel like "Jews of Europe"', *The Independent*, 4 July 2008.
11. Samuel P. Huntington, *The Clash of Civilizations and the Remaking of World Order* (New York: Simon and Schuster, 1996).
12. Gilles Kepel, *The War for Muslims' Minds: Islam and the West* (Cambridge, Massachusetts: Harvard University Press, 2004).
13. Tariq Ramadan, *Western Muslims and the Future of Islam* (New York: Oxford University Press, 2004), p. 225.
14. See Christian Joppke, 'Multiculturalism and Immigration: A Comparison of the United States, Germany and Great Britain', *Theory and Society*, 25 (1996), pp. 449–500; Christian Joppke, 'Asylum and State Sovereignty: A Comparison of the United States, Germany and Britain', *Comparative Political Studies*, 30:3 (1997), pp. 259–98; Philip Martin and James Hollifield (eds), *Controlling Im-

migration: A Global Perspective (Stanford: Stanford University Press, 1994); Gary P. Freeman, 'The consequence of immigration policies for immigrant status: a British and French comparison' in A. Messina, L. Fraga, L. Rhodebeck and F. Wright (eds), *Ethnic and Racial Minorities in Advanced Industrial Democracies* (New York: Greenwood Press, 1992); Gary P. Freeman, 'Modes of Immigration Politics in Liberal Democratic States', *International Migration Review*, 29, 4 (1995), pp. 881–902; Virginie Guiraudon, 'Citizenship rights for non-citizens: France, Germany and the Netherlands' in Christian Joppke (ed.), *Challenge to the Nation-State: Immigration in Western Europe and the United States* (Oxford: Oxford University Press, 1998); Will Kymlicka, *Politics in the Vernacular: Nationalism, Multiculturalism, Citizenship* (Oxford: Oxford University Press, 2001); Will Kymlicka, *Multicultural Citizenship: A Liberal Theory of Minority Rights* (Oxford: Oxford University Press, 1995); Will Kymlicka, *Contemporary Political Philosophy: An Introduction* (Oxford: Oxford University Press, 2001); Rainer Bauböck and John Rundell (eds), *Blurred Boundaries. Migration, Ethnicity, Citizenship* (Aldershot: Ashgate, 1998); Rainer Bauböck, Agnes Heller and Aristide Zolberg (eds), *The Challenge of Diversity. Integration and Pluralism in Societies of Immigration* (Aldershot: Avebury, 1996).

15. Sidney Tarrow, *Democracy and Disorder: Protest and Politics in Italy 1965–1975* (Oxford: Clarendon, 1989), p. 85. See Ruud Koopmans and Paul Statham, 'Migration and Ethnic Relations as a Field of Political Contention: An Opportunity Structure Approach' in Ruud Koopmans and Paul Statham (eds), *Challenging Immigration and Ethnic Relations Policy: Comparative European Perspectives* (Oxford: Oxford University Press, 2001).

16. Patrick Ireland, *The Policy Challenge of Ethnic Diversity: Immigrant Politics in France and Switzerland* (Cambridge: Harvard University Press, 1994).

17. A multitude of studies of extreme political behavior have generally only *referenced* institutionalist ideas, rather than comprehensively exploring a relationship systematically.

2. ALIENATION, ENGAGEMENT AND ANTI-SYSTEM BEHAVIOR

1. Daniel Bell, 'Sociodicy: A guide to modern usage', *American Scholar*, Autumn, 1966, 35, p. 699.

2. Ibid.

3. See John Schaar, *Escape from Authority* (New York: Basic Books, 1961).

4. Joachim Israel, *Alienation: From Marx to Modern Sociology* (Boston: Allyn and Bacon, 1971), p. 11 (original italics).

5. Jürgen Habermas, 'The Postnational Constellation and the Future of Democracy' in *The Postnational Constellation: Political Essays*, trans. ed. Max Pensky (Cambridge: MIT Press, 2001), p. 64. Walker Connor, 'A Nation is a Nation, is a State, is an Ethnic Group, is a...', *Ethnic and Racial Studies*, 1 (1978), p. 379.

6. David Held, *Global Transformations: Politics, Economics and Culture* (Cambridge: Polity Press, 1999), pp. 90–91 and John Brieully, *Nationalism and the State* (Manchester: Manchester University Press, 1982), p. 365.

7. See Montserrat Guibernau, 'National identity and modernity' in A. Dieckhoff and N. Gutiérrez (eds), *Modern Roots: Studies of National Identity* (Aldershot: Ashgate, 2001), pp. 73–94.

8. See discussion of this point in Habermas, 2001, p. 108.

9. See Steven Vertovec, 'Transnationalism and identity', *Journal of Ethnic and Migration Studies* 27, 4 (2001), pp. 573–82.

10. Arjun Appadurai, 'Sovereignty Without Territoriality: Notes for a Post-National Geography' in Patricia Yeager (ed.), *The Geography of Identity* (Ann Arbor: The University of Michigan Press, 1996), p. 57.

11. Ibid.

12. Ibid., pp. 48–9.

13. Ibid. See Montserrat Guibernau, 'Globalisation and the nation-state' in Montserrat Guibernau and John Hutchinson (eds), *Understanding Nationalism* (Cambridge: Polity Press, 2001), pp. 242–68.

14. See Charles Tilly, *Contention and Democracy in Europe, 1650–2000* (Cambridge: Cambridge University Press, 2004); Michael Mann, *The Sources of Social Power: Volume 2, The Rise of Classes and Nation States 1760–1914* (Cambridge: Cambridge University Press, 1993); Ernest Gellner, *Nations and Nationalism* (Ithaca: Cornell University Press, 1983); Michael Mann, *The Dark Side of Democracy: Explaining Ethnic Cleansing* (Cambridge: Cambridge University Press, 2005).

15. See Zygmunt Bauman, *Intimations of Postmodernity* (London: Routledge, 1992).

16. Stuart Hall, 'Ethnicity: Identity and Difference' in Geoff Eley and Ronald Grigor Suny (eds), *Becoming National* (Oxford: Oxford University Press, 1996a), p. 339.

17. Hall, 1996a, p. 347.

18. James Mayall, *Nationalism and International Society* (Cambridge: Cambridge University Press, 1990), p. 45.

19. See Montserrat Guibernau, *Nations Without States: Political Communities in a Global Age* (Cambridge: Polity Press, 1999), p. 177.

20. Sir Ivor Jennings, *The Approach to Self-Government* (Cambridge: Cambridge University Press, 1956), p. 56.

21. Brian Barry, 'Statism and Nationalism: A Cosmopolitan Critique' in I. Shapiro and L. Brilmayer (eds), *Global Justice: Nomos XLI* (New York: New York University Press, 1999). Also see Christopher Hobson, 'Beyond the End of History: The Need for a "Radical Historicisation" of Democracy in International Relations', *Millennium*, 37, 3 (2009), pp. 631–57.

22. Ibid.

23. David Jacobson, *Rights Across Borders* (London: Johns Hopkins, 1996), p. 4.

24. Stephen Castles, *Ethnicity and Globalization* (London: SAGE Publications, 2000), p. 191. Favell makes the point that we are faced with a question of Hobbesian vintage: 'How can a political system achieve stability and legitimacy by rebuilding communal bonds of civility and tolerance—a moral social order—across the conflicts and divisions caused by the plurality of values and individual interests?' [Adrian Favell, *Philosophies of Integration: Immigration and the Idea of Citizenship in France and Britain* (New York: Palgrave, 1998), p. 2.]

25. See John Locke *Second Treatise of Government*, ed. C.B. Macpherson (Indianapolis: Hackett, 1998) especially Sec. 95–8, pp. 52–3.
26. Locke, Sec. 96, p. 52.
27. See Stuart Hall, 'Cultural Identity and Diaspora' in Jonathan Rutherford (ed.), *Identity: Community, Culture, Difference* (London: Lawrence and Wishart, 1990), p. 222.
28. Arjun Appadurai, 'Disjuncture and Difference in the Global Cultural Economy' in David Held and Anthony McGrew (eds), *The Global Transformations Reader* (Malden, MA: Polity Press, 2000), p. 236.
29. Ibid.
30. Locke, Sec. 96, p. 52.
31. John Stuart Mill, 'On Liberty' in *Mill: The Spirit of the Age, On Liberty, The Subjugation of Women*, ed. Alan Ryan (New York: W.W. Norton and Company, 1997), p. 84. Similar fears of the tyranny of the majority were also expressed by Alexis de Tocqueville in *Democracy in America*, trans. and ed. Harvey C. Mansfield and Delba Winthrop (Chicago: University of Chicago Press, 2000).
32. Mill, p. 85.
33. Danielle Archibugi and David Held, 'Introduction' in Danielle Archibugi and David Held (eds), *Cosmopolitan Democracy: An Agenda for a New World Order* (Cambridge: Polity Press, 1999), p. 6, and Held, 1999, p. 101.
34. Soysal, 1996, p. 4.
35. Karl Marx, *Early Writings*, trans. T.B. Bottomore (London: C.A. Watts, 1963), p. 69.
36. Bertell Ollman, *Alienation: Marx's Conception of Man in Capitalist Society* (Cambridge: Cambridge University Press, 1971), pp. 131–2.
37. Anthony Giddens, *Capitalism and Modern Social Theory* (Cambridge: Cambridge University Press, 1971), p. 22.
38. Karl Marx, *The Holy Family* (or *Critique of Critical Critique*), trans. R. Dixon, (Moscow: Foreign Languages Publishing House, 1956), p. 157.
39. Karl Marx and Friedrich Engels, *Economic and Philosophical Manuscripts of 1844*, trans. Martin Milligan (Moscow: Foreign Languages Publishing House, 1959), p. 76.
40. Ibid ., p. 70.
41. Ibid., p. 70–71, and see Giddens, p. 30.
42. Karl Marx and Friedrich Engels, *Economic and Philosophical Manuscripts of 1844*, p. 79.
43. Giddens, p. 44.
44. Giddens, p. 41.
45. Giddens, p. 5.
46. See Ollman, pp. 217–18.
47. Annual Local Area Labour Force Survey 2001/02, Office for National Statistics, http://www.statistics.gov.uk/CCI/nugget.asp?ID=1089&Pos=2&ColRank=2 &Rank=768.
48. Sarah Touahri, 'Facing unemployment, Moroccans in Spain return home', *Maghrebia*, 6 August 2008, http://www.magharebia.com/cocoon/awi/xhtml1/en_GB/features/awi/features/2008/08/06/feature-02.

49. Giddens, p. 229.
50. Émile Durkheim, *The Division of Labour in Society*, trans. George Simpson, Free Press (London: Collier Macmillan, 1964), p. 44.
51. Ibid., p. 129.
52. Ibid., p. 179.
53. Ibid., p. 129.
54. Ibid., p. 267.
55. Émile Durkheim, *On Suicide: A Study in Sociology*, ed. George Simpson (London: Routledge & Kegan, 1952), p. 209.
56. Giddens, p. 102.
57. Clearly a variety of other normative groups, like Evangelical Christians, have also exploited the enhanced connectivity provided by global technologies. However, each successive example further demonstrates the point being made: there is a cacophony of normative communities competing for adherence in the public sphere.
58. Israel, p. 19.
59. See Robert Dahl, *Democracy and its Critics* (New Haven, CT: Yale University Press, 1989), pp. 16, 122.
60. Held, 2006, p. 125.
61. Ibid., pp. 131–2.
62. Ibid., p. 145.
63. Joseph Schumpeter, *Captialism, Socialism and Democracy* (London: Allen and Unwin, 1943), pp. 284–5.
64. Ibid., p. 269.
65. Ibid., p. 257.
66. Ibid.
67. Ibid., p. 251.
68. Dahl, pp. 120 and 129.
69. Schumpeter, pp. 254–6.
70. Henrietta Moore, 'The benefits of doubt' in London Design Council, *Touching the State* (London: London Design Council, 2005), p. 60.
71. Moore, p. 62.
72. Alexis de Tocqueville, *Democracy in America*, trans. and ed. Harvey C. Mansfield and Delba Winthrop (Chicago: University of Chicago Press, 2000).
73. L.J. Hanifan, 'The rural school community center', *Annals of the American Academy of Political and Social Science* 67 (1916), pp. 130–38.
74. Robert D. Putnam, (with Robert Leonardi and Raffaella Nannetti), *Making Democracy Work: Civic Traditions in Modern Italy* (Princeton, NJ: Princeton University Press, 1993), p. 173.
75. Robert D. Putnam, 'E Pluribus Unum: Diversity and Community in the Twenty-first Century', *Scandinavian Political Studies*, 30, 2 (2007).
76. More recent researchers like Seeman, Feuer, McDermott and Herberg choose to disregard such structural considerations, and instead operationalize the idea within a range of cognitive states and attitudes. See Melvin Seeman, 'On the meaning of alienation', *American Sociological Review*, 24 (1959), p. 786; L. Feuer, 'What is

alienation? The career of a concept'; I.M. Stein and A. Vidich (eds), *Sociology on Trial* (Englewood Cliffs, NJ: Prentice Hall, 1963); J. McDermott, 'Technology: The opiate of the intellectuals', *New York Review of Books*, 1969, XIII (31 July), pp. 25–35; and W. Herberg, 'Alienation, Dissent, and the Intellectual', *National Review*, July 30 (1968), pp. 738–9.

77. Olsen, Marvin E., 'Two Categories of Alienation', *Social Forces*, 47, 3 (1969), p. 291.

78. Also see Ferdinand Tönnies' concept of *Gemeinschaft*. It is often translated as 'community'; but its character is closer to that of a family. [See Ferdinand Tönnies, ed. Jose Harris, *Community and Civil Society* (Cambridge: Cambridge University Press, 2001).] *Gemeinschaften* are more engaged with the pursuits of the larger group than they are with their own. Unified by shared norms and values, this homogeneous association could be based on common land, faith or blood. *Gesellschaft* is often translated as 'civil society' or just 'society'. Heterogeneous *Gesellschaften* lack a set of common norms or values, and are more concerned with their own self-interest than they are loyal to the greater community. Derived from the division of labor, the incentives of the market galvanize the *Gesellschaften* to bond interdependently with his fellows but only for the sake of his personal self-fulfilment.

79. For a brief history of the idea of alienation, see Josephson, Eric and Mary Josephson, *Man Alone: Alienation in Modern Society* (New York: Dell, 1962) and also Bell, Daniel, 'The Rediscovery of Alienation: Some Notes Along the Quest for the Historical Marx', *Journal of Philosophy*, 56 (November 1959), pp. 933–952. Further works unmentioned in this section from this time period include McDill, Edward L. and Jeanne Ridley, 'Status, Anomia, Political Alienation, and Political Participation', *American Journal of Sociology*, 68 (September 1962), pp. 205–213; and Meier, Dorothia Meier and Wendell Bell, "Anomia and Differential Access to the Achievement of Life Goals," *American Sociological Review*, 24 (April 1959), pp. 189–202.

80. Nisbet, Robert A., *The Quest for Community* (New York: Oxford University Press, 1953), p. 15.

81. Seeman, Melvin, 'On the Meaning of Alienation', *American Sociological Review*, 24 (1959), pp. 783–791.

82. Zeller, Richard A., Arthur G. Neal, and H. Theodore Groat, 'On the Reliability and Stability of Alienation Measures: A Longitudinal Analysis', *Social Forces*, 58, 4 (1980).

83. Finifter, Ada W. 'Dimensions of Political Alienation', *American Political Science Review*, 64, 2 (1970), pp. 389–410.

84. Schwartz, David C., *Political Alienation and Political Behavior* (Chicago: Aldine, 1973), p. 3.

85. Johnson, Frank (ed.), *Alienation: Concept, Term and Meaning* (New York: Seminar Press, 1973).

86. The word 'panchreston,' however, is from Hardin, George, 'Meaninglessness of the word protoplasm', *Scientific Monthly*, 82 (1956), pp. 112–120.

87. Thompson, Wayne E. and John E. Horton, 'Political Alienation as a Force in Political Action', *Social Forces*, 38, 3 (1960), p. 193.

88. See Olsen, p. 291; and Zeller, et al., p. 1202.

89. Roberts, Bruce R. 'A confirmatory factor-analytic model of alienation,' *Social Psychology Quarterly*, 50, 4 (1987), pp. 346–351.

90. Muller, Edward N., Thomas O. Jukam, and Mitchell A. Seligson, 'Diffuse Political Support and Antisystem Political Behavior,' in *American Journal of Political Science*, 26, 2 (1982), pp. 240–264.

91. It is worth noting that, in defining 'anti–system' *political parties*, Capoccia makes a distinction between 'ideological anti–systemness' and 'relational anti–systemness'. He argues that 'ideological anti–systemness' regards a political party's opposition to the democratic system, while 'relational anti–systemness' regards the party's opposition to the values of the democratic system. This study is concerned with both forms of 'anti–systemness' as it is expressed in individual actors' behavior. See Giovanni. C. Capoccia, 'Anti–System Parties: A Conceptual Reassessment', *Journal of Theoretical Politics*, 14 (2002), pp. 9–35.

92. This diagram is partially based on one created by Stephen Koff. See Stephen Koff, 'The Political Use of the Concept of Alienation' in Frank Johnson (ed.), *Alienation: Concept, Term and Meaning* (New York: Seminar Press, 1973), pp. 269–93.

93. See David Held, *Models of Democracy*, second edition (Palo Alto: Stanford University Press, 1996), p. 251.

3. APARTISM: EXPLAINING ANTI-SYSTEM BEHAVIOR

1. In one of the first studies, Hutnik found that 80 per cent of British Muslim respondents selected Islam as important to their identity in a 1985 survey—before the polemics of the 1991 Gulf War and the 1989 Rushdie affair fanned the flames of identity politics further. (Nimmi Hutnik, 'Aspects of Identity in a Multi–Ethnic Society' in *New Community* [1985, 98].) More recently, the 2001 British Home Office Citizenship Survey found that religion ranked second only to family as the most important factor identifying Muslim respondents—compared to Christians, who ranked their religion seventh on average. (Maria O'Beirne, 'Religion in England and Wales: Findings From the 2001 Home Office Citizenship Survey', Home Office Research, Development and Statistics Directorate, March 2004, http:// www.homeoffice.gov.uk/rds/pdfs04/hors274.pdf.)

2. See *The Sunday Times*, 'The Enemy Within', leader in *The Sunday Times*, 13 August 2006, http://www.timesonline.co.uk/article/0,,2088–2310296,00.html. Others perceive Muslims' attachment to Islam as an affront to the secular state. See Asad, pp. 159–160.

3. Prominently, as of 2005, there were only 305 Muslims serving in the 184,000-strong, British armed forces. (BBC News, 'Striving for "Truly British" armed forces', 17 November 2005, 17:13 GMT, http://news.bbc.co.uk/1/hi/uk/4440360. stm. Also see Asifa Hussain, 'British Pakistani Muslims' Perceptions of the Armed Forces', *Armed Forces & Society*, 28, 4 (2002), 601–18. Anti–democratic Islamist groups in the UK issued a fatwa that those who join the British army are apostates and those who fight in Iraq or Afghanistan or elsewhere against Muslims are apostates because of their war against Muslims. See 'Draft Report on Young Muslims

and Extremism', UK Foreign and Commonwealth Office/Home Office, April 2004.) In another example, some British Muslim doctors and medical students refused to learn about or treat alcohol-related illnesses and sexually-transmitted diseases because they said that doing so defies their religious beliefs. A small number also refused to examine patients of the opposite sex because they said it is forbidden by the Quran. (Daniel Martin, 'Muslim medical students refuse to learn about alcohol or sexual diseases', *The Daily Telegraph*, 7 October 2007.) *Al-Muhajiroun*, a now-forbidden underground group of British Muslims, has encouraged members to reject obligations to British civil society because, they said, all non-Islamic cultural goods are naturally menacing to true Islam.

4. See Christopher Caldwell, *Reflections on the Revolution in Europe* (New York: Random House, 2009).

5. Tariq Modood, *Multiculturalism* (Cambridge: Polity 2007), p. 142.

6. See A.S. Asani, '"So That You May Know One Another": An American Reflects on Pluralism and Islam', *The ANNALS of the American Academy of Political and Social Science*, 588, 1 (2003) pp. 40–51, and M.A.M. Khan, *American Muslims: Bridging Faith and Freedom* (Beltsville, Maryland: Amana Publications, 2002).

7. Iftikhar H. Malik, *Islam, Nationalism and the West* (Hampshire: Macmillan, 1999), pp. 3–4.

8. Modood, 2007, p. 143.

9. Malik, 1999, p. 3.

10. Modood, 2007, pp. 143–4.

11. Masadul Hasan, *Reconstruction of Political Thought in Islam* (Lahore: Islamic Publications, 1988), pp. 12–13.

12. Bhikhu Parekh, 'Religion and Public Life' in Tariq Modood (ed.), *Church, State and Religious Minorities* (London: Policy Studies Institute, 1997), p. 21.

13. Nielsen, 1999, p. 70.

14. Joselyn Cesari, *When Islam and Democracy Meet* (New York: Palgrave Macmillan, 2004), p. 44.

15. Nielsen, 1999, p. 70.

16. Nielsen, 1999, p. 74.

17. Ibid.

18. See Gilles Kepel, *Allah in the West: Islamic Movements in America and Europe* (Stanford: Stanford University Press, 1997); Tahir Abbas, 'Introduction: Islamic Poltical Radicalism in Western Europe' in Tahir Abbas (ed.), *Islamic Political Radicalism: A European Perspective* (Edinburgh: Edinburgh University Press, 2007), p. 10; Gema Martin Munoz (ed.), *Islam, Modernism and the West: Cultural and Political Relations at the End of the Millennium* (London: I.B. Tauris, 1999); Parveen Akhtar, '(Re)Turn to Religion and Radical Islam' in Tahir Abbas (ed.), *Muslim Britain* (London: Zed Books, 2005), p. 165.

19. Henry Brady, Sidney Verba and Kay Lehman Schlozman, 'Beyond SES: A Resource Model of Political Participation', *American Political Science Review*, 89 (1995a), pp. 271–94. However this model is not only relevant to Muslims. Also see G. Parry, G. Moyser and N. Day, *Political Participation and Democracy in Britain* (Cambridge: Cambridge University Press, 1992).

20. Stephen Castles, *Ethnicity and Globalization* (London: SAGE Publications, 2000), pp. 88 and 191.

21. Tariq Modood and Richard Berthoud, *Ethnic Minorities in Britain* (London: Policy Studies Institute, 1997).

22. Meindert Fennema and Jean Tillie, 'Political participation and political trust in Amsterdam: Civic Communities and Ethnic Networks', *Journal of Ethnic and Migration Studies*, 24, 4 (1999). Also see Togeby, Lise, 'Migrants at the Polls: An Analysis of Immigrant and Refugee Participation in Danish Local Elections', *Journal of Ethnic and Migration Studies*, 25, 4 (1999), pp. 665–84.

23. Rahsaan Maxwell, 'Muslims, South Asians and the British mainstream: A national identity crisis?', *West European Politics*, 29, 4 (2006), pp. 736–56.

24. Ibid.

25. Marieke Slootman and Jean Tillie, *Processes of Radicalisation*, paper published by the Institute for Migration and Ethnic Studies, Universiteit van Amsterdam, October 2006, p. 42.

26. Quintan Wiktorowicz, *Radical Islam Rising: Muslim Extremism in the West* (Maryland: Rowman and Littlefield, 2005), p. 91.

27. Maxwell, 2006. A more recent study by Gallup and the Coexist Foundation found that while only one in ten Muslims in Britain see themselves as integrated into the rest of society, 77 per cent said they identified with Britain—a higher figure than the half of the public as a whole who said the same. See Steve Doughty, 'Just one in 10 British Muslims feel integrated into society, study claims', *The Daily Mail*, 8 May 2009, http://www.dailymail.co.uk/news/article-1178794/Just-10-British-Muslims-feel-integrated-society-study-claims.html;jsessionid=A82C5D913C59603C65CEF86CEF86A99A#ixzz0MhkroRBy.

28. Slootman and Tillie, p. 42.

29. Talal Asad, *Formations of the Secular: Christianity, Islam, Modernity* (Stanford: Stanford University Press, 2003), p. 5. For a primer on discursive discrimination, see Kristina Boreus, 'Discursive Discrimination: A Typology', *European Journal of Social Theory* 9, 3 (2006), pp. 405–24.

30. For more on this, see Jorgen Nielsen, *Muslims in Western Europe* (Edinburgh: Edinburgh University Press, 2004).

31. Cesari, 2004, p. 2. Asad, 2003, p. 159 (cite).

32. Humayun Ansari, *'The Infidel Within': Muslims in Britain Since 1800* (London: C. Hurst and Co., 2004), p. 8.

33. Iftikhar H. Malik, *Islam Nationalism and the West* (New York: St Martin's Press, 1999), p. 20.

34. The essentialist discourse is manifested in the actions and rhetoric of people who group all Muslims as one. This has been called the Bin Laden Effect, whereby all Muslims are cast in the role of the enemy, transforming them into scapegoats for the entire society. And indeed, in the weeks after September 11, Muslims were globally targeted during a period of reprisals. See Cesari, 2004, p. 35.

35. Edward N. Said, 'Islam Through Western Eyes', *The Nation*, 26 April 1980.

36. Sadaf Rizvi, 'News cultures, security and transnational belonging', *European Journal of Cultural Studies*, 10, 3 (2007), pp. 327–42.

37. Akhtar, 2005, p. 172.

38. Rachel Briggs, Catherine Fieschi and Hannah Lownsbrough, 'Bringing It Home: Community based approaches to counter terrorism', Demos, 4 December 2006. Retrieved from <http://www.demos.co.uk/files/Bringing%20it%20Home%20-%20web.pdf> on 6 February 2008.

39. See UK Foreign and Commonwealth Office/Home Office, 2004.

40. FOSIS, *The Voice of Muslim Students*, August 2005, Federation of Student Islamic Societies, London. Retrieved from <http://www.fosis.org.uk/committees/sac/documents/FullReport.pdf> on 6 February 2008.

41. See: Claire Dwyer, 'Contradictions of Community: Questions of Identity for Young British Muslim Women', *Environment and Planning* (1999) 31(1); Sarah Glynn, 'Bengali Muslims: The New East End Radicals?', *Ethnic and Racial Studies* (2002), 25(6), pp. 969–75; Y. Ali, 'Muslim Women and the Politics of Ethnicity and Culture in Northern England' in G. Sahgal and N. Yuval-Davis (eds), *Refusing Holy Orders: Women and Fundamentalism in Britain* (London: Virago Press, 1992), p. 113; Kim Knott and Sajda Khokher, 'Religious and Ethnic Identity among Young Muslim Women in Bradford' in *New Community* 19, 4 (1993).

42. Louise Archer, *Race, Masculinity and Schooling: Muslim boys and education* (Maidenhead: Open University Press, 2003) and Louise Archer, 'Muslim brothers, black lads, traditional "Asians": British Muslim young men's constructions of race, religion and masculinity', *Feminism and Psychology* 11, 1 (2001).

43. See Archer, 2003 and Saeed et al., 1999, pp. 826 and 830.

44. Marie Macey, 'Class, Gender and Religious Influence on Changing Patterns of Pakistani Muslim Male Violence in Bradford', *Ethnic and Racial Studies* 22, 5 (1999).

45. Tahir Abbas, 'Introduction: Islamic Political Radicalism in Western Europe' in Tahir Abbas (ed.), *Islamic Political Radicalism: A European Perspective* (Edinburgh: Edinburgh University Press, 2007), p. 10.

46. Samad, 1996, p. 17.

47. Ziauddin Sardar, 'Racism, Identity and Muslims in the West' in Abedin and Sardar (eds), *Muslim Minorities in the West* (London: Grey Seal, 1995), pp. 1–17.

48. See Steven Vertovec and Alasdair Rogers, 'Introduction' in Steven Vertovec and Alasdair Rogers (eds), *Muslim European Youth* (Aldershot: Ashgate, 1998), pp. 4–5 summary of anti–essentialist critique.

49. Fredrik Barth, 'Introduction' in F. Barth (ed.), *Ethnic Groups and Boundaries: The Social Organisation of Culture Difference* (London: Allen and Unwin, 1969).

50. Nimmi Hutnik, 'Aspects of Identity in Multi–Ethnic Society', *Ethnic and Racial Studies*, 9, 2 (1986), pp.150-67.

51. Abdullah Sahin, 'Attitudes toward Islam of young people in Birmingham colleges', unpublished PhD thesis, Birmingham University, in Edward Lifton, 'A Clinical Psychology Perspective on Radical Islamic Youth' in Tahir Abbas (ed.), *Islamic Political Radicalism: A European Perspective* (Edinburgh: Edinburgh University Press, 2007), p. 28.

52. Margaret Pickles, 'Muslim Immigration Stress in Australia' in Abedin and Sardar (eds), *Muslim Minorities in the West* (London: Grey Seal, 1995), p. 107.

53. Wiktorowicz, 2005, p. 99.

54. Amir Saeed, Neil Blain and Douglas Forbes, 'New ethnic and national questions in Scotland: post-British identities among Glasgow Pakistani teenagers' Ethnic and Racial Studies, 22, 5 (1999) pp. 8-44; and Y. Samad, 'The Politics of Islamic Identity among Bangladeshis and Pakistanis in Britain' in T. Ranger, Y. Samad and O. Stuart (eds), *Culture Identity and Politics: Ethnic Minorities in Britain* (Aldershot: Avebury, 1996).

55. Roger Ballard, 'The Pakistanis: Stability and Introspection' in Ceri Peach (ed.), *The Ethnic Minority Populations of Great Britain: Ethnicity in the 1991 Census*, Vol. 2 (London: Central Statistical Office, 1996).

56. Cesari, 2004, p. 25.

57. Katy Gardner and Abdus Shuker, '"I'm Bengali, I'm Asian and I'm Living Here": The Changing Identity of British Bengalis' in R. Ballard (ed.), *Desh Pardesh: The South Asian Presence in Britain* (London: C. Hurst and Co., 1994) p. 164.

58. See Akhtar, 2005, p. 167.

59. Hamid, p. 152.

60. See the theory of structural relations in Anthony Giddens, *New Rules of Sociological Method*, second edition (Palo Alto: Stanford University Press, 1993); and Anthony Giddens, *The Constitution of Society: Outline of the Theory of Structuration* (Cambridge: Polity, 1984).

61. Ted Robert Gurr, *Why Men Rebel* (Princeton: Princeton University Press, 1970), p. 23.

62. Ibid., p. 13.

63. Ibid., p. 24.

64. Ibid.

65. Sidney Verba, Kay Lehman Schlozman and Henry E. Brady, *Voice and Equality: Civic Voluntarism in American Politics* (Cambridge: Harvard University Press, 1995b), p. 269; Schlozman, Verba and Brady, 'Participation's not a paradox: The view from American activists', *British Journal of Political Science* 25 (January 1995), pp. 1–36. Also see Sidney Verba and Norman Nie, *Participation in America: Political Democracy and Social Equality* (New York: Harper and Row, 1972).

66. Verba, Schlozman and Brady, 1995b, pp. 271–2.

67. Slootman and Tillie, 2006.

68. See Alexander L. George and Timothy J. McKeown, 'Case Studies and Theories of Organizational Decision Making', *Advances in Information Processing in Organizations* 2 (1985), pp. 21–58, cited by Gary King, Robert Keohane and Sidney Verba, *Designing Social Inquiry: Scientific Inference in Qualitative Research* (Princeton: Princeton University Press, 1994).

69. Jorgen Nielsen, *Muslims in Western Europe* (Edinburgh: Edinburgh University Press, 1992), pp. 114–15.

70. Roy, 2004, p. 117.

4. INTEGRATED YET APART: BANGLADESHIS IN LONDON'S EAST END

1. Robert Putnam, Lecture to Government 90qa, Faculty of Arts and Sciences, Harvard University, 10 March 2003.

2. Interviewed 2 April 2008 (Tayyib).
3. Interviewed 6 May 2008 (Zubair).
4. Tower Hamlets Council, Borough Statistical Data, http://www.towerhamlets. gov.uk/data/discover/ data/borough-profile/data/borough-profile/population/ data/age-gender.cfm.
5. Spatial distribution of Bangladeshis in the East End has been shaped in part by the discriminatory housing policies of the 1980s, and the persistent hostility of the white working class. For more information about this, see John Eade and David Garbin, 'Changing Narratives of Violence, Struggle and Resistance: Bangladeshis and the Competition for Resources in the Global City', *Oxford Development Studies*, 30, 2 (June 2002) p. 139.
6. Interviewed 12 June 2008 (Fadhil).
7. Interviewed 15 May 2008 (Ridwan).
8. Interviewed 28 April 2008 (Yasir).
9. Ibid.
10. Interviewed 18 April 2008 (Zakaria), 16 May 2008 (Amjad) and 2 May 2008 (Zamil).
11. Interviewed 19 May 2008 (Qadim).
12. Interviewed 9 May 2008 (Yusuf ZB).
13. Interviewed 15 May 2008 (Ridwan).
14. Interviewed 22 April 2008 (Tayyib).
15. Interviewed 9 June 2008 (Bilal).
16. Interviewed 2 May 2009 (Uqbah).
17. Interviewed 22 April 2008 (Tayyib).
18. Interviewed 2 May 2008 (Zamil)
19. Interviewed 28 April 2008 (Zaid).
20. Interviewed 2 May 2008 (Faisal).
21. Interviewed 9 June 2008 (Bilal).
22. Interviewed 18 June 2009 (Yusuf).
23. Interviewed 15 May 2008 (Ridwan).
24. Interviewed 2 May 2008 (Zamil).
25. Interviewed 18 April 2008 (Zakaria).
26. Interviewed 2 May 2009 (Uqbah).
27. Interviewed 24 June 2008 (Ismail).
28. Sarah Glynn, 'The Spirit of '71—how the Bangladeshi War of Independence has haunted Tower Hamlets', *Socialist History Journal*, 29 (2006), pp. 56–75.
29. Yunus Samad, 'The politics of Islamic identity among Bangladeshis and Pakistanis in Britain' in Terence Ranger et al. (eds), *Culture, Identity and Politics: Ethnic minorities in Britain* (Aldershot: Avebury, 1996), pp. 93–4.
30. Halima Begum and John Eade, 'All Quiet on the Eastern Front? Bangladeshi Reactions in Tower Hamlets' in Tahir Abbas (ed.), *Muslim Britain: Communities Under Pressure* (London: Zed Books, 2005), p. 184.
31. Samad, 1996, p. 94.
32. Ibid.
33. Ibid., p. 95.

34. Glynn, 2006.
35. See Pnina Werbner, 'Theorising Complex Diasporas: Purity and Hybridity in the South Asian Public Sphere in Britain' in 'Islam, Transnationalism and the Public Sphere in Western Europe', special issue of *Journal of Ethnic and Migration Studies* 30, 5 (2004), p. 899; and David Garbin, 'Bangladeshi Diaspora in the UK: some observations on socio-cultural dynamics, religious trends and transnational politics', paper presented at the Conference on Human Rights and Bangladesh, SOAS, 17 June 2005, p. 3, and Eade and Garbin, 2002, pp. 144–6.
36. Interviewed 19 May 2008 (Qadim).
37. Interviewed 18 June 2008 (Yusuf).
38. Interviewed 19 May 2008 (Qadim).
39. Interviewed 18 June 2008 (Yusuf).
40. Eade and Garbin, 2002, p. 140.
41. Ibid.
42. Ibid.
43. Ibid., p. 142.
44. Garbin, 2005, p. 5.
45. See John Eade, 'Reconstructing places: changing images of locality in Docklands and Spitalfields' in J. Eade (ed.), *Living in the Global City* (London: Routledge, 1997), pp. 127–45.
46. Interviewed 18 June 2008 (Yusuf).
47. Interviewed 13 March 2008 (Zaki).
48. Interviewed 16 May 2008 (Amjad).
49. Interviewed 19 June 2008 (Viq).
50. Interviewed 9 June 2008 (Bilal).
51. Interviewed 15 May 2008 (Ridwan).
52. Interviewed 2 May 2008 (Ghalib).
53. Interviewed 18 June 2008 (Yusuf).
54. Ibid.
55. Interviewed 16 May 2008 (Jalal).
56. Justin Gest and Andrew Norfolk, 'British Imams "failing young Muslims"', *The Times*, 7 January 2009, http://www.timesonline.co.uk/tol/comment/faith/article3142525.ece.
57. Interviewed 10 June 2008 (Karim).
58. Interviewed 19 April 2008 (Omar).
59. Interviewed 24 June 2008 (Naz).
60. Interviewed 19 June 2008 (Viq).
61. Interviewed 19 April 2008 (Omar).
62. Interviewed 16 June 2008 (Calim).
63. Interviewed 24 June 2008 (Pir).
64. Interviewed 16 May 2008 (Amjad).
65. Interviewed 15 May 2008 (Ridwan).
66. Interviewed 1 May 2008 (Ebrahim).
67. Interviewed 19 April 2008 (Omar).
68. Interviewed 9 June 2008 (Bilal).

69. Interviewed 19 June 2008 (Viq).
70. Interviewed 22 April 2008 (Tayyib).
71. Interviewed 1 May 2008 (Ghalib).
72. For a discussion about this overlapping of seemingly distinct contexts, see Steve Vertovec, 'Young Muslims in Keighley, West Yorkshire: cultural identity, context and "community"', *Migration*, 33, pp. 119–38.
73. See John Eade, 'Identity, Nation and Religion: Educated Young Bangladeshi Muslims in London's "East End"', *International Sociology*, 9, 3, pp. 377–94.
74. Interviewed 16 May 2008 (Jalal).
75. Interviewed 15 May 2008 (Ridwan).
76. Interviewed 18 April 2008 (Hanif).
77. Interviewed 19 May 2008 (Qadim).
78. Interviewed 24 June 2008 (Naz).
79. Interviewed 12 May 2008 (Jalil).
80. Interviewed 12 May 2008 (Jalal).
81. Interviewed 18 April 2008 (Zakaria).
82. Werbner, 2004.
83. Ibid.
84. Interviewed 18 June 2008 (Yusuf).
85. See Louise Archer, 'Muslim brothers, black lads, traditional Asians: British young men's constructions of "race", religion, and masculinity', *Feminism and Psychology*, Vol. 11, No. 1, pp. 79–105; and see Claire Dwyer et al., '"From cricket lover to terror suspect"—challenging representations of young British Muslim men', *Gender, Place and Culture*, 15, 2 (April 2008), pp. 117–36.
86. Interviewed 30 April 2008 (Mahir).
87. Interviewed 24 June 2008 (Ismail).
88. Interviewed 2 May 2008 (Ghalib).
89. Interviewed 1 May 2008 (Ebrahim).
90. Interviewed 12 May 2008 (Jalil).
91. Interviewed 22 April 2008 (Tayyib).
92. Interviewed 19 April 2008 (Omar).
93. Interviewed 16 June 2008 (Calim).
94. Interviewed 9 June 2008 (Bilal).
95. Interviewed 15 May 2008 (Ridwan).
96. Interviewed 2 May 2008 (Faisal).
97. Olivier Roy, *Globalised Islam* (London: C. Hurst and Co., 2002), pp. 124–25.
98. Interviewed 16 June 2008 (Calim).
99. Interviewed 18 June 2008 (Yusuf).
100. Ibid.
101. Interviewed 1 May 2008 (Zubair).
102. Interviewed 19 May 2008 (Qadim).
103. Meeting on 6 May 2008 at Toynbee Hall.
104. Meeting on 7 June 2008 at John Knox Church.
105. Interviewed 24 June 2008 (Ismail).

106. Interviewed 19 June 2008 (Viq).
107. Ibid.
108. Meeting on 12 June 2008 at Ponler Street.
109. Meeting on 6 May 2008 at Toynbee Hall.
110. Meeting on 12 June 2008 at Ponler Street.
111. Youth Sanctuary Project Blog, http://www.yspyouth.blogspot.com/ accessed 12 June 2008.
112. Ibid.
113. Meeting on 6 May 2008 at Toynbee Hall.
114. Ibid.
115. Youth Sanctuary Project Blog, http://www.yspyouth.blogspot.com/ accessed 12 June 2008.
116. Interviewed 28 April 2008 (Yusuf).
117. Interviewed 16 June 2008 (Calim).
118. Interviewed 9 June 2008 (Bilal).
119. Interviewed 24 June 2008 (Ismail).
120. Interviewed 19 May 2008 (Qadim).
121. Interviewed 2 May 2008 (Ghalib).
122. Interviewed 19 June 2008 (Viq).
123. Interviewed 24 June 2008 (Naz)
124. Interviewed 13 March 2008 (Zaki).

5. ON THE INSIDE LOOKING OUT: MOROCCANS IN SOUTHERN MADRID

1. Interviewed 20 July 2008 (Hasan).
2. Interviewed 16 September 2008 (Alfonso).
3. The Spanish birth rate is one of the lowest in Europe at 1.26, according to Mohamed Khachani, 'La Emigración Marroquí en España', Economía Exterior, No. 28, Primavera (2004), p. 139.
4. Ivan Briscoe, 'Dreaming of Spain: Migration and Morocco' on www.openDemocracy.net, posted 27 May 2004, accessed 14 July 2008.
5. Interviewed 24 August 2008 (Majid).
6. Gloria Laura-Tamayo D'Ocon, 'Inmigración Marroquí en la Comunidad de Madrid' in Atlas de la Inmigración Magrebí en España (Madrid: TEIM, 2004), p. 346.
7. Bernabé López García, 'La periferización de los Marroquíes en la Comunidad de Madrid' in Atlas de la Inmigración Magrebí en España (Madrid: TEIM, 2004), p. 347.
8. According to Rickard Sandell, 'La Inmigración en España: ¿problema u oportunidad?' in Área: Demografía y Población, 13, 27 (January 2005), there were approximately 967,188 unauthorized immigrants in Spain in 2003. The study did not break the figure down by sending country.
9. Centro de Investigaciones Sociológicas, 'Barómetro Noviembre 2006', Esudio #2662, Opiniones y Actitudes CIS 60, Pregunta 16, 18 November 2006.

10. In 1886, there were 150,000 Spaniards counted in Algeria—many of whom were seasonal migrants. That trend would end at the turn of the twentieth century, when thousands of Spaniards moved to the Western Hemisphere, particularly Cuba and Argentina. The next exodus took place between 1960 and 1975, joining others from 'the South' to industrialized European metropolises in Germany, Switzerland, France, Belgium, the Netherlands and the United Kigdom. See Isabel Bodega et al., 'Recent Migrations from Morocco to Spain', *International Migration Review*, 29, 3, p. 802.

11. Kitty Calavita, 'A "reserve army of delinquents"': The criminalization and economic punishment of immigrants in Spain', *Punishment and Society*, 2003, no. 5, 5 (2003) pp. 403–4.

12. For further information and a chronology of important political decisions that affected Moroccan migrants, see Bodega et al., 2002, p. 815.

13. Interviewed 11 September 2008 (Ana Planet).

14. Ibid.

15. Interviewed 18 September 2008.

16. Interviewed 16 September 2008 (Alfonso).

17. Interviewed 3 August 2008 (Walid).

18. Bodega et al., 2002, p. 807.

19. Interviewed 31 August 2008 (Gamal).

20. As interviewed by Victor Morales Lezcano, 'Inmigración Africana en Madrid: Marroquíes y Guineanos (1975–1990)' (Madrid: UNED, 1993), p. 70.

21. Interviewed 2 September 2008 (Shabir).

22. Interviewed 6 September 2008 (Mohamed).

23. Víctor Pérez-Díaz, Berta Álvarez-Miranda and Elisa Chuliá, *La Inmigración Musulmana en Europa: Turcos en Alemania, Argelinos en Francia y marroquíes en España (Muslims in Europe: Turks in Germany, Algerians in France, Moroccans in Spain)*, (Barcelona: Fundación La Caixa, July 2004).

24. Interviewed 18 September 2008.

25. Ibid.

26. Interviewed 18 September 2008.

27. Ibid.

28. José Antonio Rodríguez García, *La Inmigración Islámica en España: Su problemática Juridical* (Madrid: Editorial Dilex, 2007), pp. 141 and 167.

29. Interviewed 18 September 2008.

30. Víctor Pérez-Díaz et al., 'Volumen 15: La Inmigración Musulmana en Europa: Turcos en Alemania, Argelinos en Francia, y Marroquíes en España', *Collección de Estudios Sociales* (Fundación La Caixa, 2004). Accessed via http://obrasocial.lacaixa.es/estudiossociales/vol15_es.html.

31. Sonia Varedas Muñoz, 'Sobre el Asociacionismo Marroqui en España y participación de los Inmigrantes' in *Atlas de la Inmigración Magrebí en España* (Madrid: TEIM, 2004), p. 407.

32. Ibid., p. 408.

33. Ibid.

34. Interviewed 20 August 2008 (Yousef).

35. Interviewed 6 September 2008 (Mohamed).
36. Interviewed 2 September 2008 (Jordí Moreras).
37. Interviewed 9 July 2008.
38. Interviewed 1 August 2008 (Tariq).
39. Interviewed 7 August 2008 (Sadik).
40. Interviewed 10 August 2008 (Omar).
41. Interviewed 20 August 2008 (Yousef).
42. Interviewed 31 August 2008 (Gamal).
43. Interviewed 10 August 2008 (Omar).
44. Interviewed 7 August 2008 (Sadik).
45. Interviewed 26 August 2008 (Zahir).
46. Jordi Moreras, 'La Religiosidad en Context Migratorio: Pertenencias y Observancias' in *Atlas de la Inmigración Magrebí en España* (Madrid: TEIM, 2004), p. 413.
47. Interviewed 26 July 2008 (Rachid).
48. Interviewed 2 September 2008.
49. Lezcano, 1993, pp. 105–6.
50. See Elena Arigita, 'al-Adl wa-l-Ihsan in Spain: Exploring New Frames of Reference', paper presented to Middle Eastern Studies Association, November 2009.
51. Interviewed 16 September 2008 (Rafiq).
52. Ibid.
53. Ibid.
54. Interviewed 8 August 2008 (Usman).
55. Interviewed 2 September 2008 (Shabir).
56. Interviewed 17 September 2009 (ATIME).
57. Interviewed 17 September 2009 (ATIME).
58. Interviewed 17 August 2008 (Ana Planet).
59. Interviewed 7 August 2008 (Sadik).
60. Gema Martín Muñoz, 'El Islam en España Hoy' in Luisa Martín Rojo et al. (eds), *Hablar y Dejar Hablar (Sobre racism y xenofobia)* (Madrid: Universidad Autónoma de Madrid, 1994), pp. 219 and 225.
61. Interviewed 26 July 2008 (Rachid).
62. Interviewed 2 August 2008 (Idris).
63. Interviewed 2 August 2008 (Kalid).
64. Interviewed 11 August 2008 (Amir).
65. Interviewed 2 August 2008 (Kalid).
66. Carlos Giménez Romero, 'Marroquíes en España: un perfil sociocultural' in *Atlas de la Inmigración Magrebí en España* (Madrid: TEIM, 1996), cited in Mohamed Khachani, 'La Emigración Marroquí en España', *Economía Exterior*, No. 28, Primavera 2004, p. 138. Such reports rebuff the laughably oblivious view that 'there is no Islamophobia in Spain', as argued by Javier Noya in 'Spaniards and Islam', *Real Instituto El Cano*, ARI 105/2007, 28 November 2007, from http://www.realinstitutoelcano.org/wps/portal/rielcano_eng/Content?WCM_GLOBAL_CONTEXT=/Elcano_in/Zonas_in/Image+of+Spain/ARI105-2007.
67. Interviewed 19 August 2008 (Mahmud).
68. Metroscopia, 3.5.

69. Metroscopia, 5.2.
70. Interviewed 25 August 2008 (Nasir).
71. Interviewed 20 July 2008 (Hakim).
72. Interviewed 7 August 2008 (Sadik).
73. Interviewed 8 August 2008 (Usman).
74. Muñoz, 1994, p. 226.
75. Ibid., pp. 226–7.
76. Moreras, 2004, p. 412.
77. Interviewed 26 August 2008 (Zahir).
78. Ibid.
79. Interviewed 6 September 2008 (Mohamed).
80. Ibid. Mirroring the reaction of other Muslims in Europe, many Muslims have sought to defend the vilified identity by embracing it further. Several of the more pious respondents say that they have become more religious in recent years. This reflects the trend captured by the Metroscopia survey, which shows that from 2006 to 2007 alone regular practice among Muslims in Spain rose from 41 per cent to 49 per cent of respondents—a level matched by Catholic Spaniards in 1976 (48 per cent), which has since fallen to 20 per cent.
81. Ibid.
82. Interviewed 8 August 2008 (Usman).
83. Interviewed 30 July 2008 (Qasim).
84. Interviewed 3 August 2008 (Walid).
85. Interviewed 11 August 2008 (Amir).
86. Interviewed 31 August 2008 (Gamal).
87. Interviewed 10 August 2008 (Omar).
88. Interviewed 30 July 2008 (Anwar).
89. Bravo López, 'El Musulmán como alter-ego irreducible: La expansion del discurso culturalista' in *Atlas de la Inmigración Magrebí en España* (Madrid: TEIM, 2004), 433.
90. Ricard Zapata-Barrero, 'The Muslim Community and Spanish Tradition' in Tariq Modood et al., *Multiculturalism, Muslims and Citizenship: A European Approach* (New York: Routledge, 2006), p. 145.
91. Ibid., p. 146.
92. Ibid., p. 147.
93. Ibid.
94. Interviewed 18 September 2008.
95. Interviewed 22 August 2008 (Akil).
96. Interviewed 23 August 2008 (Wasam).
97. Interviewed 22 August 2008 (Akil).
98. Interviewed 11 August 2008 (Amir).
99. Interviewed 1 August 2008 (Yusuf).
100. Interviewed 22 August 2008 (Akil).
101. Interviewed 15 September 2008 (Abbas).
102. Interviewed 2 August 2008 (Kalid).
103. Interviewed 28 July 2008 (Abdullah).

104. Interviewed 20 July 2008 (Hakim).
105. Interviewed 24 August 2008 (Majid).
106. Interviewed 7 August 2008 (Sadik).
107. Interviewed 25 August 2008 (Nasir).
108. Berta Álvarez-Miranda, 'Here and There: Transnational and Community Links between Muslim Immigrants in Europe', *Real Instituto Elcano*, posted 8 May 2007. Based on the Muslims in Europe Survey. See: http://www.realinstitutoelcano.org/documentos/288.asp.
109. Interviewed 17 September 2009 (ATIME).
110. Interviewed 2 September 2008.
111. Interviewed 26 July 2008 (Rachid).
112. Interviewed 16 August 2008 (Mahmud).
113. Interviewed 9 August 2008 (Saad).
114. Interviewed 15 September 2008 (Abbas).
115. Interviewed 3 August 2008 (Walid).
116. Interviewed 2 September 2008 (Shabir).
117. Interviewed 22 July 2008 (Said).

6. STRUCTURE AND PERCEPTION: COMPARING THE LONDON AND MADRID CASES

1. See Joselyn Cesari, *When Islam and Democracy Meet* (New York: Palgrave Macmillan, 2004), p. 44; and Jorgen Nielsen, *Muslims in Western Europe* (Edinburgh: Edinburgh University Press, 2004), pp. 70–74.
2. Interviewed 20 July 2008 (Hakim).
3. Interviewed 28 July 2008 (Abdullah).
4. Interviewed 5 August 2008 (Yasir).
5. Interviewed 1 August 2008 (Rashid).
6. Interviewed 1 August 2008 (Tariq).
7. Interviewed 15 September 2008 (Abbas).
8. Interviewed 9 August 2008 (Saad).
9. Interviewed 5 August 2008 (Yasir).
10. Ronald Inglehart and Pippa Norris, 'Muslim Integration into Western Cultures: Between Origins and Destinations', Faculty Working Paper Series, Harvard University Kennedy School of Government, March 2009.
11. See Gilles Kepel, *Allah in the West: Islamic Movements in America and Europe* (Stanford: Stanford University Press, 1997); Tahir Abbas, 'Introduction: Islamic Poltical Radicalism in Western Europe' in Tahir Abbas (ed.), *Islamic Political Radicalism: A European Perspective* (Edinburgh: Edinburgh University Press, 2007), p. 10; Gema Martin Muñoz (ed.), *Islam, Modernism and the West: Cultural and Political Relations at the End of the Millenium* (London: I.B. Tauris, 1999); Parveen Akhtar, '(Re)Turn to Religion and Radical Islam' in Tahir Abbas (ed.), *Muslim Britain* (London: Zed Books, 2005), p. 165.
12. Henry Brady, Sidney Verba and Kay Lehman Schlozman, 'Beyond SES: A Resource Model of Political Participation', *American Political Science Review*, 89

(1995a), pp. 271–94. Also see G. Parry, G. Moyser and N. Day, *Political Participation and Democracy in Britain* (Cambridge: Cambridge University Press, 1992).

13. Ayoub Korom Ali, 'Forced out, looking inwards: Britain's Bangladeshis', *New Statesman*, 22 January 2007, accessed via http://www.newstatesman.com/politics/2007/01/britain-bangladeshis-number on 31 March 2009.

14. Greater London Authority, 'Health in London', 2002 Review of London health strategy high level indicators (London: GLA, 2002).

15. Ibid.

16. Toynbee Hall, 'Snapshot', Toynbee Hall, London, 2006, accessed on 31 March 2009 via www.toynbeehall.org.uk/core/core_picker/download.asp?id=92&filetitle=Key+statistics+about+Tower+Hamlets

17. Interviewed 9 June 2009 (Bilal).

18. Ibid.

19. Interviewed 19 June 2008 (Viq).

20. Interviewed 16 June 2008 (Calim).

21. Bernabé López García, 'La Evolución de la Inmigración Marroquí en España (1991–2003)' in *Atlas de la Inmigración Magrebí en España* (Madrid: TEIM, 2004), p. 217.

22. Ibid.

23. Mohamed Khachani, 'La Emigración Marroquí en España', *Economía Exterior*, 28, Primavera 2004, p. 137.

24. See Talal Asad, *Formations of the Secular: Christianity, Islam, Modernity* (Stanford: Stanford University Press, 2003), p. 5; Edward N. Said, 'Islam Through Western Eyes', *The Nation*, 26 April 1980, http://www.thenation.com/doc/19800426/19800426said; Humayun Ansari, *'The Infidel Within': Muslims in Britain Since 1800* (London: C. Hurst and Co., 2004), p. 8. For a further primer on discursive discrimination, see Kristina Boreus, 'Discursive Discrimination: A Typology', *European Journal of Social Theory* 9, 3 (2006), pp. 405–24.

25. Iftikhar H. Malik, *Islam Nationalism and the West* (New York: St Martin's Press, 1999), p. 20.

26. Kerry Moore, Paul Mason and Justin Lewis, 'Images of Islam in the UK: The Representation of British Muslims in the National Print News Media 2000–2008', Cardiff School of Journalism, Media and Cultural Studies report, 7 July 2008. See also L. Fekete, 'Anti–Muslim racism and the European Security State', *Race and Class* 46, 1 (2004), pp. 3–29.

27. Ibid.

28. Ibid.

29. Elizabeth Poole, *Reporting Islam* (London: I.B. Tauris, 2002) in 'Muslims in the EU: Cities Report', EU Monitoring and Advocacy Program, Open Society Institute, 2007, p. 47.

30. 'New study highlights discrimination in use of anti–terror laws', Press Release, Institute of Race Relations (2 September 2004) in 'Muslims in the EU: Cities Report', EU Monitoring and Advocacy Program, Open Society Institute, 2007, p. 47.

31. Saied R. Ameli, Syed Mohammed Marandi, Sameera Ahmed, Seyfeddin Kara and

Arzu Merali, 'The British Media and Muslim Representation: The Ideology of Demonisation', Islamic Human Rights Commission, 26 January 2007.

32. Interviewed 28 April 2008 (Omar).
33. Interviewed 12 June 2008 (Fadhil).
34. Interviewed 16 June 2008 (Calim).
35. Interviewed 22 April 2008 (Tayyib).
36. Teun A. Van Dijk, 'El racismo y la prensa en España' in Hernández Antonio Bañón (ed.), *Discurso periodístico y procesos migratorios* (Donostia-San Sebastián: Gakoa, 2007), pp. 27–80.
37. Ibid.
38. Interviewed 18 September 2008.
39. Interviewed 10 August 2008 (Omar).
40. Interviewed 20 August 2008 (Yousef).
41. Interviewed 1 August 2009 (Tariq).
42. Interviewed 12 September (Abdel).
43. Interviewed 11 August 2008 (Amir).
44. Robert Booth, 'Minister for Terror: Gaza will fuel UK extremism', *The Guardian*, 28 January 2009.
45. Ziauddin Sardar, 'Racism, Identity and Muslims in the West' in Abedin and Sardar (eds), *Muslim Minorities in the West* (London: Grey Seal, 1995) pp. 1–17; Abdullah Sahin, 'Attitudes toward Islam of young people in Birmingham colleges', unpublished PhD thesis, Birmingham University, in Edward Lifton, 'A Clinical Psychology Perspective on Radical Islamic Youth' in Tahir Abbas (ed.), *Islamic Political Radicalism: A European Perspective* (Edinburgh: Edinburgh University Press, 2007), p. 28; Yunus Samad, 'Muslim Youth in Britain: Ethnic to Religious Identity', Paper presented at the International Conference on Muslim Youth in Europe; A. Saeed, N. Blain and D. Forbes, 'New ethnic and national questions in Scotland: Post-British identities among Glasgow Pakistani teenagers', *Ethnic and Racial Studies* 22, 5 (1999), pp. 8–44; Y. Samad, 'The Politics of Islamic Identity among Bangladeshis and Pakistanis in Britain' in T. Ranger, Y. Samad and O. Stuart (eds), *Culture, Identity and Politics: Ethnic Minorities in Britain* (Aldershot: Avebury, 1996); R. Ballard, 'The Pakistanis: Stability and Introspection' in C. Peach (ed.), *The Ethnic Minority Populations of Great Britain: Ethnicity in the 1991 Census*, Vol. 2 (London: Central Statistical Office, 1996); K. Gardner and A. Shuker, '"I'm Bengali, I'm Asian and I'm Living Here": The Changing Identity of British Bengalis' in R. Ballard (ed.), *Desh Pardesh: The South Asian Presence in Britain* (London: C. Hurst and Co., 1994), p. 164; C. Dwyer, 'Contradictions of community: Questions of identity for young British Muslim women', *Environment and Planning* 31, 1 (1999); S. Glynn, 'Bengali Muslims: the new East End radicals?', *Ethnic and Racial Studies* 25, 6 (2002), pp. 969–75; Y. Ali, 'Muslim Women and the Politics of Ethnicity and Culture in Northern England' in G. Sahgal and N. Yuval-Davis (eds), *Refusing Holy Orders: Women and Fundamentalism in Britain* (London: Virago Press, 1992), p. 113; K. Knott and S. Khokher, 'Religious and Ethnic Identity among Young Muslim Women in Bradford', *New Community* 19, 4 (1993).

46. Cesari, 2004, p. 25.

47. See Akhtar, 2005, p. 167.

48. Interviewed 3 August 2008 (Viq).

49. Interviewed 18 June 2008 (Ismail).

50. Interviewed 16 May 2008 (Amjad).

51. Berta Álvarez-Miranda, 'Here and There: Transnational and Community Links between Muslim Immigrants in Europe', *Real Instituto Elcano*, posted 8 May 2007. Based on the Muslims in Europe Survey.

52. Ted Robert Gurr, *Why Men Rebel* (Princeton: Princeton University Press, 1970), p. 23.

53. Ibid., p. 13.

54. Ibid., pp. 25–6.

55. Ibid., p. 24.

56. Ibid.

57. There are substantial groups of individuals in democracies who are neither 'anti-system' nor 'activists'—but something in between. Indeed, quite cynically, democracies are able to make decisions and policy because the vast majority of people are complacent enough to permit the government to make decisions on their behalf on most issues. But such complacency is both an acknowledgement that the system is greater than one person, and also an indication of confidence in the system. This study did not have the capacity to characterize other types of engagers also, in all the different varieties. And as it was most concerned with anti–system individuals and democratic activists, it focused on them accordingly. See Henrietta L. Moore, 'The Benefits of Doubt' in *Touching the State: What does it mean to be a citizen in the 21st Century?* (London: Design Council, 2004) and also David Held, *Models of Democracy* (Cambridge: Polity, 2006), p. 197.

58. See Usama Hasan and Justin Gest, 'Nothing Sells Papers Like a Villain', *The Guardian*, *Comment Is Free*, 18 March 2009.

7. CONCLUSION: DEMOCRACY'S OPPORTUNITY

1. Scott Shane, 'New Incidents Test Immunity to Terrorism on U.S. Soil', *New York Times*, 11 December 2009.

2. Pew Research Center, 'Muslim Americans: Middle Class and Mostly Mainstream', 22 May 2007.

3. See both Nabeel Abraham, 'The Yemeni Immigrant Community of Detroit: Background, Emigration, and Community Life' in Sameer Y. Abraham and Nabeel Abraham (eds), *Arabs in the New World: Studies on Arab-American Communities* (Detroit: Wayne State University Center for Urban Studies, 1983), pp. 109–34; and Sameer Y. Abraham, 'Detroit's Arab-American Community: A Survey of Diversity and Commonality' in Sameer Y. Abraham and Nabeel Abraham (eds), *Arabs in the New World: Studies on Arab American Communities* (Detroit: Wayne State University Center for Urban Studies, 1983), pp. 84–108.

4. Pew Research Center, 2007. For further statistical information from a more complete study by the Gallup organization, see John L. Esposito and Dalia Mogahed, *Who Speaks for Islam?* (Washington: Gallup Press, 2008).

5. Alejandro Portes and Rubin G. Rumbaut, *Legacies: The story of the immigrant second generation* (Berkeley: University of California Press, 2001); and Alejandro Portes and Rubin G. Rumbaut, *Immigrant America: A portrait*, second edition (Berkeley: University of California Press, 1996) as cited in Lori Peek, 'Becoming Muslim: The Development of a Religious Identity', *Sociology of Religion*, 66 (2005), p. 237.

6. See Karen I. Leonard, *Muslims in the United States: The state of research* (New York: Russell Sage Foundation, 2003).

7. John W. Ayers and C. Richard Hofstetter, 'American Muslim Political Participation Following 9/11: Religious Belief, Political Resources, Social Structures, and Political Awareness', *Politics and Religion*, 1 (2008), pp. 3–26.

8. Julie Tate, 'Notable homegrown terrorism plots', *Washington Post*, 11 December 2009, see http://www.washingtonpost.com/wp-dyn/content/article/2009/12/10/AR2009121004677.html.

9. Cass Sunstein, *Laws of Fear* (Cambridge: Cambridge University Press, 2005), pp. 204–5.

10. Paul Vitello and Kirk Semple, 'Muslims Say F.B.I. Tactics Sow Anger and Fear', *New York Times*, 17 December 2009.

11. Scott Glover, 'FBI monitored members of O.C. mosques at gyms, alleged informant says', *Los Angeles Times*, 29 April 2009.

12. Vitello and Semple, 2009.

13. Jerry Markon, 'FBI walks tightrope in outreach to Muslims, fighting terrorism', *The Washington Post*, 20 December 2009.

14. *Ibid.*

15. Robert Verkaik, 'Stop and search: white people held "to balance racial statistics"', *The Independent*, accessed 18 June 2009, http://www.independent.co.uk/news/uk/home-news/stop-and-search-white-people-held-to-balance-racial-statistics-1707895.html.

16. Conor Gearty, Lecture to Young Professionals in Foreign Policy, Houses of Parliament Committee Rooms, 23 June 2009.

17. See Steven Vertovec, 'Multicultural, multi–Asian, multi–Muslim Leicester: Dimensions of social complexity, ethnic organisation and local government interface', *Innovation: European Journal of Social Sciences* 7, 3, pp. 259–76.

18. Justin Gest and Andrew Norfolk, 'British Imams "failing young Muslims"', *The Times*, 7 January 2009.

19. As early as 1517, foreign-owned property was attacked in the East End of London in what were dubbed the 'Evil May Day Riots' against Flemish immigrants. In 1780, Catholics' houses in the East End were burnt to the ground, sparking the Gordon Riots in Stepney. One can only wonder how many of the arsonists were of Flemish descent.

20. Amidst the resulting vacuum of identity, nations offer emotional closeness and help recreate a new sense of community. See Montserrat Guibernau, *Nations Without States: Political Communities in a Global Age* (Cambridge: Polity Press, 1999), p. 179.

21. Roy, 2004, p. 132.

APPENDIX: NOTE ON METHODS

1. See David Collier, Henry E. Brady and Jason Seawright, 'Critiques, Responses and Tradeoffs: Drawing Together the Debate' in Henry E. Brady and David Collier, *Rethinking Social Inquiry: Diverse Tools, Shared Standards* (Oxford: Rowman and Littlefield, 2004), pp. 213–20.
2. Collier, Brady and Seawright, 2004, pp. 214–16.
3. Ibid.
4. See King, Keohane and Verba, 1994, pp. 84–9, 227.
5. See CIA, 'Spain' and 'United Kingdom,' in 'The World Factbook,' accessed via https://www.cia.gov/library/publications/the-world-factbook/; Office for National Statistics, 'Census 2001,' accessed via http://www.statistics.gov.uk/census2001/census2001.asp; European Commission, 'Eurobarometer: Europeans and their languages,' February 2006, accessed via http://ec.europa.eu/public_opinion/archives/ebs/ebs_243_en.pdf.
6. See *Atlas de la Inmigración Magrebí en España* (Madrid: TEIM, 1996) and David Garbin, 'Bangladeshi Diaspora in the UK: Some observations on socio-cultural dynamics, religious trends and transnational politics,' paper presented at the Conference on Human Rights and Bangladesh, SOAS, 17 June 2005.
7. This is meaningful because it contextualizes discursive concern for the maintenance of a purportedly rooted national identity. However, historical resistance to (or abstention from) assimilationist identity policies and Castillian/English control of civic identity forms from Basques, Catalans, Scots and the Welsh demonstrate that contested nature of these identity forms.
8. See 'London Attacks', BBC News, http://news.bbc.co.uk/1/hi/in_depth/uk/2005/london_explosions/ default.stm, posted 8 July 2008 12:57. See 'Zapatero y Aznar, ante la Comisión del 11–M' and '11M El Juicio' at http://www.elpais.com/especiales/2004/comision11m/ and http://www.elpais.com/comunes/2007/ juicio_11m/, respectively, viewed 15 February 2009.
9. Note that the northernmost part of Morocco was under a Spanish Protectorate from 1912 to 1956. It is from this region that most of the early Moroccan migrants hailed in the 1970s and 1980s. Also see 'Controlling our borders: Making Migration Work for Britain', HM Government, Home Office, http://www.archive2.official-documents.co.uk/document/cm64/6472/6472.pdf, posted February 2005; James Hampshire and Shamit Saggar, 'Migration, Integration, and Security in the UK since July 7', March 2006, http://www.migrationinformation.org/Feature/display.cfm?ID=383; Plan para la Integración Social de los Inmigrantes (España) at http://www.sappiens.com/castellano/articulos.nsf/Solidaridad/Plan_para_la_Integración _Social_de_los_Inmigrantes_(España)/CC3A70AD7A25A42C002569C40065F239!opendocument, posted 29 Decmber 2000. Also, see PSOE migration policy at http://www.psoe.es/ambito/osparticipacion ciudadana/docs/index.do?action =View & id=129228, viewed 15 February 2009.
10. See King, Keohane and Verba, 1994, p. 129 and 141.
11. See Martin W. Bauer and George Gaskell, *Qualitative Researching with Text, Image and Sound* (London: SAGE Publications, 2000), pp. 29–31.

12. See Bauer and Gaskell, 2000, pp. 32–5.
13. See King, Keohane and Verba, 1994, p. 25.
14. For a discussion, see King, Keohane and Verba, 1994, pp. 26–7, and critiques in Henry Brady and David Collier (eds), *Rethinking Social Inquiry: Diverse Tools, Shared Standards* (Oxford: Rowman and Littlefield, 2004).

BIBLIOGRAPHY

(WORKS CITED)

Abbas, Tahir, 'Introduction: Islamic Political Radicalism in Western Europe' in Tahir Abbas (ed.), *Islamic Political Radicalism: A European Perspective* (Edinburgh: Edinburgh University Press, 2007).

Abraham, Nabeel, 'The Yemeni Immigrant Community of Detroit: Background, Emigration, and Community Life' in Sameer Y. Abraham and Nabeel Abraham (eds.), *Arabs in the New World: Studies on Arab-American Communities* (Detroit: Wayne State University Center for Urban Studies, 1983), pp. 109–34.

Abraham, Sameer Y., 'Detroit's Arab-American Community: A Survey of Diversity and Commonality' in Sameer Y. Abraham and Nabeel Abraham (eds.), *Arabs in the New World: Studies on Arab American Communities* (Detroit: Wayne State University Center for Urban Studies, 1983), pp. 84–108.

Akhtar, Parveen, '(Re)Turn to Religion and Radical Islam' in Tahir Abbas (ed.), *Muslim Britain* (London: Zed Books, 2005).

Ali, Ayoub Korom, 'Forced out, looking inwards: Britain's Bangladeshis', *New Statesman*, 22 January 2007.

Ali, Y., 'Muslim Women and the Politics of Ethnicity and Culture in Northern England' in G. Sahgal and N. Yuval-Davis (eds.), *Refusing Holy Orders: Women and Fundamentalism in Britain* (London: Virago Press, 1992).

Álvarez-Miranda, Berta, 'Here and There: Transnational and Community Links between Muslim Immigrants in Europe', *Real Instituto Elcano* (Madrid: Real Instituto Elcano, 2009).

Ameli, Saied R., Syed Mohammed Marandi, Sameera Ahmed, Seyfeddin Kara and Arzu Merali, 'The British Media and Muslim Representation: The Ideology of Demonisation', Islamic Human Rights Commission, 26 January 2007.

Ansari, Humayun, *The Infidel Within: Muslims in Britain Since 1800* (London: C. Hurst and Co., 2004).

Appadurai, Arjun, 'Sovereignty Without Territoriality: Notes for a Post-National Geography' in Patricia Yeager (ed.), *The Geography of Identity* (Ann Arbor: The University of Michigan Press, 1996).

Appadurai, Arjun, 'Disjuncture and Difference in the Global Cultural Economy' in David Held and Anthony McGrew (eds.), *The Global Transformations Reader* (Malden, MA: Polity Press, 2000).

Archer, Louise, 'Muslim brothers, black lads, traditional Asians: British young men's constructions of "race", religion, and masculinity', *Feminism and Psychology*, 11, 1 (2001), pp. 79–105.

Archer, Louise, *Race, Masculinity and Schooling: Muslim boys and education* (Maidenhead: Open University Press, 2003).

Archibugi, Danielle and Held, David, 'Introduction' in Danielle Archibugi and David Held (eds.), *Cosmopolitan Democracy: An Agenda for a New World Order* (Cambridge: Polity Press, 1999).

Arigita, Elena, 'al-Adl wa-l-Ihsan in Spain: Exploring New Frames of Reference', paper presented to Middle Eastern Studies Association, November 2009.

Asad, Talal, *Formations of the Secular: Christianity, Islam, Modernity* (Stanford: Stanford University Press, 2003).

Asani, Ali S., '"So That You May Know One Another": An American Reflects on Pluralism and Islam', *The ANNALS of the American Academy of Political and Social Science*, 588, 1 (2003), pp. 40–51.

Associated Press, 'EU Sees Wide Discrimination Against Muslims', *The Guardian*, 28 May 2009.

Ayers, John W. and Hofstetter, C. Richard, 'American Muslim Political Participation Following 9/11: Religious Belief, Political Resources, Social Structures, and Political Awareness', *Politics and Religion*, 1 (2008), pp. 3–26.

Ballard, Roger, 'The Pakistanis: Stability and Introspection' in C. Peach (ed.), *The Ethnic Minority Populations of Great Britain: Ethnicity in the 1991 Census*, Vol. 2 (London: Central Statistical Office, 1996).

Barry, Brian, 'Statism and Nationalism: A Cosmopolitan Critique' in I. Shapiro and L. Brilmayer (eds.), *Global Justice: Nomos XLI* (New York: New York University Press, 1999).

Barth, Fredrik, 'Introduction' in Fredrik Barth (ed.), *Ethnic Groups and Boundaries: The Social Organisation of Culture Difference* (London: Allen and Unwin, 1969).

Bauer, Martin W. and George Gaskell, *Qualitative Researching with Text, Image and Sound* (London: Sage, 2000).

Bauman, Zygmunt, *Intimations of Postmodernity* (London: Routledge, 1992).

BBC News, 'Striving for "Truly British" armed forces', 17 November 2005.

BBC News, 'London Attacks', bbcnews.co.uk, http://news.bbc.co.uk/1/hi/in_depth/uk/2005/london_explosions/ default.stm, posted 8 July 2008, 12:57.

Begun, Halima and John Eade, 'All Quiet on the Eastern Front? Bangladeshi Reactions in Tower Hamlets' in Tahir Abbas (ed.), *Muslim Britain: Communities Under Pressure* (London: Zed Books, 2005).

Bell, Daniel, 'Sociodicy: A guide to modern usage', *American Scholar*, Autumn 1966, 35.

Biffi, Cardinal Giacomo, *Sedes Sapientiae*, no. 75, 30 September 2000.

Bloemraad, Irene, 'Of puzzles and serendipity: Doing Research with Cross-National Comparisons and Mixed Methods', chapter in Louis DeCipio, Sherrie Kossoudji and Manuel Garcia y Griego (eds.), *Research Methods Choices in Interdisciplinary Contexts: War Stories of New Scholars* (SSRC: 2005).

Bodega, Isabel, Juan A. Cebrian, Teresa Franchini, Gloria Lora-Tamayo and Asuncion Martin-Lou, *International Migration Review*, 29, 3 (Autumn, 1995), pp. 800–19.

Booth, Robert, 'Minister for Terror: Gaza will fuel UK extremism', *The Guardian*, 28 January 2009.

Boreus, Kristina, 'Discursive Discrimination: A Typology' in *European Journal of Social Theory* 9, 3 (2006), pp. 405–24.

Brady, Henry, Sidney Verba and Kay Lehman Schlozman, 'Beyond SES: A Resource Model of Political Participation', *American Political Science Review*, 89 (1995).

Brieully, John, *Nationalism and the State* (Manchester: Manchester University Press, 1982).

Briggs, Rachel, Catherine Fieschi and Hannah Lownsbrough, 'Bringing It Home: Community based approaches to counter terrorism', DEMOS, 4 December 2006.

Briscoe, Ivan, 'Dreaming of Spain: Migration and Morocco' on www.opendemocracy. net, posted 27 May 2004.

Calavita, Kitty, 'A "reserve army of delinquents": The criminalization and economic punishment of immigrants in Spain' in *Punishment and Society*, 5, (2003).

Caldwell, Christopher, *Reflections on the Revolution in Europe* (New York: Random House, 2009).

Castles, Stephen, *Ethnicity and Globalization* (London: SAGE Publications, 2000).

Centro de Investigaciones Sociológicas, 'Barómetro Noviembre 2006', Esudio #2662, *Opiniones y Actitudes CIS 60*, Pregunta 16, 18 November 2006.

Cesari, Joselyn, *When Islam and Democracy Meet* (New York: Palgrave Macmillan, 2004).

Cherti, Miryam, 'British Moroccans: Citizenship in Action', *Runnymede Trust*, January 2009.

Collier, David, Henry E. Brady and Jason Seawright, 'Critiques, Responses and Tradeoffs: Drawing Together the Debate' in Henry E. Brady and David Collier, *Rethinking Social Inquiry: Diverse Tools, Shared Standards* (Oxford: Rowman and Littlefield, 2004).

Connor, Walker, 'A Nation is a Nation, is a State, is an Ethnic Group, is a...', *Ethnic and Racial Studies*, 1 (1978).

Dahl, Robert, *Democracy and its Critics* (New Haven, CT: Yale University Press, 1989).

de Tocqueville, Alexis, *Democracy in America*, trans. and ed. Harvey C. Mansfield and Delba Winthrop (Chicago: University of Chicago Press, 2000).

D'Ocon, Gloria Laura-Tamayo, 'Inmigración Marroquí en la Comunidad de Madrid' in *Atlas de la Inmigración Magrebí en España* (Madrid: TEIM, 2004).

Doughty, Steve, 'Just one in 10 British Muslims feel integrated into society, study claims', *The Daily Mail*, 8 May 2009.

Durkheim, Émile, *The Division of Labour in Society*, trans. George Simpson, Free Press (London: Collier Macmillan, 1964).

Durkheim, Émile mile, *On Suicide: a study in sociology*, ed. George Simpson (London: Routledge & Kegan, 1952).

BIBLIOGRAPHY

Durkheim, Émile, *The Rules of Sociological Method*, trans. W.D. Walls, ed. Steven Lukes (London: Macmillan, 1982).

Dwyer, Claire, 'Contradictions of community: questions of identity for young British Muslim women' in *Environment and Planning* 31, 1 (1999).

Dwyer, Claire, Bindi Shah and Gurchathen Sanghera, '"From cricket lover to terror suspect"—challenging representations of young British Muslim men', *Gender, Place, and Culture*, 15, 2 (April, 2008).

Eade, John, 'Identity, Nation and Religion: Educated Young Bangladeshi Muslims in London's "East End"', *International Sociology*, 9, 3 (1994) pp. 377–94.

Eade, John, 'Reconstructing places: changing images of locality in Docklands and Spitalfields' in J. Eade (ed.), *Living in the Global City* (London: Routledge, 1997).

Eade, John and Garbin, David, 'Changing Narratives of Violence, Struggle and Resistance: Bangladeshis and the Competition for Resources in the Global City', *Oxford Development Studies*, Volume 30, Number 2, 1 June 2002.

Eikelman, Dale and Piscatori, James, *Muslim Politics* (Princeton: Princeton University Press, 1996).

El País, 'Zapatero y Aznar, ante la Comisión del 11–M' and '11M El Juicio' at http://www.elpais.com/especiales/2004/comision11m/.

Elger, Katrin, Ansbert Kneip and Merlind Theile, 'Survey Shows Alarming Lack of Integration in Germany', *Der Spiegel*, 26 January 2009.

Favell, Adrian, *Philosophies of Integration: Immigration and the Idea of Citizenship in France and Britain* (New York: Palgrave, 1998).

Fekete, Liz, 'Anti–Muslim racism and the European Security State', *Race and Class* 46, 1 (2004), pp. 3–29.

Fennema, Meindert and Jean Tillie, 'Political participation and political trust in Amsterdam: civic communities and ethnic networks', *Journal of Ethnic and Migration Studies*, 24, 4, (1999).

Feuer, Lewis, 'What is alienation? The career of a concept', in I.M. Stein and A. Vidich (eds.), *Sociology on Trial* (Englewood Cliffs, NJ: Prentice Hall, 1963).

Fish, Steven, 'Islam and Authoritarianism', *World Politics* 55, 1 (2002), pp. 4–37.

Fishkin, James, *Democracy and Deliberation: New Directions for Democratic Reform* (New Haven: Yale University Press, 1991).

FOSIS, *The Voice of Muslim Students*, August 2005, Federation of Student Islamic Societies, London.

Freeman, Gary P., 'The consequence of immigration policies for immigrant status: a British and French comparison' in A. Messina, L. Fraga, L. Rhodebeck and F. Wright (eds.), *Ethnic and Racial Minorities in Industrial Democracies* (New York: Greenwood Press, 1992).

Freeman, Gary P., 'Modes of Immigration Politics in Liberal Democratic States', *International Migration Review*, 29, 4 (1995).

Garbin, David, 'Bangladeshi Diaspora in the UK: Some observations on socio-cultural dynamics, religious trends and transnational politics', paper presented at the Conference on Human Rights and Bangladesh, SOAS, 17 June 2005.

García, Bernabé López, 'La evolución de la Inmigración Marroquí en España (1991–2003)' in *Atlas de la Inmigración Magrebí en España* (Madrid: TEIM, 2004).

García, Bernabé López, 'La periferización de los Marroquíes en la Comunidad de Madrid' in *Atlas de la Inmigración Magrebí en España* (Madrid: TEIM, 2004).

García, José Antonio Rodríguez, *La Inmigración Islámica en España: Su problemática juridical* (Madrid: Editorial Dilex, 2007).

Gardner, Katy and Shuker, Abdus, '"I'm Bengali, I'm Asian and I'm Living Here": the Changing Identity of British Bengalis' in Roger Ballard (ed.), *Desh Pardesh: The South Asian Presence in Britain* (London: C. Hurst and Co., 1994).

Gearty, Conor, Lecture to Young Professionals in Foreign Policy, Houses of Parliament Committee Rooms, 23 June 2009.

Gellner, Ernest, *Nations and Nationalism* (Ithaca: Cornell University Press, 1983).

George, Alexander L. and McKeown, Timothy J., 'Case Studies and Theories of Organizational Decision Making', *Advances in Information Processing in Organizations* 2 (1985), pp. 21–58.

Gest, Justin, 'Q. How many of 100 Britons passed the citizenship exam? A. Not one', *The Times*, 29 September 2007.

Gest, Justin and Norfolk, Andrew, 'British Imams "failing young Muslims"', *The Times*, 7 January 2009.

Giddens, Anthony, *Capitalism and Modern Social Theory* (Cambridge: Cambridge University Press, 1971).

Giddens, Anthony, *The Constitution of Society: Outline of the Theory of Structuration* (Cambridge: Polity, 1984).

Giddens, Anthony, *New Rules of Sociological Method*, second edition (Palo Alto: Stanford University Press, 1993).

Glover, Scott, 'FBI monitored members of O.C. mosques at gyms, alleged informant says', *Los Angeles Times*, 29 April 2009.

Glynn, Sarah, 'Bengali Muslims: The new East End radicals?', *Ethnic and Racial Studies* 25, 6 (2002), pp. 969–75.

Glynn, Sarah, 'The Spirit of '71—how the Bangladeshi War of Independence has haunted Tower Hamlets', *Socialist History Journal*, 29 (2006), pp. 56–75.

Greater London Authority, 'Health in London', 2002 Review of London health strategy high level indicators (London: GLA, 2002).

Guibernau, Montserrat, *Nations Without States: Political Communities in a Global Age* (Cambridge: Polity Press, 1999).

Guibernau, Montserrat, 'National identity and modernity' in A. Dieckhoff and N. Gutiérrez (eds.), *Modern Roots: Studies of National Identity* (Aldershot: Ashgate, 2001).

Guibernau, Montserrat, 'Globalisation and the nation-state' in Montserrat Guibernau and John Hutchinson (eds.), *Understanding Nationalism* (Cambridge: Polity Press, 2001).

Guiraudon, Virginie, 'Citizenship rights for non-citizens: France, Germany and the Netherlands' in Christian Joppke (ed.), *Challenge to the Nation-State: Immigration in Western Europe and the United States* (Oxford: Oxford University Press, 1998).

Gurr, Ted Robert, *Why Men Rebel* (Princeton: Princeton University Press, 1970).

Habermas, Jürgen, 'The Postnational Constellation and the Future of Democracy' in *The Postnational Constellation: Political Essays*, trans. ed. Max Pensky (Cambridge: MIT Press, 2001).

Hall, Stuart, 'Cultural Identity and Diaspora' in Jonathan Rutherford (ed.), *Identity: Community, Culture, Difference* (London: Lawrence and Wishart, 1990).

Hall, Stuart, 'Ethnicity: Identity and Difference' in Geoff Eley and Ronald Grigor Suny (eds.), *Becoming National* (Oxford: Oxford University Press, 1996a).

Hampshire, James and Saggar, Shamit, 'Migration, Integration, and Security in the UK Since July 7', March 2006, http://www.migrationinformation.org/Feature/display.cfm?ID=383.

Hanifan, L. J., 'The rural school community center', *ANNALS of the American Academy of Political and Social Science* 67, 1 (1916).

Hardin, Garrett, 'Meaninglessness of the word protoplasm', *Scientific Monthly*, 82 (1956).

Hasan, Masadul, *Reconstruction of Political Thought in Islam* (Lahore: Islamic Publications, 1988).

Hasan, Usama and Justin Gest, 'Nothing Sells Papers Like a Villain', *The Guardian, Comment Is Free*, 18 March 2009.

Haynes, Jeff, *Democracy in the Developing World. Africa, Asia, Latin America and the Middle East* (Cambridge: Polity Press, 2001).

Held, David, *Models of Democracy*, second edition (Palo Alto: Stanford University Press, 1996).

Held, David, *Global Transformations: Politics, Economics and Culture* (Cambridge: Polity Press, 1999).

Held, David, *Models of Democracy*, third edition (Cambridge: Polity, 2006).

Herberg, W., 'Alienation, dissent, and the intellectual', *National Review*, 20 July 1968.

Hervieu-Leger, Daniele, 'The Transmission and Formation of Socio-Religious Identities in Modernity', *International Sociology* 13, 2 (June, 1998).

HM Government, 'Controlling our Borders: Making Migration Work for Britain', Home Office, http://www.archive2.official-documents.co.uk/document/cm64/6472/6472.pdf, posted February 2005.

Hobson, Christopher, 'Beyond the End of History: The Need for a "Radical Historicisation" of Democracy in International Relations', *Millennium*, 37, 3 (2009), pp. 631–57.

Hüetlin, Thomas, 'Muslims in Britain: Feeling Foreign At Home', *Der Spiegel*, 14 (August 2006).

Huntington, Samuel P., 'Will More Countries Become Democratic?', *Political Science Quarterly*, 99, 2 (1984), pp. 193–218.

Huntington, Samuel P., *The Clash of Civilizations and the Remaking of World Order* (New York: Simon and Schuster, 1996).

Hussain, Asifa, 'British Pakistani Muslims' Perceptions of the Armed Forces' in *Armed Forces & Society*, 28, 4.

Hutnik, Nimmi, 'Aspects of identity in multi–ethnic society', *Ethnic and Racial Studies*, 9, 2 (1986), pp. 150–67.

Inglehart, Ronald and Norris, Pippa, 'Muslim Integration into Western Cultures: Between Origins and Destinations', Faculty Working Paper Series, Harvard University Kennedy School of Government, March 2009.

Institute of Race Relations, 'New study highlights discrimination in use of anti–terror laws', Press Release (2 September 2004).

Ireland, Patrick, *The Policy Challenge of Ethnic Diversity: Immigrant Politics in France and Switzerland* (Cambridge: Harvard University Press, 1994).

Ireland, Patrick, *Becoming Europe: Immigration, Integration, and the Welfare State* (Pittsburgh: University of Pittsburgh Press, 2004).

Israel, Joachim, *Alienation: From Marx to Modern Sociology* (Boston: Allyn and Bacon, 1971).

Jacobson, David, *Rights Across Borders* (London: Johns Hopkins, 1996).

Jennings, Sir Ivor, *The Approach to Self-Government* (Cambridge: Cambridge University Press, 1956).

Johnson, Frank, 'Alienation: Concept, Term and Word' in Frank Johnson (ed.), *Alienation: Concept, Term and Meaning* (New York: Seminar Press, 1973).

Johnson, Frank, 'Overview and Introduction' in Frank Johnson (ed.), *Alienation: Concept, Term and Meaning* (New York: Seminar Press, 1973).

Joppke, Christian, 'Multiculturalism and Immigration: A Comparison of the United States, Germany and Great Britain', *Theory and Society*, 25 (1996).

Joppke, Christian, 'Asylum and State Sovereignty: A Comparison of the United States, Germany and Britain', *Comparative Political Studies*, 30, 3 (1997).

Khan, M.A. Maqtedar, *American Muslims: Bridging Faith and Freedom* (Beltsville, Maryland: Amana Publications, 2002).

Kedourie, Elie, *Democracy and Arab Political Culture* (London: Frank Cass & Company, 1994).

Kepel, Gilles, *Allah in the West: Islamic Movements in America and Europe* (Stanford: Stanford University Press, 1997).

Kepel, Gilles, *The War for Muslim Minds: Islam and the West* (Cambridge, Massachusetts: Harvard University Press, 2004).

Khachani, Mohamed, 'La Emigración Marroquí en España' in *Economía Exterior*, 28, Primavera 2004.

Khuri, Richard, *Freedom, Modernity and Islam* (Syracuse: Syracuse University Press, 1998).

King, Gary, Robert Keohane and Sidney Verba, *Designing Social Inquiry: Scientific Inference in Qualitative Research* (Princeton: Princeton University Press, 1994).

Knott, Kim and Khokher, Sajda, 'Religious and Ethnic Identity among Young Muslim Women in Bradford' in *New Community*, 19, 4 (1993).

Koff, Stephen, 'The Political Use of the Concept of Alienation' in Frank Johnson (ed.), *Alienation: Concept, Term and Meaning* (New York: Seminar Press, 1973).

Koopmans, Ruud and Statham, Paul, 'Migration and Ethnic Relations as a Field of Political Contention: An Opportunity Structure Approach' in Ruud Koopman and Paul Statham (eds.), *Challenging Immigration and Ethnic Relations Policy: Comparative European Perspectives* (Oxford: Oxford University Press, 2001).

Labaree, Robert V., 'The risk of "going observationalist": Negotiating the hidden dilemmas of being an insider participant observer', *Qualitative Research*, 2, 1 (2002), pp. 97–122.

Leonard, K.I., *Muslims in the United States: The state of research* (New York: Russell Sage Foundation, 2003).

Lewis, Bernard, 'Legal and Historical Reflection in the Position of Muslim Populations Under Non-Muslim Rule' in Bernard Lewis and Dominique Schnapper (eds.), *Muslims in Europe* (London: Pinter Publishers, 1994).

Lewis, Bernard, *The Multiple Identities of the Middle East* (New York: Schocken Books, 2001).

Lezcano, Victor Morales, 'Inmigración Africana en Madrid: Marroquíes y Guineanos (1975–1990)', (Madrid: UNED, 1993).

Liberson, Stanley, *Making it Count: The Improvement of Social Research and Theory* (Berkeley: University of California Press, 1985).

Liebkind, Karmela, 'Concluding Remarks' in Karmela Liebkind (ed.), *New Identities in Europe: Immigrant Ancestry and the Ethnic Identity of Youth* (Aldershot: Gower, 1989).

Locke, John, *Second Treatise of Government*, ed. C.B. Macpherson (Indianapolis: Hackett, 1998).

López, Fernando Bravo, 'El musulmán como alter-ego irreducible: La expansion del discurso culturalista' in *Atlas de la Inmigración Magrebí en España* (Madrid: TEIM, 2004).

Macey, Marie, 'Class, Gender and Religious Influence on Changing Patterns of Pakistani Muslim Male Violence in Bradford' in *Ethnic and Racial Studies* 22, 5 (1999).

Mahmood, Saba, 'Secularism, Hermeneutics, and Empire: The Politics of Islamic Reformation' in *Public Culture*, 18, 2 (2006).

Malik, Iftikhar H., *Islam Nationalism and the West* (New York: St Martin's Press, 1999).

Mann, Michael, *The Sources of Social Power: Volume 2, The Rise of Classes and Nation States 1760–1914* (Cambridge: Cambridge University Press, 1993).

Mann, Michael, *The Dark Side of Democracy: Explaining Ethnic Cleansing* (Cambridge: Cambridge University Press, 2005).

Markon, Jerry, 'FBI walks tightrope in outreach to Muslims, fighting terrorism', *The Washington Post*, 20 December 2009.

Martin, Daniel, 'Muslim medical students refuse to learn about alcohol or sexual diseases', *The Daily Telegraph*, 7 October 2007.

Martin, Philip and James Hollifield, (eds.), *Controlling Immigration: A Global Perspective* (Stanford: Stanford University Press, 1994).

Marx, Karl, *The Holy Family* (or *Critique of Critical Critique*), trans. R. Dixon (Moscow: Foreign Languages Publishing House, 1956).

Marx, Karl and Friedrich Engels, *Economic and Philosophical Manuscripts of 1844*, trans. Martin Milligan (Moscow: Foreign Languages Publishing House, 1959).

Marx, Karl, *Early Writings*, trans. T.B. Bottomore (London: C.A. Watts, 1963).

Maxwell, Rahsaan, 'Muslims, South Asians and the British mainstream: A national identity crisis?', *West European Politics*, 29, 4 (2006), pp. 736–56.

Mayall, James, *Nationalism and International Society* (Cambridge: Cambridge University Press, 1990).

McDermott, John, 'Technology: The opiate of the intellectuals', *New York Review of Books*, XIII (July 31, 1969).

Melvin, Don, 'Europe works to assimilate Muslims', *Atlanta Journal Constitution*, 17 December 2004.

Mill, John Stuart, 'On Liberty' in *Mill: The Spirit of the Age, On Liberty, The Subjugation of Women*, ed. Alan Ryan (New York: W.W. Norton and Company, 1997).

Milmo, Cahal, 'Muslims feel like "Jews of Europe"', *The Independent*, 4 July 2008.

Mizruchi, Ephraim, *An Introduction to the Notion of Alienation* in Frank Johnson (ed.), *Alienation: Concept, Term and Meaning* (New York: Seminar Press, 1973).

Modood, Tariq and Berthoud, Richard, *Ethnic Minorities in Britain* (London: Policy Studies Institute, 1997).

Modood, Tariq, 'British Muslims and the politics of multiculturalism' in Tariq Modood et al., *Multiculturalism, Muslims and Citizenship* (Oxon: Routledge, 2006).

Modood, Tariq, *Multiculturalism* (Cambridge, Polity 2007).

Moniquet, Claude, 'Hearing before the Subcommittee on Europe and Emerging Threats', US House of Representatives, First Session, 109th Congress, 27 April 2005.

Moore, Henrietta, 'The benefits of doubt' in London Design Council, *Touching the State* (London: London Design Council, 2005).

Moore, Kerry, Paul Mason and Justin Lewis, 'Images of Islam in the UK: The Representation of British Muslims in the National Print News Media 2000–2008', Cardiff School of Journalism, Media and Cultural Studies report, 7 July 2008.

Moreras, Jordi, 'La religiosidad en context migratorio: Pertenencias y observancias' in *Atlas de la Inmigración Magrebí en España* (Madrid: TEIM, 2004).

Muñoz, Gema Martín, 'El Islam en España Hoy' in Luisa Martín Rojo et al. (eds.), *Hablar y Dejar Hablar (Sobre racism y xenofobia)* (Madrid: Universidad Autónoma de Madrid, 1994).

Muñoz, Gema Martín (ed.), *Islam, Modernism and the West: Cultural and Political Relations at the End of the Millennium* (London: I.B. Tauris, 1999).

Nielsen, Jorgen, *Muslims in Western Europe* (Edinburgh: Edinburgh University Press, 2004).

Noya, Javier, 'Spaniards and Islam', *Real Instituto El Cano*, ARI 105/2007, 28 November 2007.

O'Beirne, Maria, 'Religion in England and Wales: Findings from the 2001 Home Office Citizenship Survey', Home Office Research, Development and Statistics Directorate, March 2004.

Office for National Statistics, 'Annual Local Area Labour Force Survey 2001/02', http://www.statistics.gov.uk/CCI/nugget.asp?ID=1089&Pos=2&ColRank=2&Rank=768.

Ollman, Bertell, *Alienation: Marx's Conception of Man in Capitalist Society* (Cambridge: Cambridge University Press, 1971).

Open Society Institute, 'Muslims in the EU: Cities Report', EU Monitoring and Advocacy Program, 2007.

Open Society Institute, http://www.eumap.org/topics/minority/reports/eumuslims/index, EUMAP Programme.

Pan, Esther, 'Europe: Integrating Islam', Council on Foreign Relations, 13 July 2005.

Parekh, Bhikhu, 'Religion and Public Life' in Tariq Modood (ed), *Church, State and Religious Minorities* (London: Policy Studies Institute, 1997).

Parekh, Bhikhu, *Rethinking Multiculturalism: Cultural Diversity and Political Theory* (Basingstoke: Macmillan, 2000).

Parry, Geraint, George Moyser and Neil Day, *Political Participation and Democracy in Britain* (Cambridge: Cambridge University Press, 1992).

Pearl, David and Werner Menski, *Muslim Family Law* (London: Sweet and Maxwell, 1998).

Peek, Lori, 'Becoming Muslim: The Development of a Religious Identity', *Sociology of Religion*, 66 (2005).

Pérez-Díaz, Víctor, Berta Álvarez-Miranda and Elisa Chuliá, *La inmigración Musulmana en Europa: Turcos en Alemania, Argelinos en Francia y Marroquíes en España (Muslims in Europe: Turks in Germany, Algerians in France, Moroccans in Spain)* (Barcelona: Fundación La Caixa, July 2004).

Pew Research Center, 'The Great Divide: How Westerners and Muslims View Each Other', 22 June 2006.

Pickles, Margaret, 'Muslim Immigration Stress in Australia' in Syed Z. Abedin and Ziauddin Sardar (eds.), *Muslim Minorities in the West* (London: Grey Seal, 1995).

Poole, Elizabeth, *Reporting Islam* (London: I.B. Tauris, 2002).

Portes, Alejandro and Rumbaut, Rubin G., *Immigrant America: A portrait*, second edition (Berkeley: University of California Press, 1996).

Portes, Alejandro and Rumbaut, Rubin G., *Legacies: The story of the immigrant second generation* (Berkeley: University of California Press, 2001).

Putnam, Robert D. (with Robert Leonardi and Raffaella Nannetti), *Making Democracy Work: Civic Traditions in Modern Italy* (Princeton, NJ: Princeton University Press, 1993).

Putnam, Robert D., 'E Pluribus Unum: Diversity and Community in the Twenty-first Century', *Scandinavian Political Studies*, 30, 2 (2007).

Ramadan, Tariq, *Western Muslims and the Future of Islam* (New York: Oxford University Press, 2004).

Rizvi, Sadaf, 'News cultures, security and transnational belonging', *European Journal of Cultural Studies*, 10, 3 (2007), pp. 327–42.

Romero, Carlos Giménez, 'Marroquíes en España: un perfil sociocultural' in *Atlas de la Inmigración Magrebí en España* (Madrid: TEIM, 1996).

Roy, Olivier, *Globalized Islam: The Search for a New Ummah* (New York: Columbia University Press, 2004).

Runnymede Trust, *Islamophobia: A Challenge for Us All* (London, 1997).

Saeed, Amir, Neil Blain and Douglas Forbes, 'New ethnic and national questions in Scotland: Post-British identities among Glasgow Pakistani teenagers', *Ethnic and Racial Studies*, 22, 5 (1999), pp. 8–44.

Sahin, Abdullah, 'Attitudes toward Islam of young people in Birmingham colleges', unpublished PhD thesis, Birmingham University, in Edward Lifton, 'A Clinical Psychology Perspective on Radical Islamic Youth' in Tahir Abbas (ed.), *Islamic Political Radicalism: A European Perspective* (Edinburgh: Edinburgh University Press, 2007).

Said, Edward N., 'Islam Through Western Eyes', *The Nation*, 26 April 1980.

Samad, Yunus, 'The Politics of Islamic Identity among Bangladeshis and Pakistanis in Britain' in T. Ranger, Y. Samad and O. Stuart (eds.), *Culture Identity and Politics: Ethnic Minorities in Britain* (Aldershot: Avebury, 1996).

Sandell, Rickard, 'La inmigración en España: ¿problema u oportunidad?' in *Área: Demografía y Población*, 13, (27 January 2005).

Sappiens, 'Plan para la Integración Social de los Inmigrantes (España)', http://www.sappiens.com/castellano/articulos.nsf/Solidaridad/Plan_para_la_Integración_Social_ de_los_Inmigrantes_(España)/CC3A70AD7A25A42C002569C40065F239!op endocument, posted 29 December 2000.

Sardar, Ziauddin, 'Racism, identity and Muslims in the West' in Syed Z. Abedin and Ziauddin Sardar, *Muslim Minorities in the West* (London: Grey Seal, 1995), pp. 1–17.

Schaar, John H., *Escape from Authority* (New York: Basic Books, 1961).

Schumpeter, Joseph, *Capitalism, Socialism and Democracy* (London: Allen and Unwin, 1943).

Seeman, Melvin, 'On the meaning of alienation', *American Sociological Review*, 24 (1959).

Shane, Scott, 'New Incidents Test Immunity to Terrorism on U.S. Soil', *New York Times*, 11 December 2009.

Siddiqui, Kalim, 'Muslim Manifesto: A Strategy for Survival', accessed via <http://www.muslimparliament.org.uk/MuslimManifesto.pdf>, 2 February 2008.

Slootman, Marieke and Tillie, Jean, *Processes of Radicalisation*, paper published by the Institute for Migration and Ethnic Studies, Universiteit van Amsterdam, October 2006.

Soft Guides, http://www.softguides.com/madrid_guide/maps/graphics/madrid-map-001.gif on 30 January 2009.

Soysal, Yasemin, *Limits of Citizenship: Migrants and Postnational Membership in Europe* (Chicago: University of Chicago Press, 1996).

Sunday Times, The, 'The Enemy Within', leader in *The Sunday Times*, 13 August 2006.

Sunstein, Cass, *Laws of Fear* (Cambridge: Cambridge University Press, 2005).

Tarrow, Sidney, *Democracy and Disorder: Protest and Politics in Italy 1965–1975* (Oxford: Clarendon, 1989).

Taspinar, Omer, 'Europe's Muslim Street', Brookings Institution, March 2003.

Tate, Julie, 'Notable homegrown terrorism plots', *Washington Post*, 11 December 2009, see http://www.washingtonpost.com/wp-dyn/content/article/2009/12/10/AR2009121004677.html.

Tilly, Charles, *Contention and Democracy in Europe, 1650–2000* (Cambridge: Cambridge University Press, 2004).

Togeby, Lise, 'Migrants at the polls: An analysis of immigrant and refugee participation in Danish local elections', *Journal of Ethnic and Migration Studies*, 25, 4 (1999), pp. 665–84.

Tönnies, Ferdinand, ed. Jose Harris, *Community and Civil Society* (Cambridge: Cambridge University Press, 2001).

Torrance, John, *Estrangement, Alienation and Exploitation* (London: Macmillan, 1977).

Touahri, Sarah, 'Facing unemployment, Moroccans in Spain return home', *Magharebia*, 6 August 2008.

Tower Hamlets Council, Borough Statistical Data, http://www.towerhamlets.gov.uk/data/discover/ data/borough-profile/data/borough-profile/population/data/age-gender.cfm.

Toynbee Hall, 'Snapshot', Toynbee Hall, London, 2006.

UK Foreign and Commonwealth Office/Home Office, 'Draft Report on Young Muslims and Extremism', April 2004.

Van Dijk, Teun A., 'El racismo y la prensa en España' in Hernández Antonio Bañón (ed.), *Discurso periodístico y procesos migratorios* (Donostia-San Sebastián: Gakoa, 2007), pp. 27–80.

Varedas Muñoz, Sonia, 'Sobre el asociacionismo Marroqui en España y participación de los inmigrantes' in *Atlas de la Inmigración Magrebí en España* (Madrid: TEIM, 2004).

Verba, Sidney and Norman Nie, *Participation in America: Political Democracy and Social Equality* (New York: Harper and Row, 1972).

Verba, Sidney, Kay Lehman Schlozman and Henry E. Brady, 'Participation's not a paradox: The view from American activists', *British Journal of Political Science* 25 (January 1995a), pp. 1–36.

Verba, Sidney, Kay Lehman Schlozman and Henry E. Brady, *Voice and Equality: Civic Voluntarism in American Politics* (Cambridge: Harvard University Press, 1995b).

Verkaik, Robert, 'Stop and search: white people held "to balance racial statistics"', *The Independent*, accessed 18 June 2009, http://www.independent.co.uk/news/uk/ home-news/stop-and-search-white-people-held-to-balance-racial-statistics-1707895.html.

Vertovec, Steven, 'Multicultural, multi–Asian, multi–Muslim Leicester: Dimensions of social complexity, ethnic organisation and local government interface' in *Innovation: European Journal of Social Sciences*, 7, 3 (1994), pp. 259–76.

Vertovec, Steven and Rogers, Alasdair, 'Introduction' in Steven Vertovec and Alasdair Rogers (eds.), *Muslim European Youth* (Aldershot: Ashgate, 1998).

Vertovec, Steven, 'Young Muslims in Keighley, West Yorkshire: cultural identity, context and "community"', *Migration*, 33 (2000), pp. 119–38.

Vertovec, Steven, 'Transnationalism and identity', *Journal of Ethnic and Migration Studies* 27, 4 (2001).

Vitello, Paul and Kirk Semple, 'Muslims Say F.B.I. Tactics Sow Anger and Fear', *New York Times*, 17 December 2009.

Weber, Max, 'Science as a vocation' in H.H. Gerth and C.W. Mills (eds.), *From Max Weber* (New York: Oxford University Press, 1972).

Werbner, Pnina, 'Theorising Complex Diasporas: Purity and Hybridity in the South Asian Public Sphere in Britain' in 'Islam, Transnationalism and the Public Sphere in Western Europe', special issue of *Journal of Ethnic and Migration Studies* 30, 5 (2004).

Wiktorowicz, Quintan, *Radical Islam Rising: Muslim Extremism in the West* (Maryland: Rowman and Littlefield, 2005).

Youth Sanctuary Project Blog, http://www.yspyouth.blogspot.com/, accessed 12 June 2008.

Zapata-Barrero, Ricard, 'The Muslim Community and Spanish Tradition' in Tariq Modood et al., *Multiculturalism, Muslims and Citizenship: A European Approach* (New York: Routledge, 2006).

Zeitlyn, Benji, 'Migration from Bangladesh to Italy and Spain', SAMRen, July 2004, http://www.samren.org/Fellowships/papers/Beji.pdf.

INDEX